Still WATERS

CYNTHIA PERKINS

To Lynda, 11/12/19
May you walk with the Shepherd.
God's Blessing
A. Cynthia Perkins

WestBow Press
A DIVISION OF THOMAS NELSON & ZONDERVAN

Copyright © 2017 Cynthia Perkins.

All rights reserved. No part of this book may be used or reproduced by any means, graphic, electronic, or mechanical, including photocopying, recording, taping or by any information storage retrieval system without the written permission of the author except in the case of brief quotations embodied in critical articles and reviews.

NKJV: Unless otherwise noted scriptures are taken from the New King James Version®. Copyright © 1982 by Thomas Nelson. Used by permission. All rights reserved.
ANT: Scripture quotations marked AMP are from The Amplified Bible, Old Testament copyright © 1965, 1987 by the Zondervan Corporation. The Amplified Bible, New Testament copyright © 1954, 1958, 1987 by The Lockman Foundation. Used by permission. All rights reserved.
NLT: Scripture quotations are taken from the Holy Bible, New Living Translation, copyright ©1996, 2004, 2007 by Tyndale House Foundation. Used by permission of Tyndale House Publishers, Inc., Carol Stream, Illinois 60188. All rights reserved.
RSV: [Scripture quotations are] from the Revised Standard Version of the Bible, copyright © 1946, 1952, and 1971 the Division of Christian Education of the National Council of the Churches of Christ in the United States of America. Used by permission. All rights reserved.

WestBow Press books may be ordered through booksellers or by contacting:

WestBow Press
A Division of Thomas Nelson & Zondervan
1663 Liberty Drive
Bloomington, IN 47403
www.westbowpress.com
1 (866) 928-1240

Because of the dynamic nature of the Internet, any web addresses or links contained in this book may have changed since publication and may no longer be valid. The views expressed in this work are solely those of the author and do not necessarily reflect the views of the publisher, and the publisher hereby disclaims any responsibility for them.

Any people depicted in stock imagery provided by Thinkstock are models, and such images are being used for illustrative purposes only.
Certain stock imagery © Thinkstock.

ISBN: 978-1-9736-0366-5 (sc)
ISBN: 978-1-9736-0365-8 (e)

Library of Congress Control Number: 2017915291

Print information available on the last page.

WestBow Press rev. date: 12/07/2018

To My Husband Kent

Who has always encouraged me to become the best I can be.
His encouragement comes not just from his mouth,
but he proves it with his actions of
respect, financial support, teamwork, prayer, and love,
as my husband, my minister,
and my partner in the work of spreading
the Gospel of Jesus Christ.
He loves me as
Christ loves the Church and gave Himself for Her.

TO GOD BE THE GLORY!

Foreword

"I'll Walk with God"

I'll walk with God, from this day on,
His helping hand I'll lean upon
This is my prayer, my humble plea,
May the Lord be ever with me.

There is no death, though eyes grow dim
There is no fear when I'm near to Him.
I'll lean on Him forever
And He'll forsake me never.

He will not fail me as long as my faith is strong,
Whatever road I may walk along.

I'll walk with God, I'll take His hand.
I'll talk with God, He'll understand;
I'll pray to Him, each day to Him
And He'll hear the words that I say.

His hand will guide my throne and rod,
And I'll never walk alone while I walk with God!

Words by Paul Francis Webster; music by Nicholas Brodsky
Copyright 1952, 1954 (Copyrights Renewed) WB Music Corp.
All rights reserved
Used by Permission of Alfred Publishing, LLC

Preface

This project has been under construction for over thirty years. The desire to write memories, thoughts, experiences, and prayers has come from the Scripture and the devotionals I read every day, plus everyday prayer and supplication. God's Word has magnified the spiritual wisdom of the devotionals, and over time, with the mixture of the above elements of life, came the Spirit's outpouring of this devotional.

STILL WATERS is a book that exemplifies God's Way: Jesus, who is The Way. That's all—-God's Way. He is the Way to go on our walk, here, in time.

God's timing is perfect! He provided everything that was necessary for my walk with Him. He stationed me in places I never dreamed I would be to teach, speak, train, and learn, and to practice every day's step of faith in Him. I never could have guessed the places that I would be sent to glean life's knowledge and experiences so that I would know how to write these lessons concerning His infinite love for us and our love for Him.

When it came time to finalize this book and prepare for printing, He sent just the right professional people to help. This was His validation of the project. Through these bits of His loving encouragement, He is saying to me, "I love you, and I am with you as you write in My Name!"

Thank you my Shepherd, the Lord, who without there would be no walking *through the valley of the shadow of death*—we would stay there, and die in that dark shadow. Thank you Lord for eternal life, for the promise that we will *dwell in the house of the Lord forever.*

I love you, Lord.

Ackowledgments

To those who have prayed for, nurtured, and helped in the writing of *Still Waters*:

>My husband, Kent Perkins

>My girls and their families: Ann Marie & Sig Brown and

>Keri Lynn & Jacob Lawson

>My grandchildren, Brodie & Audrey Anna Brown and Dewey Wayne & Lucille Lynn Lawson.

>The Church

>Yvonne Barnes

>Desi Branson Eakle

>Jackie King

>Shauna J. Smith

>Delia Sprague

>Katie Cogburn

>Tammy Cady

Edited by
Joshua Danker-Dake

Introduction

This book is an in-depth study of Psalm 23. It is intended to be read in order, as each section builds upon the last in exploring our spiritual life in this world.

It begins with lying down, continues with walking in the paths of righteousness, and concludes with dwelling in the Lord's house forever.

Each section draws on the Lord, who is our Shepherd now, throughout time, and into eternity.

Psalm 23 is a melodious song that touches us in a place deep in our inner being. Music of all kinds can affect us in that same way. Throughout Still Waters you will see a music note that denotes a musical reflection or suggestion of listening to accompany the devotion. We hope this will move you to a deeper understanding of this Psalm, as you walk through the valley of the shadow of death to dwell in the house of the Lord forever.

Throughout the ages, scripture has been set to music so that God's people may identify the Father, the Shepherd, and the Spirit as their source of help. All of the songs in Still Waters (including most of the Psalms) can be found on social media for your convenience to listen and/or sing along each day, with each devotional. Remember the Lord, our Shepherd sings over us. So we can sing over Him.

Contents

PART I
He Makes Me to Lie Down in Green Pastures

January 2

February 38

March 70

Part II
He LEADS Me Beside the Still Waters

April 104

May 137

PART III
He Restores My Soul

June 172

July 206

PART IV
He Leads Me In The Paths Of Righteousness

August 242

September 275

PART V
Eternity Now

October 318

November 354

December 392

PART I

He Makes Me to Lie Down in Green Pastures

**The Lord is my shepherd;
I shall not want
He makes me to lie down in green pastures**

January

January 1

> "Oh come, let us worship and bow down; let us kneel before the Lord our Maker. For He is our God, and we are the people of His pasture and the sheep of His hand." (Psalm 95:6–7)

DOWN

One of the most important lessons one must learn in living life as the Shepherd teaches is the lesson of "lying down." This is the position of learning obedience—the obedience of a life which is led by the Shepherd.

In the New Testament, we find the Shepherd teaching His disciples: "He who has become a disciple in the Kingdom of Heaven is like a person who brings out of the storehouse the new teachings as well as the old" (Matthew 13:51–52). He is saying that the Old Testament was not to be spurned "for the sake of the new." Rather, the new insights gleaned from His parables were to be understood in light of the old truths, and vice versa.

In the new covenant, the Shepherd takes His Father's commandments—the Old Testament's logical law—and adds the Spirit's heart. For example, in the new covenant, one must lay down his or her life.

He says we must give up our lives, hate our lives, die to ourselves, and deny ourselves. Our initial reaction to the Shepherd's New Testament words is, "Really?" Sure. It sounds scary, and to make matters worse, the world says, "Live life my way and strive for personal gratification and personal success!" But, my Shepherd says all of this is "the foolishness of the world."

Lying here, looking up into His face, I realize the Shepherd can gently show me, and teach me, how He will protect and lead me. He will provide for me and break the chains of sin and death through His mercy and grace. I can live in faith without fear. I can live in peace without death. I can have an eternal life of joy.

My goals and objectives become one statement: "Thy will be done on earth as it is in heaven." I am lifted up by my Shepherd to walk in the newness of life; I have a heavenly life here. Psalm 23 makes known to me, there is life always—-and furthermore, there is hope always—because of my Shepherd. Starting now, lying in His pasture, I am learning how to dwell in the house of the Lord forever.

Listen as He describes the scene: "My sheep hear My voice and I know them, and they follow me. And I give them eternal life; and they shall never perish" (John 10:27–28). Follow the Shepherd on this journey down the paths of righteousness, through the valley of the shadow of death, and into the dwelling of the house of the Lord.

Cynthia Perkins

So sing PSALM TWENTY-THREE:

The Lord is my shepherd; I shall not want;
He makes me to lie down in green pastures;
He leads me beside the still waters. He restores my soul;
He leads me in the paths of righteousness for His name's sake.
Yea, though I walk through the valley of the shadow of death,
I will fear no evil, for You are with me;
Your rod and Your staff, they comfort me.
You prepare a table before me in the presence of my enemies;
You anoint my head with oil; my cup runs over.
Surely goodness and mercy shall follow me all the days of my life;
And I will dwell in the house of the Lord forever.

January 2

"Let your eyes look straight ahead, and your eyelids look right before you."

THE FACE

Oh, the joy of looking up! His face is perfect. I can't see to the right or to the left—only up, because I'm lying down. My Shepherd is here taking care of me!

When one is born, there is only the face of the mother and father. One is lying in their arms, held close and protected. There are no cares or worries. There is only trust, comfort, and nurturing.

Now, in this position, one becomes secure, protected, and intimate with the Lord, my Shepherd. Here, the last abyss of one's nature has been satisfied…the impression left is of the strong, strong sanity our Lord, the Shepherd gives.

Lying here in His green pasture, looking up into my Shepherd's face, I receive His blessings, I will come to know His words and sense the manifestation of an intimate spiritual union coming to fruition. Only Him do I see. All the world is oblivious to me.

He said, "Now I lay you down to rest and receive My instructions for the rest of time here in the valley of the shadow of death. Then I will gather you, lifting you into My arms as we walk over the threshold from death to life. There you will be eternally with the Father, the Spirit, and Myself."

To close our lesson, we will all sing WHEN I LOOK INTO YOUR HOLINESS. This is a perfect verse to sing while looking at the glorious face of the Lord, my Shepherd.

When I look into Your holiness
When I gaze into Your loveliness
When all things that surround
Become shadows in the light of You.
I worship you, I worship You.
The reason I live is to worship You.

(Cathy and Wayne Perrin, 1981)

January 3

"We should serve in the newness of the Spirit." (Romans 7:6)

REMADE

In Oswald Chambers' book *My Utmost for His Highest,* he tells us, we cannot keep one ounce of self in our lives, when we decide to become the Shepherd's. "Our Lord never patches up our natural virtues, He re-makes the whole person on the inside." Once the Lord is my Shepherd, He begins reshaping me. It is the only way to be remade.

How extremely sad is the abuse of this psalm. Sung and read at millions of gravesides, memorials, and funeral services for millions of people who denied the Savior's bidding to come. They refused to let Him "make them to lie down," and, sadly, because of their resistance, He could not remake them from the inside out.

As a young child, I was made to take naps. Mother needed some time from her children, and we needed to keep a positive attitude through the rest of the day. So we had to lie down. The minute she shut the bedroom door, we groaned aloud about having to take a nap. We would whine and gripe until mother would yell, "If I hear one more sound in there …" Then we got quiet and quickly fell asleep because we lay down. Our attitudes were so much better the rest of the day because we had rest.

Now, I am the Shepherd's, and He makes me to lie down—to learn to rest in Him. Once I relinquish myself to Him, the Lord becomes my Shepherd. I will have an exciting and glorious journey through this life because I am remade.

It is said that as children, we do most of our growing while we sleep. Also, while we sleep we are down. The same applies to our spiritual growth. As He begins to remake me, I learn to have glory in my Shepherd, and I can put no person, especially myself, above Him. In this position, I can grow in Him and be remade!

So sing "Where He Leads Me":

I can hear my Savior calling,
"Take thy cross and follow, follow Me."
Where He leads me I will follow,
I'll go with Him, with Him, all the way.

(E. W. Blandy, 19th Century)

January 4

But Jesus called them to Him and said, "Let the little children come to me, and do not forbid them; for of such is the kingdom of heaven. Assuredly, I say to you, whoever does not receive the kingdom of God as a little child will by no means enter it." (Luke 18:16–17)

A LITTLE CHILD

The Shepherd said I must "become converted as a little child." Lying here and looking up at Him sends me back to my childhood. I would lie down in the pasture and look up at those fluffy clouds. I felt the light breeze moving the grass ever so gently. The sun peeked in and out of the clouds.

Lying here like a little child in these green pastures and looking up, I see the face of my Shepherd before my eyes, and I know He is my everything. The Shepherd provides all; He meets my every need. As babies trust in the one who gave them life, I trust in the one who gives us, His sheep, new life.

I'm lying here uncomplicated, helpless, having no resources, no agenda, no accomplishments, and no achievements. Just humble faith. I am converted, convinced, and consumed. Knowing the one who makes me to lie down in green pastures, is the Lord, my Shepherd.

So I'm happy to lead us all in singing SHEPHERD OF LOVE:

Shepherd of Love, You knew I had lost my way;
Shepherd of love, You cared that I'd gone astray
You sought and found me, placed around me
Strong arms that carried me home;
No foe can harm me or alarm me—Never again will I roam!
Shepherd of love, Savior and Lord and Guide.

Shepherd of love, contentment at last is mine;
Deep in my heart there's peace and joy divine.
The future's brighter, burden's lighter,
My cup runs over each day;
Your grace supplied me now provides me
all that I need for the way.
Shepherd of love, Savior and Lord and Guide.
Shepherd of love, Forever I'll stay by Your side.

(John W. Peterson Music Company, copyright 1966. All rights reserved. Used by permission.)

January 5

"He breathed on them." (John 20:22)

BREATHE

While lying here, there are no words spoken, just the presence of my protector and guide. I do not need to say a word. Absolute exuberance fills my body and soul. I am calm because He is taking care of everything.

The truth is, my Shepherd meets every need. My heart is regenerated and reborn because I humbly lie at the feet of my Shepherd. He has promised when I obey Him, by laying my life down, He will then lift it up, and bear all of life with me. He will carry the weight of my world on His shoulders.

This lesson is where I learn to breathe. My very being—soul, mind, and spirit—receives fresh air from His presence. If I wanted to get up, I could not! His Glory is too powerful, His splendor too commanding, His brilliance too prevailing. His glory pounds out the beat of my heart and delivers oxygen to my lungs.

A good example is the feeling one has when facing a warm fire on a really cold night. The warmth of the fire reflects heat, and one's face begins to glow. One becomes comfortable and cozy and begins resting and breathing slowly and easily. This picture of complete comfort depicts the sweet countenance of His goodness, when He, the Shepherd, makes me to lie down in green pastures.

Every breath that I breathe belongs to Him. All of my being, all of my life, is lived in His presence. We will all sing "Breathe":

This is the air I breathe, this is the air I breathe
Your holy presence, living in me.

This is my daily bread, this is my daily bread.
Your very word, spoken in me.
And I, I'm desperate for you.
And I, I'm lost without you.

(Marie Barnett, copyright 1995)

January 6

"Fear not!" (Luke 1:13)

FEAR NOT

Everyone lives in fear. We feel fear of rejection or fear of loneliness. We feel fear of being hurt or fear of being unloved. Most of us are determined not to be taken advantage of—we become "sue-happy" due to our desire to retaliate. We must have payback! Never faith—just fear!

My Shepherd makes me to *lie down* in His pasture so He can show me and tell me in this life, there is no "fair," and with Him there is "no fear." He has a rod and staff. The rod is used to keep me in line or beat off those who would harm me. The staff is to catch me if I fall or need medical attention, or if at any time I'm in danger, He can quickly grab me up into His arms.

With Him, there is an assurance that I am protected, loved, guided, and safe. No harm will come to me. For my Shepherd *is*. That's all. My needs are met completely.

Therefore, when it is time to get up and follow Him, my Shepherd will lead me down a path of right living in His good, acceptable, and perfect will! How wonderful to have peace, joy, and an absolute fear free life. We never have to be worried about ..."fair." So today, tomorrow, and until eternity, I will ... "Fear not!"

"Before you" He trod all the path of woe,
He took the sharp thrusts with His head bent low.

He knew deepest sorrow and pain and grief,
He knew long endurance without relief,
He took all the bitter from death's deep cup,
He kept not a blood-drop but gave all up.
Before you and for you, He won the fight
To bring you to glory and realms of light.

(*Streams in the Desert*, October 6)

─✧─

The peace of our Shepherd must quiet our minds and rest our hearts. We must put our hand in His like a little child, a lamb, and let Him lead us out into the paths of the sunshine of His love. He knows the way through the woods and valley below. Let us climb up into His arms and trust Him, having faith that He leads us all the way to dwell in His house forever.

(Paraphrased from Dr. Paddington, *Streams in the Desert*, October 7.)

January 7

"Look to me, and be saved." (Isaiah 45:22)

THE SHEEP WHISPERER

"The Dog Whisperer" is a guru of dog psychology. He can change a dog's bad behaviors in a very short time. A jumpy, scared, nervous, irritable, or dangerous dog will, after the rehabilitation of the Dog Whisperer, learn discipline, respect, and love.

The most incredible change is when a dog that is a killer becomes quiet and peaceful—it is completely reborn, extraordinarily changed.

This change begins with the very first exercise in the rehabilitation process. The animal is put down on its back and held there until it becomes entirely relaxed. The transformation begins to happen when the dog humbles itself to the gentle command of the master's hand. Its body is completely at rest, becoming calm and submissive. The Dog Whisperer trains the animal to listen and trust him. He becomes the master, the alpha, the leader of the pack.

─✧─

Where have I heard this before? Yes! I heard this from my Shepherd. As He *makes me to lie down*, He puts me on my back. His hand stays on me, and I can feel His gentle touch. As I relax, I begin to let everything go, trusting in the Alpha. Then, my Shepherd begins to teach me to trust in Him for my rehabilitation.

I become calm and submissive, all rage and bitterness replaced by faith, because I trust in Him completely. As I am rehabilitated, I become a new creature, trained by His Word, obeying His commands, listening and trusting the alpha, the Lord, my Shepherd. The Shepherd whispers sweet peace to me.

These words exemplify the message of today's lesson:

Peace thy inmost soul shall fill—lying still!
(*Streams in the Desert*, October 8)

January 8

"I have strayed like a lost sheep." (Psalm 119:176, NIV)

DUMB

The truth is that sheep are dumb. They forget where they have left their babies. They get lost from the flock. They become confused when a predator confronts them, running every which way, out of control. Does this remind you of someone? Yes, it is just what we do. Certainly this is why the Shepherd's Word calls us dumb sheep.

One of the most serious problems dumb sheep have is that when a sheep turns completely on its back, it cannot get up without help. It will lie there until it dies unless the shepherd finds it and turns it over. This is called "casting" or "dumb." But what about the sheep in the Lord's flock? You got it! We are dumb!

As humans, because of sin, we are "on our backs" and cannot get up. Of course, we are all walking around. For a while, though, we can't see sin as sin. Then, suddenly, at a very early age, we begin to know the shame, guilt, and regret that sin brings. In this deadly position, we may be alive, but like sheep, we have gone astray. The Shepherd says that the life of this world brings darkness, fear, and death. Peace is not found anywhere in this world, in the valley of the shadow of death. The world's sheep cry "peace!"—but there is no peace.

Do you choose the Shepherd? Or do you choose to remain a dumb sheep? If He is *your* Shepherd, you will find yourself lying down before Him, because He put you there: lying down in His green pastures. No more a dumb sheep who chooses to go down because of the weight of the world. You must choose. "Choose this day whom you will serve. Choose life or choose death!" What will it be: the Shepherd's sheep, grateful and trusting? Or a dumb sheep, screaming, "Baaaaah"?

Be a sheep of the Lord, my Shepherd. "Cast your cares on the Lord and He will sustain you" (Psalm 55:22, NIV). This verse is included in Felix Mendelssohn's Oratorio "Elijah". So sing "Elijah":

Cast thy burden upon the Lord, and He shall sustain thee;
He never will suffer the righteous to fall: He is at thy right hand.
Thy mercy Lord is great and far above the heavens:
Let none be made ashamed that wait upon Thee.
Amen

January 9

"Your rod and Your staff, they comfort me." (Psalm 23:4)

THE ROD

The rod my Shepherd uses to protect His sheep is an interesting tool. It was described by Adrian Rogers in his sermon about Psalm Twenty-Three as an instrument made from the root of a strong tree. The root would be dried, then scraped clean. The shepherd would curve the end, making it into a big ball, and then drive nails or sharp objects into the knob. The result was a powerful tool or weapon. The nails gave him control of the sheep because the rod was used to inflict pain to correct the sheep's destructive actions. Remember—sheep are dumb.

When an especially ornery sheep would not follow the shepherd, he would use the rod to break the sheep's leg! Then he would brace and wrap the leg, and carry the sheep on his shoulders, until the leg was healed. After healing, the sheep would never leave the shepherd's side—he would follow closely, at the front of the flock, walking beside his master.

Does this remind you of someone? As Psalm 23:2 states, "He makes me to lie down." Possibly, as David, the Lord's anointed, wrote this, he was reminiscing about his time with his sheep—how he, because he loved his sheep, had to use the rod to break a leg to get one of his stubborn sheep out of harm's way, teaching him to lie down and to listen to his voice.

Oh, the mighty love of our Shepherd, to discipline us with the rod and the staff. He truly showers us with His mighty love. To end today's lesson, the Lord, my Shepherd, speaks these mighty Words: "And have you forgotten the encouraging words God spoke to you as His children? He said, 'My child, don't make light of the Lord's discipline, and don't give up when He corrects you. For the Lord disciplines those He loves, and he punishes each one He accepts as His child.'" (Hebrews 12:5–6, NLT)

January 10

"The Lord is near to those who have a broken heart, and saves such as have a contrite spirit." (Psalm 34:18)

RHABILITATION

Rehabilitation is the new life that one leads when one has taken the Shepherd as his or her own. God's Word, especially the Old Testament, shows that everyone "falls short of the glory of God." All of us are sinners in need of spiritual rehabilitation and transformation. One person who provides us with this insight was a shepherd himself: David, the shepherd boy, the king.

Before he was king, David worked as a shepherd in his father's fields. He became a shepherd at a young age, and God's Spirit was with him. He was strong and fearless, killing a bear and a lion with his bare hands and his sling.

Of course, the most famous story of David is how he killed the giant, Goliath, with his sling. The rock penetrates the giant right in the middle of the forehead, at the precise spot not covered by his helmet. We know that David trusted God to guide the stone to the target.

Before throwing the stone, David yelled, "You come with the sword and spear. But I come in the name of the Lord!" And with that announcement of faith—no more Goliath!

Yet in later years, King David did exactly what most of us do at one time or the other. He became ungrateful, slothful, and lazy. He had been given many blessings from God. He began living on the past presence of the Spirit— after all, he was the apple of God's eye.

David's spiritual indifference came because he did not remember his shepherding lessons. Stay close to the flock. Watch out for predators. Lead and protect.

King David became important in his own eyes. Life was all about him. Insurmountable trouble came, and he grew spiritually blind. He chose adultery, cheating, lying, and murder. He was the king who had forgotten the Face of his Shepherd.

Then David's Shepherd picked up His rod! He sent a messenger, a prophet, to tell King David the story of a shepherd who had one lamb. He was a poor shepherd, but he loved his lamb. A rich man stole the lamb and took it for his own. This man had many sheep, but he was greedy and just had to have the poor man's only lamb. And not only did he steal the lamb, he served it as the main dish at his banquet!

After hearing the story, King David became livid. "Where is this evil man?" He would wipe him off the face of the earth! Then the messenger (the rod) pointed to the king and said, "It is you!"

Ouch, that rod hit hard. David's pride hit the floor. He had a broken spirit and a contrite heart. His Shepherd brought him into calm submission by laying a heavy hand on him and throwing him down on his back!

David's story shows us that God rehabilitates those He loves. *He makes us to lie down.* David suffered terrible loss from the repercussions of his sin. But he never again forgot the lesson of the Shepherd's rod. We see this in Psalm 51, which he wrote afterward. May we all sing with David, CLEANSE ME:

Search me, O God
and know my heart today.
Try me O Savior,
know my thoughts, I pray.
See if there be
some wicked way in me.
Cleanse me from every sin
and set me free.

(J. Edwin Orr, 1936)

January 11

"She came trembling and falling down before Him." (Luke 8:47)

The College of the Feet Series

Lesson 1
SIMPLE

As I lie down here in His pasture, He stands before me, and I see His feet. I see the hem of His garment. This reminds us of so many events from His Word, of lessons learned at the Shepherd's feet. These lessons are taught at "The College of the Feet." The next several lessons of our Shepherd will be lessons learned as we lie here in the green pastures at His feet.

The first story from the Gospels is the story of the woman with the bleeding disorder. She is unnamed, yet her experience with the Shepherd rings true, and her message is potent for us today. Even though we don't know her name, the Shepherd searches her out and calls her "daughter."

As the story begins, she has tried for years to get help. She has spent all of her money on doctors who have not healed her. Her distress was made worse by the fact that in her society, due to the bleeding, she, by Jewish law, was ostracized by her family and the entire community. She had come to the end of earthly help, so like most humans, she finally decided to try this miracle worker she had heard about: Jesus.

She had nothing else to lose. So she took courage and made a plan to go to this man. When she found Him, she confronted His followers by pushing her way through. Her perseverance is notable: she goes out into the huge crowd that is following Him—a crowd so large that His apostles were surrounding Him to protect Him from possibly being physically harmed.

She prays her plan will work as she pushes through the crowd. She kneels down, not caring if she is hurt or harmed by the crowd. When the Shepherd is two steps in front of her, she lunges forward and falls on her face, reaching, stretching every muscle of her arms as far as she can. With her fingertips, she barely touches the hem of Jesus' garment, and instantly she is healed!

I see myself lying here in this place my Shepherd has made for me, and I touch His hem, and I am healed. It's as simple as that! At The College of the Feet, one learns how wonderful the Lord truly is. Is it the faith, the humility, the heart—or is it just the Shepherd? Possibly it is all of these. My Shepherd tells me, "your faith has made you well." The exact same thing He told her. "Go in peace and be healed from your affliction." Is it not wonderful! Is it not simple?

January 12

"Your sins are forgiven…Your faith has saved you. Go in peace." (Luke 7:48–50)
The College of the Feet Series

Lesson II
WORSHIP

As I lie here in the green pastures at The College of the Feet, my Shepherd continues His teaching about another of His sheep who knew that her questions about her sin-filled life would be answered. She was also a very brave woman, who deliberately walked into a crowded room filled with "important" men to demonstrate that her Shepherd had no bias against sinful women.

Simon, a Pharisee, had invited the Shepherd to his home, but had not even been courteous to Him. The Shepherd told him, "When I entered your home, you didn't bother to offer Me water to wash the dust from My feet. You refused Me the customary kiss of greeting, and you neglected the usual courtesy of olive oil to anoint My head."

One can imagine the hypercritical air, the wagging of tongues, and the nervousness as these men discussed this curious Jesus. The one who called Himself the Son of God. The one who healed the sick. The one who took no guff from the politically correct. The one who asked them questions they could not answer. The one who loved the children, women, poor, and unaccepted!

Just try to imagine the outrage and fury of these men as this sinful woman entered. She was a woman of the street, a prostitute. She never hesitated. She never hurried (when one keeps one's eyes on the Shepherd, one never does). As she walked from the back of the room toward Him, everyone became desperately quiet. When she reached the Shepherd, silence filled the room. She fell at His feet and begins to weep.

In the culture of that day, women were worth less than cattle and were used as servants, slaves, or sex objects. Surely the speculation went something like this: "I wonder what *she* is to Him! We know what kind of woman *she* is!" Jesus was not intimidated or embarrassed. He simply allowed her to cry. He had compassion, grace, and mercy, allowing her to worship Him in her own way, staying at His feet, weeping uncontrollably.

As she wept, she began to wash His feet. She continued to clean them until they were no longer dirty, weeping the entire time. She not only washed His feet, she kissed them, over and over.

He never said, "That's enough!" or "It's okay. It's okay." For the Shepherd knows His sheep's heart—He respected her emotions and allowed her to worship and learn at The College of the Feet. The men were angry as they whispered, "This man, if He were a prophet, would know who and what manner of woman this is who is touching Him, for she is a sinner!"

And there is more! She then dried His feet with her hair. In that time, a woman's hair was her glory. Women did not cut their hair. She showed by drying His feet with her hair a heart filled with humility. She wanted to make His foot washing an act of personal, intimate worship.

She pulled out a flask of extremely expensive oil, pouring it on the Shepherd's feet. The aroma filled the room, knocking out the stench of the sanctimonious sinners so that they could not miss the lesson being taught by a prostitute. When they left the room, the aroma stuck in their nostrils, reminding them of the precious, redeeming grace of the Shepherd.

The aroma would also remind them of His reprimand of their unrepentant, pride-filled hearts. "You love little because you have no faith to see your sin: no faith to believe that I, the Son of God, can forgive those sins, and no faith to believe in me. Her sins, and they are many, are forgiven, for she loved Me much; but one who is forgiven little shows little love."

As she knelt and worshiped, she leaned down to the ground, with her face close to the floor in total submission and in total abandonment of herself. Touching? Yes! She was touching her Masters feet! He was touching her heart and making it new.

And then the Shepherd released His own flask of expensive fragrance: Grace that poured from His own precious blood. "Your sins are forgiven. Your faith has saved you. go in peace."

Accolades are due to this worldly woman, this sinner, full of shame, for the lessons learned at the feet of the Shepherd. Make the Shepherd the priority. Worship Him in actions. Worship Him in the middle of hellish mankind. Keep your eyes on the Shepherd. Feel no fear; only perfect peace.

This lesson leaves me with hope, for I reek with sin and shame. Yet the Lord, my Shepherd, has said to me, "Your sins are forgiven." I lie in this green pasture, like she did, at The College of the Feet.

January 13

"Neither do I condemn you; go and sin no more." (John 8:11)

The College of the Feet Series

Lesson III
CONDEMED

Possibly the best-known and most beloved lesson from The College of the Feet is that of my Shepherd's mercy to the woman caught in adultery.

The religious leaders, who were trying to catch the Shepherd breaking Jewish law so that they could kill Him, set up the situation. At just the right time, they burst into the place of the rendezvous, snatched this woman up, and dragged her through the streets for all to see. They flung her at His feet. A crowd of law-abiding men gathered to help with judging. How fortunate she was to be thrown at the feet of the Shepherd. These men could not have known this was the perfect place for her to be.

The merciful Shepherd who loved her would grant her grace and forgiveness. What an extraordinary difference between man and the Son of Man. To their amazement, He knelt down beside her. Her face streamed with tears, buried in the dirt next to His sandaled feet.

He picked up a stone. Without looking up, He tossed the stone up and down several times before speaking. "He who is without sin among you, let him throw a stone at her first." Then the silence crashed in! Not one religious man could bring himself to throw the first stone because they, all of them, were sinners.

This adulterous woman could not only hear but see out of the corner of her eye some of these stones dropping to the ground. Finally, the thunderous pounding stopped. When the last person walked away, Jesus took her hand and helped her up. Every one of her accusers had disappeared.

What a wonderful lesson. The Shepherd asked her, "Where are those accusers of yours? Has no one condemned you?" She looked around, stunned, nervous, confused—but relieved "No one, Lord."

Let's stop here a minute. How did she know He was her Lord? Had she met Him before? Had someone told her about Him? I truly believe that when He bent down to her and she saw His face, she knew. Her eyes were opened. Just like all of us when our eyes meet His as we lie here. And he spoke words of grace to her: "Neither do I condemn you; go and sin no more."

Listen as the soloist sings NEITHER DO I CONDEMN THEE:

By the crowd of worshippers,
Sorry for their sins,
Was a poor wanderer,
Rudely brought in;
Scribes came and Pharisees
Anxious to see
What the meek Nazarene's
Verdict would be.

They told of her wanderings,
Making each flaw,
Spoke of her punishment,
Quoting the law,
Writing upon the ground sadly and slow,
but said He unheedingly,
Head bending low.

Neither do I condemn thee,
Precious words divine,
From the lips of mercy
Like the sweetest chime.
Wonderful words of Jesus,
Sing them o'er and o'er,
"Neither do I condemn thee,
Go and sin no more."

(Daniel Whittle, 1814–1901)

January 14

"When I saw Him, I fell at His feet as dead." (Revelation 1:17)

The College of the Feet Series

Lesson IV
FALL DOWN

Perhaps the most important point of the words "makes me to lie down in green pastures" is our new life with the Shepherd, is the beginning and the end. It is interesting He has us to lie down at the beginning of our journey, when we humbly come to Him. And we will all fall down, humbly, at His feet when we come into His blazing presence at the end of our lives.

One's very purpose in time is to "do the will of our Father," as the Shepherd said He was to do. To look to Him, to obey His direction, to immerse ourselves in His wisdom, to engage those around us to come into the fold, and to follow His leading: these are just a few of the works that emerge out of our love and obedience while following the Shepherd's lead.

What happens in the lives of those around us as we obey our Lord, our Shepherd? They make the choice to accept the Shepherd's call, for Him to come and be *their* Shepherd, or else they deny Him and make themselves lords of their own lives.

※

In my life, I have lain down at my Shepherd's feet. I lie there every day to learn. One of the reasons this is so important to me, is my children, my grandchildren, my friends, my students, my Church, my colleagues, must see me following the Shepherd. This is my personal goal: to point with my life to the Shepherd.

As those around me accept the Shepherd and are made to lie down, I fade; He becomes their all. He becomes their Way, their Truth, and their Life. And at the end of time, we will all fall down at the feet of the Shepherd.

January 15

"And He put all things under His feet." (Ephesians 1:22)

The College of the Feet Series

Lesson V
UNDER HIS FEET

Under His feet, God has put everything: the Church, family, principalities and powers, the entire earth, the heavens above. God put "all things" at the feet of the Shepherd.

Because He makes me to lie down, I can do nothing but look up and around, and I have no doubt He is over all: all the Church, all creation, all of heaven's glory, and all human life. Lying here, I understand the implications of the words to the old hymn, "The Wonder of It All."

At His feet, one feels the power of the Spirit of wisdom and revelation in the knowledge of Him. The eyes of one's understanding being enlightened. One comes to the understanding of the hope of His calling, the riches of the glory of His inheritance, and the exceeding greatness of His power toward His sheep.

I am being filled by Christ, who fills everything everywhere with His presence, for I am God's masterpiece. He has created me anew in Christ Jesus so that I can do the good things He planned for me long ago. When it is time to get up and be led, I am ready. I am not afraid and have no anxiety about tomorrow, for He leads me in the paths of righteousness.

Let us all sing the hymn THE WONDER OF IT ALL:

There's the wonder of sunset at evening,
The wonder as sunrise I see;
But the wonder of wonders that thrills my soul
Is the wonder that God loves me.

O, the wonder of it all
Just to think that God loves me.

(George Beverly Shea, 1956)

Cynthia Perkins

January 16

"...and she came and fell at His feet." (Mark 7:25)

The College of the Feet Series

Lesson VI
REQUEST

The Shepherd continues today with the College of the Feet Series, by explaining how the Syrophoenician woman came to Him, requesting help for her demon possessed daughter. She knew the Shepherd could heal her. The minute she arrived at the place where He was, she fell down at His feet—the best place in the world to be to request help.

Being a Gentile was bad enough. But being a women and a Gentile in that day and time was worse! Females were considered less then livestock—especially a Gentile girl child. This woman knew she must not be discouraged, nor fear rejection. She believed He could heal her child.

Maybe she had heard the stories about the healer or had seen one of His miraculous healings. Her first words were loud and clear: "Have mercy on me, O Lord, son of David! My daughter is severely demon-possessed." But He did not even answer her. She just kept crying out. The disciples were annoyed. They urged the Shepherd to send her away.

By not answering her, the Shepherd was making the point that one should persevere in asking Him for His help. He finally bid her to come to Him. Now the beautiful part: She came and worshipped Him, saying, "Lord, Help me!"

Always, when one worships the Lord, miracles happen. Worship means to respect, love, adore, and believe the Shepherd. This Gentile woman knew what His disciples didn't: to first worship the Lord at His feet and to keep crying out to Him.

His answer at first seems smug and somewhat rude. He replied, "It isn't right to take food from the children and throw it to the dogs." Jesus was implying that the Jews were the first to have His help. In Greek, He uses the word for *pet*, not a mangy mutt! The gentle Shepherd was tenderly drawing from her an expression of her faith to teach His grace and His compassion for *all* people. The Shepherd is no respecter of persons. He loves all the sheep of His pasture.

She was not undone. She replied, "Yes Lord, but even dogs are permitted to eat crumbs that fall beneath their master's table." Her response was characterized by a complete absence of pride and self-reliance. She humbly admitted her place in society, but she knew the Shepherd was not limited to society's decisions. He said, "Woman, your faith is great. Your request is granted."

Yes, Jesus grated this faithful Gentile woman her request. Her daughter was instantly healed. Again, a woman learned from the Shepherd a lesson about faith. Another miracle at The College of the Feet.

The Lord, my Shepherd, shows His love to all of us. My Lord, our gentle Shepherd. Sing with me GENTLE SHEPHERD:

Gentle Shepherd, come and lead us
For we need you to help us find our way.
There's no other we can turn to
Who can help us face another day

(Gloria and William Gaither, 1974)

January 17

"But Martha ... was worrying over the big dinner she was preparing." (Luke 10:40, TLB)

The College of the Feet Series

Lesson VII
CONTROLLING

Today, my Shepherd is teaching a lesson we learn from two of His dearest friends, the sisters Mary and Martha. Mary understood class at The College of the Feet. Nothing could deter her from sitting at His feet and listening to His words.

But Martha, worried about all the events which were part of her everyday life. She felt that Mary was disrespectful, by not helping prepare for this special occasion. This event was upon them, and Martha was feeling out of control. She began whining and complaining about the situation to none other than Jesus.

The Shepherd answered Martha, saying Mary understood, He was the Messiah. He explained that He was always teaching about God, His Father. She should understand, Mary wasted no time in quietly sitting at His feet, learning about His mission; for He would not be with them much longer.

One sister was focused *on the Lord*; the other was focused *on her work for the Lord*. It isn't hard to grasp which one had given complete control of her life to the Shepherd, because she lay at His feet. The other kept control of her life to do *her* good works for the Lord.

The Shepherd said, "My dear Martha, you are so upset over all these details! There is really only one thing worth being concerned about. Mary has discovered it—and I won't take it away from her."

She took a course at The College of the Feet.

Being controlling like Martha produces worry and fear, and no peace. Being controlled by the wonderful fellowship and worship of my Shepherd brings a life filled with good works—a life taught at The College of the Feet.

January 18

"For He who is mighty has done great things for me." (Luke 1:49)

The College of the Feet Series

Lesson VIII
MARY THE MOTHER, AND THE CHILD

At the College of the Feet, one of the greatest lessons to be learned is taught by none other than the mother of our Shepherd, Mary, as she stands beside her Son. Listen as this story unfolds with grace and mercy—not just for Mary, but for all.

What her story brings to the table is the most magnificent truth ever told in the history of mankind. As I lie here humbly at His feet, looking into Mary's Son's face—my Shepherd's face; *her* Shepherd's face—I realize this lesson of grace and mercy is absolute perfection and the greatest testimony of the sovereignty of God, His Father.

Mary's story begins with joy but soon unfolds to sadness. The sadness is not what one would think—Mary standing weeping at the foot of Jesus' cross. You might say, "Are you kidding? There could never be a worse place for a mother to be than at her son's feet while He is being crucified!"

But the saddest place in Mary's story actually came before the cross.

After the miraculous beginning of her Son's life, Mary lost her way. She forgot the beautiful expression of magnifying her God. She forgot enduring the humiliation of the pregnancy. She forgot her child's celebrated birth in a stable in the middle of an unfamiliar and crowded town. She forgot the joy and blessing she had felt knowing that the very Son of God, the long-awaited Messiah, would be her child.

Even the visit to her cousin Elizabeth, who was also miraculously pregnant with John the Baptist, the forerunner of the Messiah, was somehow forgotten. These women must have certainly been scared and excited as they discussed the news of these special babies about to be born, and how they were blessed to play a major role in God's redemption plan, but as often happens in life, life happens, and Mary got lost.

The Bible does not tell the exact time of Mary's descent. It came slowly. Going downhill in life is sometimes slow and deceiving, and it can happen without you realizing the change. Suddenly, life comes hard, and one awakens to the realization of what they have become. Just as the Shepherd has taught, most sheep somehow go astray and get lost.

After Jesus' birth, the next time we see the family together is when Jesus was twelve, and we find him in the temple. His parents are angry because they started home, and without permission, Jesus stayed behind to teach the teachers. He was scolded, and the Bible says, Mary "pondered these events in her heart." One would have thought she would have known exactly what He was doing there, but she did not seem to understand His actions or His explanation.

Eighteen years later, Jesus is thirty, and He and His mother are attending a wedding feast in Cana. At the wedding, Mary took pride in her Son: she wanted to show Him off. When the wedding party became short of wine, she told Jesus to make the water into wine. Jesus honored her and made the best wine that anyone had ever tasted. He did not embarrass her, nor tell her, "Mom, this is not the time or the place." He was gentle with her and obedient. He knew she soon would be brought to the reality of who He was, the Lamb that would be sacrificed for the sins of the whole world.

When we next see Jesus and His mother, Jesus is teaching in the temple in Nazareth. Mary went with her sons, his half-brothers, to the temple. It was so crowded, she had to send word to tell Him, He should come home! He was embarrassing her because He was becoming a rebel against the Jewish leaders by claiming He was the long-expected Messiah, and repudiating the arrogance of the Scribes, Pharisees, and Sadducees. Possibly, Mary also feared for her family's safety. In that day, if one of the family members went against these leaders, the entire family could die.

Wouldn't it have been great if Gabriel could have flown in right at this moment and restated his first announcement to Mary, "Do not be afraid!"? Surely this would have jogged Mary's memory, and she would have known the answer to the question her son had asked when He was twelve: "Do you not know that I must be about my Father's business?" She would have remembered His father wasn't Joseph, but Abba, God, Jehovah!

Just three short years later, the day came when Mary went to the College of the Feet. One can speculate that Mary ran to help her Son when she was told He had been arrested. Certainly, the reality came flooding back: "God's Son, my son has to die? He is the sacrificial lamb? Oh, God, help our Son!" Early in the morning, she watched as He was beaten and scourged. He was lied about. He was mocked and spat upon and finally sentenced to death by crucifixion. She had to witness the cruelty of man expressed with all of Satan's forces—and sin placed upon the shoulders of her precious, innocent Son, at His Father's direction.

Then they nailed Him to the cross, lifted it up and pounded the cross into the hard rock hole. Mary stood there at His feet! His precious feet that made their way to the hill of Calvary, so He could be crucified for her sins. At the College of the Feet of her Son, Mary learned the final lesson: He was not just her Son; He was her Savior, her Lord. Gabriel's words, spoken to her and Joseph, came flooding back: "You shall have a Son and call Him Jesus, and He shall save His people from their sins." Mary immediately realized her Son was doing exactly that! The Son of God was then and there taking away the sins of the whole world. She learned this lesson at the College of the Feet.

As both Jesus' mother and sheep, Mary received grace and redemption. She got a Ph.D. in Grace and Forgiveness from the College of the Feet of her own Son.

January 19

"For the Lord gives wisdom..." (Proverbs 2:6)

Lessons from the Shepherd

Lesson I
WISDOM

The Lord my Shepherd looked at me and said,

> For I the Lord give wisdom;
> from My mouth come knowledge and understanding;
> I store up sound wisdom for the upright;
> I am a shield to those who walk uprightly;
> I guard the path of justice and preserve the way of My saints.
>
> (Proverbs 2:6-8)

He sits down beside me and continues.

> The law of the Lord is perfect, converting the soul;
> The testimony of the Lord is sure, making wise the simple.
> The statutes of the Lord are right, rejoicing the heart.
> The commandment of the Lord is pure, enlightening the eyes;
> The fear of the Lord is wisdom, enduring forever;

> The judgments of the Lord are true and righteous altogether;
> More to be desired then gold, yea, than much fine gold;
> All are sweeter than honey and the honeycomb.
> Moreover by them your servant is warned,
> and in keeping them there is great reward.
>
> (Psalm 19:7–11)

He gently stands and takes a deep breath, looking at His creation—me.

※

When class in this pasture is finished and I arise to follow my Shepherd, these lessons will follow me all the days of my life, as I will dwell in the house of the Lord forever.

January 20

> "She is a tree of life to those who take hold of her, and happy are all who retain her." (Proverbs 3:18)

Lessons from the Shepherd

Lesson II
TAKE HOLD

The Shepherd says, "Do you want to be happy?" "Yes!" I shout. He smiles and begins the lesson. "Take hold of Wisdom tightly. Hold on to Her. Let Me explain."

> Blessed are those who find wisdom,
> those who gain understanding,
> for she is more profitable than silver
> and yields better returns than gold.
> She is more precious than rubies;
> nothing you desire can compare with her.
> Long life is in her right hand;
> in her left hand are riches and honor.
> Her ways are pleasant ways,
> and all her paths are peace.
> She is a tree of life to those who take hold of her;
> those who hold her fast will be blessed.
>
> (Proverbs 3:13–18, NIV)

He begins to walk slowly back and forth, continuing the lesson.

> My child, do not let wisdom and understanding out of your sight,
> preserve sound judgment and discretion;
> they will be life for you, and ornament to grace your neck.
> Then you will go on your way in safety, and your foot will not stumble.
> When you lie down, you will not be afraid;
> when you lie down, your sleep will be sweet.
> Have no fear of sudden disaster
> or of the ruin that overtakes the wicket,
> for the Lord will be at your side
> and will keep your foot from being snared.
>
> (Proverbs 3:21–26, NIV)

The Shepherd sits down and looks directly into my eyes. "Wisdom will keep your foot from being caught in a trap. As a Shepherd, I have seen traps before. They are dangerous and can maim and kill."

He stands and opens His arms wide, continuing: "Trust in Me with all your heart; do not depend on your own understanding. Seek My will in all you do, and I will direct your path" (Proverbs 3:5–6).

I am learning Wisdom from my Shepherd. I am happy to take hold of Wisdom.

January 21

"I am the Good Shepherd." (John 10:11)

Lessons from the Shepherd

Lesson III
THE GOOD SHEPHERD

In today's lesson, the Lord has placed Himself upon the side of the hill and is seated. I must look up to see Him. He gently waves His hand to indicate that He is beginning the lesson.

"I am the Good Shepherd. The good shepherd gives His life for the sheep. But a hireling, he who is not the Shepherd, one who does not own the sheep, sees the wolf coming and leaves the sheep and flees; and the wolf catches the sheep and scatters them. The hireling flees because he is a hireling and does not care about the sheep." (John 10:11–13)

He stands and walks toward me. "I am the Good Shepherd; and I know My sheep, and am known by my own. As the Father knows me, even so I know the Father; and I lay down My life for the sheep. And other sheep I have which are not of this fold; them also I must bring, and they will hear My voice; and there will be one flock and one Shepherd." (John 10:14–16)

As He finishes speaking these words, tears flood my eyes. He is the only *good* this world has. He has laid down His life for me! He smiles, and then continues.

"Therefore My Father loves Me, because I lay down My life that I may take it again. No one takes it from Me, but I lay it down of Myself. I have power to lay it down, and I have power to take it again. This command I have received from My Father." (John 10:17–18)

I raise my hand. He acknowledges me. "Dearest Shepherd," I praise Him by saying, "how powerful and awesome this lesson, expressing how much you love me, and the power of that love you demonstrated through your death and your resurrection. I thank God that you are my Good Shepherd." Tears fill my eyes, and I softly cry.

January 22

"My Sheep hear My voice." (John 10:27)

Lessons from the Shepherd

Lesson IV
THE VOICE

One very important lesson that my Shepherd teaches as I lie in the pasture is how to know His voice. The sound of His voice is extremely comforting. I know His voice because it rises above everything. His voice is not loud, yet it never disappears underneath the noise of the world's foolishness. Because He is my Shepherd, His voice is like the voice of a mother. A child can be in dire straits, crying profusely, and the mother can call out to the child—hearing the mother's voice, the child becomes calm. The Lord, my Shepherd begins today's lesson, saying:

> My sheep hear My voice,
> and I know them,
> and they follow Me.
> And I give them eternal life,
> and they shall never perish;
> neither shall anyone snatch them out of My hand.

My Father, who has given them to Me, is greater than all;
and no one is able to snatch them out of My Father's hand.
I and My Father are one.

(John 10:27–30)

My Lord, my Shepherd, will never allow harm to me. He and His Father—*my* Father—protect and keep me safe. Nothing can snatch me away from my Shepherd. He and His Father are in sovereign control of all things. His voice brings blessed assurance to my life now and for eternity. His voice is not heard in the fire, tornado, or thunderstorm. It is in a still, small voice that urges me to know Him. His is The Voice.

January 23

"I will feed My flock, and I will make them lie down." (Ezekiel 34:15)

Lessons from the Shepherd

Lesson V
THE GENUINE SHEPHERD

Today, the Shepherd will explain how some who call themselves shepherds are actually counterfeit. They look like shepherds. They act like shepherds. They dress, walk, and sound like shepherds, but they are actually wolves! The Shepherd teaches us to recognize these counterfeit shepherds.

He begins the lesson:

> Indeed I Myself will search for My sheep and seek them out. As a shepherd seeks out his flock on the day he is among his scattered sheep, so will I seek out My sheep and deliver them from all the places where they were scattered on a cloudy and dark day. And I will bring them back them out from the peoples and gather them from the countries, and will bring them to their own land; I will feed them on the mountains of Israel, in the valleys and in all the inhabited places of the country. I will feed them in good pasture, and their fold shall be on the high mountains of Israel. There they shall lie down in a good fold and feed in rich pasture on the mountains of Israel. I will feed My flock, and I will make them lie down. I will seek what was lost and bring back what was driven away, bind up the broken and strengthen those sick.

I will make a covenant of peace with them, and cause wild beasts to cease from the land; and they will dwell safely in the wilderness and sleep in the woods. I will make them and the places all around My hill a blessing; and I will cause showers to come down in their season; there shall be showers of blessing.

(Ezekiel 34:11–16; 25–26)

The Shepherd stands and walks to me and bends down, looking directly into my face.

You are my flock, the sheep of my pasture.
And I am your God.

(Ezekiel 34:30)

January 24

"They were …like sheep having no shepherd." (Matthew 9:36)

Lessons from the Shepherd

**Lesson VI
COMPASSION**

The Lord, my Shepherd, has such compassion. He is also called the "Son of Man" because He chose to became fully human, with all the emotions of humanity. Today He teaches about compassion and gentleness.

He says, "I must go to the lost sheep. I must go to the cities and villages, teaching and preaching the gospel of the kingdom, and healing every sickness and every disease among the people. When I see them, I am moved with compassion for them, because they are weary and scattered, like sheep having no shepherd" (Matthew 9:35–36).

He looks straight at me and says, "The harvest truly is plentiful, but the laborers are few. Therefore pray to the Lord of the harvest to send out laborers into His harvest" (Matthew 9:38).

We are to have the same compassion and grace as our Shepherd, to search for the lost and hurting, to preach and teach the gospel of the Kingdom. I must join my Shepherd in showing the lost, the Way is to follow Him. I understand, that these sheep's spiritual needs, are more desperate than their physical needs.

I look to my Shepherd and respond with exuberant compassion. "Here I am, Lord, send me!" Today our Shepherd will sing a special song. He said He will sing the hymn SO SEND I YOU. As the Father has sent Him, so He sends us.

So send I you to labor unrewarded
To serve unpaid, unloved, unsought, unknown,
To bear rebuke, to suffer scorn and scoffing
So send I you to toil for Me alone.

So send I you to leave your life's ambition,
To die to dear desire, self-will resign,
To labor long, and love where men revile you
So send I you, to lose your life in Mine.

(Margaret Clarkson, copyright 1954, EMI CMG MUSIC)

January 25

"I heard the voice of the Lord…" (Isaiah 6:8)

Lessons from the Shepherd

Lesson VII
THE ANSWER: "HERE I AM!"

My relationship with my Shepherd must be one of conditioning myself to always be attuned to God. But I am mostly void of any listening, except to my own opinion. "The majority of us have no ear for anything but ourselves. We cannot hear a thing God says. To be brought into the zone of the call of God is to be profoundly altered" (Oswald Chambers, *My Utmost For His Highest*).

My prayer is for my Shepherd to open my ears and my heart to really listen. In the position of lying down, as *my* Shepherd teaches me, I not only hear, but I listen.

The Shepherd begins the lesson. "Today, I want you to learn to listen. I will give you an example of one of my sheep who had to learn to listen. His name is Moses. Moses had to learn the lesson of humility before he became the great leader of My people. Because he took matters into his own hands and murdered an Egyptian, he had to run for his life to a foreign country. It took forty years of desert shepherding for Moses to learn to listen to Me."

The Shepherd waves His hands toward the mountain. "There, in the wilderness, Moses found a wife, a family, and a flock of sheep. Interesting, the irony that he would become My chosen shepherd for

My people. While out in the deep wilderness, I set a fire that did not burn anything. The angel of the Lord appeared to him as a blazing fire in a bush. That would be Me. Moses was amazed because the bush was engulfed in flames, but it didn't burn up. When I the Lord saw that I had caught Moses' attention, I called to him from the bush, 'Moses! Moses!' 'Here I am!' Moses replied" (Exodus 3:2–6).

The Shepherd looked up and said, "Notice, My sheep, that first you must give me your attention, then listen. Moses had to continue his work, yet he had to turn away from the ordinary details of life to see that in the middle of the ordinary come the extraordinary details of God. When stubborn Moses finally placed his eyes on God My Father and Me, *then* he had the strength to respond with 'Here I am.'"

"My child! My child!" the Shepherd calls. Without hesitation, I answer, "Here I am!"

January 26

"Therefore since we have been made right in God's sight by faith…" (Romans 5:1, NLT)

Lessons from the Shepherd

Lesson VIII
MADE RIGHT

The war with God is over. He reconciled us to himself by asking His son to die for our sins. Because the Shepherd was also the Sacrificial Lamb, the war between heaven and hell was won by heaven. He paid the entire price, and we are now reconciled with God.

Today, in our Shepherd's lesson, He shares the evidence of our reconciliation. He made it clear that as His sheep I have:

    *Peace with God
    *Grace
    *The hope of glory
    *Divine love
    *Freedom from divine wrath
    *Joy in the Lord

He explains that when I begin the journey down the *Paths of Righteousness*, there will be hardships and tribulations. These events in my life are put there for the purposes of finding joy, developing faith, and coming to know the Holy Spirit as I have come to know my Shepherd. Joy comes now by praising Him in every situation. Faith comes by hearing His Word.

He says, "You should glory in tribulations because tribulation builds perseverance, and perseverance builds character. Your character is living proof of your hope" (Romans 5:3–4).

He looks at us and continues, "It has been said that 'Character is what you are in the dark.' In other words, character is 'right living' by Me and My Father's Word. One must become Christlike *all* the time: in the light of day and the darkness of night."

He says, "My peace I give to you. Let not your heart be troubled, and neither be afraid (John 14:27). While you were still My enemies, you were restored to friendship with God by My death; by My resurrected life you are certainly to be delivered from eternal punishment. So now all of you can rejoice in the wonderful new relationship with God that comes through Me. By what was done for you on Calvary, you have been made right."

I respond, "Oh, my Shepherd, in Thee do I put my trust." We all shout with joy, lifting our hands, heads, and hearts with praise.

January 27

"The Ten Commandments were given so that all could see the extent of their failure to obey God's laws." (Romans 5:20, TLB)

Lessons from the Shepherd

Lesson IX
I (Me)

We sheep are not sinners because we sin. We sin because we are sinners. These words tell us exactly who we are: sinners without hope. It is discouraging to see the entire world bound in sin and shame. I know I'm a sinner because I just want to take my Shepherd's name and yet I continue to do what I want to do. That is sin! Sin is what *I* want to do!

Immediately, though, my Shepherd makes me to lie down in His pasture to teach me to follow Him in the path of righteousness for *His Name's* sake, I am to bring honor to His name.

To be released from sin, the *me* must be gone. It's not about *me*. The *me* must go. *Me* is a born sinner. *Me* cannot escape sin, death, and hell. In fact, when I took the Shepherd as Lord, *Me* had to die. *Me* could no longer live. *He* must live; *Me* must die.

Listen as He teaches. "When you died with Me on the cross, you became united with Me—I, who was raised from the dead. As a result, you can produce good fruit—that is, good deeds for God. Now you have been released from the law of sin and death, for you died with Me, and you are no longer captive to its power. Now you can really serve God by the new way—the Spirit."

To hate sin and to desire the will of *my* Shepherd is my goal, so in all I do, it may be to God's glory.

"If I am rightly devoted to the Lord Jesus, *my* Shepherd, I have reached the sublime height where no one ever thinks of noticing me. All that is noticed is that the power of God comes through me all the time." (Oswald Chambers, *My Utmost For His Highest*, November 16)

Praise be to God! Now I am a saint, not a sinner. For I am no more. *Me* has been changed to *my Shepherd*.

January 28

"And the Holy Spirit helps us in our distress." (Romans 8:26, NLT)

Lessons from the Shepherd

Lesson X
HELPER

In my Shepherd's lessons, He makes it quite clear, how in this world, there will be troubles and tribulations. Never are we out of the hemisphere of sin and shame until we are finally out of time and into eternity. Our Shepherd has expressed the glorious relationship of the Spirit that currently lives in me. And as I learn these lessons, I have come to grasp the knowledge, how in all difficult situations, my help comes from the Lord, my Shepherd, and from the Spirit. Let's listen as He begins today's lesson.

"The Holy Spirit helps you in your distress. You don't even know what you should pray for, or how you should pray. The Holy Spirit pleads on your behalf when the pain is so great it cannot be expressed in words. And the Father who knows all hearts knows what the Spirit is saying. The Spirit pleads on your behalf for God's own will to be done in that moment."

"My Father God's will is good, acceptable, and perfect. Why should you then desire *your* will? Because you are comfortable with *I* and you believe you know what is to be done in every situation. You have faith and trust in *you*. This unbelief in a sheep's life causes the Spirit and Myself much grief because we are unable to get through to be of help. We will not push ourselves on any sheep. It is your choice to be with us."

We all sit in silence, contemplating His words.

Being alone with *my* Shepherd is when He begins to expose my life and to reveal the truth about me. To get through the noisy congestion of my head, he *makes me to lie down.*

"I must get sick unto death of myself, until there is no longer any surprise at anything God can tell me about myself. I cannot touch the depths of meanness in myself. There is only one place where I am right, and that is in Christ Jesus." (Oswald Chambers, *My Utmost For His Highest*, June 21)

I must call out to my Shepherd, who is my Savior. He hears and He saves. It's as simple as that.

We all bow our heads and pray.

January 29

"There are six things the Lord hates, yes, seven are an abomination to Him." (Proverbs 6:16)

Lessons from the Shepherd

Lesson XI
ABOMINATION

My Shepherd, the Lord, does not mince words about what is disgusting to Him. He teaches Wisdom's words, expressing what is sickening and horrible in our lives. Today He explains seven sins that are detestable in the sight of God the Father.

The Shepherd begins. "Here is a description of worthless and wicked people: they are constant liars, signaling their true intentions to their friends by making signs with their eyes, feet, and fingers. Their perverted hearts plot evil. They stir up trouble constantly. But they will be destroyed suddenly, broken beyond all hope of healing."

"There are six things I and My Father hate." He looks away then quietly turns back. "No, seven: and I detest them."

a proud look
a lying tongue
hands that kill the innocent
a heart that plots evil
feet that race to do wrong
a false witness who pours out lies
a person who sows discord among brothers

The worthless person, the scoundrel my Shepherd is speaking about, is a term which came to be used of the Devil himself. Wisdom, in contrast, provides direction, protection, and boundaries for all of life's circumstances. Otherwise there will be hell to pay—now as well as eternally. An "abomination" is defined as something horrible. Wisdom uses the exact same definition for hell!

If I choose hell, I am a living abomination. Those six—no, seven things—that my Shepherd hates I will do if I choose *Me* instead of the Shepherd. So, I choose *my* Shepherd!

January 30

"Come to Me, all you who labor and are heavy laden, and I will give you rest."
(Matthew 11:28)

Lessons from the Shepherd

Lesson XII
REST

As I lie here listening to the teachings of the Lord my Shepherd, I am watching every move He makes. His gentle spirit inspires me to digest His every word. One would think that He would want us sitting up tall and attentive, ready to take notes, excitedly raising our hands to answer His questions. However, this is not His teaching method. He gently speaks and inspires with His perfect words. When I am in this position of calm submission, He speaks to me.

Listen to the lesson for today:

> Come to Me,
> all you who labor and are heavy laden,
> and I will give you rest.
> Take My yoke upon you and learn from Me,
> for I am gentle and lowly in heart,
> and you will find rest for your souls.
> For My yoke is easy and My burden is light.
> (Matthew 11:28–30

"If you feel the burden of life, come. Only when you relinquish your life and realize that you are spiritually bankrupt and have not the slightest possibility of saving yourself can you come to me. No works, no doing—just Me. Here in my arms you find rest. Here you will become rooted and grounded in My grace. Here you will become filled with all the fullness of God, the Spirit, and Myself."

My response is calm submission. He fills me with a deep well of joy unspeakable, full of glory—complete peace, refreshing freedom, and rest.

January 31

"There are four things which are little on the earth, but they are exceedingly wise."
(Proverbs 30:24)

Lessons from the Shepherd

Lesson XIII
FOUR LITTLE THINGS

One of the main objectives of my Shepherd is to have Wisdom teach me understanding. Today, she is our guest teacher. As I lie here in the beauty of this pasture, His creation is a perfect classroom for Wisdom's lesson. She is a powerful teacher.

Wisdom begins her lesson by calling up these wise creatures: the ant, the rock badger, the locust, and the spider. She gently touches each one as she speaks:

> There are four things which are little
> on the earth,
> but they are exceedingly wise:
> The ants are a people not strong,
> yet they prepare their food in the summer;
> The rock badgers are a feeble folk,
> yet they make their homes in the crags;
> the locusts have no king,
> yet they all advance in ranks;
> the spider skillfully grasps with
> its hands,
> and it is in kings' palaces.
> (Proverbs 30:24–28)

"These creatures are small, but very wise. They have a great work ethic. They have been given instinct by Me which provides for their family and their survival. They are not strong but are very wise. They show how I, Wisdom, am strong, and filled with power."

I am dumbfounded as I look at each of these creatures. Ants I always try to squash, but the rest go right back to working and are never discouraged. The badger I never get to see because he knows how to hide. The locust, I see only the empty shell stuck to the bark of a tree. The spider and her web are always everywhere in my house even though I work constantly to get rid of them. These four creatures survive because of Wisdom, their Creator, my Shepherd.

I understand my Shepherd's point. They may be small, but these creatures are strong and wise. I am learning wisdom from these "four little things."

February

February 1

NKJV Matthew 22:37-38 "Jesus said ... 'You shall love the Lord your God with all your heart, with all your soul, and with all your mind, and with all your strength. This is the first and great commandment."

Lessons from the Shepherd

LESSON XIV

THE HEART

The Shepherd just announced today's lesson is about His number one commandment. Sounds serious. Here in the pasture, surrounded by His serene creation, He is teaching the most serious of His lessons, while I lie here in this calm, submissive state, I am ready to learn.

"The greatest is the commandment of relinquishing the whole person to the Father. Not only should one relinquish all themselves, but love God more than themselves. One must love God with all their heart, with all their soul, with all their mind, and with all their strength."

"The heart is the organ that pumps the blood and without it one is physically dead. However, as we will see, a person may be spiritually dead, but still physically alive. This happens if the heart is not pumping in the spiritual, and emotional realms."

He leans in ... "The heart is also in the front of the body and exposed to everything. It is often used as a target to kill both emotionally or physically. It is the central part of a person's body."

"The heart is the basis of emotional life, and the source and center of all emotions. The heart is where the deepest and most sincere feelings are located." He stands, and says. "The heart proves a person's character, as expressed by ... 'it's the heart of the matter'."

My Shepherd walks forward and again sits down. "Furthermore, the heart provides the ability to feel humane and contains altruistic feelings. It shows love and admiration. The heart is accredited with showing a person's spirit, courage, and determination. A drawing of a heart is used to signify true love between a man and a woman, or a beloved person or friend ... I heart you."

As I listen, I am beginning to understand what *my* Shepherd teaches about our Father desiring my heart. For me to be His, or He to be mine, I must first give my heart. I must love with my heart before I can reach soul, spirit and strength.

Tomorrow we will continue learning another specific part of commandment number one ... "love with - the HEART."

February 2

NKJV Matthew 22:37 "You shall love the Lord your God …"

Lessons from the Shepherd

LESSON XV

AGAPE

Today the Shepherd continues with the explanation of the first and most important commandment. "Love the Lord your God. This love I speak about is *AGAPE* love. *AGAPE* means the love that I have shown by doing the will of *my* Father. It is a sacrificial love, shown by obedience and selflessness. It is love of God, myself, and The Holy Spirit that transcends into love for humanity. Without *AGAPE* love, there would be no love for humanity. Only this love will transform the human spirit into complete obedience to God's will."

As I listen to my Shepherd, I realize this love is generated by the abandonment of myself. He begins to teach the characteristics of *AGAPE*:

> *If human love does not carry a man/woman beyond themselves,*
> *it is not love.*
> *If love is always discreet, always wise,*
> *always sensible and calculating,*
> *never carried beyond itself, it is not love at all.*
> *It may be affection, it may be warmth of feeling,*
> *but it has not the true nature of love in it.*
> *Abandonment to God is of more value than personal holiness.*
> *Personal holiness focuses the eye on our own whiteness;*
> *we are greatly concerned about the way we walk and talk and look,*
> *fearful lest we offend Him.*
> *Perfect love casts out all that when once we are abandoned to God.*
> *We have to get rid of this notion - - - "Am I of any use?"*
> *and make up our minds that* **we are not**, *and we may be near the truth.*
> *It is never a question of being of use, but to being of value to God Himself.*

(Oswald Chambers, February 21)

"Remember! "Perfect love casts out all fear. There is no fear in Love. *AGAPE* Me - - - with all your heart, soul, mind and strength."

My life in the ordinary, little things, the daily grind, must provide the evidence to all, and to God *my* Father, that I am abandoned to Him. I respond to *my* Shepherd … "I *AGAPE* You Lord."

February 3

NKJV Matthew 22: 37-38 "You shall love the Lord your God ... with all your soul ..."

Lessons from the Shepherd

LESSON XVI

SOUL

Today's lesson continues with the greatest commandment. My Shepherd is teaching about the *AGAPE* love found only in Him and His Father. This love should manifest itself, by complete abandonment of a person's entire being. Today He focuses on our soul.

The soul is a part of our being unfamiliar to us. Let's listen as the Lord explains how and why we should ... "love the Lord our God with all of our soul ..."

"Soul has several meanings," He explains. "First; is the nonphysical aspect. These include: thoughts, feelings, consciousness and will. These are the deepest and most private thoughts that are completely hidden, and concerns a person's emotional and moral nature."

He turns and looks toward the heavens. "Physically the soul is described as the *spirit* that survives death. The soul of a human is the part that continues after death into eternity. The old hymn titled ... **Where the Soul Never Dies**, is a great example describing how the soul is eternal."

Looking back toward us He continues. "Finally, the soul is descriptive of spiritual or emotional depth, and sensitivity in a person's life especially their actions."

"Many poems and hymns have given tribute to My constant care in human tragedy and suffering by embracing the word *soul*. Examples are: *Be Still my Soul*: *My Soul is Anchored in the Lord*: *Sunshine in my Soul*: *Praise, my Soul, the King of Heaven*: and *Set my Soul Afire*. All of these titles are descriptive of the essence of a person, their entire being, transformed by the Holy Spirit breathing new life, into his or her soul."

"As a shepherd, David, who is the apple of My eye, expressed the 'soul' in his Psalm. His hundredth third and hundredth fourth Psalm both begin ... *Bless the Lord, O my soul* promoting blessing and exaltation to *My* Father, God, with everything you've got. Your entire being must become completely submerged in God's amazing grace!"

Now I understand. *AGAPE* the Lord *my* Father for ... *He restores my very soul.*

Let us all sing WHERE THE SOUL NEVER DIES:

To Canaan's land I'm on my way,
Where the soul (of man) never dies;
My darkest night will turn to day,
Where the soul (of man) never dies.
No sad farewells,
no tear dimmed eyes,
Where all is peace and joy, and love,
and the soul never dies.

(By W. M. Golden, Copyrighted, 1914)

February 4

NKJV Matthew 22: 37-38 "You shall Love the Lord your God … with all your mind …"

Lessons from the Shepherd

LESSON XVII

MIND

Our lessons about the first commandment are continuing. Today He is teaching about the mind. This is probably one of the hardest lessons to learn, and the most important, because a person's mind is controlled by his or her will. The mind is where sin's seeds are planted and begin to grow.

My Shepherd has added a completely new commandment to the ten commandments. With this new commandment, He is "upping the ante," teaching that the very thought of sinful intentions, is just as evil as the act itself. The Lord has set the standard higher than the Old Testament law, to show us His blood must flood the mind, and cleanse it.

My Shepherd is sitting on the hill. He begins the lesson: "You have heard it said to those of old 'you shall not murder' … but I tell you that whoever is angry with his brother without a cause shall be in danger of the judgment … You have heard it said you shall not commit adultery, but I say to you that whoever looks at a woman to lust for her, has already committed adultery in his heart. You have heard it said an eye for an eye, and a tooth for a tooth, but I tell you if anyone slaps you on your right cheek, then turn the other to him also. If anyone wants to sue you and take away your tunic, let him have your cloak also. And whoever compels you to go one mile, go with him two."

He stands and leans in, raising His voice, "You have heard it said 'you shall love your neighbor and hate your enemy!' But I say to you love your enemies. Bless those who curse you. Do good to those who hate you, and pray for those who spitefully use you, and persecute you. Do not lay up for yourself treasures on earth, but lay up for yourself treasures in heaven, for where your treasure is there will your heart be also. Therefore I say to you do not worry about your life, but seek first the Kingdom of God and His righteousness, and all these things will be added to you."

Everyone catches their breath and lays completely still, and totally silent. Wow! I pray. Oh God let His mind, the Lord *my* Shepherd's mind, be in me!

February 5

NKJV Matthew 22: 37-38 "You shall love the Lord your God ... with all of your strength."

Lessons from the Shepherd

LESSON VXIII

STRENGTH

The lesson from my Shepherd today is a difficult one to understand, because in this world "strength" means "strong." Our culture worships winning through strength: with guns, muscles, warfare, or by out smarting the enemy are just a few of the power tools used for human earthly strength. Today however, *my* Shepherd is teaching the truth about being strong.

He begins by repeating the first Commandment that one should ... "Love the Lord your God with all your heart, soul, mind and strength." Then He shocks us with saying that strength comes in weakness, and in gentleness. I had never heard of this. To be strong one must be weak; to be strong, one must be gentle?

He begins this lesson by explaining strength through humility. "You must humble yourself to the Lord then He will lift you up." (James 4:10) I begin to think, when do I humble myself with my family, my job, my possessions, or myself? Do these worldly matters cause me to feel strong and courageous? Hardly. My family is all over the place: my job is up and down: food only makes me feel good for a few hours, suddenly, I'm hungry again. Am I allowing these human aspects of life to control, and have authority over my life? There is absolutely no strength in these. They are but for a moment, then they are gone with the wind.

My Shepherd sits down and begins to explain how true strength only comes by Him.

God blesses those who realize their need for him.
For the Kingdom of Heaven is given to them.
God blesses those who mourn,
for they will be comforted.
God blesses those who are gentle and lowly,
for the whole earth belongs to them
God blesses those who are hungry and thirsty
for justice, for they will receive it in full.
God blesses those who are merciful,
for they will be shown mercy.
God blesses those whose hearts are pure,
For they will see God.
God blesses those who work for peace,
For they will be called the children of God.
God blesses those who are persecuted because they live for God,
for the Kingdom of Heaven is theirs.

Be very glad! Be very happy about these things.
For a great reward awaits you in heaven!"

He smiles and says … "Warning: The "HUMBLE" might not get rewards here on earth, but in HEAVEN!"

In summary if I possess humility, I will: mourn. I will be gentle and lowly. I will be hungry. I will be thirsty. I will be merciful. I will be pure. I will be peaceful. I will be persecuted because of *my* Shepherd. Then I am strong and rewarded with eternal life in the heavens! Therein lies true strength, no fear, only … JOY UNSPEAKABLE AND FILL OF GLORY:

I have found His grace
is all complete
It supply-eh every need.
But I sat and learn
at Jesus' feet for I'm free, yes free, indeed.
It is joy unspeakable and full of glory,
Oh the half has never yet been told.

(By Barney Elliott Warren, 1867-1951, Copyright 1900)

February 6

NKJV Luke 10: 27 Jesus said ... "A second commandment is equally important, 'Love your neighbor as yourself.'"

Lessons from the Shepherd

LESSON XIX

MY NEIGHBOR

Today is the last lesson about the greatest commandment. My Shepherd tells us how we are to love our neighbor as we love ourselves. The question was asked ... "Who is my neighbor?" And *my* Shepherd answered in a story called "The Good Samaritan."

A Jewish man was traveling on a trip from Jerusalem to Jericho,
and he was attacked by bandits.
They stripped him of his clothes and money,
beat him up, and left him half dead beside the road.
By chance a Jewish priest came along:
but when he saw the man lying there,
he crossed to the other side of the road and passed him by.
A temple assistant walked over and looked at him lying there,
but he also passed by on the other side.
Then a despised Samaritan came along,
and when he saw the man, he felt deep pity.
Kneeling beside him, the Samaritan soothed his wounds
with medicine and bandaged them.
Then he put the man on his own donkey
and took him to an inn, where he took care of him.
The next day he handed the innkeeper two pieces of silver
and told him to take care of the man.
'If his bill runs higher than that,' he said,
'I'll pay the difference the next time I am here.'

"Now," the Shepherd asked ... "Which of these three would you say was a neighbor to the man who was attacked by bandits?" I said, "The one who showed him mercy." And *my* Shepherd said, "Yes, now go and do the same." (NLT Luke 10: 28-39)

All people are my neighbors. One must have a righteous abhorrence of all that is base and corrupt - - - not a spiteful, personal loathing of individuals. Godly hatred is marked by a broken-hearted grieving over the condition of the sinner, tempered by a genuine love for all of mankind. My *Agape* is resting in God my Father, His Son, and the Holy Spirit. My heart, mind, soul, and strength to love my neighbor is in God. Therefore I can love the unlovely. Who are the unlovely? Everyone, but especially me!

February 7

NKJV Matthew 6:5 "And when you pray …"

LESSONS ON PRAYER

PRAYER

My Shepherd has stated soon He will have us leave this lovely green pasture. He said many of the lessons taught here, while lying down, will be about the power of prayer. Listen as He begins to teach.

"Prayer has complete power in the spiritual realm, and is the most powerful weapon in the warfare against the evil one. Prayer not only changes things, it changes people, and especially the one praying. Prayer provides strength to live now and for eternity with God our Father."

"Prayer invokes the Holy Spirit to rule and reign in our lives. Prayer proves that one's faith is in the Holy Father. Mountains are moved by prayer: sinners are saved through prayer: God's will is engaged by prayer. Physical, mental, emotional, and spiritual healing occurs through prayer power. While here in *the valley of the shadow of death,* live your life in auspicious prayer."

Continuing, He leans in:

And now about prayer. When you pray, don't be like the phony
religious people who love to pray publicly on street corners
and in the churches or synagogues where everyone can see them.
I assure you, that is all the reward they will ever get.

But when you pray, go away by yourself, shut the door behind you,
and pray to your Father secretly. Then your Father,
who knows all secrets will openly reward you.

Always ask for God's help. Pray in My name.
Pray without stopping. Pray with the right motives,
according to God's good and perfect will.
Pray with an attitude of humility. Pray without doubting.
(Paraphrased from the NLT Matthew 6:5-7)

He stands smiles, walks towards us and says … "Keep on asking, and you will be given what you ask for. Keep on knocking, and the door will be opened. For everyone who asks, receives. Everyone who seeks finds. The door is opened to everyone who knocks. All of this in worship to God My Father, your Father, place everything in His hands."

Prayer is the sweet aroma that reaches My Father's nostrils, as we worship at His throne of grace.

THE DIFFERENCE

I got up early one morning
and rushed right into the day;
I had so much to accomplish
that I didn't have time to pray.

Problems just tumbled about me
and heavier came each task;
"Why doesn't God help me?" I wondered
He said, "But you didn't ask."

I wanted to see joy and beauty
but the day toiled on, gray and bleak;
I wondered why God didn't show me.
He said, "But you didn't seek."

I tried to come into God's presence;
I used all my keys at the lock.
God gently and lovingly chided
"My Child, you didn't knock."

I woke up early this morning
And paused before entering the day.
I had so much to accomplish
That I had to take time to pray.
(Author Unknown)

February 8

NKJV Matt. 26:39 Jesus said, "Yet not as My will, but as You will."

RELINQUISHMENT

"God absolutely refuses to violate our free will, and therefore, unless self-will is voluntarily given up, even God cannot move to answer prayer!" *My* Shepherd wants His sheep to realize His will, is the only *good, acceptable*, and *perfect will*. He is very intense. If this lesson is not learned now, while we lie in His green pastures, then when we get up, we could lose our way, and turn from faith, to honor and obey our own will.

The prayer of relinquishment insists; I want You Lord, *my* Shepherd, more than I want … what this earthly life has to offer. The prayer of relinquishment is the prayer of faith in action. The relinquishment prayer acknowledges whatever my Shepherd decides will be all right with me. Fear leaves, because faith believes in the one who rules everything, made everything, and sustains everything.

Fear blocks prayer. Fear is evil. The Word of the Shepherd says over and over ..."Fear Not." *My* Shepherd says ... "Resist not evil." Fear comes when I act without trusting Him. Jesus encourages us to take His hand and walk up to fear and look that fear straight in the face, knowing that He and His Father's power obliterates the evil of fear, and replaces it with powerful godly peace. Because the act of placing ones' life in His hands, is to Him the sweet music of the essence of faith.

The Shepherd turns and speaks with complete love on His face... "I have told you these things, so that in me you may have peace. In this world you will have trouble. But take heart! I have overcome the world."

"When I was about to be arrested in the garden and die on the cross, I would not flee. Instead, I knelt to pray in that dark and lonely garden under the olive trees. In My prayer that night, I gave *My* sheep, for all time, the perfect example of the prayer of relinquishment. I had been given humanity, as well as divinity. Part of the humanity was My free will. I chose to use My free will to leave the decision to My Father as to whether I must die by execution on the cross."

"I knew only one prayer could release the power needed to lift a sin-ridden world: Dear Father, all things are possible to You, Please - - - let me not have to drink this cup. **Yet it is not what I want, but what You want.**"

My Shepherd leans down and with tears in His eyes says: "The will of my Father, and *My* will were, and always will be the same! My prayer was answered as the cup of tribulation, in all its horror was spilled upon Me. Grace was lavishly released and poured out, an undeniable power has been flowing from My Cross and Me, the **Sacrificial Lamb** ever since."

I breathe deeply, turn over on my face, and weep, praying the prayer of relinquishment.

February 9

NKJV John 17: 1 "He looked up to heaven and said ..."

THE PRAYER

My Shepherd prayed ...

Father ... I am praying ... for all who will ever believe in me
because of their testimony
My prayer for all of them is that they will be one,
just as you and I are one, Father - - -
that just as you are in me and I am in you so they will be in us,
and the world will believe you sent me.

*I have given them the glory you gave me,
so that they may be one, as we are - - -
I in them and you in me, all being perfected into one.
Then the world will know that you sent me
and will understand that you love them as much as you love me.
Father, I want these whom you've given me to be with me,
so they can see my glory.
You gave me the glory because you loved me even before the world began!*

*O righteous Father, the world doesn't know you,
but I do, and these have known you sent me.
And I have revealed you to them and will keep on revealing you.
I will do this so that your love for me may be in them, and I in them.*

The prayer of *my* Shepherd is that I and all of His sheep will be one. This must also be my prayer, and my thought. For when we get up to leave this pasture, we must be ready to face *the valley of the shadow of death.* The Shepherd's prayer proves that we, the sheep of His pasture, need to be loyal to Him and to each other.

With His love we will celebrate His glory. We celebrate by demonstrating love for each other. The Shepherd will continue to *lead us down the path of righteousness,* until we come to dwell in the *House of the Lord forever.*

February 10

NKJV Luke 18:1 "I must always pray and not loose heart!"

PRAY ALWAYS

Before leaving this position I must learn with *my* Shepherd, prayer is not a trivial part of the journey. Prayer is continual. Prayer never ceases. Prayer pursues God *my* Father's plan and His will for my life. Prayer covers me in time of trouble and persecution. *My* Shepherd teaches that prayer is simply speaking to Him and the Father, and exhibiting trust instead of anxiety, peace instead of despair, joy instead of distress.

My Shepherd teaches, when I pray mountains are moved. Battles are won. Miracles are seen, and death is no more.

Prayer is faith in action. Prayer is the belief that says … "I trust God." Prayer is when one dives into the pool of life with the Shepherd, leaving everything of the human element behind.

Warning: our Father absolutely refuses to violate our free will, and that therefore, unless self-will is voluntarily given up, even God cannot move to answer prayer. (Catherine Marshall, Beyond Ourselves)

We have learned that fear is a barrier erected between us and God our Father, blocking His power. Fear is a giant in our world. Our Shepherd's Word says over and over … "Fear Not." In God's eyes, fear is evil because it demonstrates our lack of trust in Him.

One sheep put it this way … "Admit the possibility of what you fear most, and lo and behold, as you stop fleeing. As you force yourself to walk up to the fear, as you look it full in the face, never forgetting that God and His power are still the supreme reality, the fear evaporates." (Catherine Marshall, Beyond Ourselves)

"My Father's will is good, perfect and acceptable. That is why we should actively place ourselves into His hands.. The sweet music called *The Essence of Faith*."

> *I trust the good will, the love of my God. I'll open my arms and my*
> *understanding to what He has allowed to come to me.*
> *Since I know that He means to make all things work together for good,*
> *I consent to this present situation with Hope for what the future will bring.*
> *Thus acceptance leaves the door of Hope wide open to God's*
> *creative plan.* (Catherine Marshall, Beyond Ourselves)

The Lord, *my* Shepherd is the greatest example of one trusting the Father. He has been given genuine humanity, as well as divinity. Part of that humanity was His free will. He choose to use His free will to leave the decision to His Father as to whether He must die by execution. He knew that only one prayer could release the power that was needed to save a sin-ridden world. It is: "Dear Father, all things are possible to You. Please---let me not have to drink this cup. **Yet it is not what I want, but what You want**". In these words Jesus deliberately set himself to make His will and God's will the same, and peaceful power has been flowing from His cross ever since!

February 11

NKJV I Thessalonians 5:17 "Pray without ceasing."

POSTURE

Today my Shepherd will teach a lesson about the physical aspect of prayer. He has said "posture" announces to His Father the attitude of the person praying.

> "There are three physical postures that are important in
> prayer:1) Kneeling 2) Standing 3) Prostrating.
> All three of these make known to God one's attitude of worship."

He begins the lesson. "Lift up your eyes and behold who hath created these things. It is true that looking to the heavens puts the things on earth into perspective. When one sees the creation of the heavens, one realizes the glory of our Father. We cannot help but to turn over our body, soul, and spirit to someone bigger than us." (Isaiah 11:26)

"Another position of prayer is lifting up our hands. Psalms 134 says … 'Lift up your hands … and praise the Lord.' As your hands are lifted, lift up me, *your* Shepherd. If I be lifted up, I will draw all people to me."

"Next bow your head before your God, our Father. The bowing of one's head shows humility and complete submission. Exodus 4:31 says 'The people believed, they bowed their heads and worshiped.'"

"As I was praying so desperately before my crucifixion, before the onslaught of Satan, and all of his demons, I fell on my face and prayed! This is the third position, prostrating. Many of my sheep have an issue of pride, and never embrace this position of prayer, although it is a perfect position showing such humility, belief and faith."

"As we study these positions of prayer, remember with all of your being worship, honor, and praise Me and the Father, as this is the heart of my witness to the world" He sits and bows his body.

We fell on our faces and prayed.

February 12

NKJV II Chronicles 6:13 "He knelt down on his knees before the assembly …"

KNEEL

The Shepherd continues with lessons on prayer. Today He is teaching about kneeling in prayer. Listen as He begins.

"Today's lesson is to teach you of the strength of being down on your knees. As I do the will of *my* Father, I always begin with praying alone, and many times I come to Him on my knees."

"A lesson of this position of prayer is found in the example of King Solomon's dedication of God's temple. There in that glorious event He 'knelt down on his knees before all the assembly of Israel, and spread out his hands toward heaven … ' Here we see Solomon's demonstration of a position of intense prayer."

"Solomon prayed 'Lord God of Israel, there is no other God in heaven or on earth like You, who keep Your covenant and mercy with Your servants who walk before You with their hearts.' As the prayer continued, the glory of the Lord filled the temple, fire came down from heaven, as the glory of the Lord became so thick and dominate in the room that those administering the service could not continue!"

"When all of the congregation saw how the fire came down, and the presence of the Lord in the temple, they bowed their faces to the ground on the pavement and worshiped and praised the Lord."

The Shepherd knelt down and said … "Kneeling brings about a breaking down of self, that perpetuates into God's mighty love. As King David, Solomon's father said 'Oh come, let us worship and bow down; let us kneel before the Lord our maker. For we *are* the people of His pasture, and the sheep of His hand.'"

The Shepherd kneels … "Follow Me!" He says. And we kneel and pray.

February 13

NKJV I Samuel 1:26 "I am the woman who stood by you here, praying to the Lord."

STAND

Today we continue the lessons on the posture of prayer. Our Shepherd explains how one can pray in a standing position. He has a guest with Him, a beautiful young woman.

"We come today to teach another position of prayer. Our guest today is Hannah. I'm sure you have read about her. Hannah is a mother of faith. Hannah was barren for a time, yet throughout this barrenness, with much heartache and grief, she persisted in prayer. She remained devoted to her God. I'll let her explain."

She steps to the front and begins. "As I stood before God, I prayed so intently, that the priest Eli accused me of being drunk!" she smiles. "Even with His accusation I did not back down from my praying. I sought a contract with God. I pledged that if He would give me a son, I would give back to Him the precious life of my child. My Father honored my boldness, and sent me a precious son. I named him Samuel."

"At a very young age I took my only son, to be raised in the house of the Lord. Because of prayer, he grew to become a powerful man of God. He became a great prophet to the Kings of God's people. Due to constant obedient faith through prayer, when he was very young, God the Father, spoke directly to him."

"Here is the Prayer I prayed." She stands and lifts her head and hands, looking into the heavens.

O Lord of hosts, if You will indeed look on the affliction
of Your maidservant and remember me,
and not forget Your maidservant,
but will give Your maidservant a male child,
then I will give him to the Lord all the days of his life,
and no razor shall come upon his head.

(NKJV I Samuel 1:11)

"I requested special attention and care from the Lord, my Father. I had faith He would provide the request." We all could feel her faith as the Shepherd put His arm around her. They smiled.

I begin in silence to pray … "May I stand, in prayer and complete devotion and discipline to Thee, oh God my Father, believing as Hannah does, that all things are possible through You."

February 14

NKJV Nehemiah 8:6 "And they bowed their heads and worshiped the Lord with their faces to the ground."

PROSTRATE

Today is the final lesson concerning the positions of prayer. The Shepherd will teach about falling down and bowing prostrate before our Father.

The Shepherd's voice is soft and emotional as He begins the lesson. "As I went to the cross I knew the physical pain it would entail. I also knew the heavy burden that would be upon Me, for *all* sins ever committed would be placed upon My shoulders."

"My disciples did not have a clue what they were about to experience, and Satan and all of his demons were in for the kill. As we left the upper room I knew there was no way to handle this history changing event, except through the infinite power of our Father." He looks toward the mountains, and continues.

"That night when we reached the garden, all my disciples were tired so I told most to rest, but took My three leaders, Peter, James and John with me further into the isolated section of the garden. I needed to be alone. I had to pray!"

He looked tenderly into the heavens … "I tried to express how undone I was and asked My disciples if they would help keep watch for those coming to arrest me. After they sat down, I moved further into the dark, and I fell on my face before our Father praying … 'Oh My Father, if it is possible, let this cup pass from me, nevertheless not as I will, but your will be done.' I prayed three times falling on my face before our Father."

He smiled as tears of joy fell down His face. "I, the Shepherd, gave My life for you My Sheep. Paying the price with My blood, for the sins of this world for all time. My Father consoled Me that night, the Spotless Sacrificial Lamb, who brought salvation to the entire world. Through prayer the joy of Our Lord became the victory. Sin and shame was and is, forever overcome."

Look at His face, shining as the noonday sun. He is pure "Joy!" The Lord who is *my* Shepherd.

February 15

> NKJV Daniel 9:3 "Then I set my face toward the Lord God to make request by prayer and supplications, with fasting ..."

PRAYER POWER

The Shepherd is continuing His lessons on prayer. For the next few days He will be teaching about the power of prayer. He calls it ... "Prayer Power!"

He begins by giving examples of prayer power. Those examples are standing in front of us. Listen as He speaks.

"To begin today's lessons I will introduce several of my prayer warriors. First is Daniel." Daniel says "Hello." The Shepherd continues. "Daniel is one of my dearly beloved prophets, who lived on earth at a time of Israel's captivity. Daniel obeyed *my* word even in the mist of severe persecution. Daniel was scrutinized, spied upon, and eventually thrown into a den of lions where it was thought that he would experience a horrible death. Yet, because of his faith in Me, and his life of obedient prayer, not even hungry lions could touch him." He laughs, and we all laugh with Him.

"Daniel was so covered with the power of prayer, that My Father sent the most powerful angel in response to his prayer request. It took Gabriel two days to get there due to a battle with the evil one. Gabriel assured Daniel that he was 'greatly beloved' by God. He gave him ... 'skill to understand.' Gabriel told Daniel that ... 'at the beginning of his supplication the command went out, and he was commanded to come!'"

"Daniel not only prayed to the Lord, but he also set his face toward God with fasting, sackcloth and ashes."

"As one can see, My Father gave prayer as the power that connects Himself to each and every individual that is His child." The Shepherd gives Daniel a huge hug. We all clap and praise our Shepherd.

As I pray and give thanks to God for His Son, *my* Shepherd, I am beginning to understand prayer power.

February 16

NKJV Daniel 6:10 "With his windows open … he knelt down on his knees three times that day, and prayed."

STRENGTH

"Daniel had no fear in his commitment to His Lord God, our Father." The Shepherd continues … "Daniel was in another country, where people worshiped pagan gods. God had honored his obedience by causing King Darius to acknowledge Daniel as one of his best men, and set him as one of three governors over his kingdom."

"Eventually, because of Daniel's Godly Spirit, the king decided to set Daniel over the entire kingdom. The king's court broke out in a jealous rage. As the officers engaged in an evil plot to kill him, they used his faithfulness in honoring and worshiping the Lord as their accusation against him."

"Daniel continued with his daily routine of obedient prayer." The Lord pauses and takes a deep breath, leans in and begins to speak. "Daniel did not resist the evil plot of the officers of Darius' court. He continued his obedient prayer, three times a day. In the upper room, of his home, with the windows open, for all the kingdom to see, he knelt down on his knees and prayed giving thanks before our God."

The Shepherd smiles at Daniel, then continues. "It is interesting how Daniel my servant knew he was in trouble, the first thing he did in prayer was to give thanks."

"The men of the court all gathered to watch Daniel and then reported to the King the law that Daniel had broken."

"The next scene was when Daniel was thrown into a den of lions," The Shepherd laughs a kind roaring laugh. The kind of laugh that makes all of us laugh. "But I came and shut the mouth of My creatures. Daniel was innocent! My Father loves and protects His obedient children. What fun I had that day as the King announced his honor to My Father, because Daniel could not be stopped even by the roaring lions!"

Daniel prayed:

*Blessed be the name of God forever
and ever, For wisdom and might are His.
And He changes the times and the seasons;
He removes kings and raises
kings; He gives wisdom to the wise
and knowledge to those who have understanding.
He reveals deep and secret things;
He knows what is in the darkness, and light dwells with Him.
I thank You and praise You, O God of my fathers ... (Daniel 2:20-23)*

What Valor! What Honor! Daniel ends the lesson ... "Prayer does not fit us for the greater works; prayer is the greater works." (Oswald Chambers)

We all stand and pray a prayer of thanks to God our Father for His strength. We lift our hands toward the Lord, *my* Shepherd, and pray.

February 17

NKJV I Kings 18:37 "Hear me, O Lord, hear me, that this people may know that you are the Lord God ..."

MIGHT

The Shepherd begins the lesson. "One of the most exciting times of My Word was during the days of the prophets. At these times, much of My Father's and My power was demonstrated to the sheep in marvelous and mysterious ways. Especially when they prayed!"

"Today we have with us Elijah the prophet." Elijah smiles and acknowledges us. What a strong and wild looking man. "Elijah is one of those rough and tough prophets of old." He points to Elijah as He speaks. "He is wild and shaggy. He wore skins. With fire and enthusiasm, he always said what God told him to say, whether it was politically correct or not. Yet, when a widow who gave him refuge son died, he was tender, and filled with compassion, bringing the boy back to life."

"He was by nature a recluse. Only appearing before men to deliver a message from God and to enforce it by a miracle, and then disappearing from sight again." (Unger's Bible Dictionary) Listen as Elijah expounds upon the power, and might of prayer."

As Elijah steps forward, his presence is overwhelming. He begins ... "One specific day I was deployed by God to go to King Ahab and his wife Jezebel was extremely evil. They were worshiping false gods due to Jezebel's pride, and Ahab's selfishness. To this day they are both known as the most evil king and queen ever! I challenged them to come to Mt. Carmel, and there to have a *Battle of the Gods,* with Bale's prophets one of their gods against me, the prophet of God!"

"They accepted and the day of the contest came." As he continued he could not keep from laughing. "I proposed that two oxen be slain, and each laid on a separate altar, one for Bale, and one for Jehovah. Whichever sacrifice was consumed by fire from heaven, would determine which god the children of Israel would serve!"

"I was calm and confident; the sixty three prophets of Bale in splendid apparel, yelled vain repetitions. They cut themselves while uttering maddening cries. They danced their choreographed routine all morning - - nothing happened. I began to taunt them … 'Maybe if you could be louder, because it appears your god is meditating, or on a long journey, or sleeping; and you must wake him!' By evening, the prophets of Bale were spent. Absolutely nothing happened!"

"Then I stepped up and asked servants to bring gallons of water and drench both sacrifices with water, until all the trenches were full and everything was soaking wet. Then I PRAYED!"

"I shouted the prayer … 'Oh Lord, the God of Abraham, Isaac, and Israel, today let it be known that Thou art God in Israel, and that I am Thy servant, and that I have done all these things at Thy Word.'"

"Immediately fire fell from heaven and consumed the burnt offering, even the wood, and the stones! The fire consumed the dust and literally licked up the water that was in the trench. This was no ordinary fire! It was the Holy Ghost Fire!"

A standing ovation emerged as we shouted, clapped, whistled and praised our God, our Father, for His mighty work. WHAT POWER; WHAT STRENGTH; WHAT MIGHT - - - PRAYER.

February 18

NKJV John 11:25 "I am the Resurrection and the Life."

THE FORCE

My Shepherd continues to teach the lesson of prayer. If these lessons are not learned while lying here, our power will be limited as we *walk through the valley of the shadow of death.*

"Today our lesson shows prayer power in the weakest of persons, a woman. There she comes, walking toward us through the green pastures. I am the force by which one has life and the first person that I told this to was this woman." He smiles … "Can you imagine the trouble that I caused at a time when women were not even considered as worthy enough to be counted in a public assembly?"

The woman is now standing beside the Shepherd. He gently hugs her. "May I introduce Martha. She and her sister Mary and brother Lazarus are my dearest friends. I will let her explain the power of prayer lesson she learned while one of my followers."

She smiles and begins. "Lazarus my brother became sick and he died. So I sent someone to tell *my* Shepherd. However, He did not come immediately. I learned afterward that He purposely came late. It is interesting that our Shepherd's timing is always perfect. His and the Father's plan was to use Lazarus' death to glorify *your* Shepherd, because immediately following His miracle, He would die and raise Himself from the grave."

She looks at the Shepherd with love and compassion then continues. "When He and His disciples arrived, Lazarus had been dead and buried for four days. I was crying and told Him that if He had been there, Lazarus would not have died. He told me that Lazarus would rise again."

"He said, 'I am the resurrection and the life. He who believes in me though he may die he shall live. And whoever lived and believes in me shall never die. Do you believe this? I said I believe that you are the Christ, the Son of the living God, who is come into the world."

The Shepherd put His hand on her shoulder as she shed tears and continued. "My Shepherd began to weep. He was broken hearted because we were so confused. It broke His heart knowing that with the miracle that He was about to perform, He would bring Lazarus back from heaven to one day again go through death."

She continued. "He ordered them to move the stone. We all looked into His face with intensity so strong it was hard to breathe. No one defied Him. His power exploded so strongly that everyone took a step back and did not make a sound."

"He prayed, lifting His eyes to heaven. 'Father, I thank You that You have heard Me. And I know You always hear me.' He yelled in a voice of thunder, *'Lazarus come forth*!' And Lazarus came out in grave clothes, and with a foul smell!"

We all jumped up praising our Shepherd and our Father. Prayer Power! Wow! Martha a woman, a friend; Elijah a powerful misfit prophet; Daniel the King's right hand man; and Lazarus the man who died and came back to life! Oh what a Savior, the Lord, *my* Shepherd.

February 19

NKJV Acts 2:17 "In the last days, says God, 'I will pour out my Spirit on all flesh.'"

ENGAGE THE SPIRIT

The Shepherd will now teach us about YHWH, or *Spirit of God*. He explained that this name that defines Him is pronounced as simply *the Spirit*. The Spirit connects us to God by taking our prayers to the throne.

Listen as the Shepherd explains. "I know all of you have met the Spirit. Today I want to explain in more detail the Spirit's purpose. If you are My sheep, He is indwelling you, and He takes your prayer to the very throne of our Father, then He actually translates each word into the exact emotion and message that the praying sheep wants to convey."

"The Spirit moves upon the hearts and consciences of all persons, revealing truth with His power wherever it is known, and even where it is not known, affording some measure of divine light and gracious influence." (New Unger's Bible Dictionary)

Now listen as the Spirit steps forward and speaks. His demeanor is one of comfort and joy.

"I convict all of sin; I graciously aid you in repentance and faith; I regenerate, comfort, and sanctify all believers. I also bear witness to all who accept God, and who are adopted as God's children. I execute the miracle of indwelling to all believers who have accepted the Shepherd as Lord; and transform in all of you a new, and divine life. I am in you. And most importantly, I am greater and more powerful than the ruler of this world!"

He leans in … "It is important that you understand that you must engage Me. Always pray without ceasing. Pray and never loose heart. Give yourself continually to prayer. In everything, by prayer and supplication let your request be made known." He smiles.

His presence is calming and peaceful. "The Shepherd has prayed for you, and has given you Me, the Comforter, so I can be with you, and in you, forever. I will lead you into all Truth. The world at large cannot receive Me, for it isn't looking for Me, and doesn't recognize Me, but you do, for I live with you now! The Shepherd and the Spirit stand shoulder to shoulder."

I see now, as I lie here calm and submissive, the pouring out of the Spirit, seals power for our journey with the Lord, *my* Shepherd.

February 20

NKJV Acts 1: 8 "You shall receive power when the Holy Spirit has come upon you …"

RECEIVE

Today the Shepherd continues teaching about the job of the Spirit.

"The Spirit's work in you, is to bring you into union with Me, and all other believing sheep. Altogether, My sheep are called the Bride. He also dwells perpetually within every believer, sealing every believer for the day of redemption."

"He is your Helper. He is sent in My name from My Father. He is the Spirit of Truth, which is another name for Me. He guides you into all Truth; because He does not speak on His own authority, but whatever He hears Me speak, He speaks. He tells you of things to come; He glorifies Me. He will take of what is Mine and declare it to you." (John 16:12-15)

The Shepherd turns, looks up to the Father and then slowly continues. "The Spirit convicts the world of sin, of righteousness and of judgment: of sin because they do not believe in me; of righteousness because I am with my Father, and judgment, because the ruler of this world is judged." (John 16: 8-11)

He points to the Spirit. "He was sent to you in My name, He is here to teach you all things and help you remember all things that I say to you as you walk on this journey *through the Valley of the Shadow of Death.*"

The Spirit simply smiles as the Shepherd begins to pray: both lifting Their faces to heaven … we follow:

> *Father, I desire that they also whom You gave Me may be with Me where I am, that they may behold My glory which You have given me. Righteous Father, the world has not known You, but I know You; and these know that You sent Me! And I have declared to them Your name, and will declare it, that the love with which You loved me may be in them, and I in them.*

The Shepherd, the Spirit, and the sheep all rejoice in this love that is overwhelming.

February 21

NKJV Luke 24:49 "Behold I send the Promise ..."

THE PROMISE

Today we begin our lesson by continuing to become knowledgeable about the work of the Spirit. The Shepherd teaches how the Spirit is often called *The Promise.* Because on our journey, *through the Valley of the Shadow of Death,* He is promised to indwell us, and we become empowered by His indwelling presence.

The Shepherd has confirmed that *the Promise* came in a new way, in the New Covenant, providing the power to continue and preserve us, as we continually walk with our Shepherd in a new life.

Here are several of the New Covenants Spirit's provisions:

The Spirit ...
- ... Was part of the Incarnation (Luke 1:35)
- ... Declared the Truth about Christ (John 16:13,14)
- ... Endowed believers with power to witness (Acts 1:8)
- ... Poured out God's Love (Romans 5:5)
- ... Intercedes for every believer (Romans 8:26)
- ... Distributes giftedness for ministry (I Corinthians 12:4-11)
- ... Empowers believers with characteristics for Godly living (Galatians 5:22-23)
- ... Strengthens believers within (Ephesians 3:16)
- ... Seals the believer in Christ (Ephesians 4:30)
- ... Guides the believer (Romans 8:14)

God the Father never defaults on His promises. The greatest, most powerful, exciting, miraculous promise is the gift of the Spirit, who dwells in us, as *we walk through the valley of the shadow of death!*

Our every prayer is lifted by the Spirit to the *Thrown of Grace*. We have power through Him to overcome time and death. Through Him we will *fear no evil*. Never should we fear evil because He is with us. He is with us inside and out. This is *The Promise*.

February 22

NKJV Acts 1:8 "And you shall be witnesses to Me ... to the ends of the earth."

WITNESS

The Shepherd continues to teach that prayer power is from the Spirit. He said we would be *martus*, the Greek word for witness. However, due to many previous witnesses being killed for their faithfulness to the Shepherd, the word *martus* became synonymous with *martyr*. A *martyr* is a person who is put to death for his or her belief.

"Being a witness was, is, and continues to be costly to any of My sheep. History proves, many have suffered torture and death, because they were My witnesses."

"You are to bear witness of Me in all you do. Your life should be a reflection of Me, *your* Shepherd. The Spirit inside of you makes sure that My life shows through what you do. Your life is like a letter written on you, that anyone can read."

"As you pray, your lives will radiate with Godly speech, good works, and righteous character, because you engage the power of the Spirit living within you. As one sheep wrote 'The true test of the Spirit will not be the way we act, but the way we react to the daily frustrations of life.'" (The Women's Study Bible, quote by Beverly LeHay)

He stands and raises His voice. "The manifestation of the Spirit's witness in us, is when a believer, the sheep of My pasture, becomes in character, and actions, increasingly more like Me, *your* Shepherd. My witness to My Father is calm submission, as I *walk through the valley of the shadow of death*. And you, the sheep of my pasture, must do likewise to be My witness, and a witness for our Father." He sits down.

I want to be a witness for the Lord, *my* Shepherd. So that all who see me, will see the Shepherd.

February 23

NKJV Psalm 66:18 "If I regard iniquity in my heart, the Lord will not hear me."

FIRE

To have access to Him, the Shepherd says that one must be pure in heart. The Shepherd tells us of one of His special sheep, King David, who is considered the "apple" of God the Father's eye. David had committed adultery and murder, yet he would not confess, and refused to recognize these sins, and became stiff-necked and unrepentant.

The Shepherd said that King David began to shrivel up inside for not admitting these sins. He covered them up with lies and manipulation, sacrificing his people's spiritual status, his character as a Godly king, and the power he had been given by God to rule God's children.

The Shepherd stands an exclaims ... "Listen! The eyes of the Lord are over the righteous, and His ears are open unto their prayers; but the face of the Lord is against them that do evil." (I Peter 3:12)

"King David admitted 'I have sinned against the Lord.' Not against those he had abused in his sin, but against God! David nailed it, ultimately sin is against God My Father!"

"When the spirit, the Comforter came, He convicted the world of sin. (John 16:9) The fire of the Spirit must purify your hearts and minds. When confessing your sins: He will be faithful and just, to forgive your sins, and cleans you from *all* unrighteousness." (I John 1:9)

"In conclusion," the Shepherd said, "one of my prophets explained the fire of the Spirit, take heed to His words:

> *The Lord isn't too weak to save you. And He isn't getting deaf! He can hear you when you call! But the trouble is that your sins have cut you off from God. Because of sin He has turned His face away from you and will not listen anymore." (Isaiah 59:1-2)*

King David learned his lesson. He said ... "Where can I go from your Spirit?" (Psalm 138:7)

The Spirit is the Fire of restoration and preservation! He dwells in me.

February 24

NKJV Acts 2: 2 "And suddenly there came a sound from heaven, as a rushing mighty wind ..."

WIND

The Spirit is described as wind; and His presence as air. The Spirit is the breath of spiritual life. This life-giving air is prayer. The following is a good example of the power the Shepherd describes as the essence of the Spirit's power.

I live in a state that is called "Tornado Alley." The tornadoes here are mighty and ruthless. They come quickly and pick up and destroy anything that is in their path. Everyone who has survived one says that *it sounded like a freight train!* There is complete stillness right before it hits. Then suddenly, the powerful wind, with its' horrendous sound, sucks everything up into itself.

This analogy brings insight to the Shepherd's words about the Spirit's power when a lamb is ... "praying always with all prayer and supplication in the Spirit." (Ephesians 6:18)

The Spirit is the wind, and the air, the oxygen of those who are the Shepherd's sheep. With His breath He sucks up the heart expressions of that lamb, and with His powerful wind lifts the prayers straight to heaven, dropping them at the throne of grace!

The Shepherd said ... "Be unceasing in prayer - - - praying always with persistence If prayer ceases one dies spiritually. Their Spiritual lungs collapse. Spiritual oxygen is provided only by the Spirit."

The Spirit, the Holy Wind, lifts me up, and sustains me in every way as *I walk through the Valley of the Shadow of Death I will fear no evil."* And, *goodness and mercy shall follow me all the days of my life.* Praise the Shepherd our Father for the Spirit Wind I breathe through praying.

February 25

NKJV Matthew 6: 9 "In this manner, therefore, pray ..."

SPIRIT WORK

As we pray, the Spirit gains control. Our Spiritual life in us is sustained through prayer. Prayer provides for us spiritual oxygen. Every Spiritual breath we take sustains a healthy, Godly life.

"We look upon prayer as a means of getting *things* for ourselves; the **Bible** idea of prayer is that we may get to *know* God Himself." (Oswald Chambers)

The Shepherd desires complete submission. After submitting, we are able to plunge into obedience, with complete assurance that the Spirit's intercession takes the pilgrimage, the mission, the work, the need, and presents it to the Lord God. Then, His good and perfect will, in His good and perfect timing, for each and every finite circumstance, can and will be done.

"To be" - - - not "to do" the work of God, should be our goal. We are the work of God. By praying, a child of God is not conscious of the will of God, because he or she *is* the will of God. A child of God never prays to be conscious that God answers prayer, he is restfully certain that God *always* does answer prayer." (Oswald Chambers)

The following describes the Spirit's work through us as we live a life of prayer:

>   He convicts of the Truth of the Gospel
>   He empowers us to witness
>   He destroys the power of sin
>   He guides the believer
>   He gives assurance of salvation
>   He intercedes
>   He comforts
>   He shows us our sins
>   He leads and controls our lives

The Shepherd closes the class, lifting His eyes to heaven … "Father glorify Your own name!" The Father answered: "I have already glorified it …!"

February 26

NKJV Galatians 5:25 "Since we live by the Spirit, let us keep in step with the Spirit."

BARRIER

The Shepherd begins today's lesson by speaking very forcefully. "There is a barrier that comes between the power of prayer, the Spirit, and us. This barrier is sin. Sin literally means … **missing the mark.** My Father has instructed each and every sheep to obey Him. He and I both have stressed that If you love us, you *will* keep our commandments!"

"My Father has given absolutes in His instructions for living. He sent me to earth, to live out these instructions in front of all humanity. I became the *Sacrificial Lamb* for all sin for all time. Death and hell is defeated because of My intervention. I set the standard of excellence for right living. Everyone MUST come to me and accept My Will, My Way, My Truth, and My Life, or live with sin, shame, and destruction."

He waves His hand over all of us. "The choice is up to each and every person. The bequest is in place. All are welcome to accept the gift. To accept *My* gift means acceptance of *My* will, forgiveness of sin, and eternal life with Me, in heaven. To reject all of this still means eternal life; however, not with Me, but without Me, in hell!. To desire one's own will - - - is a sin that demands hell." He looks to the heavens, then back at us.

"I have said all along, that no one is righteous; not one person. Right living can only come through being in *My* will. A person's will is transformed into *My* will when they accept Me as Lord and Savior of their life. You have done this. You are the sheep of *My* pasture."

Quietly the Shepherd continues. "All persons who insist on living in sin will be barred from receiving prayer power. Sin, transgressions, unrighteousness, all cause the tragedy of eternal separation from My Father. Therein lies the barrier of prayer that will not be heard." He quietly sits down.

May there never be a barrier between me and *my* Shepherd.

February 27

>NKJV Psalm 51:7 "Purge me ... and I shall be clean; Wash me, and I shall be whiter than snow ... Create in me a clean heart, O God, and renew a steadfast spirit within me."

PURGE

Today the Shepherd is pleading for us to trust and obey His direction in all we do. "Our sins come between us and God and makes it impossible to recognize His presence. They are like mud and dirt thrown on a window pane, shutting out the sunlight."

The Shepherd leans in and begins the lesson. "Every sin narrows the stream of His love by which life and vitality flows to us, thus blocking the Spirit's comfort. Often we do not understand the connection between our lack of productivity and the sin that so easily constrains us. Sin separates the conscious mind from the subconscious, so that we are in conflict with ourselves."

The Shepherd walks over to the edge of the field, turns and continues. "God reaches down to hold your hand. With your other hand you touch the lives of fellow human beings. Some are My sheep, others are not. Only as both connections are made, can the power flow. Sin will break the connection every time. and without that connection all is dark."

He raises His voice. "Sin *MUST* be dealt with. One must be honest and candid with God about all sins and failures. Drop all excuses and explanations. Be as specific as possible in confession. Know what sin is by studying the sinless Savior. Then when a counterfeit deed confronts you, immediately recognize that it is not the Truth - that would be ME!"

"When you follow your own inclinations, your life will produce evil. The following list will help evaluate yourself, and your motives of self will: impure thoughts, eagerness for lustful pleasure, idolatry, Spiritism (that is, encouraging the activity of demons), hatred and fighting, jealousy and anger, constant effort to get the best for yourself, complaints and criticisms. You will have the feeling that everyone else is wrong except those in your own little group. There will be wrong doctrine, envy, murder, drunkenness, wild parties, and all sorts of selfish endeavors." We are all quiet, contemplating how sin so easily entangles ones' life. (Galatians 5:19-21)

Right now I feel these strong emotions. I feel sadness for the Shepherd's desire to protect and guide such incorrigible sheep; and I feel a desire to fall down at His feet and praise Him who purged me from the onslaught of evil and sin.

February 28

NKJV Matthew 11:29 "Take My yoke upon you, and learn of Me."

WHINE

Overcoming sin will be the topic of today's lesson. We will learn not to whine about the results of our choices, but to allow the Shepherd to help us in our time of need. He said that He will carry all of our burdens.

My Shepherd begins the lesson. "Whom the Lord loves, He chastens! How petty is your complaining! I will bring you into the place where you can have communion with our Father and Me. I am asking you to take one end of the yoke, for My yoke is easy. Get alongside Me, and we will pull together."

"To you that have no might I will increase your strength. The Father comes and takes you out of your sentimentality, and turns all into victory and praise. The only way to know My strength, which is given by the Father, is to take My yoke upon you as you are learning about Me."

"My joy is your strength. The fact that the peace, light, and the joy of your Father are there, is proof that you, and He, are carrying the burden. The burden placed on our shoulders squeezes our lives, like the press squeezes grapes, and out comes the refreshing drink. No power on earth or in hell can conquer the Spirit of God in a human spirit, it is an inner *unconquerableness*." (Oswald Chambers)

"If you are whining about your burdens, throw them over to Me, Your Shepherd. It is a crime to be weak in God's strength."

I think about when the "all about me" kicks in, I cannot forgive myself for the sin that I committed, or I begin to only think about myself, and how stupid I am. I am now learning that I can take these sins, and throw all of them onto Him, for He cares for me.

He confronts me, and leads me back to the path of right living. Oh what a Savior, *my* Shepherd. Let us sing this very thought O WHAT A SAVIOR:

> *Once I was straying in sin's dark valley*
> *No hope within could I see*
> *They searched through Heaven*
> *And found a Savior*
> *To save a poor lost soul like me.*
>
> *O what a Savior, O hallelujah*
> *His heart was broken on Calvary*
> *His hands were nail scarred*
> *His side was riven*
> *He gave His life-blood for even me.*
> *(By Marvin P. Dalton, 1906-1987, Copyright 1948)*

February 29

NKJV James 4:8 "Draw nigh to God, and He will draw nigh to you."

TRANSACT

He stands tall as He begins to teach. The Shepherd begins the lesson with much intensity.

"It is essential for Me to allow My sheep the freedom to act as they choose. The responsibility of choosing My way must be left to the individual. No sheep can act for another. The evangelical message ought always to lead each individual sheep to act. The paralysis of refusing to make righteous choices, which begins with choosing Me, leaves a sheep exactly where they were before. It is foolishness that stands in the way of all of those who have been convicted by My Spirit, but choose disobedience. Immediately a sheep propels themselves over into My arms, that very second they live the life of grace."

"Never allow a Truth of God that is brought to your attention to pass without acting on it. Record it, with ink or with blood. The feeblest sheep who transacts business with Me is emancipated. The instant one acts; **ALL THE ALMIGHTY POWER OF GOD IS ON THEIR BEHALF!** When one comes up to the Truth of God and confesses their wrong, but goes back again and then one comes up to it again, and again goes back. Finally then they learn they have no business going back. My Word encourages them to come clean by coming to Me. I, their Shepherd can then transact business. My word "come" means "transact."

He sits down and leans in and says … "Come unto Me. The sad reality is that most times the last thing that a sheep does is come; but all sheep who do come, know that in that second, the supernatural rush of the life of God invades them instantly. The dominating power of the world, the flesh and the devil is paralyzed, not by the act of coming, but because one's act has linked on to God and His redemptive power, through Me, your Shepherd!" (Oswald Chambers)

Oh, *my* dear Shepherd. What a joy it is to come, to draw near, and to believe, through faith, that you are our Savior, the Lord, *my* Shepherd.

March

March 1

> NKJV Galatians 5: 16, 22-25 "I say then: Walk in the Spirit ... the fruit of the Spirit is love, joy, peace, long-suffering, kindness, goodness, faithfulness, gentleness, self-control ... and those who are Christ's have crucified the flesh with its passions, and desires. If we live in the Spirit, let us also walk in the Spirit."

LESSONS ON THE LIFE IN THE SPIRIT

LEAD

The Shepherd has made it clear that when we acknowledge sin and come to Him we are to walk in the Spirit. He has stated how the flesh does not desire the Spirit. Therefore, when we rise up to walk, we must walk in the Spirit. We must walk circumspectly, wisely, redeeming the time, because the days are evil, we must Constantly praise God for everything, giving thanks always, and be constantly filled with the Spirit.

The Shepherd gives nine Godly ingredients that characterize Him, and must characterize us. They are: love, joy, peace, long-suffering, kindness, goodness, faithfulness, gentleness, and self-control. Each ingredient is found in the SPIRIT FRUIT.

This is crucial for the life of His sheep because the fruit of the Holy Spirit affects the believer's relationship with God our Father, others, and ourselves. This fruit is evidence of salvation, and the genuine work of the Holy Spirit in each sheep's transformed life. The actions of all who claim the Lord as their Shepherd are wrapped up in the FRUIT OF THE SPIRIT. The true sheep of the Lord's pasture, exemplifies the fruit by walking, (their day to day actions), in the Spirit.

By consuming this fruit, the sheep is filled with the Holy Spirit. The Spirit controls him or her. As a result of the Spirit fruit, the sheep becomes a communicator of God's love toward the entire flock.

As we get up from this green pasture to continue the trip through the *valley of the shadow of death*, we are led by the Spirit while walking with the Shepherd. By doing so, we reflect the character of *my* Good Shepherd BY THE FRUIT OF THE SPIRIT.

March 2

NKJV Galatians 5: 22 "But the fruit of the Spirit is love ..."

FIRST INGREDIENT

LOVE

The Shepherd speaks about ingredient of love with extreme seriousness.

Love is the first ingredient of the Fruit of the Spirit. This love, called "Agape," means the love of the will. It does not mean love of emotion. Agape is the love that we must chose to have for the Shepherd, and then for all others.

The Shepherd begins the lesson. "The love that I bring to you and have shown to you is the essence of Agape. Remember 'You shall love the Lord your God with all your heart, with all your soul, mind and strength, and love your neighbor as yourself.'"

"I told you to love one another; as I have loved you. Agape proves to all that you are My sheep. If you love Me, you will keep My commandments. As the Father loved Me, I also have loved you; abide in My love. If you keep My commandments, you will abide in My love, just as I have kept My Father's commandments, and abide in His love."

He puts His hand on His heart. "This is My commandment; that you love one another as I have loved you. Greater love has no one than this, to lay down one's life for his friends. You are my friends if you do whatever I command you. You did not choose Me but I chose you, and appointed you that you should go and bear fruit, and that your fruit should remain, that whatever you ask the Father in My name He may give you. These things I command you, that you love one another."

He smiles. "For God so loved the world that He gave Me, His only begotten Son, that whosoever believes in Me should not perish, but have everlasting life. For God did not send Me into the world that the world would be condemned, but that the world through Me might be saved." He stops and lowers His head.

The Shepherd ends the lesson leaning down looking into our eyes: "If you say 'I love God,' and hate someone, you are a liar. Those who love God **must** love their brother or sister also." The first ingredient of the Fruit of the Spirit is love. Without **love** the Spirit Fruit rots!

As I ponder the magnitude of *my* Shepherd's Agape. I realize what has made Him seem radical to this world, is what I must emulate. It is not power, money, or fame, but the unfathomable depth of His love that has no end, and been defined as ... "too high, too deep, too wide for us to ever know its infinity." I must lay down my life, pick up the cross, and follow the Lord - - - *my* Shepherd.

March 3

NKJV I John 4:8 "For God is Love."

GODLOVE - AGAPE

Love is God. For the Shepherd says … "God is love …" The Shepherd also has said that the greatest of these nine ingredients is Agape *love*. The other eight ingredients may be put into the actions of love:

Joy is love exulting
Peace is love in repose
Long-suffering (patience) is love on trial;
Gentleness is love in society;
Goodness is love in action;
Faith is love on the battle field;
Gentleness (meekness) is love at school;
Self-control is love in training;

Agape love is not an emotion. It is a decision. The love *my* Shepherd lavished out upon us was a decision of His own will. God our Father did not force Him to love us with His life. *My* Shepherd looked at us and he said "Forgive them, for they do not know what they are doing." After the way we treated Him, if we still do not recognize His amazing grace love, then we should all stand up from His green pasture, and head out our own way!

Tragically most don't recognize His Agape. The world is blind to the Shepherd. The world does not see His love because it likes its own way. That's why the Shepherd has called us sheep, (the dumbest animals alive). Humans desire to be in control of what they believe to be their life. The world has no Agape, because Agape comes through His power and the act of relinquishing ones entire being to the Spirit's control. This is why Agape *must* be the first ingredient.

Our Father first loved us. He knitted me in my mother's womb, and He planned for me. I am wonderfully made. Every hair on my head is numbered. He protects, guides, feeds and nurtures me. He provides everything I need to live and to find peace in this world. He prepares for my eternal residence. I am from love (Agape), of love (Agape), for love (Agape).

As I lie her in the green pastures, I cannot imagine living and dying without His Agape. The precious Agape love of the Lord, *my* Shepherd.

March 4

NKJV I John 4:7 "Dear friends, let us practice love."

PRACTICE AGAPE

Listen as He teaches. "Dear friends, let us practice loving each other, for love comes from God, and those who are loving and kind show that they are the children of God. If a person isn't loving and kind, it shows that they do not know God, for God is love. God showed how much He loved you by sending Me, into this wicked world to bring to you eternal life through My death. In this, you see what real love is: it is not your love for God, but His love for you. He sent Me, His Son, to satisfy His anger against your sins. Dear sheep, since God loved you so much, surely you ought to love each other too. For though you have not yet seen God, when you love each other, God lives in you and His love within you grows ever stronger."

He sits down and continues … "He has put His Holy Spirit into your hearts as proof to you, that you are living with Him, and He with you; furthermore, you have seen with your own eyes and now tell all the world that God sent Me, His Son, to be your Savior. Anyone who believes and says I Am the Son of God, has God living in him or her, and is living with God. You know how much God loves you, because you have felt His love, and because you believe Him when He tells you that He loves you dearly. *God is love!* Anyone who lives in love is living with God, and God is living in them."

The Shepherd moves His hands over all of us. "As you live with Me, your love grows more perfect and complete; so you will not be ashamed and embarrassed at the day of judgment, but can face our Father with confidence and joy because He loves you and you love Him too. There is no need for fear of someone who loves you perfectly; His perfect love for you eliminates all dread of what He might do to you. If you are afraid, you are not fully convinced that He really loves you. So you see, your love for Him comes as a result of His loving you first."

"If anyone says, 'I love God,' but keeps on hating their brother and sister, they are liars; for if they do not love their brother or sister who is right there in front of them, how can they love God whom they have never seen? For the Father has said, that one must not only love Him, but their brother or sister also." He sits back and smiles. (I John 5:7-21, NKJ)

My Shepherd invites us to pray. The love flows through His words. He looks up to heaven and says … "Father, thank you for hearing me." Laying here we can't help but to look to the heavens and worship the loving Lord, *my* Shepherd.

March 5

NKJV I Corinthians 12:31 "And I will show you a still more excellent way!"

THE GREATEST

The lesson continues on Agape, the love of God. He begins ... "This lesson was taught by My apostle Paul. As you listen, apply it to yourself."

*If I speak in the tongues of men and of angels, but have not love,
I am a noisy gong or a clanging cymbal.
And if I have prophetic powers, and understand all mysteries
And all knowledge, and if I have all faith,
So as to remove mountains, but have not love, I am nothing.
If I give away all I have, and if I deliver my body to be burned,
but have not love, I gain nothing.*

*Love is patient and kind; love is not jealous or boastful;
it is not arrogant or rude.
Love does not insist on its own way; it is not irritable or resentful;
it does not rejoice at wrong, but rejoices in the right.
Love bears all things, believes all things, hopes all things, endures all things.*

*Love never ends; as for prophecies, they will pass away;
as for tongues, they will cease; as for knowledge, it will pass away.
For our knowledge is imperfect and our prophecy is imperfect;
but when the perfect comes, the imperfect will pass away.*

*When I was a child, I spoke like a child,
I thought like a child, I reasoned like a child;
when I became a man, I gave up childish ways.
For now we see in a mirror dimly, but then face to face.
Now I know in part; then I shall understand fully,
Even as I have been fully understood.*

So faith, hope, and love abide, these three;
but the greatest of these is love.
(I Corinthians 13)

Tears fill all our eyes, as His love pours on us like rain. Listen to LET IT RAIN:

Let it rain let it pour, let my life be secure
in your love, in your love.
Let it rain on my face let my soul be embraced
by your love, by your love.
let it, let it, rain.
(By Cynthia Perkins)

March 6

NKJV Jeremiah 31:3 The Lord says … "Yes, I have loved you with an everlasting love."

LOVE IS ETERNAL

The love that God the Father, God the Son, and God the Spirit bestows on us is so powerful, so strong, and so perfect, that words cannot explain agape. His love never started; it just was. No time limit was, or is, or ever can be put on love, for this love is eternal.

Love cannot be put away. Evil never destroys His Love. Disease and sickness is impotent because of this love; hell, Satan, and all his cohorts have no power because of this love. All sin has been paid for by Love. Death has been destroyed because of love! The Shepherd put it this way "Death has no sting. The grave has no victory. The gift of My Father is eternal life through Me, His Son."

Love is everlasting so that when strong winds blow upon it, flames ignite. When covered over with the dirt of mankind's sins, the fire refuses to be snuffed out. Love's fire, the Spirit, will not be extinguished. Agape is the eternal flame of our Father, the Shepherd, and the Spirit, three in one; the Holy Trinity of Love!

Just as the will of the world is hell, God's is heaven. His will is Good and Perfect. When we step into this glorious place of constant fellowship with the Trinity, we will completely understand His eternal love. For Love (Agape) is eternal.

We will all now praise our Father and sing with the Shepherd the hymn THE LOVE OF GOD:

The love of God is greater far
than tongue or pen can ever tell,
It goes beyond the highest star
And reaches to the lowest hell;
The guilty pair, bowed down with care,
God gave His Son to win:
His erring child He reconciled
And pardoned from his sin.

O love of God, how rich and pure!
How measureless and strong!
It shall forevermore endure
The saints' and angels' song.
(By Frederick M. Lehman 1868-1953, Copyright, 1917)

March 7

NKJV Galatians 5:22 "But the fruit of the Spirit is ... Joy ..."

SECOND INGREDIENT

JOY

Today's lesson is one of joy. "Joy flows out of the love that must rule the life of My sheep. Joy is as a deep rooted vine that grows from the heart, soul, and mind of Agape love from the Father and I. Joy is not a hilarious happy matter, that makes us happy for a few moments, and then disappears. Joy becomes the outflow of My sheep's life, a life overflowing **with joy**, that pours out agape love onto everyone who comes in contact with it!"

"Don't rejoice in successful service, but rejoice because you are rightly related to Me. In keeping your relationship right with Me, whatever circumstances you are in, and whoever you find yourself with day by day, though you I will open the floodgates of joy and they then will be the recipients. My sheep may never know the joyful service that they bring to others. The lodestar of the saint is God Himself, not estimated usefulness. It is the work that *God* does through your outpouring of joy that counts; not what *you* do for Him." (Oswald Chambers, August 30)

He smiles and continues. "I said to My disciples on the way to My crucifixion, My joy is set before me, because, the Agape love will be spilled over into doing the miraculous work of obliterating sin, shame, death and hell for eternity. So … Count it all joy when you come into perilous situations, for My joy is your strength!"

"When starting the Church, My disciples were a testimony of this joy. After they were whipped, abused, and persecuted, they would burst out in song! Those hearing their singing and praise; seeing them worship in the pit of hell; were dumbfounded at such a joyful response to torture. Through the joy in the middle of such terror, many sinners came to repent, and accept me as their Savior."

He begins to gently laugh … "Being full of joy makes this life a blessing. One will acknowledge the sovereign Father's hand in all of life and in death. For in all of these situations and circumstances, God keeps His promises. All things work together for the good for My sheep that love Me, and are called according to My Word. Whatever you do, remember this promise."

The Shepherd begins to lead us in singing - - - I'VE GOT THE JOY:

I've got the joy, joy, joy, joy,
down in my heart.
Where!
Down in my heart.
Where!
Down in my heart.
I've got the joy, joy, joy, joy,
down in my heart.
Where!
Down in my heart to stay.
(By George Willis Cooke 1848-1923)

March 8

NKJV Galatians 5: 22 " …peace."

THIRD INGREDIENT

PEACE

The Shepherd continues.

"As My sheep you will find your refuge in this world to be My peace. My peace I leave with you. My peace I give you; not as the world gives do I give to you. Let not your heart be troubled, neither let it be afraid. Through your love and obedience, joy filled strength will overflow, and your mind will be stayed on Me."

"Fear and anxiety: cares and concerns will dissipate. Worry: is *the paralysis of faith*. If one worries, one immediately takes out My love and peace. For there is NO FEAR IN LOVE. Perfect love casts out fear. I have issued many promises saying that worry does not change anything. It only draws one away from My Father, and His faithfulness in bringing solutions to life's issues."

"Therefore, I say to you, do not worry about your life, what you will eat or what you will drink; nor about your body, what you will put on. Is not life more than food and the body more than clothing?" He points toward the sky, we all follow looking up. "Look at the birds of the air, for they neither sow nor reap, nor gather into barns: yet your heavenly Father feeds them. Are you not of more value than they?" He looks at us, pointing His finger at each of us as He speaks … "Which of you by worrying can add one cubit to their stature? So, why do you worry?"

He waves His hand over the meadow below, by the stream. "Look at the lilies of the field how they grow: They neither toil nor spin; and yet I say to you that even Solomon, the richest king ever to live, in all his glory was not arrayed like one of these. Now if God so clothes the grass of the field, will He not much more clothe you?" He pauses and there is a moment of complete silence. Gently He says "Please; have faith. For your Father knows that we need all of these things."

"Seek first the kingdom of My Father, and His righteousness, and all these things shall be added to you. I demonstrate perfect peace, not as the world offers, but as *I Am* offers. My peace passes all understanding. I Am the Prince of Peace." (Paraphrased from Matthew 6:25-34)

We are all mesmerized. Not one word was spoken, everyone still, in the presence of the Prince of Peace, *my* Shepherd, the Lord.

March 9

NKJV Galatians 5:22 " …patience (an even temper/forbearance)."

FOURTH INGREDIENT

PATIENCE

The Shepherd leans down and connects with His sheep. We cannot look away, for He commands our eyes to look only at Him.

"Patience," He begins … "is a vital ingredient in the Spirit fruit, because it deals with constant faith in the Father and belief in His sovereignty for all of mankind, through time and eternity. Patience is seldom found in the character of those on earth. God, our Father demonstrates patience to all of mankind."

"God has perfect timing. He waits patiently, for He knows exactly what, when, how and where. His plans for all mankind, are good, and perfect. Now you are being made to lie down in this pasture." He waved His hand over the jeweled green landscape. "Ironic isn't it, how We must go to such extremes to get your attention?"

"Godly Patience is that calm unruffled temper with which the individual of God bears the evils of life. Patience manifests itself by a sweet submission to the providential appointments of God, and fortitude in the presence of the duties, and conflicts of life. Patience saves one from discouragement in the face of evil; aids in the cultivation of Godliness, and in the development of Christian character; and, continued till the end, will result in the reward of eternal life." (Romans 2:7 / James 5: 7-8)

"A prime example of patience's usefulness in the Spirit Fruit, is Job. Job showed patience by trusting in God's sovereignty. The theme of his story rests in the wisdom, and justice that overshadowed his excessive suffering. Job was given by God to Satan, for a time of testing. Satan had accused God of bribing Job with great blessings."

"God proved His love for Job, by God making it known to him, the quest is never— "Why?" in suffering, but ... *Who is in charge while suffering?* When the *Who?* is God, then the gnawing *Why?* is moderated. The believer can be like a weaned child with his mother, who has learned to **wait for and trust in his mother to give him what he needs at just the right time.**" (The Women's Bible)

The Shepherd looks at us with tender mercy in His eyes. "God is not in charge of only the good things that happen; nor impotently observing as bad things happen; but He is sovereignly in control of all things weather, good and or bad. He permits His children to endure testing. One who only accepts the good from God's hand risks rejecting Him completely when things do not work out as desired. Such a limited acceptance of God's wisdom is foolish."

"This is why, as the storms of life come at you, My voice will be heard, quiet, and to the point ... PEACE! BE STILL!"

The Lord, *my* Shepherd instills in me His love, through the ingredient of patience in the Spirit Fruit. I will need patience as I obey Him, following as He leads down *the paths of righteousness.*

March 10

NKJV Galatians 5: 22 "Kindness ..." (In the Greek *Chrestotes* meaning: *Mellowed with age. *Nothing harsh or painful.)

FIFTH INGREDIENT

KINDNESS

"Kindness" the fifth ingredient of the Spirit fruit ... can only be accomplished by a sheep who has assimilated the first four ingredients of the Spirit fruit into their character. Kindness does not just happen: kindness must be practiced. When you regurgitate ... love, joy, peace, and patience, kindness becomes an outpouring."

"Notice I said *SHOW* kindness. Kindness is an action. One becomes kind by imitating Me and God, the Father. So be imitators of Us, walking in love, as I do in loving you ... Let all bitterness, wrath, anger, clamor, and evil speaking be put away from you. Be kind to each another, tenderhearted, forgiving one another, even as God, through Me, forgave, and continues to forgive you."

The Shepherd explains further. "I have stated over and over in My Word, speaking is one of the most effective tools in relationships. Speaking is either good or evil. Sweetness of the lips increases learning; pleasant words are like a honeycomb, sweetness to the soul and health to the bones; the words of the pure are pleasant. Speech is powerful. Wisdom, speaks My Word, and teaches control of the tongue. She speaks words of kindness, so study Her."

"Communication is not only verbal, but also nonverbal. The intent of a message is mostly communicated non-verbally. I physically showed nonverbal kindness as I went through the trial, beatings, humiliation, and death.": Speak the truth in love. Control angry words."

"Here are some guidelines. Speak words of encouragement and healing. Avoid unkind or bitter speech. Speak words of forgiveness."

He has tears in His eyes ... "Please ... be kind one to another, especially as you see your final day approaching. For each of you have a very short time to convey the message of salvation to the world. If the world sees in you the nonverbal and verbal actions of: love, joy, peace and patience, you will emanate kindness to all who come near you!"

"In summary: kindness, is in no way weak. True kindness never compromises truth, nor backs down during times of spiritual warfare. Kindness never gives in to evil, or refrains from speaking about God's goodness. Rather, kindness is a manner of speaking and acting. It is an attitude, a quality of behavior that stands firm without forcing others to their knees. I instruct you to be kind." (God's Treasury of Virtues)

We close today's lesson by praying to digest this lesson. Soon, *we will walk through the valley of the shadow of death*, and we will show to all the kindness of *my* Shepherd.

March 11

NKJV Galatians 5:22 "Goodness …" (The Greek word is "Agathosune" meaning "a character that is energized to display an active goodness. This is Goodness that "does good" toward others and in relationship to others)."

SIXTH INGREDIENT

GOODNESS

"God Is So Good …" The Shepherd plays and sings this beautiful chorus to begin the lesson. "He's so good to me." He lays down His instrument.

"Only God is good. There is no other with His goodness. You and I must imitate the Father. We become good by going about doing His *good and perfect will.* By dwelling in the goodness of God I have shown you that goodness."

"I touched the leper with my hand; I anointed the eyes of the blind; and sometimes when I was asked to speak words of healing from a distance I did not comply, but went to the sick bed and there with them, healed them. The lesson here is do good."

He shows us His hands. "Give with your own hands; show kindness with your own eyes; speak good words with you own mouth. Your own Godly goodness will have more influence than a whole library of tracts, donations, or sermons preached!"

He stands. "Throughout my earthly life I went from village to town doing good. Never let danger or difficulty, be a deterrent. Goodness requires both courage and restraint. The truly good and Godly person does whatever is necessary to right a wrong. Take note of My actions as I moved toward people with kindness and confronted them when they were engaged by evil. My response was always goodness! My words and actions are always intended to move evil doers toward My Father, by convection, not away from Him through harmful condemnation." (God's Treasurer of Virtues)

As *my* Shepherd bowed His head, He leads us in the same song He opened the class with, GOD IS SO GOOD:

God is so good.
He's so good to me.
(Attributed to Vina A. Ledin)

March 12

NKJV Galatians 5:22 "Goodness."

GOODNESS I

"The sixth ingredient of the Spirit fruit is Goodness." The Shepherd stands, breathing deeply, as though releasing more power into the lesson.

"Goodness is the opposite of evil. Goodness lights up the dark world. Goodness radiates by being right with God and living right. The righteousness of God in us is what generates the power of goodness, turning on the Light. I Am the Light."

"Goodness would not be if God the Father had not made the distinction between the two. Goodness comes from obeying the laws, and commands of our Father. Through obedience, a sheep may live a right and righteous life. Walking with Me in the Light, alleviates the darkness. Walking in the fear of the Lord, and in the comfort of the Holy Spirit demonstrates our Father's goodness."

"God's goodness is the predominate force in this world. The bad deeds of man are actually so rare, that they make the news. Law and order are the general rule. The plotters of evil are outnumbered by the planners of good. All of you sheep, obeying the Lord God as I do, setting the examples even unto death, are the conductors of goodness. By your testimonies and examples of righteousness goodness cannot be ignored."

"My Word, the Bible, is the number one book in the world: Christianity is the number one belief in the world: more believe in Me than any other god: death has been overcome, and eternal life has been proven by resurrection! Nothing can ever separate you from My love. All the powers of hell itself cannot keep God's love away. Your fears for today, or your worries about tomorrow cannot keep God's love away."

"So what can naysayers ever do to such wonderful goodness? If God is on our side, who can ever be against us? God keeps His promises. His sovereign goodness is indispensable. For I am God the Son!"

Again we sing GOD IS SO GOOD:

God is so good;
God is so good;
God is so good;
He's so good to me."
(Anonymous/Unknown)

March 13

NKJV Galatians 5:22 "Goodness ..."

GOODNESS II

The Shepherd's continues His teaching on goodness.

"You, My sheep are the world's seasoning. If you lose your flavor, what will happen to the world? You yourselves will be thrown out and be trampled under as worthless."

"You are the world's light, a city on a hill, glowing in the night for all to see. Don't hide your light! Let it shine for all; let your good deeds glow *in the valley of the shadow of death* for all to see, so they will praise your heavenly Father."

"Don't misunderstand why I have come. It isn't to cancel the Old Testament laws, and the warnings of the prophets. No, I came to fulfill them, and to make them all come true. With complete earnestness I have said every law in the book will continue until its purpose is achieved."

"And so if anyone breaks the *least* commandment, or teaches others to, he shall be the least in the Kingdom of Heaven, but those who teach God's laws and obey them shall be great in the Kingdom of Heaven. I warn you, unless your goodness, and your righteousness is greater than the hypocritical Scribes and Pharisees self-righteousness, you cannot enter the Kingdom of Heaven!"

He walks through the middle of the flock and continues ... "Under the Mosaic law, 'If you kill, you must die.' But I have added to that rule, and tell you that if you are only angry, or harbor malice against someone, you are in danger of being brought before the court. If you curse someone, you will be in danger of hell's fire! Furthermore, if you are worshiping God, and suddenly remember that a friend has something against you, leave, and immediately go and apologize, and be reconciled to them, and then come and offer your sacrifice to God."

He walks back to the front of the class, turns and leans into us. "The laws of Moses said, 'You shall not commit adultery.' But I say, anyone who even looks at a woman with lust in his eye has already committed adultery with her in his heart. So if your eye, even if it is your best eye, causes you to lust, gouge it out and throw it away. It is much better for part of you to be destroyed than for all of you to be cast into hell. If your hand, even your right hand, causes you to sin, cut it off and throw it away. Better that, than you find yourself in hell."

He pauses, then softly continues ... "These words of mine bring light to the darkness because goodness out shines the bleak shadows of this valley of death."

We are all amazed at His teachings. His way is good and perfect!

March 14

NKJV Galatians 5:22 "Goodness."

GOODNESS III

Our lessons on goodness continues. Today the Shepherd is intense. "The law of Moses says, 'If a man gouges out another's eye, he must pay with his own eye. If a tooth gets knocked out, knock out the tooth of the one who did it. But I say, don't resist violence! If you are slapped on one cheek, turn the other too. If you are ordered to court, and your shirt is taken from you, give your coat too. If the military demands that you carry their gear for a mile, carry it two. Give to those who ask, and don't turn away from those who want to borrow." (Matthew 5:38-45)

"There is a saying, 'Love your friends and hate your enemies.' But I say, **Love your enemies!** Pray for those who persecute you! In that way you will be acting as true sheep of your Father in heaven, for He gives His sunlight to both the evil and the good, and sends rain on the just and the unjust. If you love only those who love you, what good is that? Even scoundrels do that much. If you are friendly only to your friends, how are you different from anyone else? Even the heathen do that. *But you are to be perfect, even as your Father in heaven is perfect."*

He looks up, then shouts! "Take care! Don't do your good deeds publicly, to be admired, for then you will lose the reward from your Father in heaven. When you give a gift to a beggar, don't shout about it as the hypocrites do, blowing trumpets in the streets to call attention to their acts of charity! I tell you in all earnestness, they have received all the reward they will ever get. When you do a kindness to someone, do it secretly. Don't tell your left hand what your right hand is doing and your Father who knows all secrets will repay you."

"Your heavenly Father will forgive you if you forgive those who sin against you; but if you refuse to forgive them, He will not forgive you."

"If your eye is pure, there will be sunshine in your soul. But if your eye is clouded with evil thoughts and desires, you are in deep spiritual darkness." He points His finger at us ... "You cannot serve two masters: God and money. For you will hate one and love the other." (Luke 6:27-36)

We all smile and praise Him: For His goodness endures forever!

March 15

NKJV Galatians 5:22 "Goodness."
GOODNESS IV

The Shepherd continues today, explaining His goodness. "Will all your worries add a single moment to your life? And why worry about your clothes? Look at the field Lilies! They don't worry about theirs. Yet King Solomon in all his glory was not clothed as beautifully as they. If God cares so wonderfully for flowers that are here today and gone tomorrow, won't He more surely care for you, oh you of little faith? So don't worry about having enough food and clothing. Why be like those lost sheep? They take pride in all these things and are deeply concerned about them. But your heavenly Father already knows perfectly well that you need them. And He will gladly give them to you if you give Him first place in your life. So don't be anxious about tomorrow. God will take care of your tomorrow. Live one day at a time." (Matthew 6:25-34)

He stands crossing His arms. "Don't criticize, and you won't be criticized! Just as you judge and criticize and condemn others, you will be judged and criticized and condemned, and in accordance with the measure you deal out to others it will be dealt out again to you. Should you say, 'Friend, let me help you get that speck out of your eye?' When you can't even see because of the board in your own? Hypocrite! First get rid of the board. Then you can see to help your brother and sister. Don't give pearls to swine! They will trample the pearls and turn and attack you; and do not give dogs what is holy." (Luke 6:37-42 / Matthew 7:6 NLT)

"Keep asking and it will be given you; keep on seeking and you will find; keep on knocking and the door will be opened to you, for everyone who asks, receives. Anyone who seeks finds. If only you will knock, the door will open. If a child asks his father for a loaf of bread, will he be given a stone instead? If he asks for fish, will he be given a poisonous snake? Of course not!"

The Shepherd looks toward the entire group. "And if you hardhearted, sinful sheep know how to give good gifts to your children, won't your Father in heaven even more certainly give good gifts to those who ask Him for them? Do for others what you want them to do for you. This is the teaching of God the Father from the Old Testament." (Matthew 11:9-13, NLT paraphrased)

He sits down again and speaks softly, and with extreme emotion says ... "Heaven can be entered only through the narrow gate! The highway to hell is broad, and its gate is wide enough for all the multitudes who choose its easy way. But the Gateway to Life is small, and the road is narrow, and only a few ever find it and enter." He pauses and softly cries.

"Beware of false teachers who come disguised as harmless sheep, but are wolves and will tear you apart. They can be detected by the way they act, just as you can identify a tree by its fruit. You need never confuse grapevines with thorn bushes; or figs with thistles! Different kinds of fruit trees can quickly be identified by examining their fruit. A variety that produces delicious fruit never produces an inedible kind! And a tree producing an inedible kind can't produce what is good! So the trees having the inedible fruit are chopped down and thrown on the fire. Always remember; the way to identify a tree or a sheep of Mine, is by the kind of fruit produced." (Matthew 7:13-20 NLT)

We listened intently to the Shepherd's words of what true goodness entails. As the Shepherd finishes the lesson, we begin preparing to go forth and to do good works.

March 16

NKJV Galatians 5:22 "Goodness."

GOODNESS V

The Shepherd waves His hand over the flock, motioning that He is continuing His teaching of God's goodness. "Not all who talk like My sheep are. They may refer to Me as 'Lord,' but won't get to heaven. At the judgment day, many will say to me 'Lord, Lord, we told others about you and used Your name to cast out demons, and to do many other great miracles.' But I will reply, 'you have never been Mine. Go away, for your deeds are evil.'"

"All who listen to My instructions and follow them are wise, like a sheep who builds their house on solid rock. Though the rain comes in torrents, and the floods rise, and the storm winds beat against it, it won't collapse, for it is built on rock. Those who hear My instructions and ignore them are foolish, like sheep who builds their houses on sand. When the rains and floods come and storm winds beat against their house, they will fall with a mighty crash." He slaps His hands together and we jump. (Matthew 7:24-27 NLT)

"So be wise and good, with God's goodness. Never be overcome by evil, but overcome evil with good. Our Father made the world and you." He looked around at His handiwork and said … "It is good! God blesses without reservation. His mercies are new every morning. His grace is sufficient for all." (Romans 12:9-21)

The Shepherd quietly stands and walks away, finished with today's lesson. As I watch Him go, I am reminded of so many things. God the Father's goodness meets every need. Every part of life is secured. He changes our hearts to soft hearts filled with His love.. He sends the Spirit to live and breathe in us.

I'm reminded of a poem that expresses how His goodness penetrates us in each and every *dot and tittle* of life, making us to shine like diamonds for Him.

A diamond in the rough, Is a diamond sure enough.
Before someone ever found it, It was made of diamond stuff.
But when it's found, And when it's ground,
And when it's burnished bright
That diamond just everlastingly flashes out its light.
(Anonymous)

March 17

NKJV Romans 10:17 "Consequently faith comes from hearing, and hearing through the word about Christ."

SEVENTH INGREDIENT

FAITHFULNESS

Today the Shepherd is discussing the seventh ingredient of the Spirit's fruit, *faithfulness*. He has stated that faith comes by hearing His word. If one has developed in their lives the first six ingredients - - -love, joy, peace, patience, kindness and goodness - - - than faithfulness emerges.

The Shepherd is teaching us faithfulness by being faithful. He is ever faithful to me and all of the other sheep. Not one of His promises, has failed to be true, and He has said … "My word will never fail." THE GOOD SHEPHERD lays down His life for His sheep. He gave His life so we will live eternally with our Father.

The Shepherd has shown us that many have remained faithful, even unto death. His word teaches that followers who by faith have accepted Him, and who are living out faith by their actions, are considered the heroes of faith. Their lives exemplify faith by trust, and confidence in what the Shepherd and the Father promised. The result is a life filled with faithfulness, and perseverance. Faith is the essential response to the grace of God.

The Shepherd has provided a list of some of those who are among the champions of faith, who remained in faithful, active duty. These men and women lived and died providing a Godly example in word, conduct, love, spirit, trust and purity. He has titled the list "Heroes of Faith."

He believes the study of these men and women of faithfulness, will provide inspiration and encouragement for all of His sheep, to remain faithful to the Shepherd.

Still Waters

The Shepherd explained: "Without faith it is impossible to please God. For all of the just shall live by faith. We, the sheep of His pasture must not draw back but, we must believe. Those who come to God must believe that He is, and that He will reward those who diligently seek Him." (Hebrews 11:6)

→‹—

Faith and Trust lead to eternal life and a home with *our* Shepherd; *my* Shepherd.

March 18

NKJV Hebrews: 11:4 "By faith …"

FAITHS HEROES

The Heroes of faith are an exciting group. Today the Shepherd takes us back with a history lesson to the beginning, those who have gone before us living and dying by faith. Listen as He teaches.

"By faith, we know that the world and the stars, in fact, all things were made at God's command; and that they were made from nothing!"

"It was by faith Abel offered to God a more excellent sacrifice than Cain did. Enoch trusted God too, and that is why God took him away to heaven without dying."

"Noah was another who trusted God. When he heard God's warning about the future, Noah believed Him, even though there was then no sign of a flood, and wasting no time, he built the ark and saved his family."

"Abraham trusted God, and when God told him to leave home and go far away to another land, … Abraham obeyed … Abraham did this because he was confidently waiting for God to bring him to that strong heavenly city whose designer and builder is God. Sarah, too, had faith, and because of this she was able to become a mother in spite of her old age."

"These men and women of faith died without ever receiving all that God had promised them; but by faith they saw it all awaiting them on ahead and were glad, for they agreed that this earth was not their real home, but that they were just strangers visiting down here."

"It was by faith that Isaac knew God would give future blessings to his two sons, Jacob and Esau. By Faith Jacob, blessed each of Joseph's two sons. By faith, Joseph, as he neared the end of his life, confidently spoke of God bringing the people of Israel out of Egypt, to a promised land."

"Moses thought that it was better to suffer for the promised Christ than to own all the treasures of Egypt."

"It was faith that brought the walls of Jericho tumbling down. Rehab the harlot, did not die with all the others that refused to obey God because she had faith" (Hebrews 11)

"Whirr! Let me get my breath." He smiles … "The faith of these sheep, lead to perseverance that won God's approval, and while in the valley of the shadow of death, none of them received all that God had promised, by faith, they knew that God was preparing the grandest of rewards, an eternal, heavenly home!"

"Since you sheep have studied such a huge crowd of men and women of faith watching you from the grandstands, strip off anything that slows you down or holds you back, and especially those sins that wrap themselves so tightly around your feet and trip you up; and run with patience the particular race that God has set before you." We all stand with Him, excited about the faith race.

So much joy; and faith. That is … "the essence of things hoped for, and the evidence of things not seen." I pray, I am, and will be, recorded as a **Hero of Faith**.

March 19

NKJV Hebrews 11:38 "Now the just shall live by faith; …"

FAITH RACE

Faith is a race. We lay aside all evil and sin, and we run. The **Faith Race** is an endurance race. It is Jesus the Shepherd who is the coach. We must see how He endured His race to the finish line of His death, burial and resurrection. Now, His race is finished, He is waiting in the winner's circle at the right hand throne of our Father God, to welcome His sheep as they cross the finish line.

Never let your eyes be taken away from Jesus' face. He gave His life's blood for you and me. As we look to Jesus the author and finisher of our faith, doubts and fears that we face are overcome by the power in the blood of the Sacrificial Lamb, our Shepherd.

He disciplines us, as we train in the Spirit fruit. We develop our body, soul and spirit to run this race with the same goals and objectives as that of our Lord, our Shepherd.

I'm reminded of the words from a movie called "Chariots of Fire," about the endurance race of the Olympics. The runner stated to a friend … "When I run I feel God's pleasure in me." As the Shepherd coaches us, and we run in the Spirit, we know He is pleased, because we feel His pleasure.

When we leave this pasture to run the race, it must be by faith. We take the baton of His will, His Word and His Truth. We are never focused on who or what is around, but only on what the coach is telling us to do. We are in complete obedience, never looking back. We are pressing on to the mark of excellence to be crowned with the Crown of Life.

Almighty God is our coach and trainer sustaining us. He never leaves us nor forsakes us!

Those of us running, carry the torch of the light of faith. We, the sheep of His pasture, cannot lose. We win this faith race! FAITH IS THE VICTORY:

Faith is the victory,
faith is the victory.
O glorious victory
that overcomes the world.
(By John H. Yates, 1837-1900)

March 20

NKJV Matthew 21:21-22 "I say unto you, if you have faith as a grain of mustard seed, you will say to this mountain … 'Move from here to there' and it will move; and nothing will be impossible for you."

SEED

The Shepherd teaches us that faith must be out of the source of God's will, and not our own. If our faith is small, even the size of a teeny, tiny mustard seed, great power, enough to move mountains, will come. He uses the mountain as a metaphor to help us see that as we look at a literal mountain, it would seem impossible to move it; however, with God as our source of faith and strength … "nothing is impossible."

The mountains of our evil emotions, perilous mind, hard hearts, and physical problems are more difficult to move then literal mountains. Our Shepherd knows this, and that is why He is here demonstrating the faith that can move these mountains.

The Shepherd explains to us that faith can be deficient if it is based in anything besides our Father. True faith is not seen by physical eyes. So as a sheep, I must believe without seeing or knowing the outcome of my faith. The faith I should exhibit is a *blind* faith that is obedient as it works the works of the Father.

One summer I was at a huge convention. I went into the women's restroom, and while standing in line, I noticed another woman standing in the middle of the room. She had finished and come out of the stall, but she just kept standing there until the long line was gone and it was my turn. When I came out of the stall she was still there! As I asked "Are you ok? Do you need me to help you in anyway?" She said "No. I'm just waiting for my friend to come and guide me for I am blind." At that moment her friend came in and she put her hand in the hand of the guide and out the door they went.

What impressed me, was the blind lady stayed in the same place, faithfully believing that her friend would come. She never seemed afraid, or worried about standing there. As people bumped into her, and walked around her, she never asked for anyone to help her. She was content to wait for her friend, knowing that she would come.

Faith is just like that; *knowing* without *seeing*. *My* Shepherd said, "Faith is being sure of what we hope for; and evidence of what we cannot see."

Being faithful and having faithfulness now, while in the Lord's pasture, will not happen if the first six ingredients of the Spirit's fruit are not intact: love, joy, peace, patience, kindness, and goodness all employ faithfulness. The lovely blind lady proved by her patience, peace, goodness, and joy, that she was acting out her *blind* faith. That is exactly what I can do, because the Lord, is *my* Shepherd.

March 21

NKJV II Corinthians 5:7 "For we walk by faith and not by sight."
FAITH SIGHT

The Shepherd will soon have His flock to stand and prepare for the journey where He will lead us on the *path of righteousness.* As we walk down that path we will be walking by faith and not by sight, always keeping our eyes on the Author and Finisher of our faith. We have no worry or fear of what is ahead, taking one step at a time, as His light leads the way.

Today the Shepherd explains the faith walk. "To walk with Me in My light, is just like these sandals made with a candle holder in the toe." He holds them up. "As one takes a step, the candle lights just enough area to provide light for the next step. My light will always be there to lead you. There is only enough light to let you see My feet as you follow me."

"Faith is blind, but My light is so bright, it should block out all of these circumstances: evil, danger, and darkness. When you walk in the light as I am in the light, you will have fellowship with the flock, because My blood has cleansed you from sin, you have been washed and are now as white as snow."

"There was a blind man who lived in one of the towns I went through, while here on earth. He had been blind since birth. When I healed him I told him 'Your faith has saved you.' This man had been born blind, yet he had seen me before I healed his blindness! He had faith that opened his eyes and saved his soul from hell. How much more important is being saved from hell, than having ones sight restored? It takes faith for both." He smiles as He ends the lesson.

In our humanity, we do not know what the next moment holds. Living and dying are all out of our hands. I may predict, all of my life's journey, yet I never know what lies ahead. The sovereign Shepherd is the only one who knows the answer to life's questions here *in the valley of the shadow of death*.

With faith I can see. There, up there He is, the Lord, *my* Shepherd!

March 22

NKJV Hebrews 11:6 "Without faith it is impossible to please God."
IMPOSSIBLE

The Shepherd has made it clear that faith pleases the Father. Without faith, His sheep become sickly and feeble. He has said that we are sheep that have gone astray. Wolves in sheep's clothing, the darkness of sin, shame, and evil, stifle the Spirit. Therefore, by faith we must *walk through the valley of the shadow of death*.

Both the Shepherd and our Father, want us to believe every Word of the Bible. Its Words bring strength for life. The Word gives us the ability to sever the ties to the world. We are the sheep of His pasture, carrying out His will for all eternity.

Faith is the shield for this life. Faith protects us from all worldly attacks by the evil one. We, the sheep, by faith, become confident, knowing we please the Father and *our* Shepherd.

The Shepherd looks up and says … "The Father knows you. He planned every minute detail of your being. He is Omniscience; Omnipresence; and Omnipotent. Let us all sing of the fact that God Himself brings us to faith, that pleases Him. 'For without faith it is **impossible** to please God.'"

Everyone let's sing:

PSALM 139
*O Lord you have searched me
and know me.*

*You know my sitting down
and my rising up;*

*You understand my thought afar off.
You comprehend my path and my lying down,*

And are acquainted with all of my ways.
For there is not a word on my tongue,
but behold, O Lord, you know it altogether.

You have hedged me behind and before,
and laid your hand upon me.

Such knowledge is to wonderful for me
It is so high, I cannot attain it.

I believe. We shout, "Amen, and Amen!"

March 23

NKJV James 2:17 "Faith without works is dead!"

DEAD FAITH

Listen as the Shepherd's teaching us the absolute necessity of faith being a verb; faith means action.

"What does it profit, my brethren, if someone says he has faith but does not have works? Can faith save him? If a brother or sister is naked and destitute of daily food, and one of you says to them, 'Depart in peace, be warmed and filled,' but you do not give them the things which are needed for the body, what does it profit? Thus also faith by itself, if it does not have works, is dead."

"But someone will say, 'You have faith, and I have works.' Show me your faith without your works, and I will show you my faith by my works. You believe that there is one God. You do well. Even the demons believe and tremble! But do you want to know, O foolish sheep, that faith without works is dead? Was not Abraham our father justified by works when be offered Isaac his son on the alter? Do you see that faith was working together with his works, and by works faith was made perfect? And the scripture was fulfilled which says, 'Abraham believed God, and it was accounted to him for righteousness.' And he was called the friend of God. You see then that a sheep is justified by works, and not by faith only. For as the body without the spirit is dead, so **faith without works is dead!**" (James 2:14-26)

The Shepherd takes a deep breath and explains further … "True faith ignites when it is put into action. A person of faith leaves behind a trail of complete devotion to Me and My Father. Nothing will separate a person of faith from me."

He stands, and continues. "So now, since we have been made right in God's sight, by faith in His promises, you can have real peace with Him because of what I, the Lord have done, and am doing for you. For because of your faith, I have brought you into this place of highest privilege where you now stand, and you confidently and joyfully look forward to actually becoming all that God has in mind for you to be."

"You can rejoice also when you run into problems and trials, for you know that they are good for you---they help you learn to be patient. And patience develops strength of character, and helps you trust God more each time you use it, until finally your hope and faith are strong and steady. For you know how dearly God loves you, and you feel this warm love everywhere within you, because God has given you the Holy Spirit to fill you hearts with His love." (Romans 5:1-11)

These words of comfort, from the Lord, *my* Shepherd. The Shepherd, makes me feel strong. The Shepherd turns and says, "Let us pray." He looks up and begins to pray … "Dear Father, God, My sheep hear My voice, and I know them, and they follow Me. **And I give them eternal life, and they shall never perish; neither shall anyone snatch them out of My hand.**" (John 10:27-28)

March 24

NKJV Isaiah 40:11 "He will feed His flock like a shepherd; He will gather the lambs with His arm, and carry them in His bosom, and gently lead those who are with young."

EIGHTH INGREDIENT

GENTLENESS

A sheep who is a teacher of God's word explains gentleness, the eighth ingredient of the Spirit fruit.

The Greek word translation of "gentleness" is *prautes*. The Greeks used it when referring to people or things that demonstrated a certain soothing quality---like an ointment that took the sting out of a burn. *Prautes* described the controlled conduct of one who had the power to act otherwise.

"Remember, our goal is balance. Not just tough. That alone makes a man cold, distant, intolerant, unbearable. But tough and tender, gentle, thoughtful, teachable, considerate. Both, like Christ." (God's Treasury of Virtues)

Gentleness is the right kind of toughness. Gentleness marks God's sheep, separating them from all other sheep.

Peter, the first apostle and leader of the apostles, explains gentleness by examining how a woman radiates with inner beauty by being gentle: "Your beauty should not come from outward adornment, such as braided hair and the wearing of gold jewelry and fine clothes. Instead, it should be that of your inner self, the unfading beauty of a gentle and quiet spirit, which is of great worth in God's sight. For this is the way the holy women of the past who put their hope in God used to make themselves beautiful." (I Peter 3:3-4)

Now, listen to the Shepherd: "I will feed My flock. I will gather the lambs in My arms, and carry them in My bosom, and gently lead those who are with young. Tenderly I will lead you in the path of righteousness and *through the valley of the shadow of death.*"

I praise My Shepherd in song: Sing GENTLE SHEPHERD:

Gentle Shepherd, come and lead us,
For we need You to help us find our way.
Gentle shepherd, come and feed us,
For we need Your strength from day to day.
There's no other we can turn to
Who can help us face another day;
(By William and Gloria Gather, Copyrighted 1974 by Capitol CMG pub.)

March 25

NKJV Matthew 5:5 "Blessed are the meek, for they shall inherit the earth."

GENTLENESS - MEEKNESS

Today's lesson begins with this illustration.

"A wild horse which has been tamed to accept a saddle and harness or bridle is a picture of the Biblical concept of meekness. Meekness means not easily provoked. The horse has become a tame animal. He naturally is a strong steed with nostrils flaring, who holds his head proudly, poised to move with speed and power, but under the control of the master's hand. Nothing can hinder this steed from doing the master's bidding. In full control, yet powerful, he inherits the earth because he is meek."

"Meekness is not a weakness!" He continues explaining. "It is the gentle sheep who is filled with honor to do the direct orders I give. One cannot be weak and be gentle. It is impossible! I have constantly said 'Be strong in Me, and in the power of My might.'"

"Through the exercising of My will, one achieves an inner peace, because I do the will of My Father. As I hear, I judge, and my judgment is just; because I seek not My own will, but the will of My Father who has sent me. If I bear witness of Myself, My witness is not true." (John 5:30-31)

"The sheep who bears God's likeness of meekness, is easily directed by God, exemplifying a gentleness in outward demeanor; while at the same time, continues to demonstrate great Spiritual strength." (God's Treasury of Virtues)

He moves to the rock and sits down, continuing: "I say, don't get involved in foolish arguments which only upset people and make them angry. God's people must not be quarrelsome; they must be gentle, patient teachers of those who are wrong. Be gentle when you are trying to teach those who are mixed up concerning the truth. For if you talk meekly and courteously to them, they are likely, with God's help, to turn away from their wrong ideas and believe what is true. They will come to their senses and escape from Satan's trap of sin. Then, they will begin doing My will, that is one and the same as My Father's will." (II Timothy 2:23-26 NLT `)

The Shepherd looks up to the heavens, gently looking to God His Father.

He said, "The meek will inherit the earth ..." and I know I can have gentleness by following His direction as I *walk through the valley of the shadow of death,* for the Gentle Shepherd leads me.

March 26

NKJV Romans 13:14 "Ask the Lord Jesus to help you live as you should."

GENTLENESS

The Shepherd continues to explain about the ingredient of gentleness in the Spirit's fruit. "There is nothing so brazen and unsettling as a person out of control. Whether it be an attitude, or emotions. It flashes a neon sign of self-indulgence, and pride."

"Listen to Me! Now it is time to awake out of sleep, for now your salvation is nearer than when you first believed. The night is far spent, the day is at hand. Therefore, cast off the works of darkness, and put on the armor of light. You must walk properly as in the day, not in revelry, and drunkenness, not in lewdness and lust, not in strife, and envy. But put your sin and shame on Me, *your* Shepherd, and make no provision for the flesh, to fulfill its lust."

"True gentleness is strength under the control of the Spirit. Don't be drunk with the world's pharmaceuticals, but be filled with the Spirit. We must study the Scripture, learning from the examples of those who have proven this ingredient of the Spirit fruit in their lives. Your lives must exemplify theirs."

Be in control - Spirit control. When it is time to leave the Lord's pasture, I must follow the footsteps of Jesus, *my* Shepherd. Let us all sing the hymn FOOTSTEPS OF JESUS:

Sweetly, Lord, have we heard Thee calling,
"Come, follow Me!"
and we see where thy footprints falling,
lead us to Thee.

Footprints of Jesus that make the pathway glow;
We will follow the steps of Jesus
where'er they go.
(By Mary B.B Slade, 1826-1882)

March 27

NKJV Philippians 2:5 "Let this mind be in you …"

HORIZONTAL

It has been said that meekness is not horizontal but vertical. Meekness is our attitude and relationship toward God our Father. If meekness was what man did on his own, we would bend to the strongest person's will.

Moses was a meek person. His meekness can only be attributed to the fact He followed every command of God. He trusted God's word. Because of his faith, he dealt gently with God's people, the Israelites.

The Shepherd, demonstrated by His life, what Moses, and others like him knew they should be as followers of the Shepherd:

> He who is the Bread of Life began His ministry hungering.
> He who is the Water of Life ended His ministry thirsting.
> Jesus hungered as a man, yet fed the hungry as God.
> He was weary, yet He is our rest.
> He paid tribute, yet He is the King.
> He was called a devil, but He cast out demons.
> He prayed, yet He hears prayer.
> He wept, and He dries our tears.
> He was sold for 30 pieces of silver, yet He redeems sinners.
> He was led as a lamb to the slaughter, yet He is the Good Shepherd.
> He gave His life, and by dying He destroyed death.

Throughout His life on earth, Jesus was a man of striking contrasts. He reflected both His genuine humanity and His full deity. On the Sunday before He died, one might have expected Jesus, the King, to enter Jerusalem on a mighty steed, but He chose instead a lowly donkey. He came as the Sacrificial Lamb; the Savior who chose to die.

The Shepherd leaned down and gently spoke to us ... "Let this mind be in you, which is in Me: I, being in the form of God, thought it not robbery to be equal with God: But made Myself of no reputation, and took upon me the form of a servant, and was made in the likeness of men." (Philippians 2:5, NKJ)

He is a gentle, and kind servant to us, meek and lowly in heart, and we must learn to do the same as we live like *my* Shepherd.

March 28

>NKJV Proverbs 16:32 "Better a patient person, one with self-control than one who takes a city."

NINTH INGREDIENT

SELF-CONTROL

Our lesson on the last ingredient of the Spirit's fruit is about SELF-CONTROL. Listen as He begins. "Self-control, makes all of the other ingredients effective. Paul, My apostle, used the Greek word, *egkrateia,* rooted in *Kratos,* meaning to have strength in control of self. The only way to control self is by surrendering to Me and giving up personal control. My control in you becomes the foundation of your self-control."

"The Holy Spirit is called the wind. Therefore, My sheep, have self-control, because the Spirit is a tunnel which channels its extreme power to lead you into the Truth and self-control. The Spirit comes in filling your very being, urging you in the direction of His Word and Wisdom, keeping you in the Way of righteousness."

"My sheep do not gain Me through self-control; you, gain self-control through Me, your Shepherd. It is My love that constrains you to My way."

"If you accept Me, the fruit of the Spirits first ingredient love, springs into action. You follow My way. You obey My words. You then are set free from disobedience and sin and are free to do My will, and to not feel the tyranny of making choices, destructive to both yourself, and others. Love Me, and do as you like, for you will like what I like, and you will have self-control."

I prayed … "Lord, God may I be in Thee, and Thou be in Me. In the precious name of *my* Shepherd, Jesus, Amen

March 29

NKJV Romans 6: 15 "God's grace has set us free."

SHEPHERD CONTROL

To live as the Lord *my* Shepherd did, filled with the Spirit, with complete assurance of His Father, with no pretense nor selfishness existing in Him, is *my* goal. Seeing the steady training and discipline resonating in Him teaches me how to live this life engaging self-control and discipline.

My Shepherd was never out of control. Even in the cleansing of the temple, when He used the whip, spoke loudly, and pushed over the money tables, He contained perfect Spirit-filled control. His anger was righteous. He knew He was the Temple, and the Sacrifice. All the frills and taboo of those temple leaders, were not of God. They reeked with selfish, out-of-control religiosity.

Jesus, by His love, cleansed the temple of mediocrity, and chaos. He restored peace, and announced His house should be a house of prayer. He has told us His house is each of us, His sheep. He comes to live in us. The Spirit fills us. We pray constantly, never ceasing, always giving thanks to God our Father.

Listen as the Shepherd explains. "Sin is no longer your master, for you no longer live under the requirements of the law. Instead, you live under the freedom of God's grace."

"Well then, since God's grace has set you free from the law, does this mean you can go on sinning? Of course not! Don't you realize, you become the slave of whatever you choose to obey? You can be a slave to sin, which leads to death, or you can choose to obey God, which leads to righteous living. Thank God! Once you were slaves of sin, but now you wholeheartedly obey this teaching we have given you. Now you are free from your slavery to sin, and you have become slaves to righteous living." (Romans 8:2-11 NLT)

Still Waters

The Shepherd smiles. We all begin to clap and cheer! What joy to be free! So sing! I AM FREE:

I am free to run
I am free to dance
I am free to live for you
I am free, I am free
(By Jon Egan, Copyright 2004)

March 30

NKJV Roman 6:23 "For the wages of sin is death, but the free gift of God is eternal life through Christ Jesus our Lord."

DARKNESS

It has been said that a person's true character is what one does in the dark. *My* Shepherd has said, we are the light. Therefore, if the character I exemplify is of the light, then **my** character is the same character as **my** Lord, *my* Shepherd. Though the world's darkness surrounds me, I will illuminate darkness, because of His Light. His light in me pierces the darkness. Each of **my** words, thoughts, and actions, ignites or extinguishes that light. Self-control, is the light from the lighthouse on the hill, shining for all of the flock to see. It is the light which all eyes must look, to see the glory of God, our Father..

"I am the light of the world." He begins his teaching. "So if you follow Me, you won't be stumbling through the darkness, for living light will flood your path."

"If one is not controlled by love for Me, than the Light goes dark. The world loves darkness better than Light. With the darkness comes evil that hardens hearts. When sin rules there is no Light. What emerges from sin is darkness due to disobedience and eternal damnation!"

"For a sheep must say to God 'Thy will be done.' We have a choice: to walk in the light as He is in the light. Then we have fellowship with God, our Father, and all the other sheep of His pasture." He smiles. "We could call it *FELLOWSHEEP.*"

My Shepherd says not to give Satan a foothold in my life. If he is given a foothold, the crack immediately becomes a crevasse, then a gully, and finally the entire life collapses and comes crashing down through the tunnel, slithering into the bottomless pit, and living there for eternity!

Praise the Lord, *our* Shepherd, this is not the end for those of us who choose the Shepherd as their Lord and Savior. For *my* Shepherd has said, "When you were slaves to sin, you were free from the obligation to do right. And what was the result? You are now ashamed of the things you used to do, things which end in eternal doom. But now you are free from the power of sin and have become slaves to do the good work of God. Now you do those things which lead to holiness and result in eternal life. For the wages of sin is death, but the free gift of God is eternal life through Me, Christ Jesus, the Lord."

We shout and jump up and clap! Praising our Shepherd. Again we stand and sing, I AM FREE.

March 31

NKJV Isaiah 40:11 "Like a Shepherd He will tend His flock."

WHERE HE LEADS THE FLOCK FOLLOWS

Today is our last day on the lessons concerning the ingredient of gentleness in the Spirit fruit. Our Shepherd is beginning to speak. His eyes, clear, and filled with love and grace.

"I am the good Shepherd. The good Shepherd lays down His life for the sheep. I am *your* Shepherd, you shall not be in want. Our Father, God is our God for ever and ever; I will be your guide even to the end. I tend My flocks because I Am the Good Shepherd; I gather the lambs in My arms and carry them close to My heart; I gently lead those which have young."

He smiles and continues … "I Myself will tend My sheep and have them lie down. I will search for the lost and bring back the strays. I will bind up the injured and strengthen the weak, but the sleek and the strong I will destroy. I will Shepherd the flock with justice. May the God of peace, who through the blood of the eternal covenant brought Me back from the dead, equip you with everything good for doing His will, and may I work in you what is pleasing to Me, to whom be glory for ever and ever. And when I appear again, you will receive the crown of glory that will never fade away."

He stands and lifts His hands toward heaven. "For I, am your Shepherd; I lead you to springs of living waters. And our Father God will wipe away every tear from your eyes." He has us all stand to begin our walk to the *still waters*.

We are all standing, preparing for the trip. There is a quiet anticipation. To travel through this *valley of the shadow of death,* with the Shepherd, will be one, exciting trip. Come, go with us!

PART II

He LEADS Me Beside the Still Waters

April

April 1

NKJV Psalm 23:2 "He leads me beside the still waters …"

THE POND

Ponds are still. Never extremely deep. You can walk across most ponds. Ponds are not used for water sports like skiing, or boating.

Ponds are vital for life on a farm or ranch. Ponds are found in the desert oasis.

Ponds are often dug. Others are natural. Families built their pastures, homes, and barns around ponds, because they are essential in droughts, fire and provide drinking water for animals.

My Shepherd leads us to the *still waters* because we must replenish to prepare our soul for the life journey ahead. *Still Waters* is an convenient place for a sheep to drink. If the waters were hurling, twirling, or rushing by, it could be more difficult, and even scary to try to drink. We sheep are scared of everything because we are extremely dumb, so the Shepherd brings us to the *still waters* to drink, for it is a matter of life or death.

Listen, He is speaking … "Drink up, drink freely … we have a long and dangerous journey ahead."

The Shepherd is the *Water of Life.* His Water is contained, calm, and has easy access. It is a restful water; peaceful water; a water that restores us and gives strength and nourishment to all who drink. Our entire being is baptized in His *Water of Life.* Once we drink we will never thirst again!

After I am finished *laying down in the green pasture*, becoming humbled, calm, submissive, and rested, I got up thirsty, ready to drink of Christ the Shepherd's … *Water of Life.* He leads me now to the *still waters.*

April 2

NKJV Psalm 23:2 "He leads me beside the still waters."

HE LEADS ME BESIDE THE STILL WATERS

We are now preparing to leave the green pasture, and get ready for the trip. Our Shepherd is calling … "Come follow me." He is leading us beside the *still waters* to drink the *Water of Life.* The Shepherd said, if we drink of His water, we will never thirst again.

As we get ready for the trip, we are filled with anticipation. Also, the Water restores us, enabling our souls to be saved, as we are preparing for the *walk through the valley of the shadow of death*. The Spirit is calling, saying … "Come: and let all who desire take the *Water of Life* freely. And let all who thirst come to the water." (Revelations 22:17)

As we gather around the *still waters* to drink, the Shepherd will continue teaching us concerning Himself, and how His Water preserves us spiritually.

He said, "One day my disciples and I were traveling from Galilee and we went through Samaria. When I came to the city called Sychae, I sat down at Jacob's well, named after the shepherd Jacob. It was the hottest part of the day, and I had plans to visit with one of the women of the community, who came at noon to draw her water. She intentionally came late in the day, so she would avoid the neighborhood ladies."

He moved to the weeping willow tree by the water and leaning on it, He continued teaching. "My disciples were hungry and went to purchase food. As I arrived, she came to draw her water."

"I said, 'Please give Me a drink.' She said 'How is it that You being a Jew, ask a drink from me, a Samaritan woman.' For Jews had no dealings with Samaritans. I said, 'If you knew the gift of God and who it is who says to you, 'Give Me a drink,' you would have asked Him, and He would have given you living water.'"

"She said, 'Sir, you have nothing with which to draw, and the well is deep! Where then do you get this living water? Are you greater than our father Jacob, who gave us the well, and drank from it himself, as well as his sons and his livestock?'"

"I smiled, and looking into her soul, I said… 'Whoever drinks of this water will thirst again, but whoever drinks of the Water I shall give him, will NEVER thirst. But, the water, I shall give to this person, will become in them a fountain of water springing into everlasting life.'"

"She immediately responded… 'Sir, give me this water so I may not thirst, nor come here to draw.' Then I begin to tell her about her life … 'You go call your husband, to come here.' She looked down, avoiding My eyes … 'I have no husband.' I said, 'You have well said, 'I have no husband,' 'for you have had five husbands, and the one, whom you now have, is not your husband!'"

"She very sheepishly replied … 'Sir I perceive that you are a prophet.' I replied. 'Woman believe Me the hour is coming, and now is, the true worshipers will worship the Father in Spirit and Truth; for the Father is seeking such to worship Him. God is Spirit, and those who worship Him must worship in Spirit and Truth.'"

"I know the Messiah is coming, who is called Christ. When He comes, He will tell us all things." I told her: a Gentile woman; I was the Messiah: *I WHO SPEAKS AM HE.* (NLT John 4:1-26)

We all jumped to our feet and clapped and cheered. The first person *my* Shepherd told He was the Messiah, was a woman! What grace. What love. Oh God my Father, I love Your Son, *my* Shepherd.

April 3

NKJV John 4: 14 Jesus said, " …but whoever drinks of the water I shall give them, will never thirst …"

COME

The Lord, *my* Shepherd tells us to come with Him to the waters. He leads us to the *still waters*. The Spirit says "come." Both are calling.

After our time spent lying down in the pasture, maturing and growing, we now need refreshment. The water He leads us to is not a rushing stream or flowing river, deep and scary, but a pond which is safe and small, quiet and serene. This is a place where it is easy for the Shepherd to see all of us as we drink.

"Come to the Water." He calls. "I want you to drink because the journey is long, treacherous, and weary. This water I offer is of the Spirit. He fills you, and protects and refreshes you daily." My Shepherd knows His sheep. He encourages us to be completely at His bidding, trusting Him to fill us up with the *Life Water*, for the paths ahead.

The Shepherd sings this song to us. The song expresses how He will never leave, nor forsake us. And we should come to Him the *Water of Life*. COME TO THE WATER:

You said you'd come and share all my sorrows
You said you'd be there for all my tomorrows …

And Jesus said,
"Come to the water, stand by my side
I know you are thirsty, you won't be denied
I felt every tear drop, when in darkness you cried.
and I strove to remind you, It's for those tears I died."
(By Marsha Stephens 1969)

His voice is so gentle. We are moved to tears. Who can resist the Shepherd's *Water of Life*.

April 4

KJV Psalm 62:1 "Truly my soul silently waits for God."

BE STILL MY SOUL

The water that we drink from the pond is the *Living Water* of the Shepherd. He *is* the *Water of Life*. As I drink, complete peace comes in and fills me. Fear does not abide when a sheep has their fill of *Life Water*.

As we drink, the Shepherd walks around all of us watching for anything that would harm or attack us. He has His angels, all the heavenly host, at His disposal, to do His bidding. His guardian angels have surrounded us.

He, the *Water of Life*, has the Spirit to help guide, direct and comfort us at all times. He is the Spirit of peace that passes all understanding; a peace that calms and levels our emotions. A peace that says ... "Look to the Shepherd ... follow Him without fear, worry, or anxiety."

As we drink, the Lord, *my* Shepherd is at our side. He protects us, and sits our feet firm on this place.

The song of worship we will sing is perfect for our time here filling up with the Water of Life. On our journey through *the valley of the shadow of death* we will never thirst again.

He begins to conduct us as we sing BE STILL MY SOUL:

> *Be still, my soul; the Lord is on your side*
> *Bear patiently the cross of grief or pain.*
> *Leave to thy God to order and provide.*
> *In every change He faithful will remain.*
> *Be still, my soul; Thy best, Thy heavenly friend*
> *Thro' thorny ways leads to a joyful end.*
>
> *Be still, my soul; Thy God doth undertake*
> *To guide the future as He has the past.*
> *Thy hope, Thy confidence let nothing shake;*
> *All now mysterious shall be bright at last.*
> *Be still, my soul; the waves and winds still know*
> *His voice who ruled them while He dwelt below.*

Be still, my soul! The hour is hastening on
When we shall be forever with the Lord,
When disappointment, grief, and fear are gone,
Sorrow forgot, love's purest joys restored.
Be still, my soul; when change and tears are past,
All safe and blessed we shall meet at last.
By Katharina Von Schlegel 1697

He, the Lord, *my* Shepherd has given us Himself to drink. My soul is still.

April 5

NKJV Revelation 22:17 "Let any who thirst come."

SPIRIT AND BRIDE SAY COME

Today, the Spirit and the Bride, also called the Church, are here with the Shepherd and they are calling for all who thirst to come. The invitation is one, unto which I have answered "yes." I now tell all those I know to come to the *Living Water*.

The invitation is to all the world - - - everyone! The invitation is all inclusive! Whatever has happened; is happening; or will happen in a sheep's life, the invitation is still open. The Shepherd says … "Drink of Me … the … *Water of Life*. I give water which is a spring, welling up to eternal life, sent down from heaven. So, whoever desires, let them take freely of the *Water of Life*. If anyone thirst, let them come to me and drink." (NLT John 4:13-15/ John 7:37)

"My sheep hear My voice, and I know them, and they shall never perish; neither shall anyone snatch them out of My hand. My Father, who has given you to me, is greater than all, and no one is able to snatch you out of My Father's hand. I, and My Father are one." (NKJV John 10:27-30

The Spirit and Bride, stand strong as the Shepherd continues. "I am the Alpha and the Omega, the Beginning and the End. I will give of the fountain of the *Water of Life* fully to those who thirsts. He who overcomes shall inherit all things, and I will be their God and they shall be My people." (NKJV Revelation 21:6-7)

This is the only perfect invitation. Who could resist? Who can ignore so great a salvation? Who is not thirsty for a joyful, free, peaceful, Spirit-filled eternal Life! The Spirit and the Bride reach out their arms and say----- "COME!"

Today, in the closing of this lesson, around the *still waters*, the Spirit and the Bride will lead us in the invitation hymn, JUST AS I AM:

Just as I am without one plea
But that Thy blood, was shed for me.
And that Thou bidd'st me come to Thee
Oh Lamb of God I come, I come.

Just as I am, and waiting not
To rid my soul of one dark blot,
To Thee whose blood can cleanse each spot,
O Lamb of God I come, I come.
(By Charlotte Elliott 1789-1871)

April 6

NKJV II Corinthians 5:17-20 "Be reconciled to God."

RECONCILIATION

Our Shepherd is continuing to fill us with *Life Water*. As we drink of His *Water*, He teaches us that we also drink of His blood which was given to sustain us as we *walk through the valley of the shadow of death.*

"If anyone is in me, they are a new creation; old things have passed away, behold all things have become new. Now all things are of God, who has reconciled you to Himself through Me, and has given you the ministry of reconciliation, God in Me, reconciling the world to Himself, not imputing their trespasses to them, and has committed to you the Word of reconciliation."

"Now then you are ambassadors for Me, as though God were pleading through all of you; We implore all on My behalf, to be reconciled to God. For He made Me who knew no sin, to be sin for all, enabling all in Me, to become the righteousness of God."

He turns and walks to the center of the pond. (No one is surprised. We know He walks on water.) "You then as workers together with Me, should also plead with all, not to receive the grace of God in vain. For God said … 'In an acceptable time I have heard you, and in the day of salvation I have helped you.'"

The Shepherd lifts up His head and shouts - - - "Now *is* the accepted time! Now *is* the day of salvation!" (NKJV II Corinthians 5:17- 6:3)

―※―

We are preparing to go and proclaim the *good news* of the gospel of our Shepherd … *my* Shepherd. May we be filled with the water of life, and then go forth, on *the paths of righteousness,* to preach the *good news* of the gospel of peace.

April 7

NKJV John 4:14 "The water that I shall give them shall be in them a well of water."

LIVING WATER

Listen … "If anyone thirsts, let them come to Me and drink." He is beginning today's lesson. "They who believe in Me, as the Scripture has said, from their hearts will flow rivers of *Living Water*. Your heart is the main stream of those emotions. Fill your heart with My *Living Water*."

The *Living Water,* of *our* Shepherd comes through the Spirit when we believe. Through the Spirit, our inner being will have a life-flowing source of satisfaction. Life becomes easy, as easy as the stars shinning in the darkest night: or the birds singing in the middle of a thunder storm: because the source of our lives is Him, the *Water of Life.* (NKJV John 7:37-38)

He continues … "Today I will read a passage from one of My sheep which further explains, Me, the *Living Water*."

Never allow anything to come between yourself and Jesus
Christ, no emotion, experience; nothing must keep you from the one
great sovereign Source. Think of the healing and far-flung rivers nursing
themselves in our souls! God has been opening up marvelous truths to our minds, and every point
He has opened up is an indication of the wider power of the river He will flow through us. If you
believe in Jesus, you will find that God has nourished in you mighty torrents of blessing for others.

Jesus says, out of you will flow rivers of living water.
It is not a blessing passed on, not an experience stated, but a river
continually flowing. Keep at the Source, guard well your belief in the Shepherd and
your relationship to Him and there will be a steady flow for other lives …

Is it not too extravagant to say that out of an individual believer
rivers are going to flow? 'I do not see the rivers,' you say.
Never look at yourself from the standpoint of - Who am I?
In the history of God's work you will nearly always find

that it has started from the obscure, the unknown, the ignored,
but the steadfastly true to Jesus Christ, the Lord, my Shepherd.
(Oswald Chambers, September 6 and 7)

What joy, the *Living Water* brings to our life. We all bow and pray, thanking our Father for *my* Shepherd, His Son.

April 8

NKJV Isaiah 12:3 "With joy you shall draw from the well of salvation."

LESSONS ON FILLING UP

LESSON I
AMBASSADORS

The Shepherd will teach several lessons He describes as *filling up*, because we should be holy and filled with the Spirit. He said these will be lessons to encourage us to *drink* from the well of salvation.

"Realize you are ambassadors for Me, as though God were pleading through you. Be scrupulous in your behavior, giving no offense which can tarnish the ministry. In all things, present yourselves as ministers of God; as ambassadors of Christ, and fellow workers for God, no unwarranted behavior should damage the sheep." As He speaks, He stands in the middle of the *still waters.*

The Shepherd shows us a list of the many issues we will face as we journey on as ministers of God. "Be of My Father in much patience, in tribulations, in needs, in distresses, in fasting: by purity, by knowledge, by long-suffering, by kindness, by the Holy Spirit, by sincere love, by the word of truth, by the power of God, by the armor of righteousness on the right hand and on the left: by honor and dishonor, by evil report and good report, as deceivers, and yet true: as unknown, and yet well known: as dying, and behold we live: as chastened, and yet not killed, as sorrowful, yet always rejoicing as poor, yet making many rich: as having nothing, and yet possessing all things." (NLT II Corinthians 5:20-6:10)

He takes a deep breath continuing with much intensity ... "We are the temple of the living God. Our Father said:

I will dwell in them
And walk among them
I will be their God,
And they shall be My People ...

I will be a Father to you
And you shall be My sons and daughters ...
(NLT II Corinthians 6:16-18)

My Shepherd smiles as He finishes. The joy of the Father is in His words of complete ownership of us, His sheep. The Lord God takes care of me.

April 9

NKJV Galatians 2:20 "I am crucified with Christ. It is not I who lives but Christ lives in me."

LESSON II

STILL

The lesson learned from the Shepherd here beside the *Still Waters* must be internalized before moving on to the *paths of righteousness*. The Shepherd has named it the hardest lesson of all, because it demands complete annihilation of the sheep's will, and replacement with the will of the Shepherd. He calls it being *crucified* with Him!

Therefore, the sheep must focus completely on the Shepherd. He's told us "Fix your eyes on me, the Author and Finisher of your faith." He states over and over throughout His lessons that we should ... "Be still and know that He is God!" (NKJV Hebrews 12:2/ Psalm 46:10)

The Shepherd knows His sheep desire to drink where the water is slowly stirring, gently flowing, and has easy access. He, the Gentle Shepherd, is this peaceful Water. We drink of Him, and He fills us with the peace, joy, mercy, and grace of the Spirit. It is an intimate, refreshing, Shepherd drink.

Filling up with the *still waters* of Life, we never thirst again. All fear, subsides, and He alone is our refuge and strength. All earth's sin and shame are destroyed by His flowing, luscious, peaceful Water.

To drink, one must be still, because it is an uncomfortable situation when one tries to drink while on the run. This is why the Lord, our Shepherd, tells us to fill up of the *Water*, because the journey *through the valley of the shadow of death* is rough, hot and dry. Death will certainly come, but a death which is futile, because of the cup of the *Water* of our Lord.

So here we are to drink, and be filled of the *still waters* He provides for us. Preparing our hearts, souls and minds for the journey ahead ... until that day we drink anew with Him in His, and our Father's Kingdom.

I bow my head, being very still, I softly cry.

April 10

NKJV Romans 8:34 "It is Christ who makes intercession for us ..."

LESSON III

STILL

The Shepherd provides the Spirit's intercession. The Shepherd and the Spirit literally put themselves in our place! In times, of trouble as we walk through *the valley of the shadow of death* the Shepherd and the Spirit dissipate all evil and darkness. Therefore, we walk with complete security. Nothing can touch us because of Their intercession. At every sharp curve in darkness, at the edge of the steep cliffs, the Shepherd and the Spirit carry us, lead us, push us, holdout their hands to take ours, and grab us before we fall to our death.

The Shepherd constantly cries out ... "Fear not ...! I will never leave you nor forsake you. Fear not little lamb, I will carry your burden, feed and water you. Be bold, be strong, I am with you."

The Spirit will help us in every infirmity. When we cannot talk or explain, He hears and knows exactly what we are trying to say, and what is happening. He takes the issue directly to the Father, and They provide the help that is needed.

When we sheep get on our backs, and all fours are sticking up, and we cannot get up nor move, the Shepherd picks us up returning us to a standing position and leads us home. Our Shepherd and the Spirit guide, guard, and keep us on the journey. At the end, a banquet is prepared for us, and goodness, and mercy, will follow us right to the door of the *house of the Lord*.

My soul will be still and know He is with me. I'm looking forward to dwelling *in the house of the Lord forever*.

April 11

NKJV Psalm 40:1 "I wait patiently for the Lord."

LESSON IV

HE ... STILL

The Shepherd was dreading the torture of the cross. In addition to the most painful of deaths, the Father loaded Him down with all of man's sins. The Spiritual aspect of His death was such a load, an indescribable weight; so the burden of sin, was worse than the physical torturous shedding of the blood!

Adding the evil to it all, Satan and his demons were dancing and playing dissonant tunes; no melody, just sheer horrendous noise! God, His Father, turned away His face from Him, because He could not stand to look at the despicable evil curse of sin and shame of all mankind, laid on His Son's back. And to make matters worse the very ones He loved, and had spent the last three years training for the ministry, turned their backs on Him, running away. Peter denied he ever knew Him, and Judas revealed to the enemy who He was by the kiss of death. Rejection! Rejection! Rejection!

Yet, through all of this *Jesus was still*. He never once disobeyed, blamed, or cursed. He could have screamed, "I Am the Healer, the Miracle Worker, the Son of God! I Am your Friend! I'm your Shepherd, holy and compassionate! I made you! I knew you in your mother's womb! By My will you are here! I LOVE YOU!"

Not once did He ever give a sign of fear to anyone. They were clueless to His agony. Even when He tried to tell them that He would be going soon, they were disconnected, aloof and thinking only about themselves.

Our Shepherd went as the *Lamb* to the slaughter! He came to be the *Sacrificial Lamb*. He only asked the Father if He could see any other way that the payment for the sins of the world for all time, could be made! The question was asked alone, in a dark garden, as a humble prayer, falling on His face in agony!

Talk about being still! Most of us would have become like Jonah and hit the ship to another continent, to get away from God's order to save this evil world. There would be NO stillness. We would cry ... "This is SO unfair! I'm out of Here! I'm done!"

Jesus, *our* Shepherd, was so very still. He knew the outcome was victory over the evil one and his cohorts. The price would be paid for the sins of all mankind, once, for all of time. Victory was His, the Father's, the Spirit's and His sheep.

Now, beside the *still waters*, we learn to be still in our souls, for He is at our side ... He is our example. As He is still; so are we.

April 12

> NLT Matthew 26:38 / Luke 22:44 "Then He said to them, 'My soul is exceedingly sorrowful, even to death. Stay here and watch with Me ... For He was in such agony of spirit that He broke into a sweat of blood, with great drops falling to the ground as He prayed more and more earnestly."

LESSON V

AGONY

"Every human being can get through into the presence of God now because of what the Son of Man went through." Our Shepherd, *my* Shepherd came as a Lamb to the slaughter. He, being the Son of Man, was ready to explode as the *Salvation* of the world. He paid the price for sin. The cost? His life. "The centre of salvation is the Cross of Jesus and the reason it is so easy to obtain salvation is it cost God so much." (Oswald Chambers)

"The cross did not happen to Jesus: He came for that purpose. He is 'the Lamb slain from the foundation of the world!'" The cross became the Gate! The cross became the Door! Every human may enter through that gate into union with God, because of the sacrificial Lamb, *my* Shepherd.

The agony, was made even more harsh, due to the fact that He was cursed because He died on that cross. He said ... "My soul is crushed with horror and sadness to the point of death." (NKJV Matthew 26:38)

He stands in front of His sheep, the Savior, the Lord who is *my* Shepherd. I do not deserve Him. I went through no physical agony to receive the grace that I have been given. His grace covers me, because His blood covers me. The price was paid for all sin for all time, until eternity. Jesus died long ago, but still, until the earth is burned up and recreated and He returns, the blood covering stands. It brings salvation for me, and all who accept Him as both Lord and Savior.

The agony of the poured out blood sacrifice of Calvary's Lamb, is the tsunami of love, the wave of redemption, that covered all sin and death; completely obliterating Satan, and his team's war-game. Jesus paid it all.

We all turn and join in the hymn, JESUS PAID IT ALL:

Jesus paid it all
all to Him I owe;
Sin had left a crimson stain,
He washed it white as snow
(By Elvina M. Hall 1820-1889)

April 13

NKJV I Peter 2:24 "Who His own self bore our sins in His own body on the tree."

LESSON VI

THE CRASH

God and sin at the cross crashed and when sin hit the Savior all hell broke loose, and death was finished. The Spirit came to be with us and in us and therefore, we have perfect peace. The Shepherd is teaching us to be *still* and to drink of Him and to eat of Him. Then as our inside pours out, the deeds will be of the Spirit, and not of the flesh.

The crash at the cross changed everything which once was. Death died; sin is covered; fear and evil are caught and held captive by the slaying of the Lamb.

The Cross of Jesus is the revelation of God's judgment on sin.
Never tolerate the idea of martyrdom about the Cross of Jesus
Christ. The cross was a superb triumph in which the
foundations of hell were shaken. There is nothing more certain
in Time or Eternity than what Jesus Christ did on the Cross:
He switched the whole of the human race back into a right
relationship with God. He made Redemption the basis of
human life, that is, He made a way for every son
of man to get into communion with God.

The Cross is not the cross of a man but the Cross of God, and the Cross of God
can never be realized in human experience. The Cross is the exhibition of the
nature of God, the gateway whereby any individual of the human race can enter
into union with God. When we get to the Cross, we do not go through it;
we abide in the life to which the Cross is the gateway.

The cross is the point where God and sinful man merge with a CRASH
and the way to life is opened - - - but the crash is on the heart of God.

(Oswald Chambers, April 16)

The cross of *my* Shepherd saved me from the cross of this world. We know that the journey *through the valley of the shadow of death* has been paved with the Crash of the Cross!

April 14

NKJV Mark 4:39 "Peace ... be still."

LESSON VII

STORMS

The peace that our Shepherd supplies, is the peace which cannot be understood. It is the peace that delivers us from life's storms. There is an old Proverb that says: "All sunshine makes a desert." If there were no storms, discomfort, hard work, sickness nor death, we would just become more complacent and self-seeking, and never become thirsty for the *Water of Life*.

In today's lesson, our Shepherd will be teaching us how we should go through these storms. Some of the storms will be physical and some will be spiritual.

He begins ... "The first storm My disciples and I encountered was a physical storm. It happened on one excruciatingly tiresome day of teaching, healing, and feeding approximately 15,000 people. After I sent the multitude home, I instructed My disciples to get into a boat and head to the next city where we would be working. I went out alone, up the mountain to rest and to pray."

"By evening a storm blew in and I saw the boat in the middle of the sea. My disciples were straining at rowing because the waves were so boisterous, and they were afraid the boat would capsize. I decided to walk out, on the water to where they were, and comfort them."

"I got to them right in the middle of the storm, and when they saw Me walking on the stormy sea, their fear turned to complete shock and horror because they thought I was a ghost. They cried out, and I called to them, telling them to be of good cheer." He smiled, and in a deep, loud voice demonstrated His words; 'It is I; do not be afraid.'"

He looks at us with deep love and compassion and continues ... "Peter, my aggressive disciple, said, with much confidence, 'Lord, if it is you, command me to come to you on the water' I said 'Come.' Peter got out of the boat and walked on the water toward me. At first he kept his eyes directly on Me, but when he realized he was actually walking on the water, fear emerged. Then his eyes turned from Me to the storm! He begin to sink yelling 'Lord save me!' I put out My hand and lifted him up out of the waves, and the deep, dark water. As I pulled him to safety, I said loud enough for all of them to hear… 'O you of little faith, why did you doubt?'"

"As we climbed into the boat the winds ceased, and the storm became still and at peace. All of My disciples came and worshiped Me, exclaiming to Me, that I was truly God's Son." (NLT Mark 4)

He leaned toward us continuing … "Today you are here by these *still waters* worshiping, learning, and being filled with the *Water of Life*. I will never leave you or forsake you. I will catch you when you fall. Worship Me and have faith in My Words; drinking of the *Water of Life*. For I am the Chief Shepherd, and I supply all your needs." (NKJV Jeremiah 23: 3 - 4)

Oh to be in the presence of *my* Shepherd, and to hear the message of His Word, His basking in love He has for all of His Sheep. I bow my head and pray.

April 15

NKJV Revelations 22:4 "They shall see His face; and His name shall be in their foreheads."

LESSON VIII

REFLECTION

Standing by the *still water*, and leaning over, I look into it and see myself. It is, of course, not like looking into a mirror, but it clearly shows my face. As I'm looking at my reflection, suddenly another reflection is by mine! It is the reflection of Jesus *my* Shepherd. He is right beside me. We then look at each other and laugh.

I know really how it should always be, when any person looks at me, they should always see the Shepherd. He should be the reflection which comes from my body, soul, mind and strength. As I drink from the *Water of Life* I become a reflection of Him.

I am so in love with Jesus, He shines out of me. My life reflects Him. For in Him I live, and breathe, and have my being. As the apostle said, "I am made all things to all men, that I might by all means save some." The Shepherd helps Himself to my life. To live for Jesus is to live in Him, a holy and devoted life which is abandoned to the Shepherd, *my* Shepherd.

As I am in love with Jesus, and as I look at our reflections, my face disappears from the water and His remains. His working in me brings me to working for Him. Because the mainstream of my life runs out of the main stream of the *Water of life*, all who look at me see Him. The Lord, *my* Shepherd.

The song that I am about to sing reflects the person of *my* Shepherd. This song is in honor of the One who fills me to the point I look like Him. So, with that said … "I GIVE YOU JESUS:"

If the ship of your life, is tossing on the sea of strife,
you need someone.
If you feel so all alone and your house is not a home
you need someone.
If it seems life isn't fair and there's no one left to share all your lonely
days and nights when things just don't turn out right.
And you want someone to care, and someone to just be there,
you need someone.

If the pressures all around, keep your spirits to the ground;
You need someone.
If your body is in pain, And your health you can't regain;
You need someone
If at times you have tried, with all the strength you have inside;
And it seems that you have failed, Remember on that cross he nailed
All the bitterness and grief, To give you love and sweet relief
He is that someone that you need.

I Give you Jesus, He's the Peace that passes all understanding
I Give you Jesus, He's the perfect Love that casteth out all fear
I Give you Jesus, He's the water that you drink
and never thirst again.

My friend, I Give you Jesus.
(By Becky Fender/ No Matter What Woman Publishing / ASCAP)

April 16

NKJV Psalm 95:6-7 "Oh come, let us worship and bow down; let us kneel before the Lord our maker for He is our God, and we are the people of His pasture, and the sheep of His hand."

OASIS

The Shepherd leads us to the *still waters* is an oasis for our lives. As we moved from the *green pastures* He told us these words: "Oh come, let us worship and bow down, let us kneel before the Lord our Maker for He is our God, and we are the people of His pasture, and the sheep of His hand."

Here at the water's edge is our oasis of worship: here we drink of the *Water of Life*. As we kneel, we rest in the Lord. We wait patiently for Him to rejuvenate us completely, from the inside out. For when we worship and bow down, humble and obedient to our Lord, we find our souls at rest; the oasis of *our* Father God, and the Spirit of Truth.

The *Water of Life* becomes an oasis that continually provides strength, courage, and comfort for the walk through *the valley of the shadow of death*. We kneel before Him and worship. Constant worship and prayer provides peace, righteous living, and confidence for our journey ahead.

My Shepherd leads us in an oasis of praise, as we continue filling up of the *Water of Life*. PSALM NINETY FIVE:

Oh come let us sing to the Lord.
Let us shout joyfully to the rock of our salvation.
Let us come before His presence with Thanksgiving.
Let us shout joyfully to Him with psalms.
For the Lord is the great God.

April 17

NKJV Psalm 23:2 "He leads me beside the still waters."

HE - THE LORD: JEHOVAH-SHALOM (PEACE)

One of the Shepherd's names in the Hebrew is *Jehovah-Shalom* meaning "Peace." The *Water of Life* actually pours His peace into our lives.

"The world shouts peace!" He begins the lesson..." But there is no peace. I bring peace which passes all understanding: a peace which cannot be understood by the world. My peace filling you, My sheep, is the peace which invades the human soul with a comfort which takes no notice of the world, death, nor hell. My peace is perfect!"

As we drink, He continues providing instructions for the coming journey ... "Go to the lost sheep ... and as you go preach, saying the 'Kingdom of Heaven is at hand.' Heal the sick; cleanse the lepers; raise the dead; cast out demons. Freely you have received, freely give. Provide neither gold nor silver in your money belts, nor a bag for your journey, nor two tunics, nor sandals, nor staff, for a worker is worthy of their food. Now, whatever city or town you enter, inquire who in it is worthy, and stay there till you go out. And whoever will not receive you nor hear your words, when you depart from that house or city, shake off the dust from your feet." (NKJV Matthew 10:6-15)

Jehovah-Shalom, God our Father of peace has spoken clearly what is expected of His sheep as we journey through *the valley of the shadow of death*.

So, as we gather around this cool, clear water, the Shepherd moves us with the power of His Word, and the *peace that passes all understanding*. The trip will be one of complete dependence on Him. For with Him, the Lord, *our* Shepherd, all things will be possible because all is provided.

I pray that we all will drink our fill of the *Water of Life*, who is *the Lord, my Shepherd*. I love you Jesus, and I will sing MY JESUS I LOVE THEE:

My Jesus I love Thee, I know Thou art mine
To Thee all the follies of sin I resign.
My gracious Redeemer, my Savior art Thou.
If ever I love Thee, my Jesus tis now.
(By William R. Featherstone 1846-1873)

April 18

NKJV John 14:27 "Let not your heart be troubled, and neither let it be afraid."

THE LORD: JEHOVAH-SHALOM

In preparation for our journey, He says. "I am sending you out as sheep among wolves. Be as wise as serpents and as harmless as doves. But beware! For you will be arrested and tried, and whipped. Yes, and you must stand trial before governors and Kings for My sake. This will give you the opportunity to tell them about Me, yes, to witness to the world." He turns His back, and waits, finally turning around to speak with tears in His eyes. "When you are arrested, don't worry about what to say at your trial, for you will be given the right words at the right time. For it won't be you doing the talking it will be the Spirit of your heavenly Father speaking through you!" (NLT Matthew 10:19-20)

His voice becomes very quiet as He continues … "Everyone will hate you because you belong to me. But all of you" … He waves His hand taking in all of us … "who endure to the end shall be saved. When you are persecuted in one city, flee to the next. I will return before you have reached them all!" These words sound somewhat scary, but we all know that His peace provides His banner of love covering. (NLT Matthew 10:22-23)

With fire in His eyes He continues … "A student shares his teacher's fate. The servant shares his master's fate. And since I, the Master of the household, have been called 'Satan' how much more will you! But don't be afraid of those who threaten you, for the time is coming, when Truth will be revealed. What I tell you in the dark, speak in the light; and what you hear whispered in your ear shout it from the housetops! Don't be afraid of those who can kill only your bodies, but also your souls!" His voice becomes loud like a trumpet blast ... "Fear only God who can destroy both soul and body in hell!" (NLT Matthew 10:24-28)

Pausing, He takes a deep breath ... "So listen. Whoever confesses Me before men, then I will also confess before My Father who is in heaven. But whoever denies Me before men, that person I will also deny before My Father who is in heaven." (NLT Matthew 10:32-33)

With that said, we all bowed our heads and knelt by the *still waters*, quietly giving thanks to our Father for *my* Shepherd, who fills our soul with the *Shalom* of the *Water of Life*.

April 19

NKJV Matthew 10:34 "I came not to bring peace, but a sword!"

SPIRIT SWORD

"Today, I bring to you a writing from My flock about the *sword of the Spirit* and how it cuts out the heart of the problem of sin's deadly infiltration of our souls."

Never be sympathetic with the soul whose case makes you come to the conclusion that God is hard. God is more tender than we can conceive, and every now and again He gives us the chance of being the rugged one that He may be the tender One. If a person cannot get through to God, it is because there is a secret thing he does not intend to give up, I will admit I have done wrong, but I no more intend to give up that thing than fly. It is impossible to deal sympathetically with a case like that: we have to get right deep down to the root until there is no more antagonism and resentment against the message. **People want the blessing of God, but they will not stand the thing that goes straight to the quick.**

If God has had His way with you, your message as His servant is merciless insistence on this one line; cut down to the very root, otherwise there will be no healing. Drive home the message until there is no possible refuge from its application. Begin to get at people where they are until you get them to realize what they lack, and then erect the standard of Jesus Christ for their lives, "Jesus Christ says you must." "But how can we be?" "You cannot unless you have a new Spirit."

There must be a sense of need before your message is of any use. Thousands of people are happy without God in this world. If I was happy and moral till Jesus came, why did He come? **Because that kind of happiness and peace is on a wrong level: JESUS CHRIST CAME TO SEND A SWORD THROUGH EVERY PEACE THAT IS NOT BASED ON A PERSONAL RELATIONSHIP TO HIMSELF** (Oswald Chambers, December 19)

The Shepherd looks straight into our eyes and asked… "Where are you getting your peace? It must come from the Spirit or it is not of Me." We all smile as He smiles. The Spirit's Sword brings peace through the Word, who is *my* Shepherd.

April 20

NKJV John 14:27 "My peace I leave with you."

NO HEART TROUBLE

To begin today's lesson the Shepherd is quoting one of His sheep:

When you really see Jesus, I defy you to doubt Him. When I defy you to trouble your mind, it is a moral impossibility to doubt when He is there. Over time you get into personal contact with Jesus, His words are real. "My peace I give unto you," it is a peace all over from the crown of the head to the sole of the feet, an irrepressible confidence. Your life is hid with Christ in God, and the imperturbable peace of Jesus Christ is imparted to you. (Oswald Chambers)

"At My human birth, the proclamation was issued; 'Glory to God in the highest, and on earth PEACE, goodwill toward all men.' Now this very peace has come to fruition by My blood that was shed as the Sacrificial Lamb. The atonement has given to you, My sheep, the Spirit, who is the *Peacemaker*."

"If I abide in you, and you abide in me, there is perfect peace. Many cry, 'peace, peace,' but there is none. Peace only comes through Me, the Lord, *your* Shepherd. I came and preached peace to you who were afar off and to those who were near. For through Me you all have access by one Spirit to your Father, and this Truth brings peace." (NKJV Jeremiah 6:14)

"You shall not hunger nor thirst anymore; the sun shall not strike you, nor any heat; for the Lamb who is in the midst of the throne will Shepherd you and lead you to living fountains of waters. And God, our Father, will wipe away every tear from your eyes, because of Jehovah - Shalom!" (NKJV Revelation 7:16-17)

He had us all stand, then He said. Please sing with Me. We sing … MASTER, THE TEMPEST IS RAGING:

The winds and the waves shall obey Thy will.
Peace, be still! Peace, be still!
Whether the earth of the storm-tossed sea,
Or demons, or men, or whatever it be,

No waters can swallow the ship where lies
The Master of ocean, and earth, and skies;
They all shall sweetly obey Thy will,
Peace! Peace! be still!
(By Mrs. M. A. Baker 1831-1921)

April 21

NKJV Matthew 4:18-22 "Follow me and I will make you fishers of men."

LESSONS ON FISHING

FISHING … FOR MEN?

Here beside the *still waters*, the Shepherd is teaching us how to fish! We are fishing for mankind (sheep)! He said to follow Him, and He will make us **fishers of men.** This is going to be interesting, because *all* of His sheep are to be fishers of men. These next few lessons will be fun and exciting as our Lord teaches us to **fish for men**.

Jesus said, "When I began My three years of ministry, I started by calling My disciples to follow Me. The first four I called, were men whose occupation was fishing: Simon, who later was called Peter; Andrew, Peter's brother; and James and John, also brothers. They became the leadership of My disciple team."

"One day as they were working on their fishing boats on the Sea of Galilee, I called to them … 'Follow Me and I will make you fishers of men.' They immediately left their fishing boats and their families."

"Then began the training for a new kind of fishing, catching men, women, and children for the Kingdom of Heaven. The apostles learned these lessons by watching Me."

"The fun and hard part about the lessons on fishing for men, was learning to obey My commands. The day I called them, I begin by asking Simon to take the boat out into the deep. Simon said, they had fished all night and had caught nothing. Finally, reluctantly, he followed My direction. He said, 'Sir, we worked hard all night and didn't catch a thing. But, if you say so, we'll try again.'"

Jesus cheerfully laughed with a gleam in His eye. "When they followed My directions and went out into the deep, and cast their nets exactly as I told them to do, they caught a large number of fish. In fact, they yelled for their other partners to bring their boats to help with the load, because their boats began to sink!"

Sharing the joy that the Shepherd had in performing a miracle for His first catch, the disciples, He slaps His knee as He tells His fishing story (with no usual fishing story embellishments).

Cynthia Perkins

"Without any hesitation, they took their boats to shore, and there they left them and followed Me."

⸻

Now comes the hard part …

April 22

NKJV Matthew 4:18-24 "**If you follow Me** … I will make you fishers of men."

LESSONS ON FISHING

THE TRAINING

Today the Shepherd has the apostle Peter. with Him. He is a tremendous fisherman of fish, and of men.

How exciting to have him here to help with our lesson. The Shepherd is beginning. "Today Peter will teach about how one should catch fish, and how fishing pertains to your job of catching mankind for the Kingdom. While we are by the *still wate*rs is the best time to learn this lesson." Peter smiles at the Shepherd, and begins the lesson.

"To be a fisher-person one must prepare to fish. Preparation takes time, and money. To be successful, one must map-out places to fish, and then find those good fishing holes. To just go off without a plan, is a waste of time and energy. To be a successful fisherman, one must do homework, finding the right fishing spot, fishing times, and fishing equipment."

He turns and sits down. "The water should be around 60 degrees, or else the fish will not bite. The best places to cast the nets, or rods, is an important decision. The weeds, around fallen trees, bushes, or rock ledges that are under the water, are great places to try to catch, because fish feed, spawn, or rest in these areas. Around, and under docks or bridges, are also places where fish hang out.

"And what about the bait?" He holds up several packages of bait. "The color, texture, smell, live or synthetic, and the size … etc., are some of the very important issues to be acknowledged while choosing bait."

The Shepherd shakes His head, in recognition that there is so much to fishing, then He adds this to Peter's lesson. "All of this fishing scenario is the same for you My sheep, My disciples, who are commanded to catch all of mankind for the Kingdom. You should know where, and how you can accomplish My commend, and how to catch with the gospel those that I send to you, and also know how to reel them in from the ocean of sin."

"I'm sending you to preach the Kingdom of God and to heal the sick … whatever house you enter stay there, and from there depart. I give you authority and power over all demons, and to cure diseases. It is written, and thus it was necessary for Me to suffer and to rise from the dead the third day, and repentance and remission of sin should be preached in My name to all Nations, beginning now. This is My premise, all of My sheep be trained to catch fish called *mankind*." (NKJV Luke 9:2-6/ 24:46-49)

These specific instructions are given for all of us to catch our crop of fish. We are the fishermen for the Lord, *my* Shepherd. The Shepherd and Peter are singing for us the chorus I WILL MAKE YOU FISHERS OF MEN:

> *I will make you fishers of men,*
> *fishers of men, fishers of men.*
> *I will make you fishers of men*
> *if you follow me.*
> (By Harry D. Clarke, Copyright 1927)

April 23

NKJV Matthew 4:18-24 "I will make you fishers of men."

LESSONS ON FISHING

FISH

Peter, the fisherman continues our lessons on *fishing*. "To fish for men correctly takes much research and experience. Trying different techniques, skills, or theories, has to be done to achieve the goal of catching a stringer full of fish. A truly great fisherman studies, educating themselves with research, and listening to those teachers who are well versed in catching fish. A good fisherman never goes to fish unprepared."

"Today's lesson is based on catching fish, these techniques man also used to catch mankind. The following list are steps that a fisherman would take in preparation for catching fish. But remember, this is really an analogy of becoming a prepared fisher-person for the Shepherd's Kingdom:

Number One: *EQUIPMENT*

>A fisherman must have equipment which is in working condition and ready for the fisherman at all times.

Number Two: *BAIT*

>To catch fish, bait is pertinent. Not any bait, but the kind of bait which will entice the fish to strike.

Number Three: *VARIETY*

> A fisherman must decide what kind of fish are in that particular area of the water. If a fisherman goes out to fish for a particular kind of fish, and those fish are not to be found, then the equipment, bait and time have been wasted. The fisherman must know what kind of fish he or she is trying to catch.

Number Four: *CLOCK, TIME, AND WEATHER*

> Early morning or late night is the best time to fish. In the heat of the day, fish usually hide to stay cool. If it is too cold, stormy, or windy, it is not a good time to fish.
>
> A good fisherman plans for the weather, clock time, and seasons.

Number Five: *EXTRA PREPARATION*

> Boats, nets, stringers, extra poles, hooks, lines and proper clothing make a fishing day productive and many more fish can be caught.

Number Six: *ATTITUDE*

> An attitude of patience, quietness, perseverance and intensity makes for a good fisherman. A good fisherman is not greedy nor narcissistic. He gives God the glory for providing the catch."

Peter sits down and the Shepherd takes a moment to just talk very personally with us. "Now let me ask all of you a very important question … If all of these steps are used to catch fish-fish, then how much more astute should you sheep be as fishers of men?"

"You are to know the Truth, that is Me, and to study to show yourselves to God fishers of man who are not afraid, those who can handle My Word! It is My commandment, for you to go into all this whole, world, and there preach and teach the gospel to every creature. In every place be assertive in the Way of My Father, the Way I am leading you and have taught you. You must be one as I and My Father are One. My Father must be in you, as I am in Him, and He is in me. The Father wants the world to know He sent Me, and He loves you all just as He loves the Shepherd, Me, His Son." (NKJV Mark 16:15 / John 14:6 / 17:21)

There is not a dry eye as we hear and feel the love and care our Shepherd provides for all of His sheep. Here by the *still waters*, we prepare to go and be fishers of men!

April 24

NKJV John 20:21 "So Jesus said to them ... "Peace to you! As the Father has sent Me, I also send you."

LESSONS ON FISHING

FISHERS OF MEN VS AQUARIUM KEEPER

The Shepherd said ... "Follow Me and I will make you fishers of men. If we do not fish for men, we are a *fishless* fisherman. So ... if we are not a fisher of men, then we must ask this question: Who are we?"

Our purpose is first to follow Him. He said ... "follow Me ..." We cannot bring the lost to Christ if we don't follow. We cannot bring the lost in, if we don't fish! The question that will be asked in eternity is simple ... "Who did you bring with you?" And to get the job done we must follow Him and go after the fish (mankind or sheep).

Look at our Lord's radical ways: He commanded that we love one another; give up our life by crucifixion; hate our father, mother, sister and brother by loving Him so much it looks that way; go into the entire world; preach, teach and baptize in His name. By being a radical like Him, we are made like Him to become fishers of men? "Follow **Me** and **I** will MAKE you ..."

Jesus makes us the sheep who catch mankind. Jesus made this statement as He began to gather the twelve men who would do just that ... fish for mankind. It was His first command as He began His three year ministry to transition from the Old, to the New covenant. My Shepherd is serious about this command ... "Follow Me. I Am the Way, the Truth and the Life. That person that loses His life for My sake, will find it; that person who finds his life will lose it."

"We have nothing to do but to fish." He continues. "Mankind are ... sheep who have gone astray. We have turned, every one, to our own way. We are to bring the sheep back to the fold by catching or by pointing them to Me as I call. I am the Door, and the Gate, of the sheepfold. They must come into the fold through Me."

Every sheep who has given their lives to Him have this quest. "Follow Me and I will make you **fishers of men**."

An aquarium is a building where people can go to look at fish. We are not to just look and admire the fish, we're told by the Shepherd that we **must** catch fish. Here by the *still waters* as He teaches us to catch the lost, we know that time is critical, and we must follow His instructions as we learn the skill and become **fishers of men**.

April 25

> NKJV Luke 15:7 "There will be more joy in heaven over one sinner who repents, than over ninety-nine just persons who need no repentance."

LESSONS ON FISHING

THE CATCH

When the Shepherd gave Peter and the others the big catch, they were overjoyed. The Shepherd said, when one person comes to Him, all of heaven rejoices.

There is the same joy when one lost sheep comes to the Lord, *our* Shepherd. That person is transformed into a new creature. Their very heart, mind and soul, is covered by the grace and the blood of Jesus Christ. Now heaven, not hell, is their home for eternity. Their name has been changed from *Sinner* to *Saint*.

In all of the Shepherd's teaching about fishing for men, we must be aware that the catch is not our doing. The catch is due to the Shepherd. He asks us to follow His directions in complete obedience, so the outcome is not ours but His. Our Shepherd is in the salvation business. Never should a sheep take credit for the catch!

When the Shepherd gave them the catch, Peter and the others at the boat fell down and worshiped Him. When one is caught for the kingdom, we should fall down and worship our Shepherd. We should rejoice and be glad because, at one time, this person was dead, but now they are alive, in Christ Jesus, our Lord, *our* Shepherd.

Listen as the Shepherd explains. "What person of you, have a hundred sheep, if they lose one of them, does not leave the ninety-nine in the wilderness, and go after the one which is lost until they find it? And when they have found it, they lay it on their shoulders, rejoicing. And when they come home, they call together their friends and neighbors, saying to them, 'rejoice with me, for I have found my sheep which was lost!' I say to all of you here, that there will be more joy in heaven over one sinner who repents than over ninety-nine just persons who need no repentance." (NKJV Matthew 18:12-13)

Jesus yells … "Look what I caught!" In His hand is *my* hand. It is *me*! They all clap for joy.

April 26

NKJV Mark 6:33 "And with many such parables He spoke the word to them as they were able to hear it."

FINAL LESSON ON FISHING

PARABLE OF FISHLESS FISHERMEN

Today the Shepherd asks a poignant question, then answers it by telling the following parable.

"Issue: Is a sheep of Mine a fisherman, if year after year they **never catch** any fish? Let me tell you this parable and you decide."

Now it came to pass that a group existed who called themselves fishermen. And lo, there were many fish in the water all around. In fact, the whole area was surrounded by streams and lakes filled with fish. And the fish were hungry. Week after week, month after month, and year after year, those who called themselves fisherman meet in meetings and talked about their call to fish, the abundance of fish and how they might go about fishing. Year after year they carefully defined what fishing means, defended fishing as an occupation, and declared that fishing is always to be a primary task of fishermen. Continually they searched for new and better methods of fishing and for new and better definitions of fishing. Furthermore they said, "Fishing is the task of every fisherman's club." They sponsored special meetings called "Fishermen's Campaigns" and "The Month for fisherman to fish." They sponsored costly nationwide and worldwide congresses to discuss fishing and to promote fishing and hear about all the ways of fishing such as the new fishing equipment, fish calls, and whether any new bait was discovered. These fishermen built large, beautiful buildings called "Fishing Headquarters." the plea was that everyone should be a fisherman and every fisherman should fish. One thing they didn't do however;
they didn't fish.
*In addition to meeting regularly, they organized a board to send out fishermen to other places where there were many fish. All the fishermen seem to agree that what is needed is a board which could challenge fishermen to be faithful in fishing. The board was formed by those who had the great vision and courage to speak about fishing, to define fishing, and to promote the idea of fishing in faraway streams and lakes where many other fish of different colors lived. Also, the board hired staff and appointed committees and held many meetings to define fishing, and to decide what new streams should be thought about. But the staff and committee members **did not fish**.*

The Shepherd's parable will be continued as tomorrow's lesson. In closing, we are all to sing with the Shepherd, and Peter, I WILL MAKE YOU FISHERS OF MEN:

I will make you
Fishers of men
If you follow Me
(By Harry D. Clarke, Copyright 1927)

April 27

PARABLE OF FISHLESS FISHERMEN

CONTINUED FROM YESTERDAY'S LESSON

The Shepherd and Peter look refreshed and ready to continue yesterday's parable. Everyone is excited to hear the rest of the story.

"Yesterday I began a parable about sheep who have been called My fishermen, yet that are **fish-less**. These fishermen, who don't catch fish, were working in every way to prepare for the fish, going to elaborate extremes to get the job done but **never** going fishing. Let's continue."

Large, elaborate, and expensive training centers were built,
whose original and primary purpose was to teach fishermen how to fish.
Over the years courses were offered on the needs of fish, the nature of fish,
where to find fish, the psychological reactions of fish, and how to approach
and feed fish. Those who taught had doctorates in Fishology. But the teachers did
not fish. They only taught fishing. Year after year, after tedious training, many were
graduated and were given fishing licenses. They were sent to do full-time
fishing, some to distant waters which were filled with fish.

Some spent much study and travel to learn the history
of fishing and to see faraway places where the founding fathers
did great fishing in the centuries past. They lauded the faithful
fisherman of years before who handed down the idea of fishing.

Furthermore, the fishermen built large printing houses to
publish fishing guides. Presses were kept busy day and night to produce
materials solely devoted to fishing methods, equipment, and programs to
arrange and to encourage meetings to talk about fishing. A speakers'
bureau was also provided to schedule special speakers on the subject of fishing.

Many who felt the call to be fisherman responded. They were commissioned and sent to fish. But like the fishermen back home, never fished. They engaged in all kinds of other occupations. They made all kinds of equipment to travel here and there to look at fish hatcheries. Some also said they wanted to be part of the fishing party, but they felt called to furnish fishing equipment. Others felt their job was to relate to the fish in a good way so the fish would know the difference between good and bad fishermen. Others felt that simply letting the fish know they were nice, land-loving neighbors, and how loving and kind they were was enough.
BUT THEY NEVER FISHED!!!

There was complete silence. We got the point! We knew we were to fish and catch for the Shepherd. We are to fish as we *walk through the valley of the shadow of death.*

I bow my head and I pray … "The Lord is *my* Shepherd … and I will fish and catch men."

April 28

NKJV Matthew 4:19 "I will make you fishers of men."

CONCLUSION OF THE "PARABLE OF FISHLESS FISHERMEN"

Today Jesus and Peter finish the parable of the "Fishless Fishermen." The Shepherd begins.

After one stirring meeting on "The Necessity for Fishermen," one young fellow left the meeting and went fishing. The next day he reported he had caught two outstanding fish. He was honored for his excellent catch and scheduled to visit all the big meetings possible to tell how he did it. So he quit his fishing in order to have time to tell about the experience to the other fishermen. He was also placed on the fishermen's General board as a person having considerable experience.

Now it's true that many of the fishermen sacrificed and put up with all kinds of difficulties. Some living near the water smelled dead fish every day. They received the ridicule of some who made fun of their fishermen's clubs and the fact that they claimed to be fishermen yet never fished. They wondered about those who felt it was of little use to attend the weekly meetings to talk about fishing. After all, were they not following the Master who said, "Follow me, and I will make you fishers of men?"

Imagine how hurt some were when one day a person suggested that those who didn't catch fish were really not fishermen, no matter

how much they claimed to be. So goes the question ... Is a person a fisherman if year after year they never catch a fish? Is one following Him if they aren't fishing?
(John M. Drescher 1929-2014, Copyright 1979)

The Shepherd looks intently at us and says. "All of you know that this is a modern day parable. However, it makes the point that if you are the sheep of My pasture, you are called to fish. You will follow me and fish for all of mankind. Now I ask the question ... 'Who have you caught lately?' If you are not **My** fisherman catching fish, then ask yourself this question...Whose am I?"

I answer with joy, raising my hand and shouting ... "I am Your fisherman. I will catch for *my* Shepherd's Kingdom."

April 29

NKJV Psalm 23:2 "He leads me beside the *still waters.*"

CALL TO ONE ANOTHER

The Shepherds stands with us at the end of the day. It is quiet, and the sounds of the still waters, are announcing the evening is upon us.

He gently waves His hand over us as He sits. We all join, sitting at the water's edge. "Before we go our separate ways for this evening, I would like to share with you a beautiful story, a folktale which is a perfect description of how we should treat each other as My sheep.

> *The alpine Shepherds have a beautiful custom of ending the day by singing to one another an evening farewell. The air is so crystalline that the song will carry long distances. As dusk begins to fall, they gather their flocks and begin to lead them down the mountain paths, singing. "Hitherto hath the Lord helped us. Let us praise His name!"*
>
> *And at last with sweet courtesy, they sing to one another the friendly farewell: "Good night! Good night!" The words are taken up by the echoes, and from side to side the song goes reverberating sweetly and softly until the music dies away in the distance.*
>
> *So let us call out to one another through the darkness, till the gloom becomes vocal with many voices encouraging the pilgrim host ... Let the echoes gather till a very storm of hallelujahs breathe in thundering waves around the sapphire throne, and then as the morning breaks we shall find ourselves at the margin of the sea of glass,*

crying, with the redeemed host, "Blessing and honor and glory be unto Him Who sitteth on the throne, and the Lamb forever and ever!"

(By Mrs. Charles E. Cowman, STREAMS IN THE DESERT, December 31)

We sing Hallelujah, with call and response. The beauty of the singing, resonating fills the green valley. Chills run up my back. Tears fill my eyes. I cannot breathe.

April 30

NKJV Revelation 7:15 "They have washed their robes and made them white in the blood of the Lamb."

LESSONS ON THE WATERY GRAVE OF BAPTISM

LESSON I
THE WASHING

The Shepherd stands at the *still waters* preparing us for the trip on the path of righteousness, baptizing us with the water and the blood. And as we rise out of that watery grave of baptism, we walk in a new eternal life. After the washing, our garments are as white as snow. Sin's stain is no more and we stand righteous, and holy before the Lord, the Shepherd.

The coming of Jesus annihilated death and brought life. The wages of sin is death, but God's gift of His Son in us, is eternal life. Salvation's transformation, and resurrection, emerged from the horror of that sacrifice. His blood pouring out provided the nourishment for the blooming of the *Rose of Sharon, our* Shepherd.

Listen as He teaches...I Am the Door of the sheepfold. All who ever came before me are thieves and robbers. I am the Door. If anyone enters by Me, they will be saved, and will go in and out and find pasture. The thief does not come except to steal, and to kill, and to destroy. I have come that they may have life, and that they may have it more abundantly. I am the Good Shepherd. The Good Shepherd gives His life for you, My sheep." (NKJV John 10:6-11)

"Because of My death and resurrection, NO DEATH!" We clap.

"So Death, where is your sting; and grave where is your victory? The sting of death is sin, but the gift of God is eternal life through Me, the Shepard, your Lord." We all look up to the Father and give thanks, clapping and shouting the name of *our* Shepherd, the Lamb of God! (NKJV I Corinthians 15:55)

The washing of regeneration, our baptism, represents the Gospel of our Shepherd. His death means we die to ourselves, as we leave the world behind. His burial means we are buried into the watery grave, as He was buried into the earthly grave; His resurrection means we are raised out of the watery grave of baptism to *walk* in newness of life.

Water baptism is the physical example of the Gospel, the ceremonial cleansing of our coming to belief in Jesus. The washing demonstrates in action the Gospel, the "Good News" of the death, burial, and resurrection of our Lord Jesus Christ, *my* Shepherd.

May

Cynthia Perkins

May 1

NKJV John 1:29 "Behold! The Lamb of God who takes away the sin of the world!"

LESSON II

WATER

Now that we have been brought to the *still water's* edge, the Shepherd's teaching today centers on baptism.

"All of My sheep know me by name, and they follow Me. They imitate Me, and one of the ways that I have commanded them to follow is in the act of baptism."

"Baptism is a sign of the seal of salvation through the Holy Spirit. Baptism is for those who have repented, turning from their wicked ways, changing their life's direction, and placing their faith in me."

"Physical baptism is a sheep's public testimony, of an inward transformation to their repentance, regeneration, and new direction. Baptism means immersion into the water representing the blood of the Lamb. My blood covers their sins, burying them in the grave of water."

"Baptism represents the gospel: My death, burial, and resurrection. One dies to self, as one turns his or her life over to Me. The immersion represents the burial, and being under the blood. Rising out of the water reenacts My resurrection and marks the new birth, and the new life 'washed' white as snow."

He gently smiles. "After the resurrection out of that watery grave, the sheep is filled with the gift of the Spirit. The Spirit's ministry is to represent the moment the believer places his or her faith and trust in Me, Christ the Savior. The Holy Spirit is a provision of security and a mark of ownership. It is a certification and a sign of approval. The Spirit is the final secure evidence in the believer's life, both to themselves and to others, of the truth of salvation." (NKJV Acts 2:38)

The Spirit is standing by the Shepherd. When John, Jesus' cousin baptized Him, *the Spir*it came to *our* Lord in the form of a dove. The dove is the symbol, for all of the Shepherd's sheep of perfect peace, which passes all understanding, and issues us into a new life.

We are all filled with "aah" and joy!

May 2

NKJV John 3:13 "Then Jesus came to John at the Jordan to be baptized by him."

LESSON III

MINE

"My cousin John baptized Me." The Shepherd begins today's lesson with the huge, hairy, wild looking man standing beside Him. "My Father had planned for John and I to be close and to be His witnesses at the same time."

"When John was inside his mother Elizabeth's womb, My mother, Mary, went to visit her. When she arrived, John jumped in his mother's womb!" All of us laughed. "He always made a fuss."

"Elizabeth, feeling his jump exclaimed 'Blessed is she who believed for there will be a fulfillment of those things which were told her from the Lord.' All that she and My mother had been told came true."

He sits down, and continues. "After John left home, He was always in the wilderness shouting to everyone about My coming. He told everyone they should 'Repent, for the Kingdom was near.'" He smiles, "He looked a sight, wearing stinky camel's hair clothes with long stringy hair. He was tall and lean from his choice of diet, locusts and honey."

"They flocked to see and hear this strange man who had no fear, but looked scary. Many came and were baptized with John's *Baptism of Repentance*."

"The day of My baptism was a highlight for My cousin and Myself. As I came over the hill to the Jordan River where John was preaching and baptizing that day, he looked up and shouted … 'Behold the Lamb, that takes away the sins of the whole world.' At first he was reluctant to do the honors. He said that I needed to baptize Him! I told him that the plan was for us to fulfill all righteousness. He was preparing the way: I Am the WAY."

"All eyes were on us as John took Me down into the water. There. I proclaimed publicly that I was God's Son, and identified Myself with all the people whom I came to save. The Trinity: the Father, the Son, and the Holy Spirit was represented as I came up out of the water, the heavens immediately opened and the Spirit came down like a dove and set on Me. Then My Father shouted 'This is My beloved Son, in Whom I am well pleased.'"

The Shepherd looked at John with pure joy on His face. "When My Father declared His pleasure with Me, I was overjoyed, because the peace of the Spirit was right beside Me. My life here would be fulfilled by Him and the Spirit. My Father loved Me, and He brought complete joy to this mission by His confirmation. For from that day forward, He declared My authority here on earth; **I Am His Son!**"

We all looked at His amazing face, and His cousin John's face, and shouted "AMEN!"

May 3

NKJV Acts 8:36 "Here is water. What hinders me from being baptized?"

LESSON IV

NOW

"Immediately following My death and resurrection, as the Church was beginning to grow, Philip, one of My witnesses, was directed by the Spirit to go toward the south, along the road which goes down from Jerusalem. This was a well-traveled road that connected the Middle East with Egypt." The Shepherd begins today's lesson with this story.

"Along his way he came upon a man sitting in a chariot, reading. As Philip got closer, he could see that the man was an Ethiopian eunuch, who was reading the Scriptures. As Philip began conversing with him, he learned that he was not only from Ethiopia, but employed by the household of Candace the queen of Ethiopia. He was a man of great authority because he was over all of her treasury and he had come to Jerusalem to worship."

"The Eunuch was reading from Isaiah the prophet. The Spirit told Philip to help this Ethiopian man with the reading of My Word. Philip said 'Do you understand what you are reading?' He answered 'how can I unless someone guides me.' So Philip went into the chariot and sit with him. The eunuch was reading:

He was led as a sheep to the slaughter
And as a lamb before the shearers is silent,
So He opened not His mouth. In his humiliation
His justice was taken away and who would declare
His generation? For His life is taken from the earth.

"The eunuch turned to Philip and asked 'Of whom does the prophet say this, of himself or of some other man.' Then Philip beginning at these verses preached to him Me, Jesus. He told him all about the Shepherd, the Lamb."

The Shepherd looks up, quiet for a moment, then He gently speaks. "As they went down the road Philip taught him. When they came to water the eunuch said 'So here is water. What keeps me from being baptized?' Philip answered 'If you believe with all your heart you may.' The eunuch said 'I BELIEVE THAT JESUS CHRIST IS THE SON OF THE LIVING GOD.'"

"Immediately the eunuch commanded the chariot to stand still and they both, Philip and the eunuch went down into the water and Philip baptized him! Then the Spirit took Philip away, and the eunuch never saw him again, but he went on down the road rejoicing and giving praise!" (NKJV Acts 8:26-40)

As I now look at these *still waters*, I know that because of the grace of our Shepherd it reflects the beauty of one's baptism. And once we are baptized, we must go on our way, following the Shepherd down the *paths of righteousness* rejoicing!

May 4

NKJV Acts 2:38 "Repent and be baptized, every one of you …"

LESSON V

FOR THE CHURCH NOW

The Shepherd has often reminded us that there are wolves that will come into the sheep fold, and spread lies about what He has commanded. One of the major doctrinal debates that has risen since the resurrection of the Shepherd and the coming of the Church age, is baptism. Most of the "wolves" have used baptism as a major source of division. Baptism was never meant to bring about heartache, division, and /or condemnation.

Christian baptism is very simple. The immersion in water in submission to the authority of our Shepherd, Jesus Christ. It is an act of obedience which commits one to a life of obedience.

The Shepherd's Word answers the following questions and concerns about baptism.

WHAT ABOUT BAPTISM?

The Shepherd teaches that baptism is a command: "I have been given all authority in heaven and earth. Therefore, go and make disciples in all the nations, baptizing them into the name of the Father and of the son and of the Holy Spirit. And then teach these new disciples to obey all the commands I have given you; and be sure of this, that I am with you always, even to the end of this world." (NLT Matthew 28:18-20)

The first sheep that made up the church were called Christians. Baptism became known as *Christian Baptism*. These Christians taught that baptism symbolizes the cleansing from sin, and washing away of the old life. The Shepherd's Word says "Go and be baptized, and be cleansed from your sins, calling on the name of the Lord."

Christian Baptism symbolizes the new birth by which one becomes a new creation in Christ. It symbolizes the beginning of the new life in Christ.

When the priest, Nicodemus came at night to interview the Shepherd about His radical teaching, he said, "Sir, we all know that God has sent You to teach us. Your miracles are proof enough of this."

The Shepherd replied, "With all the earnestness I possess I tell you this; unless you are born again, you can never get into the Kingdom of God." "Born again!" exclaimed Nicodemus. "What do You mean? How can an old man go back into his mother's womb and be born again?" Jesus replied. "What I am telling you so earnestly is this: Unless one is born of water, and the Spirit, he cannot enter the Kingdom of God." (NLT John 3:3-7)

The Shepherd will continue this lesson on baptism tomorrow. We bow for a closing prayer. The Lord, *my* Shepherd prayed.

May 5

NKJV Acts 2:38 "Repent and be baptized, every one of you ..."

CONTINUATION OF LESSON V

FOR THE CHURCH NOW

The Shepherd is explaining what baptism is and how it works toward our salvation.

"In baptism we show that we have been saved from death and doom by My resurrection; not because our bodies are washed clean by the water, but because in being baptized, we are turning to God and asking Him to cleanse our *hearts* from sin. When someone becomes a Christian they become a brand new person inside. A new life has begun!"

"*Christian Baptism* is the act which initiates the Christian into fellowship with God, the Spirit, Myself, and the Body, of Believers."

He leans into us and continues ... "Each of us becomes a part of My body. Some of us are Jews, some are Gentiles, some are slaves and some are free, but the Holy Spirit has fitted us all together into one Body. You, My sheep represent My Body. You have been baptized into My Body, washed by My blood, and have been given the same Holy Spirit by baptism."

This is the summery of His lesson. Christian baptism symbolizes the death, burial, and resurrection of Jesus, our Shepherd, and provides the new covenant. In baptism our old, evil nature dies with Him, and is buried with Him, under the blood, washed clean, then coming up out of death with Him, raised to walk in a new life. Immediately, sin's power over us is forever banished!

Our baptism birthed us into a new life, because Jesus Christ the Lamb of God was slain for our sins. Through His death, the power of our sinful nature was shattered. By baptism, our old sin-loving nature was buried! God the Father, with glorious power, brought Him back to life again. We are given this same wonderful resurrection as we come up out of that watery grave; our new life begins!

We all stand and sing ARE YOU WASHED IN THE BLOOD OF THE LAMB:

Have you been to Jesus for the cleansing power?
Are you washed in the blood of the Lamb?
Are you fully trusting in His grace this hour?
Are you washed in the blood of the Lamb?

Are you washed,
In the Blood,
In the soul cleansing blood of the Lamb?
Are your garments spotless,
are they white as snow?
Are you washed in the blood of the Lamb?
(By Elish A. Hoffman 1839-1929, Copyright 1878)

May 6

NKJV Acts 2:38 "Repent and be baptized every one of you …"

CONTINUATION OF LESSON V

FOR THE CHURCH NOW

Today's lesson is still concerning the fellowship of believers and how they become a part of the flock that belongs to the Shepherd. Listen, as our Shepherd continues to teach and explain.

Should a sheep be baptized?

"The act of baptism is commended by Me. It is the appeal to God for a clear conscience. Baptism does now also save you, not by the removing of outward body filth, but by the answer of a good and clear conscience (inward cleanness and peace) before God, through My resurrection."

"Baptism demonstrates obedience and their willingness to come under the Lordship of Me, Christ, your Shepherd ... Whoever says, 'I know Him,' but disobeys My commandments, is a liar, and the Truth is not in them."

"I was baptized to 'fulfill all righteousness.' As My sheep, you have no grounds on which to claim exemption from any divine requirement. The result of love for Me is complete and faithful obedience, which becomes the main motive of a sheep's life."

How was Christian Baptism Performed?

"My Word states that baptism is immersion. They were baptized by him in the river Jordan, confessing their sins, John the Baptist was baptizing at Aenon because there was plenty of water there."

"When I was baptized, I went up at once out of the water, and behold, the heavens were opened, and John saw the Spirit of God descending like a Dove and alighting on Me."

What Christian Baptism is not.

"*Christian Baptism* is not a guarantee of heaven. If there is not faith and repentance, water baptism is invalid. My word states that ... 'by grace are we saved through faith; and that not of yourselves; it is the gift of God, not of works, lest any person should boast."

"It is not proof to a congregation of the genuineness of a convert's faith. it is only proof to God who knows the heart and motives of the person. Remember My words ... 'No person knows the heart of any person except God our Father, and Myself.'"

"The following are some evidences that prove authentic Christianity:

- *Obedience to God's Word
- *Love for God
- *Repentance from sin
- *Spiritual growth
- *Separation from the world"

When I was a small lamb, only five years old, I was baptized. I remember that I knew that *my* Shepherd loved me. And I knew I had to belong to Him. And to this day, I testify that I knew exactly what I was doing.

May 7

NLT Matthew 28:19 "Go and make disciples in all the nations, baptizing them into the name of the Father and of the Son and of the Holy Spirit."

CONTINUATION OF LESSON V

FOR THE CHURCH NOW

The Shepherd stands before us, and reaches out His hand to begin the lesson. "There are many questions asked about Baptism. Here are the questions and My answers."

Q. Is there 'baptismal regeneration?
A. "No. Baptismal regeneration is the belief that a sheep is saved by the act of baptism itself. This cannot be, because My Word says we are saved by grace through faith, not that we are saved by baptism. Baptism is ... 'not a removal of dirt from the body, but an appeal to God for a clear conscience.'"

Q. Can a person be a Christian and not be baptized?
A. "To say *yes* is to say more than My Word says. To say *no* is to presume you are God. Once a sheep has said *yes* to Me as Savior **And** Lord, they have forfeited all rights to say no to any of My or My Father's commands. **Baptism is one of my commands!**"

Q. Why is it a requirement for a person who is a believer to be baptized in order to be a member of My Church.
A. "Because all of the examples of My early Church, baptism was a pattern of commitment and witness. It would not be following the Scriptures if less than this were allowed."

Q. How soon should a person be baptized once they have received Me as their Shepherd?
A. "The early Church's pattern in My Word is '**immediately!**'"

The Shepherd stands beside the *still waters* and says ... "When you go, make disciples of all; teaching and baptizing."

May 8

NKJV Acts 2:38-39 "Repent and let everyone of you be baptized in the name of Jesus Christ for the remission of your sins; and you shall receive the gift of the Holy Spirit. For the promise is to you and to your children, and to all who are afar off, as many as the Lord our God will call."

FINAL LESSON ON THE WATERY GRAVE OF BAPTISM

LESSON VI
PERSONAL

As the Shepherd has us stationed here by the *still waters*, filling us up of the *Water of Life*, I am constantly reminded of my own baptism.

It was in the late summer and I was five years old. I knew the Shepherd completely at this young age. I knew His love and His care. I knew that He was my Savior. Being baptized was no big leap in my faith. It was as natural as breathing. I can remember thinking baptism was obeying Jesus and it was to show Jesus, *my* Shepherd, my absolute devotion for Him.

On that baptismal day, a bright, sunny, Sunday morning, I stepped out to walk down the Church isle during the singing of the invitation hymn. Two other girls stepped out and followed as well. These girls were twelve year old twins, Helen and Ellen. As the last verse of the invitation was sung I heard a commotion and one of the ladies of the church had gotten up and made her way over to a young man in his twenties whose name was Bud Wilson. Bud was twenty five in physical age, but in his mind he was around the age of five.

Bud was the kindest and most loving person ever. Once he met you he NEVER forgot your name. Bud never missed church. If no one came to pick him up, he walked the three miles to church. And now on this day the lady told Bud … "You can be baptized if you want." He practically ran down the isle.

That's how it is with the love and care of the Shepherd. He takes us all: at five years old, twelve years old, or a man in his twenties that lived a five year old life. We all are called. "Come unto Me" *my* Shepherd says.

We all went to Cow Creek, our country Churches' baptismal, and we were washed in the blood of the Lamb! I remember all of us holding hands walking through the water holding on to each other because of the rocky bottom, it was easy to slip and fall. The water was cool, still, and quiet. At a quaint pool in the middle of the creek, we stopped and all of us were baptized.

There in the *still water's* grave of baptism, we were washed as white as snow. Those standing on the bridge begin to sing.

Yes we gather at the river
the beautiful, beautiful, river.
gather with the saints at the river
that flows by the throne of God.
(By Robert Lowry, 1826-1899, Copyright Public Domain)

We sang this hymn as we accepted the atoning grace of our Lord, our Shepherd. The minister said "I baptize you for the remission of your sins, in the name of the Father, the Son, and the Holy Spirit." Under I went. When I came up those on the bridge all sang.

Now I belong to Jesus
Jesus belongs to me
Not for the years of time alone
But for eternity.
(By Norman J. Clayton 1903-1992, Copyright 1938)

All of us that day became the *sheep of His pasture*. We all came to be washed and cleansed in the blood of the Lamb, who is *my* Shepherd.

May 9

NKJV John 4:14 "The water that I shall give them shall be in them a fountain of water springing up into everlasting life."

MUDDY PUDDLE

The source to the Spirit is the Shepherd. If we disconnect with the source, the Spirit will be stopped. The Spirit is He who flows through us, and if there is no Spirit we are stale, dry, and stinky.

The Shepherd explains … "Have you seen a muddy pond, that sits, having no flow, no vegetation, nothing of life? As time passes, bugs, dirt, rocks, land in these holes and die there. The smell is one of dirty dirt and rottenness."

"The hole dries down to nothing. The hole has no flow and no source of water coming in to give life to those who need a refreshing drink. As it completely dries up, it becomes a cracked hole. It is dangerous, and causes any man or beast who steps in it, to stumble and fall down and hurt themselves."

Our Shepherd gives us this example: "Be constantly filled, and the sweetness of the vital relationship to Me will flow out of you, My sheep, as lavishly as the river flows to the sea. Keep right at the source, and out of you will flow rivers of Living Water, irrepressible life!"

"The *Living Water* is a blessing passed on, not an experience stated, but a river continually flowing. Keep at the source, guard well your belief in Me and your relationship to the Spirit, and there will be a steady flow for other lives."

"Some sheep are like the muddy puddle, always taking in but never giving out, because they are not rightly related to the source: they've been disconnected. As surely as you receive from Me the Water, I will pour out through you a well of Life. If I am not pouring out of you, our relationship has gone awry!"

"Therefore, here is My question for all of you. Is there anything between you, the Spirit and Myself?"

One of my fellow sheep expressed the lesson for today saying:

> *Is it not too extravagant to say*
> *that out of an individual believer*
> *rivers are going to flow?*
>
> *"I do not see the rivers," you say.*
> *Never look at yourself from the standpoint of*
> *Who am I?*
> *In the history of God's work*
> *you will nearly always*
> *find that it has started from the obscure,*
> *the unknown, the ignored,*
> *but the steadfastly true to Jesus Christ.*
> *(Oswald Chambers, September 7)*

That would be me; the steadfastly true to Jesus Christ, the Lord, *my* Shepherd.

May 10

NKJV John 7:38 "Rivers of living water."

RIVERS

"If anyone thirsts, let them come to Me and drink. Those who believe in Me, out of their heart will flow rivers of *Living Water*. Your heart is the main stream of emotions. Fill your hearts with My *Living Water*!" The Shepherd continues His lessons concerning the Water of Life.

The *Living Water* comes of the Spirit when we believe in the Shepherd. Through the Shepherd's gift of the Spirit, our inmost being will possess a life giving source of satisfaction. The Source, the Shepherd, will flow out of us, to others, as the Spirit works the *Living Water*. Life becomes as easy as the lilies growing in the rockiest soil; the stars shining in the darkest night; or the birds singing in the middle of a strong thunder storm. One sheep put it this way:

A river is victoriously persistent, it overcomes all barriers.
For a while it goes steadily on its course,
then it comes to an obstacle and for a while it is baulked,
but it soon makes a pathway round the obstacle.
Or a river will drop out of sight for miles,
and presently emerge again
broader and grander than ever.

Into your life an obstacle has come,
and you do not seem to be of any use.
Keep paying attention to the source,
and God will either take you round the obstacle
or remove it.
The river of the Spirit of God overcomes all obstacles.
Never get your eyes on the obstacle or on the difficulty.
The obstacle is a matter of
indifference to the river which will flow steadily through you
if you remember to keep right at the source.

Never allow anything to come between yourself
and Jesus Christ, the Shepherd:
no emotion, or experience;
nothing must keep you from the one
great sovereign Source.
(Oswald Chamber, September 6)

Through obedience, the flow of the Spirit's work is released in us, and the mighty rivers of *Living Water* brings other sheep into the sheepfold, as we ... gather by the *still waters*.

May 11

NKJV Matthew 6:26-27 "Look at the birds of the air ... "Consider the lilies of the field."

CONSIDER

As we drink, our Shepherd continues to fill us with *Living Water*. "Consider the lilies of the field how they grow, and simply are." He waves His hand toward these beautiful flowers, growing by the pond. "Look around at the sky, the sun, the stars, and the moon. These are so beautiful."

He gently sweeps His hand over all of us. "Do not bother about being of use to others; believe on Me - pay attention to the source, and out of you will flow rivers of living water. One cannot get at the springs of their natural life by common sense. Growth in spiritual life does not depend on you watching it, but on concentration to Myself, and the Father in heaven. Our heavenly Father knows the circumstances you are in, and if you keep concentration on Him, you will grow spiritually as the lilies grow, and fly as freely as the birds of the air."

"If you are to live in Him and to be of use to His will and His way, every one of you must be in a right relationship to the Spirit, constantly drinking of the *Water of Life*. As the flow of the source runs through, nothing blocks the Spirit. Even unconsciously, you are made to be used by God every minute that you live and breathe. None of life's storms, can detour or disrupt the flow of that *River of Life* running through your life, reaching to the end of time into eternity." He gently smiles and sits down.

To close today I have asked the Shepherd if I may sing this song, CONSIDER THE LILIES:

Consider the lilies, they don't toil nor spin,
and there's not a king with more slender than them.
Consider the sparrows, they don't plant nor sow,
but they're fed by the Master who watches them grow.

We have a Heavenly father above with eyes full of mercy
and a heart full of love.
He really cares when your head is bowed low.
Consider the lilies and then you will know.
(By Joel Himphill, Copyright 1977)

May 12

NKJV II Corinthians, 4:15 "That life also of Jesus might be made manifest in our mortal flesh."

MANIFEST

Today the Shepherd reads to us about the life of the Spirit made manifest in us. Listen as He reads.

We have to form habits to express what God's grace has done in us.
It is not a question of being saved from hell,
but of being saved in order to manifest the life of the son of God
in our mortal flesh, and it is the disagreeable things
which make us exhibit whether or not we are manifesting His life.

Do I manifest the essential sweetness of the Son of God,
or the essential irritation of "myself" apart from Him?
The only thing that will enable me to enjoy the disagreeable is the
keen enthusiasm of letting the life of the Son of God manifest itself in me.
No matter how disagreeable a thing may be, say,
"Lord, I am delighted to obey Thee in this matter,"
and instantly the Son of God will press to the front,
and there will be manifested in my human life that which glorifies Jesus.

There must be no debate. The moment you obey the source,
the Son of God presses through you in that particular;
but if you debate you grieve the Spirit of God.
You must keep yourself fit to let the life of the Son of God be manifested,
and you cannot keep yourself fit if you give way to self-pity.

Our circumstances are the means of manifesting
how wonderfully perfect and extraordinarily pure the Son of God is.
The thing that ought to make the heart beat is a new way of manifesting
the Son of God. It is one thing to choose the disagreeable,
and another thing to go into the disagreeable
by God's engineering. If God puts you there, He is amply sufficient.

Keep your soul fit to manifest the life of the Son of God. Never live on
memories; let the Word of God be always living and active in you.
(Oswald Chambers, May 14)

I lift my eyes to Him and I pray. Lord God, thank You for the words you provide to shine the light so all may see Your good works. In Jesus, *my* Shepherd's name, Amen.

May 13

> NKJV Revelation 22:17 "Let the thirsty one come, anyone who wants to; let them come and drink of the *Water of Life* without charge."

DEHYDRATED

Jesus, *my* Shepherd is teaching me to drink the *Water of Life.* He is the perpetual spring that flows forever. How is this to be done? As I stand by the *still waters* here are several ways to learn how to fill up:

1) Drink and not become Spiritually dehydrated.
2) Go every day to Him in His Word.
3) Listen to Him alone, without the noise.
4) Pray without ceasing.
5) Constantly drink the Truth which the Spirit prompts.
6) When in trouble, drink up from the *still waters.*
7) Keep your mind stayed on Him.
8) Make each step a step of faith especially in complete darkness.
9) Know you have eternal life, beginning now!
10) Know peace because, death is swallowed up in victory.

Spiritual dehydration is deadly. When dehydration occurs there is extreme danger of ignoring the Spirit, and forgetting the Shepherd. When we abandon the Father, peace and comfort leave. Worry prevails and joy dissipates. Fear, anxiety, anger and human desire begin to emerge and one becomes dizzy and disoriented. Suddenly the chosen drink is not of the *Water of Life*, but the desires of sinfulness, the desires of one's own will!

At this point, the Shepherd can never quench the worldly thirst. Spiritual life becomes dead, brittle, craving after what that sheep desires, which is sin and shame. There is no riding the fence. The drink of choice becomes sinfulness, the desires of one's own will.

The sheep that has chosen the flesh instead of the Spirit, who fills up with themselves, independent of the Shepherd and God, will struggle with inferiority, insecurity, inadequacy, guilt, worry and doubts. Their gage is on Spiritual emptiness, parched and dry. The filling of the flesh eventually leads to death, because the sinful nature within us is against God. The sinful flesh can never please God.

Listen as He speaks: "You shall neither thirst anymore; the sun shall not strike you, nor any heat; for the Lamb who is with you, and in the midst of the throne, will Shepherd you and lead you to living fountains of water." (Revelation 7:16 NKJ)

The power from drinking of the *Water of Life* provides everything one needs for living a truly good and Godly life: God even shares His own glory, and His own goodness with us! As you go on in this way, you will grow strong in the Lord and the power of His might, becoming fruitful, and useful for the walk through the *valley of the shadow of death.*

May 14

NKJV Isaiah 11:28 "The everlasting God … faints not, neither is weary."

EXHAUSTED

Exhaustion means that the vital forces are worn right out. Spiritual exhaustion never comes through sin but only through service. Whether or not you stay exhausted will depend upon whether you are getting your supplies. The Shepherd explained this to Peter, His sheep.

He said to Peter, "Feed My Sheep …" but He gave him nothing to feed His sheep with. He continues. "The process of ourselves being made broken bread and poured out wine means that you have to be the nourishment for other souls until they learn to feed on God. They will drain you. Make sure you get your supply from Me, or before long you will be utterly exhausted. Before other souls learn to draw on the life of Me direct, they must draw on life through you."

"*Has the way in which you have been serving God, our Father betrayed you into exhaustion? Where did you start the service from, from your own sympathy, or from the basis of the redemption of Jesus Christ? Continually go back to the foundation of your affections, and recollect where the source of power is. You have no right to say, "O Lord, I am so exhausted." "He saved and sanctified you in order to exhaust you. Be exhausted for God, but remember that your supply comes from Him … "all My springs shall be in Thee." (Oswald Chambers, February 9)*

In light of this lesson, I am singing a beautiful song called FILL MY CUP LORD. When drinking from His well, I stay Spiritually rejuvenated and full of His love. Listen as I sing.

Fill my cup Lord,
I drink it up Lord,
come and quince this thirsting of my soul.
Bread of heaven feed me till I want no more;
Fill my cup, fill it up and make me whole.
(By Richard Blanchard, 1925-2004, Copyright 1945)

Cynthia Perkins

May 15

NKJV Psalm 34:19 "Many are the afflictions of the righteous, but the Lord delivers them out of them all."

IT IS WELL WITH MY SOUL

As we are gathered by the *still waters,* the Shepherd is using hymns to teach us several of the lessons from His Word. The hymn today has great meaning for us sheep, as we prepare to walk through the *valley of the shadow of death.* As we stand at the water's edge, let us listen as the Shepherd tells the story of the hymn written by Horatio G. Spafford.

"Horatio was a lawyer in Chicago. When the great Chicago fire consumed the Windy City in 1871, he lost a fortune. About that time, his only son, age four, succumbed to scarlet fever. Horatio drowned his grief in work, pouring himself into rebuilding the city, and assisting the 100,000 who had been left homeless."

"In November of 1873, he decided to take his wife and daughters to Europe. Horatio wanted to visit D.L. Moody's and Ira Sankey's, evangelistic meetings in England, then enjoy a vacation."

"When an urgent matter detained Horatio in New York, he decided to send his wife, Anna, and their four daughters, on ahead. As he saw them settled into a cabin aboard the luxurious French liner *Vill du Havre,* unease filled his mind, and he moved them to a room closer to the bow of the ship, then he said good-bye, promising to join them soon."

The Shepherd pauses a moment, turning away. Then gently and softly continues. "During the small hours of November 22, 1873, as the *Ville du Havre* glided over smooth seas, the passengers were jolted from their bunks. The ship had collided with an iron sailing vessel, and water poured in. The *Vill du Havre* tilted dangerously. Screams, prayers, and oaths merged into a nightmare of unmeasured terror. Passengers clung to posts, tumbled through darkness, and were swept away by powerful currents of icy ocean. Loved ones fell from each other's grasp and disappeared into foaming blackness."

"Within two hours, the mighty ship vanished beneath the waters. The 226 fatalities included his daughters. Mrs. Stafford was found nearly unconscious, clinging to a piece of the wreckage. When the 47 survivors landed in Cardiff, Wales, she cabled her husband: 'Saved alone.'"

"Haratio immediately booked passage to join his wife. En route, the captain called him aside and said, 'I believe we are now passing over the place where the *Vill du Havre* went down.' Spafford went to his cabin but found it hard to sleep. He said to himself, 'It is well: the will of God be done.' It was then he wrote this famous hymn, based on those words."

Still Waters

The Shepherd stood and said, "May we all stand and sing this great hymn. You will need to know it as *you walk through the valley of the shadow of death.* IT IS WELL WITH MY SOUL:"

When peace like a river, attendant my way,
when sorrows, like sea billows roll;
whatever my lot, thou hast taught me to say,
"It is well, It is well, with my soul."

It is well (It is well)
With my soul, (with my soul),
It is well, it is well,
with my soul.
(By Horatio G Spafford 1828-1888, Copyright 1873)

May 16

NKJV Luke 12:32 "Do not fear, little flock, for it is your Father's good pleasure to give you the kingdom."

DELIGHT

The Shepherd brings peace because He is our desire. Listen as He teaches. "Fish were made to be in the sea. Birds were made to fly in the air. You, My sheep, were made for Me. Things in this life will never satisfy you. I have told you to delight yourself in Me, and I will give you the desires of your heart. Don't get out of the element My Father created you for."

He smiles, continuing. "My names define the comfort and joy that I bring to each of you.

I Am:

Jehovah - Roi/Shepherd - The Lord is Your Shepherd.
Jehovah - Jireh/Provider - You shall not want.
Jehovah - Shalom/Peace - Leads you beside the Still Waters.
Jehovah - Rapha/Healer - Restores your soul.
Jehovah - Nissa/Present - I will fear no evil."

"To live a complete, peace filled, and contented life, is by being rooted in Me, *Jehovah*. I am the Way. The things that you ask me for and I give you, will never make you satisfied. The deepest needs of your heart will be met when *I Am* is your heart's desire. You must live, move, breath, and have your being in Me."

"There is no fear in agape love; perfect love casts out fear, because fear involves torment. You need have no fear of someone who loves you like I do - perfectly." He gently and softly continues. "My perfect love eliminates all dread of what might happen to you in this world. If you are afraid it proves that you are not fully convinced that I love you, nor that you love Me. I who is in you, is greater than the enemy-wolves who are in the world."

With these words the Shepherd, *my* Shepherd, kneels, lifting His face to the heavens. We all join Him. "May My sheep's minds be stayed on You, oh God. And, therefore, they will be kept in perfect peace because they trust Me." We all praise Him, shouting "Amen!"

May 17

NKJV Matthew 8:24 "When you pass through the waters I will be with you ..."

RAGING WATERS VS STILL WATERS

Today I will give a testimony of my experience with the Shepherd saving me from raging waters.

As a small girl living in the mountains of Oklahoma, there were constant encounters with water due to the many rivers and creeks. As the Shepherd speaks of His *still waters* and the peace that they bring, I am reminded of the other side of waters, those raging torrential waters.

These encounters bring to mind how extremely dangerous life's stormy waters will be while walking through *the valley of the shadow of death*. One such encounter was with a dear friend of mind when we were six and seven years old.

We had both gone to summer Youth Church camp, and each day we could choose swimming or horseback riding as our "activity" in the afternoon. My friend was scared of water, but she loved the horseback riding; I on the other hand, enjoyed both. So we compromised. We decided that we would switch off, one day the horses, the next day swimming.

The place we always swim at camp was the *Little River* swimming hole. We were partners. The rule was that you had to have a partner to swim. The lifeguard gave each partner a number, and when the whistle blew, we would yell out the numbers, as we held hands and jumped up.

After the swim, we had our last *buddy check*, and it was time to leave. Just as we took a couple of steps, down we went! The water was deep enough that we couldn't touch bottom. I pushed my friend down so I could go up for air, and when I did, I yelled "help!" Then she pulled me under and went up for air and I heard her yell "help!" We shifted this way about three times, then we begin to fight each other to get to the top for air! We knew we were about to drown!

Suddenly, hands grabbed me, and at the same time hands grabbed my buddy. They both pulled us up out of the hole. It was a hole that in one step forward we would have been in knee-deep water. **Only one step and we were out of the danger of drowning!**

The persons pulling us up were twin girls. We had never seen them before. They saved our lives; and I do not remember ever seeing them again. To this day, my friend, and I believe that the Shepherd and our Father sent angels to save us from drowning in a pocket of deep water.

My Shepherd is just like His angels, He pulls us out of the raging waters of life's circumstances, those deep pockets, and sits us on higher ground. There is no drowning in sorrow, fear, or worry, because when our Shepherd keeps us, He leads us by His *still waters* and comforts us in troubled times.

May 18

NKJV Matthew 8:24 "When you pass through the rivers, they shall not overflow you."

FLASH FLOODS

Another event taught me to love and trust the *still waters* of *my* Shepherd.

In the mountains where I was raised we encountered flash floods. Once it had rained for approximately five days nonstop. On the fifth day of the rains, my family decided we would go to a school function. The school was approximately twelve miles away.

The roads we lived on were dirt, and the bridges were one lane, and "low-water" (that meant they were barely above the creek or river). On the way to the school event, we did not encounter any problems, but returning home was a different story!

The school event lasted about two hours. In torrential rains we started home. As we rounded a sharp curve leading to the one lane, low-water bridge, the car hit a slick spot, and began to slide sideways. Water was everywhere!

The vehicle hit the bridge hard, bouncing high, landing in the raging water! Immediately we started floating downstream, and as the inside of our vehicle begin to fill with water, it stopped floating, and sank to the bottom.

Those inside were my dad, mom, brother, two sisters, a friend, and myself. As the water rushed in, filling up the vehicle, dad yelled for us to roll down our windows, and to climb out on top of the vehicle. Mom softly prayed … "Oh God Help us!" And my friend quietly said … "I can't swim."

Dad took my friend, putting her under his arm, and my little brother, telling him to put his arms around his neck and to "NOT LET GO!" My dad went into the water trying to swim to shore.

The night was so dark we could not see each other. The roaring of the water was so loud that we could barely hear each other.

The current took dad a distance downstream before he was able to maneuver to the bank. Mama yelled for us to climb out of the windows and get on top of the car. Dad finally, with both my brother and friend, was able to get to the bank.

Dad yelled that he was cutting a long tree branch, while explaining to mama to keep calling out to him so he could figure out just where we were, because he could not see us.

As he finally reached the bank area where we were in the water on top of the car, he held out the branch in the direction of mama's voice until she caught it. I went first, catching hold of the branch. I hung on to the branch and dad pulled me safely to shore. The same process was done for the others, just as the water covered the entire vehicle.

The true story of one of my life's experiences is a great analogy of what happens in the stormy waters of life's *walk through the valley of the shadow of death.* The Shepherd standing in front of you, gently whispering your name, reaching His hand out for you to grab and plants your feet on solid ground. He speaks peace, calming the storm. When you grab His hand He pulls you from the deep raging pit of death and hell. He again says, "Peace, be still."

And just as my earthly father pulled me from the raging stormy waters, our heavenly Father and *my* Shepherd pulls us into the shelter of His arms. **I will not be afraid**, so that others may follow my example of faith in *my* Shepherd, and drink of the *Water of Life.*

May 19

NKJV John10:11 "I Am the Good Shepherd."

THE GOOD SHEPHERD

THE LORD MY SHEPHERD IS SOVEREIGN

The Lord, *my* Shepherd standing here by us is Jehovah, the great One. In-other-words Jehovah is *my* Shepherd. The name Jehovah was so intricately sacred, that in the Jewish tradition it was only pronounced once a year. A Jewish scribe never spoke this name, and in writing the name, it could only be written with a pen once, then the pen would be discarded and a new pen must be used.

He is *my* Shepherd, the great I Am, always eternal. He rules the universe by His sovereign Deity. The Jehovah of the Old Testament is the Jesus of the New Testament. When one speaks of the Jehovah of the Old Testament, one speaks of His deity: when one speaks of the Shepherd, one speaks of His Humanity.

Our Shepherd said "I am the Good Shepherd." Because of His loving sympathy He laid down His life for His sheep. No one took it from Him. He laid it down. He said … "I have power to lay it down, and I have power to take it up again. This command I received from My Father."

As one sheep said … "It wasn't nails that held Him to the tree. It was the silver cords of love, the golden bonds of redemption. No persons killed Him; He laid down His life; He never had to die! In dying, He dealt with the penalty of sin that all of humanity must pay." (Adrian Rogers, The Secret of Satisfaction)

Listen to Him … "I Am the Good Shepherd. The Good Shepherd gives His life for His sheep. I Am the Good Shepherd; and I know My sheep and am known by My own." (John 10:11-18 NKJ)

⁓⁓

The Good Shepherd stands before us; the sovereign Jehovah God; the I Am and Ruler of the universe, *my* Shepherd.

May 20

NKJV John 10:7 "I am the Good Shepherd … I am the gate of the sheep."

THE GOOD SHEPHERD - THE GATE

Today our Shepherd will teach about "The Way" through Him, who is the *Gate* to the sheep fold. There is absolutely no other Way to enter into His sheep fold, but through the *Gate*. Many have corrupted His words, putting their own spins on them, developing their own theories, and presenting them to the sheep as though there were other ways to enter. "Be sincere," "Don't dance, or drink, or eat this or that," "Just follow me and my ways and the laws that *I* have written."

Here is what the Shepherd has said … "He who does not enter the sheep fold by the *Gate*, but climbs up some other way is the same as a thief and a robber. One who enters by the *Gate*, who is the Shepherd of the sheep, is saved. To that one the *Gatekeeper* opens the gate, and those sheep hear His voice; and He calls His own sheep *by name* and leads them out."

That is why we are here by the *still waters* preparing to go down the *path of righteousness.* Our Shepherd leads us. He knows our name. When He calls, we will answer, because we are listening for our names. We know His voice and we will follow Him, focused on Him.

He said … "You will in no way follow a stranger, but will run from him because you do not recognize their voice. You follow only the Shepherd who is Truth." (John 10:5 NLT)

In closing, today we will sing the chorus I'LL BE SOMEWHERE LISTENING FOR MY NAME. For He soon will call for us to begin our journey.

> *When my Savior calls I will answer*
> *when He calls for me I will be there*
> *when my Savior calls I will answer.*
> *I'll be somewhere listening for my name.*
> *I'll be somewhere listening.*
> (By Eduardo J. Lango, Copyright 1937)

May 21

NKJV John 10: 11 "I Am the Good Shepherd … I lay down My life."

THE GOOD SHEPHERD; THE SACRIFICIAL LAMB

We like most sheep have gone astray and have not returned to the Shepherd of our souls. So, our Shepherd had to die. His blood spilling out completed the new covenant. By His death, burial, and resurrection those sheep who hear His call and return to Him will be saved.

He became the Sacrificial Lamb, bringing to us the absolute confidence that death has died, and we are recipients of eternal life. He brought victory over death. As both the Good Shepherd, and the Sacrificial Lamb, He with certainty watches and cares for His sheep.

In today's lesson two things stand out:

1) **THE GOOD SHEPHERD DIED ONCE FOR ALL**.
    We have been sanctified under the new plan, forgiven and made clean by Christ's dying for us ONCE FOR ALL.

This is how He explained it … "Under the old agreement the priests stood before the altar day after day, offering sacrifices that could never take away our sins. I gave Myself to God for your sins as one sacrifice for all time! For by that one offering, all who accept Me are made forever perfect in the sight of God, My Father. The Holy Spirit testifies that this is so."

The Spirit said … "I will put My laws into your minds so you will always know My will, and I will write My laws in your hearts so that you will want to obey them." (NKJV Hebrews 8:10)

2) **THERE IS NO LONGER A NEED FOR A SACRIFICE.**
The Shepherd said … "When sins have been forever forgiven, and forgotten, there is no need to offer more sacrifices."

The Shepherd and the Spirit smiled at each other. We clap our hands in praise and worship for the Sacrificial Lamb, the Son of God, the Lord, *my* Shepherd.

May 22

NKJV Matthew 25:32 " …as a shepherd separates the sheep from the goats …"

THE GOOD SHEPHERD KNOWS HIS SHEEP

The Good Shepherd knows the sheep who belong to Him: His true sheep. And He knows those sheep who profess to be in His flock, but are actually those who have not confessed Him as Lord. The true sheep, those belonging to the Shepherd, do the work of the Shepherd because they love Him and obey Him in word and action. Helping other sheep is a result of their obedience.

We become quiet as the Shepherd explains. "When I, the son of Mankind, shall come in My glory, and all the angels with Me," He moves His hands in the air. "Then I shall sit upon My throne of glory. And all the nations shall be gathered before Me. And I will separate the people as a shepherd separates the sheep from the goats, and place the sheep at My right hand, and the goats at My left. Then I, the King, shall say to those at My right, 'Come, blessed of My Father, into the Kingdom prepared for you from the founding of the world. I was hungry and you fed me; I was thirsty and you gave me water; I was a stranger and you invited Me into your homes; naked and you clothed Me; sick and in prison, and you visited me."

"Then these righteous ones will reply, 'Sir, when did we ever see You hungry and feed You, or thirsty and give You anything to drink, or a stranger, and helped You, or naked and clothed You? When did we ever see You sick or visit You in prison?' And I, the King, will tell them, 'when you did it to these My brothers and sisters you were doing it to Me!"

He stands up and continues … "Then I will turn to those on My left and say, 'Away with you, you cursed ones, into the eternal fire prepared for the devil and his demons. For I was hungry and you wouldn't give Me anything to drink; I was a stranger, and you refused Me hospitality; I was naked, and you wouldn't clothe Me; I was sick, and in prison, and you didn't visit Me.'"

"Then they will reply, 'Lord, when did we ever see You hungry or thirsty or a stranger or naked or sick or in prison, and not help You?' I will answer, 'When you refused to help the least of these My brothers, you were refusing help to Me.' Then they shall go away into eternal punishment; but THE RIGHTEOUS INTO EVERLASTING LIFE." (NKJV Matthew 25:31-46)

The Shepherd asked us to bow and pray for those who are not His sheep, but believe that they can enter into His rest without following Him. Softly I cry and ask that my Father will forgive my lack of faith in Him, and that in the day of judgment I am not found wanting.

May 23

NLT Matthew 28:6 "He has come back to life, just as He said."

THE GREAT SHEPHERD

My Shepherd is the Great Shepherd because He arose!

Up from the grave He arose
with a might triumphant ore His foes.
He arose a victory from the dark domain
and He lives forever with His saints to reign
He arose, He arose, Hallelujah! Christ arose!
(By Robert Lowry 1826-1899)

The chains of sin, death, and hell are broken forever because of His resurrection. The Great Shepherd says … "Who is he who condemns? Will I? No! For it is Me who died, and furthermore is also risen sitting at the place of highest honor next to God, pleading for you in heaven. Who then can ever keep My love from you? For the Scripture tells you that for My sake you must be ready to face death at every moment of the day, you are sheep awaiting slaughter; but despite all of this, overwhelming victory is yours through Me, your Shepherd, the Christ, who loved you enough to die for you."

He sits down on the bank leaning in and waiting a moment for all of our attention. "For you are now convinced beyond doubt. You are sure that nothing can ever separate you from My love. Your fears for today, your worries about tomorrow, will never ever be able to separate you from the love of God." He quietly raises his head, stands and walks toward the path. (NLT Romans 8:34-39)

Here by the *still waters* we drink it all in. We drink of the *Life Water.* The pool is deep, cold and sweet. The Water is the Good Shepherd. Soon we will be restored, prepared to be lead down *the path of righteousness for His name's sake.*

May 24

NKJV Revelation 1:18 "I am the living One ... behold I am alive for ever and ever."

THE GREAT SHEPHERD AROSE TO LEAD

Today's lesson teaches that *my* Shepherd arose from the dead to bring about perfect peace, so that His sheep can follow His leading in doing His good and perfect will.

He begins the lesson. "*In the valley of the shadow of death* as I went about teaching, preaching, and healing the sick, I was moved with compassion. As I saw the multitudes, I hurt for them, because they were weary and scattered, like sheep having no shepherd. Therefore, you must always be moved with compassion."

He turns, looking out into the valley. "The harvest truly is plentiful, but the laborers are few. So pray to Me who is in charge of the harvesting, asking for more workers for My harvest." The shepherd walked out further toward the path, and then quietly turned and continues.

"Compassion means to feel another's pain. Here is My command, feed My flock! Gather the lambs in your arms and carry them in your bosom. Gently lead those who are with young." He walks gently toward us. "Be caring to all. Be intentional about bringing the lost into the fold. Always remember it is by the grace and goodness of our loving Father that He gave me, His only Son, to save the world!"

He bows His head and He prays ...

I do not pray for these alone, but also for those who will believe in Me
through the Word; that they all may be one, as You,
Father, are in Me, and I in You; that they also may be one in Us,
that the world may believe that You sent Me.

And the glory which You gave Me I have given them,
that they may be one just as We are One: I in them, and You in Me;
that they may be made perfect in one, and that the world may know that
You have sent Me, and have loved them as You have loved Me."
(NKJV John 17:20-26)

We all look up, seeing His compassion, knowing that all things are possible with Him as we are refreshed, preparing to begin our journey down the *paths of righteousness*.

May 25

NKJV I Peter 5:4 " ...and when the Chief Shepherd appears, you will receive the crown of glory that does not fade away."

THE CHIEF SHEPHERD

Today the Shepherd introduces another name for Himself ... the **Chief Shepherd**. The *Chief Shepherd* will appear to take us home as we finish the walk *through the valley of the shadow of death*. The *Chief Shepherd* is providing protection by overcoming death and providing eternity. He is the **King of glory**. He rules and reigns, and ends fear by providing joy and peace.

"I give you eternal life, and you shall never perish, neither shall anyone snatch you out of My hand. My Father, who has given you to Me, is greater than all, and no one is able to snatch you out of My Father's hand. I and My Father are One."

He lifts His hands toward heaven and proclaims ... "You are saved by God's grace, not works. Salvation is eternal! Behold, I Am coming quickly, and My reward is with Me, to give to everyone according to their work. I Am the Alpha and the Omega, the Beginning and the End, the First and the Last!"

Looking up to heaven He earnestly prays:

Father, the time has come.
Reveal the glory of Your Son
so that He can give the glory back to You.
For You have given Him authority
over every man and woman in all the earth.
He gives eternal life to each one
You have given Him.
And this is the way to have eternal life
by knowing You, the only true God, and
Jesus Christ, the One You sent to earth!
I brought glory to You here on earth
by doing everything You told me to.
And now, Father, reveal My glory
as I stand in Your presence,
the glory We shared before the world began.
(NLT John 17:1-5)

The Spirit covered us with His glory cloud, as we all stood and exclaimed this Word together:

Now to Him who is able to keep us from stumbling,
and to present us faultless before the presence of His glory
with exceeding joy, to God our Savior, who alone is wise,
be glory and majesty, dominion and power,
both now, and forever.
Amen

May 26

NKJV Philippians 4:7 "And the peace of God which transcends all our powers of thought, will be a garrison to guard your hearts and minds in Christ Jesus."

UNDISTURBABLE CALM

It is said that "Shallow streams make the most noise; but *still waters* run deep." That is why the Shepherd leads us to the *still waters*.

The depth of our spiritual lives provides us the peace and joy for life's journey. Peace comes through diving deep into His Word and submerging our very souls in its rich message of hope and glory. The covering of His water washes our human and spiritual bodies, both inside and out, transforming us into new creatures, filled up with the *Water of Life*, whole and clean. We are washed whiter than snow. We are made pure and preserved forever in holiness.

These deep pools are made not of water but of blood. The blood that fills the deep pool covers *all* of the sin of *all* of mankind for *all* of time. The blood shed by our Lord, *my* Shepherd expresses a love that cannot be measured. It is infinity!

This is a story that helps explain the depth of His love.

There is what is called the "cushion of the sea."
Down beneath the surface that is agitated by storms, and driven about
with winds, there is a part of the sea that is never stirred.
When we dredge the bottom and bring up the remains of animal
and vegetable life we find that they give evidence of not having been
disturbed in the least, for hundreds and thousands of years.
The peace of God is that eternal calm which, like the cushion of the sea,
lies far too deep down to be reached by any external trouble or disturbance;
and whoever enters into the presence of God,
becomes a partaker of the undisturbed and undisturbable calm.
(Dr. A.T. Pierson, Steams In the Desert, by Mrs. Charles Cowman, October 20)

We sheep need to stop the noise of the constant shallow bleating, and fill up with the deep still peaceful, undisturbed water of our Lord, *my* Shepherd.

May 27

NKJV John 14:27 "Peace I leave with you, My peace I give unto you."

DISTURBED?

Today we will move closer to the path. The Shepherd is giving us a final bit of comfort. One of His sheep reads our lesson.

*There are times when our peace is based upon ignorance,
but when we awaken to the facts of life,
inner peace is impossible unless it is received from Jesus.
When our Lord speaks peace, he makes peace, His words are ever "spirit and life." Have I ever received what Jesus speaks?* **"My peace I give unto you"** *- it
is a peace which comes from looking into His face and realizing
His undisturbedness.*

*Are you painfully disturbed just now, distracted by the waves
and billows of God's providential permission, and having, as it were,
turned over the boulders of your belief, are you still finding no well
of peace or joy or comfort; is all barren?
Then look up and receive the undisturbedness of the Lord Jesus.
Reflected peace is the proof that you are right with God
because you are at liberty to turn your mind to Him.*
**If you are not right with God, you can never turn your
mind anywhere but on yourself.**
*If you allow anything to hide the face of Jesus Christ from you,
you are either disturbed or you have a false security.*

*Are you looking unto Jesus now, in the immediate matter
that is pressing and receiving from Him peace?
If so, He will be a gracious benediction of peace in and through you.
But if you try to worry it out, you obliterate Him and deserve all you get.
We get disturbed because we have not been considering Him.
When one confers with Jesus Christ the perplexity goes,
because He has no perplexity, and our only concern is to abide in Him.
Lay it all out before Him, and in the face of difficulty,
bereavement, and sorrow, hear Him say,* **"Let not you heart be troubled."**
(Oswald Chambers, August 23)

We are all moved, and stand and cheer as our Lord, the Shepherd of peace stands at the edge of the *still waters*. He looks in each and every sheep's face pronouncing … "Peace, be still."

May 28

NKJV Galatians 2:20 "I am crucified with Christ."

KILLED

How can killing be peaceful, especially crucifixion? This can only happen when one makes the decision that their old life be crucified with Christ. Have I made the decision to kill sin? It is at this moment in life, when I decide that just as He died for the sins of the world, that sin must be crucified!

By these *still waters*, our Lord has said we must choose His life, or our life. Eternal life is in Him. Death is in sin. A sheep can choose to destroy sin and death by crucifixion. We have learned that if we are crucified with our Lord, and become renewed by drinking of the *Water of life*, then we are new sheep.

In this killing, the Spirit is allowed to come in and live inside of us. I have a new clean and holy heart. I can then proclaim with King David's song:

Search me oh God.
Know my thoughts.
try me oh Savior, see if there is
any wicked way in me,
oh my Lord My God.
(NKJV Psalm 139:23-24)

Or as another follower of the Shepherd put it:

I have entered into the glorious privilege
of being crucified with Christ until
all that is left is the life of Christ
in my flesh and blood.
(Oswald Chambers, April 10)

The results of being killed ... "I live; yet not I, **BUT CHRIST IN ME!**"
(NKJV Galatians 2:20)

When we see our sins beside the Shepherd, we all absolutely scream at the horror. Our dear Shepherd, brings to us new and everlasting life. Death, is killed and no longer has dominion over us!

Let us sing VICTORY IN JESUS:

*O victory in Jesus, My Savior, forever. He sought me and bought me, with
His redeeming blood; He loved me ere I knew Him, and all my love is due
Him, He plunged me to victory. Beneath the cleansing flood.
(By Eugene M. Bartlett, Sr. 1895-1941, Copyright 1939)*

May 29

NKJV Galatians 2:20 "I am Crucified with Christ."

SPURN

*No one is ever united with Jesus Christ
until they are willing to relinquish not sin only,
but their whole way of looking at things.
To be born from above of the Spirit of God
means that we must let go before we lay hold,
and in the first stages it is the relinquishing of all presence.
What our Lord wants us to present to Him is not goodness,
nor honesty, nor endeavor, but real solid sin;
that is all He can take from us.*

*And what does He give in exchange for our sin? Real solid righteousness.
But we must relinquish all presence of being anything,
all claims of being worthy of God's consideration.*

*Then the Spirit of God will show us what further there is to relinquish.
There will have to be the relinquishing of my claim
to my right to myself in every phase.
Am I willing to relinquish my hold on all I possess,
my hold on my affections, and on everything,
and to be identified with the death of Jesus Christ?*

*There is always a sharp painful disillusionment to go through before we
do relinquish. When a man or woman really sees themselves
as the Lord sees them, it is not the abominable sins of the flesh that shock
them, but the awful nature of the pride of their own heart against Jesus
Christ. When they see themselves in the light of the Lord,
the shame, and the horror, and the desperate conviction comes home.*

*If you are up against the question of relinquishing, go through the crisis,
relinquish all, and God will make you fit for all that He requires of you.*

(Oswald Chambers, March 8)

We all lift our voices and pray to God our Father and to the Lord, *my* Shepherd.

May 30

NKJV II Corinthians 5:17-20 "Be reconciled to God."

URGENT

Our Shepherd is continuing to fill us with *Life Water.* As we drink His blood and eat His body, we will be sustained throughout the walk *through the valley of the shadow of death.*

Listen as He preaches: "If anyone is in Me, they are a new creation; old things have passed away. Behold all things have become new. Now all things are of God, who has reconciled you to Himself through Me, and has given you the ministry of reconciliation, that is, God is in Me reconciling the world to Himself, not imputing their trespasses to them, and has committed to you the Word of reconciliation."

"Now then you are ambassadors for Me, as though God were pleading through all of you: We implore all on My behalf, to be reconciled to God. For He made Me who knew no sin, to be sin for all, that all might become the righteousness of God in Me."

He turns and walks to the center of us, His sheep. "You then as workers together with Me, should also plead with all, not to receive the grace of God in vain. For God said ... 'In an acceptable time I have heard you, and in the day of salvation I have helped you.'"

The Shepherd lifts up His head and shouts - "Behold **now** *is* the accepted time; behold **now** *is* the day of salvation!" (NKJV II Corinthians 5:17-6:2)

He now begins the process of restoration. As we go forth, filled with the Spirit's *Life Water*, may the Good News of the *gospel of peace*, fill up our entire body.

May 31

> NKJV Ephesians 3:20 "To Him who is able to do immeasurable more than all we ask or imagine, according to His power that is at work within us."

SOUL RESTORATION TO SOLE RECONCILIATION

We are now on our way to restoration. We must cut the shore line here by the *still waters,* and put our complete trust in the One who is leading.

Our next step is *soul restoration.*

This operation may hurt. He has to cut deep to pull out the sin and shame that sickens our souls.

We let this world be our anchor. So we must make the decision to cut loose, and grab hold of the Shepherd's staff. He will pull us to safety and begin the process of restoration.

All restoration begins with a good cleaning, fixing broken pieces and having a mindset that no matter what is wrong with us, or what we look like, we are worth everything to the Shepherd. Yes! The very blood of the Lord God, *our* Shepherd was spilled for our soul's restoration. He gave His life to restore ours, and to reconcile us again to our Creator God, our loving heavenly Father.

Now, on we go to our *sole reconciliation* by having our Souls Restored.

PART III

He Restores My Soul

June

June 1

NKJV Psalm 23:3 "He restores my soul …"

PERFECT RESTORATION

The complete spiritual restoration has to be finished before we embark on our journey *in paths of righteousness*.

First, *our* Shepherd provides complete restoration of our being, our very soul. Interestingly, He restores us by training. Before we can travel *in the Path of Righteousness*, He must discipline us to the point that we are trained to be **self-disciplined**.

An analogy that teaches us how the Shepherd restores us is to compare our relationship with Him to the relationship of raising children. The Shepherd said to "Start children off on the way they should go and even when they are old they will not turn from it." (NKJV Proverbs 22:6) We are *His* children, the sheep of *His* pasture, who are *His* own. On our journey, we are to be trained and disciplined to follow *Him* in every way. Where He leads we should follow.

Listen! He is starting these lessons of restoration.

"The first step to a restored soul is to understand that God, *our* Father is sovereign. He keeps His promises. God is a God who cannot lie! He is the Word: the Truth: the Creator of *all* things. We are His creation and he made us for Himself."

"Therefore, the prayer of King David, is the prayer that we shall pray each day as the training of our restoration process begins:

Who can understand his/her errors?
Cleans me from secret faults.
Keep back your servant from
presumptuous sins;

Let them not have dominion over me.
Then, I will be blameless,
and I shall be innocent of great transgressions.

Let the words of my mouth and the meditation of my heart
be acceptable in your sight, o Lord,
my Shepherd and my Redeemer.
(NKJV Psalm 19: 12-14)

The Shepherd knows how to heal and rejuvenate our souls. "Sometimes your discipline will be harsh, because our Father disciplines out of love. The Father says not to fear, for He is with you;

be not dismayed, for He is your God. He will strengthen you, yes, He will help you, and He will uphold you with His righteous right hand." (NIV Isaiah 41:10)

The Shepherd smiles His big bright smile as we all say "AMEN!"

June 2

NKJV Psalm 119:28 "You are my God, and I will praise you; You are my God I will exalt You."

TRAINING LESSONS

LESSON I
TRUST

The Shepherd begins our training by lining us all up. Today our first lesson teaches us to **TRUST** in Jesus, *our* Shepherd, and *our* Father, God.

He begins the lesson. "My Father's law provides true wisdom in revealing how to live a life pleasing to Him. Those who are humble and open to God's Truth find the way of eternal life."

"We celebrate His law and magnify His name in all the earth. Those who train, and learn from this training to discipline themselves, will experience His blessings, and are protected from sin, shame and eternal damnation. God's Word stands forever, providing light and guidance for the *paths in Righteousness* and *walk through the Valley of the Shadow of death*."

He slowly walks down the line; we stand soldier like; He speaks; it sounds like thunder: "Trust in Me with all your heart. Lean not to your own understanding. In all your ways acknowledge Me and I will direct your path. But if you refuse, if you turn away and forsake My statutes and My commandments which I have set before you, and go and serve other gods, and worship them, then I will uproot you. I will cast My name out of your sight and make it a by word … and those who see it will ask 'Why has the Lord done this?' and they will answer, 'Because they forsook the Lord God, and embraced other gods and worshiped them and served them; therefore, He has brought all calamity on them.'" (NKJV II Chronicles 7:19-22)

The Shepherd emphatically lays down the first lesson in our training of our Father God's discipline. **Trust**!

June 3

NKJV Proverbs 3:12 "For whom the Lord loves, He disciplines."

LESSON II

DISCLIPINE

In today's training the Shepherd introduces the variables in His restoration training. Each variable trains us in the self-control needed as we walk *the paths of Righteousness through the Valley of the Shadow of Death.* It is mandatory to learn discipline so these paths of righteousness are clearly marked. If sin abides in the sheep, they will stray from the righteous paths and get lost, or hurt, even die, and it could be a death that sends them to hell!

If we continue to sin, our Father will use punishment to bring us back; or He may remove His blessings; for if He does not act with discipline, we can be sure we have gone astray for good, leaving the sheepfold and the Shepherd, turning to our own way.

Again, King David, who was a lover of the Shepherd, but strayed in so many ways, wrote of this in a song. He expressed how to follow the Shepherd by recognizing his sinful nature, and then learning how to conquer it:

God is our refuge and strength.
an ever present help in trouble.

Therefore we will not fear, though the earth give way
and the mountains fall into the heart of the sea.

Though its waters roar and foam
and the mountains quake with their surging.

He says "Cease striving and know that I am God;
I will be exalted among the nations,
I will be exalted in the earth."
Amen
(NKJV Psalm 46: 1-3, 10)

God's law *provides* the wisdom that reveals how to live a life pleasing to Him, and then we *walk in the paths of righteousness, through the valley of the shadow of death.* As we take the trip, He *restores our souls.*

June 4

NKJV Samuel 15:22 "To obey is better than sacrifice."

LESSON III

TRUST AND OBEY

The Shepherd, Spirit, Wisdom, and the Church our Shepherd's Bride, stands before us. They are all a part of the process of soul restoration.

The Shepherd speaks. "We cannot, stand with these," He points to those standing beside Him. "If we do not obey, it is impossible to please God and have our soul restored.

"To obey is better than sacrifice: to obey shows *trust* in Me even though there may not be understanding of the situation. It is *faith* in action. It is taking the Word and digesting it, then putting it into action. We are to love and be in My Body, and Bride, the Church; and building one's life on Wisdom's … 'fear of the Lord.'" As He teaches He points to each of these persons.

Wisdom speaks. "Obedience *must* govern a sheep's life. Our Father's Wisdom is shown through obedience. When one knows and obeys instructions, one receives words of understanding, and acknowledges the direction of the Shepherd's training. Then justice, judgment, and equity are established in that heart, mind, body and soul. The results? A God honored life!"

"The obedient sheep has come to the realization that his or her soul is restored through discipline. Only discipline, whether spiritual or physical, can train us in the Way. The Way, *our* Shepherd is showing Godly living, now and forever."

This seems a hard lesson; however, I trust in Him, the Lord, *my* Shepherd. We are all standing to sing the hymn TRUST AND OBEY:

When we walk with the Lord
in the light of His word,
What a glory in sheds on our way!
What He says we will do,
Where He sends we will go,
Never fear, only Trust and Obey.

Trust and obey,
For there's no other way
To be happy in Jesus.
But to trust and obey.
(By John H. Sammis, 1846-1919)

June 5

NKJV Ephesians 6: 11 "Put on the full armor of God!"

LESSON IV

TRAINING

The restoring of our soul can only be accomplished by the Lord, our Shepherd. He restores our souls and then He protects that restoration. We are in a spiritual war, and the enemy is not one we can physically see. **Sin** and **shame** are our enemies. They are prompted by the ruler of this world and his army of darkness. He seeks us out, and knows exactly where to tempt us and rob our joy. He hunts for those that he can devour!

Listen as the Shepherd describes the first enemy ... **sin**. In Proverbs He likens her to beauty:

> *"Do not lust after her beauty in your heart,*
> *Nor let her allure you with her eyelids.*
> *For by means of a harlot a man is*
> *reduced to a crust of bread;*
> *And an adulteress will prey*
> *upon his precious life.*
>
> *Wounds and dishonor he will get,*
> *And his reproach will not be wiped away ...*
> *Till an arrow struck his liver.*
> *As a bird hastens to the snare,*
> *He did not know it **would cost** his life.*
> *(NKJV Proverbs 6:25 - 27, 33; 7: 23)*

The second enemy, **shame**:

> *... fornication, uncleanness, lewdness,*
> *idolatry, sorcery, hatred, contentions,*
> *jealousies, outbursts of wrath,*
> *selfish ambitions, dissensions,*
> *heresies, envy, murders,*
> *drunkenness, revelries, and the like ...*
>
> *These things I have told you before,*
> *and now I am telling you again,*
> *that those who practice such things*
> *will **not inherit the kingdom of God**."*
> *(NKJV Ephesians 5:3-5)*

I know that *I will fear no evil, for Thou, my Shepherd, art with me.*

June 6

NKJV Ephesians 6:10 "Put on the full armor of God!"

LESSON V

GOD'S ARMOR

Our Shepherd is standing before us today dressed in the **Armor of God**. Our lessons for the next few days will consist of the training for our earthly battle and how we dress in the *armor of light*, to overcome the attacks and temptations of Satan and his demonic army. Once we have these lessons we will dress in this spiritual armor every day to *walk through the valley of the shadow of death.*

Listen as He teaches. "Put on the whole armor of God every day. If you begin to become lazy and complacent in this step of training you will die spiritually!"

He grows louder. "This war is not against flesh and blood, but a war against your very soul. Without the discipline and training of a soldier of the cross, the prince and ruler of darkness will attack. and he will stop at nothing. All of the armor of God must be worn in life's battles so that you will be able to stand against all of Satan's strategies, lies, and tricks."

The Shepherd has the Spirit introduce each part of the armor. He wears the armor. He says, "Spiritual armor is like that of a Roman soldier:

* The belt holds several weapons.
* The breastplate, made of bronze, covers the entire body from neck to thigh.
* The sandals have cleats, made of sharp nails designed to give firm footing on the rugged terrain.
* The shield is oblong or oval and made from two layers of wood, covered with leather or animal hides, bound together with iron.
* The helmet is bronze and is held in place by a leather strap.
* The short two-edged sword enables the heavenly-armed soldier to attack deftly and defeat the enemy at close range.
* Pray to the Father, all the time! Plead with Him; reminding Him of your needs."

He pauses and looks up. "Please pray with Me now." We all bow the knee. He prays …

Father, My plea is not for the world
but for those You have given Me
because they belong to You.
And all of them,
since they are Mine, belong to You;
and You have given them back to Me
with everything else of yours,
and so they are My glory!
(NLT John 17: 9-10)

We all lift our heads and exactly at the same time shout "Amen!"

June 7

NKJV Ephesians 6:14 "Stand therefore, having girded your loins with truth, …"

LESSON VI

BELT

Today the Shepherd and His helpers, are continuing the explanation of His armor. The Spirit begins today's lesson by holding up a belt, called **the belt of truth**.

"This 'Belt of Truth' is for girding your belly with the Word," He points to the Shepherd. "He is the Way, and the Truth."

"The abdomen is the seat of a sheep's emotions. Emotions are not true. They are constantly moved by a sheep's will. To put Him, the Truth, around yourself deflects frivolous and self-centered emotions that you might allow yourself to believe. These self-centered emotions are lies, bringing fear and self-pity. The Truth obliterates these lies."

He smiles and continues. "To know and believe the Truth brings freedom to the believer. Then regardless of the backlash, called fiery darts, Satan and his army cannot injure the sheep who has put his or her trust, in the victory of the Shepherd's Truth."

Cynthia Perkins

We all lift up our voices and again sing VICTORY IN JESUS:

Oh victory in Jesus,
my Savior forever.
He sought me and He bought me,
with His redeeming blood.
He loved me ere I knew Him,
and all my love is due Him,
He plunged me to victory,
beneath the cleansing flood.
(By Eugene Monroe Barlett Sr 1895 – 1941)

June 8

NKJV Ephesians 6: 14 " …having put on the breastplate of righteousness …"

LESSON VII

BREASTPLATE OF RIGHTEOUSNESS

Now the Shepherd moves to the second piece of the armor, and explains its' use. He and the Spirit, are both dressed in the armor.

"The second piece of armor that you sheep soldiers must put on each day, is the breastplate. The heart is generally thought of as the seat of the soul. The heart must be protected and kept pure and righteous, because sin wants to hit at your heart. Therefore, righteousness must wrap around your heart."

The Spirit has the breastplate on. It covers His body from neck to thigh and is made of a strong bronze metal.

He continues … "A sheep does not need to seek other protection. The *Breastplate of Righteousness* protects you because of what I have done by also being Your Sacrificial Lamb."

"Therefore, the *Breastplate of Righteousness* provides cover and protection you sheep need in this war."

Still Waters

What a sight it is for all of us to see *our* Shepherd, the Lamb of God dressed in His Father's armor! We all kneel bowing before Him, our Commander in Chief-the Lord, our Shepherd. We then stand and sing MIGHTY WARRIOR:

Mighty Warrior dressed for battle
Holy Lord of all is He.
Commander in Chief
bring us to attention
Lead us into battle
to crush the enemy.
(By Kenny Gamble, 1987)

June 9

NKJV Ephesians 6:15 " …having shod your feet with the preparation of the gospel of peace."

LESSON VIII

SHOES

The Shepherd lifts up His feet to display a pair of His footwear. The Spirit stands beside Him.

"In war you must protect your feet so that they remain healthy. The battle is until earthly death; your entire life. You will march, walk, run, and climb in this battle. If your feet get soar, or injured, the battle could be lost. It is hard to fight if you cannot move quickly."

"These 'Gospel Shoes' provide comfort because they bring peace. You have no fear of harm as you are able to move about doing My Father's business of reconciliation, through spreading My gospel. My *Gospel of Peace* shoes saves all who believe and accept me as their Shepherd, from the darkness of hell."

He holds up His shoes so that we can see them. "Furthermore, these shoes keep you focused on the mission. If you fall, I will lift you; if you're hurt, I will heal you; if you die, I will raise you up! Know that these *preparation of the gospel of peace* shoes **NEVER COME OFF**!"

"These shoes are able to speed you on, as you go out to preach and teach the *Good News of the Gospel of Peace*." He smiles as He provides us all with a new pair of these shoes.

As I put on my shoes, I am at peace with God, our Father. *My* Shepherd is at my side. Therefore, I have divine confidence, knowing that I am wearing the proper shoes for the battles up ahead, as we will *walk through the valley of the shadow of dead.*

After we have all put on our shoes, he wants us to sing … I'VE GOT CONFIDENCE:

I've got confidence
God is gonna see me through.
No matter what the case may be,
I know He's gonna
fix it for me.
(By Andrae' Crouch, 1971)

June 10

NKJV Ephesians 6:16 " …**Above all,** take up the shield of faith, with which you are able to quench all the fiery darts of the wicked one."

LESSON IX

FAITH - THE SHIELD

My Shepherd is holding the long, oblong shield that He will teach about in today's lesson. It has two layers of wood covered with animal hides, bound together with iron. He begins the lesson.

"The shield can be used side by side with the entire army and form a wall of protection. Also when soaked in water, the shield can adequately defend against flaming arrows."

He steps up toward us very intense. "The enemy wants to accuse My sheep of shame, and instill doubt, fear, worry, and guilt in their minds. His fiery arrows are soaked with evil temptation tar, and set on fire with his torture. **He will not let up on the accusations**. He will accuse you **day and night** before God."

"Have no fear little lambs, for you will overcome with the *shield of faith* soaked in the blood of the Lamb; Me!" He pushes the shield over His head, high in the air. "All the fiery arrows will be quenched by the *shield of faith*. The shield of faith offers God's unlimited resources of power and wisdom. God is faithful. He will not allow you to be tempted beyond what you are able to overcome, but with the temptation He will make a way of escape, so that you may be able to bear it and win."

"By faith, you, My sheep, please God. Without faith it is impossible to please Him. Basic trust in God protects and guides you in the heat of the battle. Trust in Him with all of your heart. He will fight your battle and provide peace."

He leans in speaking very softly. "Above all, trusting in His promises is absolutely necessary to protect you from temptations of every sort of sin. All sin comes when the victim falls to the enemy's lies, and promises of pleasure, rejecting the true choice of obedience and belief in God."

We all stand and sing ... FAITH IS THE VICTOR:

> *Faith is the victory!*
> *Faith is the victory!*
> *Oh glorious victory*
> *that overcomes the world.*
> *(By John H. Yates, 1837-1900)*

June 11

NKJV Ephesians 6:17 " ...the helmet of salvation ..."

LESSON X

HELMET OF SALVATION

In this Spiritual Warfare *all* soldiers must wear *the helmet of salvation*. Head covering protects the mind from injuries. The helmet is bronze and has a leather strap. A head covering is pertinent for righteous living through one's spiritual battles.

The Shepherd begins our lesson. "The *salvation helmet* protects the head, the place of thoughts and ideas. It covers and protects the sheep from temptation that starts in the mind. Thinking evil thoughts, with the intention of carrying them out in word or deed, is sometimes just as sinful as the actual act."

He puts the helmet on His head. "The *salvation* helmet extinguishes the evil weapons used to engage the mind to perform sin. Salvation's grace and mercy brings confidence and security to the Spirit-filled warrior, and is a mighty defense against doubt, and insecurity."

"Because of My blood cover over the salvation helmet, the mind is protected. Always let this mind be in you that is in Me, Christ Jesus, your Lord, your Shepherd."

We are set apart for His purposes, having the guarantee of present, future, and eternal deliverance from every kind of evil warfare. Therefore, every day pray, and study His Word. Prepare yourself for the attacks, and may all disobedient thoughts be blown apart by the *helmet of salvation*. We all stand and sing with much exuberance! BE BOLD:

Be bold! Be strong!
For the Lord your God is with you.
I am not afraid,
For I'm walking in faith and victory!
(By Morris Chapman, Copyright 1983)

June 12

NKJV Ephesians 6:17 " ...and the sword of the Spirit—-the Word of God."

LESSON XI

THE SPIRIT WEAPON

Today the army will be training with the weapon of warfare, the **Spirit Sword.** The sword is designed as the Word. Our Shepherd is holding up this double edged sword. It is not long and slim as would be expected, but short and thick, and extremely sharp, made for up close and personal fighting. It enables the heavily-armed soldier to attack deftly, and defeat their enemy at close range.

Our Shepherd has the Spirit hold the sword as He begins the lesson. "Today as I teach you about your spiritual warfare weapon, I will tell you a story that happened to Me as I begin My preaching ministry. My Father sent me into the wilderness to prepare Me for the earthly war ahead. There Satan would meet Me with temptations."

"I did not eat or drink anything, for forty days and nights, and when the fasting was finished, I became very hungry and thirsty. Then guess who shows up? Yes it was Satan in all his glory. He always attacks when you are most vulnerable."

"His first attack came with him shooting out the Word of God, My Father. Satan **never** speaks the Truth. So He tweaked the Word just a little to see if I would be wounded by the fiery dart he shot at Me! He had perfect timing in that his attack was about bread, because I was very hungry. But I pulled out the Spirit Sword, striking him with the Truth. He gave a huge groan, and he went down!"

"The next fiery dart attack was lies about life and death. He was trying to explain how My Father would save me, if I wanted to *prove* I was His Son! Of course I was tired, so his arrow went right for the mind. I stepped toward him and struck again with the Sword of God's Word. Satan went down again, but with a huge crash!" He laughed and said, "Some of his demons had to run to help him get up."

"The third time he wanted me to take a little trip with him. He took me to the peak of a very high mountain. It was high enough that we could visualize the entire universe, and all the nations of the world. He started with his temptation arrow saying that he would give all of *his* power to Me! Trying to make Me believe he owned it! I guess in his narcissistic way, he thought I was stupid." We all roared with laughter.

"Again I cut hard with My Sword." He demonstrated. "Get out of here Satan. The Scriptures say, 'worship only the Lord God, obey only Him!' He was hit so hard that he and his army of demons all fell to the ground, jumped up, turned tail and ran, wounded and crippled. Satan was shouting at the top of his lungs that he would be back, and he would get Me."

"He thought that day was the day that I would be the Sacrifice. He just forgot the Lamb of God part!"

We all shout His praise! "I won again for all sheep for all time." We clap and clap. The Spirit waved the sword above His head, shouting "Victory!"

Our Shepherd gently smiled. "Do not be afraid little flock. For I Am the Word; I Am with God; and the Word of God. The Spirit's Sword, the Word, is the offensive weapon in My armor. It penetrates all sinful behavior. My Word is living and powerful. It is sharper than any two-edged sword, piercing even to the division of soul and spirit, and of joints and marrow, and is a Discerner of the thoughts and intent of the heart!"

We all instantly stood and gave a shout! And begin singing THE BATTLE BELONGS TO THE LORD:

In heavenly armor we'll enter the land,
No weapon that's fashioned against us will stand,
the battle belongs to the Lord!
We sing glory, honor,
power and strength to the Lord.
(By Jamie Owens-Collins, Copyright 1984)

June 13

NKJV Ephesians 6:18 " ...praying always ..."

FINAL LESSON XII

THE ATOMIC BOMB!!!

Today the Shepherd continues His teaching concerning armor, battle preparation, and strategy. The final piece of the armor is prayer. Prayer is an all-encompassing strategy for each soldier, individually and collectively. As we prepare for battle; as we suit up; as we engage; and finally as we rest from battle; prayer must *never* stop.

The Lord begins His lesson. "The Holy Spirit's power of prayer equips the soldier for any type of enemy fire. The power of prayer is stronger than the atomic bomb. Prayer enlists the Spirit to engage in the fight. God, our Father, oversees the battle. Prayer changes outcomes and provides perfect choices that must be made quickly in the heat of the battle."

He stands and looks intently at each of us. "Prayer is the blood covering, and opens the lines of communication between you and God, giving access in the midst of the battle, so that we are in constant contact. When praying, one is in constant communication with our Shepherd through the Spirit, who provides direction, intersession, and encouragement."

"Do not forget what I have told you, in Me, you will have *My* peace of mind and heart while in the battle."

We give the battle cry: "PRAISE THE LORD!" Our sergeant quieted us as He reads a poem that expresses the power of prayer needed for our daily spiritual warfare.

LOOK UP AND PRAY

If you are troubled in your heart
If you are sad today
And if the world is cold and bleak
Look up to God and pray.

Tell Him your problems pour them out
Before His mighty throne
You will not be the first to plead
You will not be alone.

However futile it may seem
How much you may despair

There always is the comfort and
The peace that comes with prayer.

If you are not to blame at all
He knows that you are true
And if you are a sheep that's strayed
He searches now for you.

He is as willing to forgive
The wrongs that you have done
As He is ready to bestow
The glory you have won.
(By Earl Boatman, Out of My Treasure)

June 14

NKJV II Corinthians 10:4 "For the weapons of our warfare are not of the flesh, but divinely powerful for the destruction of fortresses."

STRONGHOLDS

The Shepherd has told us, His sheep, that He is our *Light* and our *Salvation* so we should have no fear; He has said He is our *Stronghold,* so we live fearless. He said when our enemies and our foes attack, they will stumble and fall. The enemy has no *stronghold* against us!

He begins by speaking to us very lovingly. "Let us sing the song of our sovereign Father God, SONG EIGHTEEN:

I will love you, o Lord my strength.
The Lord is my rock and my fortress
and my deliverer;

My God, my strength, in Whom I will trust;
my shield and the horn of my salvation, my stronghold.
I will call upon the Lord, who is worthy to be praised;
so shall I be saved from my enemies.

The pangs of death surrounded me,
and the floods of ungodliness made me afraid.
The sorrows of death confronted me.
In my distress I called upon the Lord,

and cried out to my God;
He heard my voice from His temple,
And my cry came before Him, even to His ears.

He sent from above, He took me;
he drew me out of many waters.
He delivered me from my strong enemy,
From those who hated me,
for they were too strong for me.
They confronted me in the day of my calamity,
but the Lord was my support.
He also brought me out into a broad place;
He delivered me because He delighted in me.

For you will light my lamp;
The Lord my God will enlighten my darkness.
For by You I can run against a troop,
by my God I can leap over a wall.
As for God, His way is perfect;
the Word of the Lord is proven;
He is a Shield to all who trust in Him.

It is God who arms me with strength,
and makes my way perfect.
He makes my feet like the feet of deer,
and sets me on my high places.

You have also given me the shield of Your salvation;
Your right hand has held me up,
Your gentleness has made me great.
You enlarged my path under me,
So my feet did not slip.

The Lord lives! Blessed be my rock!
Let the God of my salvation be exalted.
(NKJV Psalm 18: 1-6/ 16-19/ 28-30/ 32-33/ 35-36/ 46)

No fear. Just complete silence. Still. Standing before the Lord, *my* Shepherd.

June 15

NKJV Psalm 19:7 "making wise the simple ..."

RESTORE

Through discipline the Lord restores my soul. He trains us for the war that we are in. As we *walk through the valley of the shadow of death,* the discipline is twofold.

First: He teaches us the discipline of living by His rules. Which guide us and provides direction for all who see us as His children. Our goal is to become self-controlled through the training process.

Second: Discipline is corporal punishment. Yes, God as our Father inflicts punishment. The reason for corporal punishment is as He said in His Word ... "spare the rod, and you *hate* your child." The Shepherd uses His Shepherd's staff as a tool of discipline. He has been known to induce physical pain in order to get the sheep's attention.

The Shepherd explained today that for the next several lessons He will teach God's rules of restoration. Here is the outline of what we will study:

> **Law** ... ... a rule established by authority
> **Testimony** ... ... a covenant between God and man / to be a witness
> **Statutes** ... ... a decree or edict
> **Commandment** ... a commend ... edict
> **Fear** ... ... extreme reverence or awe
> **Precepts** ... ... a rule or principle impressing a particular standard of action or conduct
> **Judgments** ... ... the mental ability to receive and distinguish relationships or alternatives; decrement

My Shepherd again tells us that all of the above edicts are true, and right living. He continues "All of these are to be desired more than gold, yes more than fine gold; Sweeter than honey and the honeycomb. Moreover, by them you are warned, and in keeping them there is great reward." (NKJV Psalm 19:10-11)

If we, His sheep keep the rules and regulations of our Father, we have blessings now, and rewards to come as we go to *dwell in the house of the Lord forever.*

June 16

NKJV Psalm 19:7 "The law of the Lord is perfect, converting the soul."

THE LAW

Today we begin the study of our Lord's law. Through the knowledge of these rules and regulations we become immersed in Wisdom. Today, Wisdom stands beside the Shepherd. With Her beauty and grace, She is teaching us how life should be lived as a wise servant of our Master. Through these edicts we may be restored to the likeness of our Father, just as we were in the Garden of Eden.

The Shepherd begins "My sheep, look around at the glory and beauty of our Father's creation. The order of glory in the earth is because our Father has set His laws in place. The heavens constantly reveal His glory, as the signature of His Word. They reveal His promises. We see His revelation of Himself in His creation. It is the physical manifestation of His divine presence, and the external form of His majesty, preeminence, and dignity." (Notes on Psalm 19 NIV The Women's Study Bible)

"Without question, everyone may observe this glorious creation which stands as a witness of God's revelation, and in so doing no sheep can miss the awesome Creator, who by His very presence, makes all things new, determining every event, and direction of this world by His sovereign power. After all, **He is God**!"

"The laws of creation amaze us: All of creation expresses His just laws of life and death. It cannot be disputed, though some will always try." Our Shepherd looks around and waves His hand over everything we see. "It is so much, so overpowering, so big, so breathtaking!" He smiles; we smile.

The Shepherd turns and stands looking at the sky. "The heavens declare the glory of God; and the firmament shows His handiwork. Day unto day it utters speech, and night unto night reveals knowledge. There is no speech nor language, where their voice is not heard. Their sound has gone out through all the earth, and their words to the end of the world." (NKJV Psalm 19:1-4) He lifts His hands to the heavens.

God's laws rule! They are undeniable. Creation declares the power of God. So, quietly in awe, we close by kneeling and praying to our Jehovah God. And, so should you.

June 17

NKJV Psalm 19:7 "The testimony of the Lord is sure, making wise the simple."

THE TESTIMONY

The next edict in restoration of the soul is understanding His testimonies. The Shepherd has expressed how the testimonies of our Father are exciting, revealing to His sheep His loving covenants. The testimonies of His witnesses, especially the heroes of faith, who lived and died in honor of our Lord and God, reveal the ever loving God, and His mercy, and grace.

Now, our Shepherd begins the lesson. "The testimony of the Lord is sure, making wise the simple. The 'simple' lamb is one whose mind is open to God's Truth. His covenant with man was stated at the beginning of His creation when He said 'I will make man in *Our* image, according to *Our* likeness.'"

"We allowed man to have dominion over the fish of the sea, over the birds of the air, over the cattle, over all the earth, and over every creeping thing that creeps on the earth. God made man in His image; in His image He created all of you, and my, you are a good looking group!" We all laugh at His compliment.

The Shepherd sits down, turning toward us. He has pure joy in His eyes. "The most important testimony, is the testimony of Myself. I Am also a covenant, and I bear witness of His undeniable love, grace, and mercy. God our Father sent Me into the world, not to condemn the world, but that the world, through Me, might be saved."

"Those of you here have become wise by accepting God's testimony and His Truth. You, His sheep, are sure of what you hope for, and confident in what you have not seen. Never doubt Him, for all of these testimonies are the acts of the Redeemer who *restores your souls*."

"There are many, many more testimonies that are provided in My Word. Wisdom comes to you simple ones by the Word of the Lord. I distribute Wisdom to whom it pleases Me to do so. From Her mouth comes understanding; She is a shield to those who walk uprightly. Because of Wisdom, you will understand righteousness, justice, equity, and learn to walk in every good path."

"He restored their soul; He restores *my* soul." I softy whisper these words as I obey *my* Shepherd's testimonies.

June 18

NKJV Psalm 19:8 "The statutes of the Lord are right, rejoicing the heart …"

STATUTES

Today, we'll be studying the next action of restoration, the Lord's statutes. Statute means … *a decree or proclamation.* These are always right; and because they are right, perfect, and good, when obeyed they bring rejoicing.

"Our statutes are the legitimacy of laws, regulations and decrees of our God. It is our duty and obligation to follow God's statutes. He has laid them down as a testament of His truth. For God is a God who cannot lie. All of His promises are true."

"Please keep God's statutes!" He gets loud … "You **must** keep His statutes! Because Truth manifests itself in Me, follow My leading. I Am Truth, because My Father is Truth, and I and My Father are One."

The Shepherd becomes very intense. "My Father; your Father, He is not only dependably accurate, but He is also accurately dependable! Know the Truth of God's statutes, and the Way, the Truth, and the Life, will be abundantly available. The Truth, Me, sets you, My sheep, **free**. For the law of the Spirit of life in Me, has made you free from the law of sin and death." (NKJV Romans 8:2)

"Freedom from sin and shame brings a miraculous joy, peace, and confidence that this world cannot explain. You are more than conquerors through Him who loved you. For neither life, nor death, nor angels, nor principalities, nor powers, nor things present nor things to come, nor height nor depth, nor any other created thing, shall be able to separate you from our God's love which is in Me, Christ Jesus your Lord." (NKJV Romans 8:38-39)

Instantly we are on our feet singing I AM FREE:

I am free to run.
I am free to dance.
I am free to live for you, I am free.
(By Jon Egan, Copyright 2004)

June 19

NKJV Psalm 19:8 "The commandment of the Lord is pure, enlightening the eyes."

COMMANDMENT

Probably the best known of these edicts are **The Ten Commandments**, or Laws of Moses. Today our lesson will deal with these very famous Lord's Commandments.

Here comes *our* Shepherd, and with Him, Wisdom, and Moses, the law giver. We shout for joy, we've heard so much about Moses.

"Today we teach about the Father's Commandments. The Word says … 'the commandments of the Lord are pure, enlightening the eyes … ' When you obey His Commandments, living by all of them, understanding that by obedience they help guide your life, you, My sheep will not be filled with the shame of sin and rebellion."

"Ask yourself this question: How can I stay pure and clean in my life? By taking heed according to My Word. With your whole heart seek the Lord; do not wander from His Commandments! His word you must hide in your heart so you will not sin against your Father."

"Today, My dear brother Moses the law giver, is here to talk about the *Ten Commandments.*" Moses begins the lesson.

"**The Ten Commandments** are also called the *Decalogue* (10-words) and are the basic principles of the Lord's covenant with Israel. The statements address each person individually. Exodus 20: 2-11 center on the individual relationship with the Lord; and verses 12-17 discuss dealing with others."

He smiles. "Now let us begin the study of these joyful commands that fill us with life and free us from shame and the chains of sin and death."

Let us listen!

June 20

NKJV Exodus 20: 1 "And God spoke all these words: 'I am the Lord your God.'"

TEN COMMANDMENTS

The Shepherd brought Moses with Him again today. It is exciting to begin studying the Law with the person called "The Great Law Giver."

He begins to teach the statements that are the ten basic principles of the Lord's covenant with His people, the children of Israel. Each commandment is short and easy to understand. Moses actually wrote the *Law* on Mount Sinai, as God spoke directly to him.

Moses begins the lesson. "The day of the delivery of these commands was an awe-inspiring day. These words, written on the tablets of stone, were the basis for God's covenant with His people for all time. They never should be forsaken. Following these commandments gives life and brings honor to all of God's people."

Moses looks off in the distance, continuing to speak. "That day the thunder and lightning, the trumpet sounds, the thick clouds, the smoke and fire and a trembling mountain, plus God's audible voice caused complete fear and terror. At the time, we did not understand that He had set us apart for this historical event."

"The Lord told His people to wash their clothes, stay off the mountain and refrain from sexual intercourse. They were commanded to follow these instructions for three days. Therefore, the Lord's people were consecrated, sanctified, and presented holy, and clean before the Lord."

"Today we begin the lessons about these ten directions for an abundant life with our God. These are to be followed in your faithful walk with the Shepherd, and our Father. The Shepherd, has said that He did not come to destroy these edicts, but to raise them up to even a higher standard."

We have not studied the relationship of **The Ten Commandments** to us who are now under the New Covenant of the Lord, *my* Shepherd. Tomorrow we begin.

June 21

NKJV Exodus 20: 2 "I Am the Lord God ..."

MOSES' COMMANDMENTS

Moses sounds like thunder as he begins today's lesson. We are dazed as his words pierce our very souls:

1) You shall have no other god's before me.
(Show respect to God and to those He has placed in authority over you.)

2) You shall not make for yourself a carved image.
(Live your life in whole-hearted devotion)

3) You shall not take the name of the Lord your God in vain.
(Guard your speech and your actions
and strive to communicate effectively and respectfully.)

4) Remember the Sabbath day, to keep it holy.
(Allow time for rest and for God, meditation, study, and relaxation.)

5) Honor your Father and your mother.
(Treat parents with respect.)

6) You shall not murder.
(Recognize God's control over life and death.)

7) You shall not commit adultery.
(Honor the vow of faithfulness to spouse and God.)

8) You shall not steal.
(Guard against taking what is not yours.)

9) You shall not bear false witness against your neighbor.
(Respond to others in integrity and respect.)

10) You shall not covet.
(Be satisfied with your own possessions and resources.)
(NKJV Deuteronomy 5: 7-21)

Moses turned and looked to the heavens, as if speaking to God without saying a word. Then turning to us he said … "Do not be afraid, God has come to test you, and that His fear may be before you, so you may not sin!"

We are totally still and quiet. No one moved as Moses' face was ablaze. I covered my eyes because his face was too bright to look at. We all were overcome with complete reverence and awe.

June 22

> NKJV Deuteronomy 10:12 "What does the Lord your God require of you, but to fear the Lord …"

THE ESSENCE OF THE LAW

Moses continues his teaching of the Lord's Commandments. He begins today's lesson by asking, and then answering an important question.

"After yesterday's reviewing of the Ten Commandments, what really does the Lord your God require of you? He requires you to fear Him, and to walk in all of His ways, and to love Him. He requires you to serve the Lord your God with all of your heart, and with all of your soul; and to keep the commandments of the Lord, and His statutes which I commend you today for your good. Indeed heaven above, and the heavens below belong to the Lord your God; also the earth with all that is in it."

He gets very loud, piercing our hearts with his eyes and his words. "Therefore, circumcise the foreskin of your heart, and be stiff-necked no longer! For the Lord your God is God of gods and Lord of lords, the Great God, mighty and awesome, who shows no partiality nor takes a bribe. He administers justice for the fatherless and the widow, and loves the stranger, giving him food and clothing. Therefore, love the stranger."

"You shall fear the Lord your God, you shall serve Him, and to Him you shall hold fast. He is your praise, and He is your God, who has done for you these great and awesome things which your eyes have seen. You shall love the Lord your God, and keep His charge, His statutes, His judgments, and His commandments always. You shall keep every commandment that I command you today, that you may be strong and that you may prolong your days."

He points his finger at all of us, "And it shall be that if you earnestly obey my Lord's commandments to love the Lord your God and serve Him with all your heart, and with all your soul, then I will give you rain for your land in its' season. I will send grass in your fields for your livestock that you may eat and be filled."

"You shall lay up these words of Mine in your heart, and in your soul, and bind them as a sign on your hand, and wear them on your forehead, between your eyes! Teach them to your children. Speak of them when you sit in your house, when you drive or walk, when you lay down, and when you rise up. You shall write them on the doorposts of your house and on your gate, that your days, and the days of your children may be multiplied in the land, like the days of heaven on earth."

He breathes deep then turns and smiles saying, "Today I set before you a blessing and a curse: the blessing if you obey the commandments of the Lord your God which I command you today; and the curse if you do not obey the commands of the Lord your God, but turn aside from the way which I command you today, and make other things your god." (NIV Deuteronomy 10:16-11:28)

He leans into us, speaking softly, "You must be careful to observe all the statutes and judgments which I set before you today!" He takes a deep breath and sits down.

After this lesson I understand why Moses is called "The most humble man on earth." He knows that only God can change hearts and minds. And he loves the Father, *my* Shepherd and the children of God.

June 23

NKJV John 15:12 "This is **My** Commandment …"

COMMANDMENT #1

Jesus, *our* Shepherd, begins to teach further about **The Ten Commandments**.

"A new commandment I give to you is that you love one another as I have loved you. By this, all will know that you are My sheep, if you love one another. Greater love has no man then this, than to lay down his life for his friend. You are My friends if you do whatever I command you."

"As the Father loved Me, I also loved you. If you keep My commandments, you will abide in My love, just as I have kept My Father's commandments and abide in His love."

"You did not choose Me, but I chose you, and appointed you that you should go and bear fruit, and that your fruit should remain, that whatever you ask the Father in My Name, He may give you."

"These things I have spoken to you, that My joy may remain in you, and that your joy may be full." The Shepherd raises His voice and shouts … "These things I command you, **THAT YOU LOVE ONE ANOTHER!**" (NAS John 15:11-17)

We all are still; and silent. The love, the joy, is overwhelming. Our Shepherd's commandment is full of grace and mercy, paid for by His choosing to be the Sacrificial Lamb of Love. His blood is the thread that binds it all together.

All of us sheep begin to sing the chorus THIS IS MY COMMANDMENT:

> *This is My Commandment*
> *That you love one another*
> *that your joy may be full.*
> *(Anonymous, Copyright 1990)*

June 24

NKJV Matthew 22:36 "Teacher, which is the greatest commandment in the law?"

THE GREAT COMMANDMENT

Today is an exciting lesson because yesterday the Shepherd was asked "Which is the greatest commandment?" We can't wait to hear His choice and explanation. I hope He chooses the one that I like best.

He smiles as He begins the lesson. "Yesterday I was asked which commandment is the greatest? I know that those who initiated this question were just trying to trick me. I will now explain."

"The commandment that is first and second are not *any* of those that appear on the list of the original *Ten Commandments!*" A murmur is heard around us, as we are startled about what He has just said. "So here they are, 'You shall love the Lord your God with all your heart, with all your soul, and with all your mind. This is the first and greatest commandment.'"

He continues. "And the second is; you shall love your neighbor as yourself."

We are all blown away. No one moves. We know to love God first, but the Shepherd just linked these two together! Loving God and ourselves is one thing, but loving our neighbor as we love ourselves, that seems a bit radical!

He continues, "The first Commandment is not possible without the second, any more than the second Commandment could stand without the first. A whole hearted devotion to God, our Father is at the heart of the Old Testament Law and My teachings! A right relationship with our Father is the beginning of everything, and produces a right relationship with others."

"If anyone says 'I love God,' and hates their sister or brother, they are liars; for those who do not love their sister or brother whom they have seen, how can they love God whom they have not seen? Those who love God must love their sisters and brothers also." He stands very still as we try to take in all He has just said. (NKJV I John 4:20-21)

The Greatest Commandment is ours to obey. If I love God, our Father; and I do; I will obey.

We will all sing THIS IS MY COMMANDMENT:

> *This is My commandment*
> *That you love one another*
> *that your joy may be full.*
> *(Anonymous, Copyright 1990)*

June 25

NKJV Proverbs 9:10 "The fear of the Lord is the beginning of wisdom."

AWE - FEAR

"You sheep have all heard the Scripture state how our Father should be feared." He begins our lesson with a smile. "Yet over one hundred times the Word says, *Be not afraid*. So, what is this fear of our Father about? Should we be shaking in our *army of the Lord boots*?" We all laugh as He cackles and slaps His leg in delight. "The fear of our Father is best understood as a reverent obedience expressed in a submissive spirit; rather than a terrifying dread."

"A fool is morally rather than intellectually defective, but the disciplined soldier knows that fearing the Lord and loving Him are not antithetical but inseparable. Fear in this sense indicates submissive reverence and not chaotic terror. To reject this *awe*, which inspires respectful obedience, is to determine to go your own way. Remember our Father has told us, 'My thoughts are not your thoughts, nor My ways your ways.'"

He stands and continues. "As a result of our reverent fear, our Father promises: goodness, riches, honor, satisfaction, a right relationship with others, long life, mercy, strong confidence and His constant attention."

You can't beat that! We all shout joyfully, and begin to sing BLESS HIS HOLY NAME:

Bless the Lord,
O my soul,
and all that is within me,
Bless His holy Name.

He has done great things,
Bless His holy Name.
(By Andrae' Crouch, Copyright 1973)

June 26

NKJV Psalm 119:159 "Consider how I love Your precepts."

PRECEPTS

The Shepherd, shows me His precepts by His life. That is why I love His precepts, because they are the standards of *His* action, and *His* conduct. We, the sheep of His pasture, must pattern our lives after Him. This should be our goal and objective for life on this earth while *walking through the valley of the shadow of death.*

He wants us to be revived by His righteousness. He restores us by disciplining Himself to His Father's ways, therefore, by observing Him, we, the sheep of His pasture, become like the Shepherd, loving Him with our whole hearts.

One sheep, King David, put it this way … "Teach me, O Lord, the way of your *statutes* and I shall keep them till the end. Incline my heart to your *testimonies*. Give me understanding, and I shall keep Your *law*. I shall keep your law continually forever and ever. And I will walk at liberty, for I seek Your *precepts*. I understand more than any other sheep because I keep your *precepts*. Make me understand the way of your *precepts*; so shall I meditate on your wonderful works." (NKJV Psalm 119:33-48)

The Shepherd validates by His behavior, how we should conduct ourselves as His lamb. The following list are some of those important precepts of our Shepherd's character that we are to follow:

* He makes no mistakes
* He speaks truth
* His will is good and perfect
* He calls the little lambs to Him

* He sacrificed His life for His sheep
* He protects, guiding His sheep
* He has an eternal home prepared for us

His precepts are a guide for our thoughts that should become our behavior. In both word and deed, we shall be like Him.

Oh what a Savior, the Lord, *my* Shepherd. We sing the hymn O WHAT A SAVIOR:

O what a Savior, O hallelujah.
His heart was broken, for you and me.
His hands were nailed scared.
His side was riven.
He gave His life's blood, for even me.
(By Marvin Dalton, Copyright 1948)

June 27

NKJV Psalm 119: 66 "Teach me knowledge and good judgment, for I trust your commands."

JUDGMENTS

The lessons on restoration of our soul will end today with the last of the laws called *Judgments*. Judgment, by us sheep, should be the mental ability to receive, and distinguish relationships, or to learn discernment.

Today our Teacher brings a lesson of the most famous of kings: King David. David understood the love, grace and mercy of our Father because he had gone astray and our Shepherd brought him back into the fold. David wrote many songs about his struggles and how he was *never* forsaken in his time of sin and sorrow.

How exciting, that here he and *my* Shepherd stand, ready to teach us about our soul's restoration. King David strong and handsome smiles and begins. "God's judgments are true and righteous. Moreover, by them you are warmed, and in keeping them there is *great* reward." (NKJV Psalm 19:9 & 11)

"Oh *my* Shepherd, who can understand their errors? Listen to my prayer and learn. Cleanse me from secret faults. Keep back your lamb from presumptuous sins; let them not have dominion over me. Then I shall be blameless, and I shall be innocent of great transgressions."

He stands and looks all around at the creation that is a perfect revelation of God and exclaims, "The heavens declare the glory of God; and the firmament shows His handiwork! Day unto day they utter speech, and night unto night they reveal knowledge. There is *no* speech *nor* language where their voice is not heard. Their sound has gone out through all the earth, and their words to the ends of the world." We clap our hands and shout for joy at his glorious description. (NKJV John 10:9-16)

He continues. "The heavens reveal His glory, His revelation of Himself to His creation, the physical manifestation of His divine presence, and the external form of His majesty, preeminence, and dignity. All of us can observe this being God reveled, and in so doing, cannot miss, this, the awesome Creator!" (NKJV Psalm 119: 1)

"The creation marks indisputable recognition of Him, and should lead all to worship the creator, God our Father, and His Son, *our* Shepherd, the Lord." David lifts his hands to the heavens, as we all jump up shouting praises.

King David's powerful responses to His glory was his falling on his face; and we follow, falling down in confession, worship and praise! As "He restores *my* soul."

June 28

> NKJV Leviticus 11:45 "The Lord spoke ... you shall be holy, for I the Lord your God am holy."

HOLY

Today the Shepherd teaches a lesson concerning holiness. The lesson shows how He restores His sheep's lives as they become holy like Himself. Holiness is commanded of the Lord. So, how in this *valley of the shadow of death* do we become and remain holy?

Our Shepherd begins the lesson as He sits down beside the road up the hill. "Holiness is a law commanded by our Father God. He has stated in the Word over and over that ... 'we are to be holy as He is holy.' Holiness is therefore not an option. Holiness is at the root of the right relationship with God our Father, and without it worship is not possible."

"The most explicit book in the Bible that explains the concept of our Lord's holiness is Leviticus. Leviticus has holiness as tis major theme, as holiness is listed over one hundred times. The young children of the Israelite nation started their education by reading the book of Leviticus."

He stands, and continues, "Our Father, is teaching in this book, that He has never, and will never, be associated with evil. Therefore, to be holy is to be separated from sin and evil." How can we do this living in this sin filled world?

Still Waters

He continues, "We then must become holy by living an obedient life of purity, separated from the world. We, His sheep, are to be in the World, but not of the world."

"Because I came as the Lamb for My Father, the *Sacrifice* and *Atonement* for sin, everyone has access to all personal and collective sins being forgiven. By this forgiveness of sin, God, our Father enables us to enjoy fellowship with Him; therefore we can be found holy!"

He takes a deep breath, then continues. "Living every day desiring His will and by obedient commitment of being separated from this world, its evil, and impurity, should be each of our heart's desire. Then establishing a right relationship with God, our Father, by living a righteous holy life will be a lifetime journey of pure joy, and abundant peace!" Our Shepherd becomes very quiet and gentle.

"We are to give *all* to our Father. There is no part or middle. Our Father has said that if we are lukewarm 'I will vomit you out of My mouth!' Being holy and clean before the Lord is commanded. One can only achieve Holiness though Me. You must join Me by being a living sacrifice, holy and acceptable before the Lord. My blood washes, cleanses, and covers you. Then you become holy as We are holy."

We all bowed our bodies to the ground and worshiped the *Sacrificial Lamb*, the Lord, *my* Shepherd.

June 29

NKJV I Samuel 2:2 "There is none holy like the Lord."

HOLINESS

The Shepherd continues to teach concerning the restoration of our souls through holiness.

"God is holiness. He is the root of holiness. Nothing can stand before our Father's holiness. In comparison with the all-transcending holiness and purity of God, all creatures which ethically and physically are the purest, are impure. The holiness of God is absolute; its' law is in the perfection of His own Being."

His head is somewhat bowed as He seems extremely humbled by the Father's holiness. "In our Father there is no possibility of sin. He hates sin. He hates it with a perfect anger and judgment. As we study His holiness we see from the very beginning of time that obedience is the key to our restoration. We are called to be set apart by believing in God's redemptive plan. Worship cannot be legitimate without living an outward dedication of the inward heart, covered by the acceptance of the blood covering, made possible through My sacrifice."

"Both character; and conduct; are to be holy. Holiness is a requirement! All of My sheep must pursue righteousness, then grace and peace may abound, and all of mankind will see and hear the gospel of our Lord in their walk through the *valley of the shadow of death.*" (NKJV Hebrews 12:14)

"Through living a life that is holy and acceptable before the Lord, a personal relationship is developed with the Father. All believers reveal to their Father the love of their commitment by the quality of their behavior, showing honor and trust in Him who sent Me to reconcile you to our Father through My atoning blood sacrifice, for all sin, for all sheep, for all time!"

"Now know, you can be holy, as He, the Lord your God, is holy."

We all stand and sing HOLY, HOLY, HOLY:

Holy, holy, holy! Lord God Almighty!
Early in the morning our song shall rise to Thee;

Holy, holy, holy! Merciful and mighty!
God in three Persons, blessed Trinity!
(By Reginald Heber 1783-1826)

June 30

NKJV Leviticus 22:22-23 "I Am the Lord who sanctifies you ... I Am the Lord."

SETTING APART - SANCTIFICATION

We are set apart by our Father, meaning we are *sanctified.* The standard of the world, is not the standard set before us by our *Holy* Father.

Our lives are to be pure in accordance with God. The "*set apart*" life of righteousness is of God, and from God. A holy life is a life that *always* chooses to do what God, our conductor, directs. We sing His song. We echo the praises as we honor and obey our Father.

My Shepherd has explained that through Him, we are forgiven and set apart from sin. We are God's saints, God's holy, sanctified people. We saints are believers whose lives have changed, we are new creatures, alias in this world, with a new mind and a new heart. We take on the likeness of our Shepherd. We are not as the world sees us; we are as Jesus our Shepherd sees us!

That change has come, through our Shepherd's being "the Lamb of God who has taken away the sins of the world." This occurs not only through our relinquishment of our will, but also by *The Holy Spirit's* work.

The Word says, "True holiness is exemplified only in God, though the Holy Spirit who empowers His children to pursue holiness, for God did not call us to uncleanness, but in holiness. Therefore those of us who reject this do not reject man, but GOD, who has given us His Holy Spirit!" (NKJV I Thessalonians 4:7-8)

We cannot make ourselves holy; but, if we desire to become holy and set apart (sanctified); our wills must be set toward following the Lord, He will make us so. The Lord never commands us to do something that He does not enable us to do. He said, "Remember, I Am the Lord who sanctifies you!"

Personally I am so glad and filled with joy that God does a mighty work in me, because I know that I cannot be holy on my own. I Praise the Lord, *my* Shepherd.

July

July 1

NKJV I Thessalonians 5:23-24 "And the very God of peace sanctify you wholly."

(From the Utmost For His Highest by Oswald Chambers)

INSTANTANEOUS AND INSISTENT SANCTIFICATION

"Today I am passing out three devotionals that have been written by one of My sheep. He has penned a description of sanctification, that really touches the heart of the matter. I want you to read them as a part of our preparation for the path ahead. They explain in no uncertain terms the soul's sanctification."

He has one of the sheep read from the first of the three.

> *When we pray to be sanctified, are we prepared to face the standard of these verses? We take the term sanctification much too lightly. Are we prepared for what sanctification will cost? It will cost an intense narrowing of all our interests on earth, and an immense broadening of all our interests in God. Sanctification means intense concentration on God's point of view. It means every power of body, soul and spirit chained and kept for God's purpose only. Are we prepared for God to do in us all that He separated us for? And then after His work is done in us, are we prepared to separate ourselves to God even as Jesus did? "For their sakes I sanctify Myself." The reason some of us have not entered into the experience of sanctification is that we have not realized the meaning of sanctification from God's standpoint. Sanctification means being made one with Jesus so that the disposition that ruled Him will rule us. Are we prepared for what that will cost? it will cost everything that is not of God in us.*
>
> *Are we prepared to be caught up into the swing of this prayer of the apostle Paul's? Are we prepared to say, "Lord, make me as holy as You can make a sinner saved by grace"? Jesus has prayed that we might be one with Him as He is one with the Father. The one and only characteristic of the Holy Ghost in a man is a strong family likeness to Jesus Christ, and freedom from everything that is unlike Him. Are we prepared to set ourselves apart for the Holy Spirit's ministrations in us?*

(Oswald Chambers, February 8)

We all agree that this does explain the essential point of our being made holy and sanctified. May all glory, honor and praise be to His name.

July 2

NKJV Matthew 11: 29 "Take My yoke upon you, and learn of Me."

INSPIRED INVINCIBILITY

Today another sheep reads the lesson from the writings of Oswald Chambers.

#2

"Whom the Lord loves, he chastens." How petty our complaining is! Our Lord begins to bring us into the place where we can have communion with Him, and we groan and say, "O Lord, let me be like other people!" Jesus is asking us to take one end of the yoke, "My yoke is easy, get alongside Me and we will pull together." Are you identified with the Lord Jesus like that? If so, you will thank God for the pressure of His hand.

"To them that have no might He increases strength." God comes and takes us out of our sentimentality, and our complaining turns into a paean of praise. The only way to know the strength of God is to take the yoke of Jesus upon us and learn of Him.

"The joy of the Lord is your strength." Where do the saints, we would say get that strength. "Oh, he, or she, has nothing to bear." Lift the veil. The fact that the peace and the light and the joy of God are there is proof that the burden is there too. The burden God places squeezes the grapes and out comes the wine; most of us see the wine only. No power on earth or in hell can conquer the Spirit of God in a human spirit, it is an inner unconquerableness.

If you have the whine in you kick it out ruthlessly. It is a positive crime to be weak in God's strength. (Oswald Chambers, April 14)

We all realize that we have the "whine" in us. Only our Lord, *my* Shepherd, your Shepherd, our Shepherd can restore our soul and stop the whine.

July 3

NKJV I John 2: 2 "And He is the propitiation for our sins: and not for ours only, but also for the sins of the whole world."

THE KEY TO THE MISSIONARY MESSAGE

The Shepherd quiets us as He again reads from Oswald Chambers this life restoring message.

#3

The key to the missionary message is the propitiation of Christ Jesus. Take any phase of Christ's work, the healing phase; the saving and sanctifying phase; there is nothing limitless about those. "The Lamb of God which taketh away the sin of the world!" that is limitless. The missionary message is the limitless significance of Jesus Christ as the propitiation for our sins, and a missionary is one who is soaked in that revelation.

The key to the missionary message is the remissionary aspect of Christ's life, not His kindness and His goodness, and His revealing of the Fatherhood of God; the great limitless significance is that He is the propitiation for our sins. The missionary message is not patriotic, it is irrespective of nations and of individuals, it is for the whole world. When the Holy Ghost comes in He does not consider my predilections, he brings me into union with the Lord Jesus.

A missionary is one who is wedded to the charter of his Lord and Master, he has not to proclaim his own point of view, but to proclaim the Lamb of God. It is easier to belong to a coterie which tells what Jesus Christ has done for me, easier to become a devotee to divine healing, or to a special type of sanctification, or to the baptism of the Holy Ghost. Paul did not say, "Woe is unto me, if I do not preach what Christ has done for me," but, "Woe is unto me, if I preach not the gospel!" This is the Gospel— "The Lamb of God, which taketh away the sin of the world!" (Oswald Chambers, October 15)

After we finished reading the sheep's message of sanctification, *our* Shepherd stood and said ... "Notice this is not about you. This is about the Father and I. I and My Father are one. I do the will of My Father. You are to give your life to Me, then you are grafted into Us. You are then found holy and acceptable." With that, He sat down

We all listen and ponder His words. Our sins are forgiven and forgotten. The Spirit indwells our hearts, souls and minds. We pray, and sing ... MY JESUS, I LOVE THEE:

My Jesus I love Thee,
I know Thou art mine.
To Thee all the follies,
Of sin I resign.
My gracious Redeemer,
My Savior art Thou.
If ever I loved Thee.
My Jesus tis now.
(By William Ralph Featherston, 1846-1873)

July 4

NKJV Psalm 23:4 "Thy rod and Thy staff they comfort me."

DISCIPLINE SUBMISSION

Another discipline that comes from the mighty hand of our Father, and the direct contact of our Shepherd, is the discipline of the flesh. This fleshly body must be brought into submission, or disciplined to the control of our Shepherd. In order to become submissive, the Father punishes those of us whom He loves, so they learn to submit to His grace and mercy.

The rod and staff are instruments, used to bring us, His sheep, to submission. These instruments are used to comfort us through physical punishment and protection. We have already been taught concerning the use of His rod. Today our Shepherd will reiterate this lesson.

Listen as he begins. He is holding His rod. "As has already been explained to you, My rod is used to protect you. It is to protect you in two specific areas: number one, from predators; and number two, from yourself." We laugh; He smiles.

"This rod makes a powerful tool used for discipline or as a weapon, because the rod is used to inflict pain. Pain corrects My sheep's destructive actions. Because you sheep are really dumb, which is proven when you do not follow Me!"

"After King David had the rod used on him, He wrote these words in his twenty-third Psalm, that this rod will make you all to lie down in green pastures. David was a shepherd, as I Am, and he was recalling the times he had to use the rod, to break a leg, or punish a stubborn sheep to make his sheep lie down and become submissive."

"Have you forgotten these encouraging words from our Father God? He said … "My child don't ignore it when the Lord disciplines you, and don't be discouraged when He corrects you. For the Lord corrects those He loves, just as a father corrects a child in whom he delights!" (NLT Proverbs 3:11-12)

With that He bowed His head to pray.

I praise God, He sustains our relationship. *With His Rod He restores My Soul.*

July 5

NKJV James 2: 10 "For whosoever shall keep the whole law, and yet stumbles in one point, he is guilty of all."

PAIN

A sheep once said that, "God whispers to us in our pleasure, speaks in our conscience, but *shouts* in our pain: it is His megaphone to rouse a deaf world." (C.S. Lewis "The Problem with Pain") Suffering forms the need to fight on our own, or heed to God's mighty hand of loving discipline and care.

* * * * *

The Shepherd begins our class. "If you endure chastening, God deals with you as His child. For what child is there whom a father or mother does not chasten? But if you are without chastening, of which *all* of you have become partakers, then you are illegitimate and NOT HIS CHILD."

"Furthermore, we have had human fathers who corrected us and we paid them respect. Shall we not much more readily be in subjection to the Father of spirits and live? For they indeed for a few days chastened us as seemed best to them, but He, our heavenly Father for our profit, that we may be partakers of His holiness." He smiles an encouraging smile.

"No chastening seems to be joyful for the present, but is painful; nevertheless, afterward it yields the peaceable fruit of righteousness to those who have been TRAINED by it." (NKJV Hebrews 12: 7-11)

We should deliberately choose to obey our Shepherd. His shedding of His blood washes us clean. When I choose to obey, all heaven breaks through the darkness of my sin and shame. I am restored!

Today the Shepherd, *my* Shepherd has us sing an invitation hymn for any who want to come for a rededication, or to become restored by the confession of their sins. We will all sing CLEANSE ME:

Search me, O God,
and know my heart today;
Try me, O Savior,
know my thoughts, I pray.
See if there be some wicked way in me;

Cleanse me from every sin
and set me free
(By J. Edwin Orr, 1912-, Copyright 1934)

July 6

NKJV Matthew 11:29 "Take My yoke upon you, and learn of Me."

CHASTENED

My Shepherd continues the lesson ... "Whom the Lord loves, He chastens. We complain sometimes when the Lord begins to bring us into the place where we have complete communion with Him, and we groan and say, 'O Lord this hurts. How can you let this happen to me? I'm Your Child.' I am asking you to take one end of My yoke, for My yoke is easy. Get alongside Me and we will pull together. If you are identified with Me, you will thank God our Father for the pressure of His hand."

"God increases strength to those who are weak by taking us out of our constant complaining, fear, and worry, and turning it into a *hallelujah* of praise." He pats His chest exclaiming. "I must say to you, the only way to know the strength of God is to take My yoke upon you and learn of Me!"

"Those who have My commandments and keep them, they are whose who love Me; and those who love Me shall be loved by My Father, and I will love them, and will reveal Myself to them. If anyone loves Me, they will keep My Word; and My Father will love them, and We will come to them, and make our abode with them." (NKJV John 14:21)

He looks up, then back at us, continuing this lesson, speaking very intensely. "Take heed to yourself, and diligently keep yourself, lest you forget the things your eyes have seen, and lest they depart from your heart. And teach them to your children and your grandchildren." (NKJV Deuteronomy 4:9)

May God be my strength and my song. For in Him we breath, move, and have our being. We will now sing another verse of CLEANSE ME:

I praise Thee, Lord,
for cleansing me from sin:
fulfill Thy word and
make me pure within.
Fill me with fire where once I burned with shame;
Grant my desire to magnify Thy name.
(By J. Edwin Orr, 1912-, Copyright 1934)

July 7

NKJV Geneses 1: 27 "God created mankind in His own image."

ORGINIAL CREATION

In order to be restored to a right relationship with the Shepherd and the Father, we must look back to the creation and the fall of mankind.

Our Father created us to be His, made in His image. We were physically and spiritually alive and in perfect union with Him. Our Father blessed man and woman and told them to, "Be fruitful and multiply; fill the earth and subdue it; have dominion over the fish, birds, and over every living thing that moves on the earth. Every tree and every green herb I have given to you for food." All of man's needs were met. He was safe and secure, having a sense of belonging, perfectly provided for in every way.

He begins to teach. "God, our Father, created man first, He was given headship as responsibility, with humility, and not a right to demand with pride. The woman was then made as his helper, so that he would not be alone in his dominion over the world. She is a part of the divine plan for fellowship, continuation of the generations, and for doing the work assigned by our Father." (Commentary page 5, NIV Women's Study Bible)

The Shepherd smiles as He continues. "When My Father said to Us, We would make man in Our image, according to Our likeness, We were filled with joy. After the creation, Our Father called Us together, and We blessed all that We had made. Then My Father God, the Spirit, and Myself saw everything made, and it was absolutely perfect. My Father exclaimed, 'IT IS GOOD!' That day all of Us and Our creation praised the Father."

"Our original plan was one of beauty and perfection." He bows His head, to regain His composure as He begins to teach about the sad part of the story.

We begin to know the problem of our demise, and why restoration is necessary! Sin came in because of human choice, and infested all of creation. I pray, "Oh God we feel the intense shame and the pain of our sins. I am sorry. Forgive me."

July 8

> NKJV Genesis 2:17 " …but of the tree of the Knowledge of Good and Evil you shall not eat, for in the day that you eat it you shall surely die."

THE FALL

The Shepherd begins the lesson. "The sad part of today's lesson is how you rejected the perfection We created and planned for your lives. As the Father finished all of creation, He told both Adam and Eve to be 'fruitful and to multiply.' The garden that we created for them was called *The Garden of Eden*." Beside Him stands Adam and Eve.

"Our Father only gave them one commandment; 'Every tree of the garden you may freely eat; but of the tree of the *Knowledge of Good and Evil*, you shall not eat, for in the day that you eat, you shall surely die!' And the rest is history.'" He looks at Adam and Eve who have tears in their eyes. They both look lovingly at the Shepherd, never once looking away. He continues.

"They ate and a process of physical and spiritual death was set in motion. Because of their disobedience, their relationship with Him was broken. They desired their own way. God forbade fellowship with them, and they were banished from His presence, to die in sin and shame."

"Does this remind you of anyone?"

All of us sheep begin to cry and morn this terrible loss. Adam held Eve close as she softly cried.

Our Lord continues, "Both physical life and spiritual death is inherited from parents. Every human being who comes into the world is born physically alive, and immediately begins to physically die. They are also born spiritually DEAD, separated from our Father God. Therefore, just as through one man sin entered the world, and death through sin, death spread to all men, because all sinned. For as by one man's disobedience many were made sinners," He points to Adam. "So also by one Man's obedience many will be made righteous." He points to Himself, stretching out His arms wide, hands open and we see the scares from those nails. "Because of My sacrifice all are given eternal life if they accept me." (NKJV Romans 5:12-21)

Adam, Eve, and *my* Shepherd smile. They look at each other with love and affection. His grace covered, and is still covering all sins for all time.

He closes the class with these words, as if He were pouring oil on each of our heads, and hearts, like *the oil of joy*. He continues. "Where sin abounds, grace abounds much more, so that as sin reigned in death, even so grace might reign through righteousness to eternal life through Me, *your* Shepherd, Jesus Christ the Lord." (NKJV Romans 5:20)

Still Waters

We all stand and sing MY JESUS I LOVE THEE:

*My Jesus I love Thee, I know Thou art mine,
For thee all the follies of sin I resign;
My gracious Redeemer, my Savior art Thou;
If ever I loved Thee, my Jesus its now.
(By William Ralph Featherstone 1846-1873)*

July 9

NKJV I Corinthians 2:14 "But the natural person does not receiver the things of the Spirit of God, but they are foolishness to them; nor can they know them because they are Spiritually discerned."

THE NATURAL SHEEP

The Shepherd tells us of the three distinct types of sheep coming out of the fall of mankind. The first is the **natural person**.

"Now, because of disobedience there are those who try to find purpose in life independent from Me. These are called people who walk after the flesh. These persons believe they are free to choose their own behavior and their own destinations."

"However, they are in complete darkness and are chained to the laws which governs the bondage of sin. They are in fact slaves to sin, not free at all! Their entire body, mind and spirit is controlled by the depravity of this world."

"These lost sheep struggle with inferiority, insecurity, inadequacy, guilt, worry and fear. Their minds are obsessed with what they desire, becoming crude and vulgar. Their own will includes: immortality, impurity, idolatry, sorcery, strife, outburst of anger, jealously, disputes, dissensions, envying, drunkenness, and carousing."

"Their bodies react by being sick. Bitterness, un-forgiveness, depression, and anxiety causes weakness and then eventually becomes actual physical pain, and sometimes death is the result."

The Shepherd turns to us and sadness fills His face. "The spirit of the natural person is dead to our Father, and they walk according to the course of the world and according to the *Prince of the Power of the Air.*" He takes a deep breath, then bows his head. (NIV Ephesians 2:2)

He leans, stressing these words. "Thus, this **natural person** is unable to fulfill the purpose for which he or she was created. They are dead. They walk in darkness and have no life because they leave Me out. Sin is inevitable. They have chosen DEATH!"

No one moved. The sadness of this truth is crushing! What a mess is this *valley of the shadow of death*.

July 10

NKJV I Corinthians 2:15 "But those who are Spiritual …"

THE SPIRITUAL SHEEP

The Shepherd, is teaching today about how we become filled with a new restored life. A life having been redeemed! For He *restores my* soul.

Listen … "I have come to bring new life from out of the darkness, for I am the *Light* of all. I shine in the darkness. All flesh may come out of their fleshly life into new life by My restoration process."

"First, one must be crucified with Me. The mind is transformed, renewed and one becomes single-minded, equipped for action. The body is understood to be the temple of God, presented as a living sacrifice, holy and acceptable as a reasonable service unto Him. The will of the flesh is given up to My will and the person becomes one of My sheep, walking after the Spirit. In My sheep, the indwelling Spirit enjoys salvation, forgiveness, assurance, security, acceptance and worth."

"And in this fallen and dark world, emotions become peace and joy. The Father has adopted you. You become My brothers, and sisters, joint hires with Me!" He laughs with joyful eyes. We join in.

"The Spiritual sheep receives his or her lifestyle from the Spirit, not from the flesh. He or she walks according to the Spirit. The description of the Spiritual person is the perfection of an abundant life! It's the model of maturity toward which you are all growing. And your Father, My Father, has made every provision for you to experience now, and forever this life of perfection."

"So, the question is: why live another way? The choice you sheep make every day is whether to live in My will, free, and restored, on the mountain top of maturity; or the depths of the fleshly valley of hell and damnation. Have you made your choice?" He ask us not to answer out loud, but to search our hearts for the answer.

Tomorrow we have a final lesson concerning restoring our soul. We all look up and pray "Father forgive us our trespasses. In Your precious name, amen."

July 11

NKJV I Corinthians 3:3 "Are you not carnal? (fleshly) ..."

THE FLESHLY SHEEP

The Shepherd speaks of His sheep who belong to Him but choose to live a life by their own will. They live a life not in the Spirit but in the flesh. Our Shepherd has brought the Spirit along today to help teach the lesson.

"I have constantly commissioned you, My sheep, not to walk, or live in the flesh, but walk and live in the Spirit. By *walk* I mean your choice of lifestyle should not be that of living according to your own sinful, selfish desires. To *walk* in the Spirit, describes a life yielded to the control of the Spirit of Truth." He and the Spirit walk toward us coming very close to us as they continue the lesson.

"The fleshly sheep is a sheep that shares My name, but their physical body as the temple of God the Father, is in sad disrepair. Many sheep continue to be victims of their flesh. They have lost their way. They are in darkness and continue to have unstable emotions."

The Spirit steps forward to speak. "These Sheep quench Me, ignoring my urges, and advice. If necessary they push me out, or to the back of their hearts, and ignore my promptings."

He continues ... "These sheep are double minded. Their ingrained fleshly habits still appeal to their mind and they desire to live independently of God and the Lord, *your* Shepherd. They have outbursts of anger, disputes, strife, immorality, idolatry, and impurity. They live a joyless, peaceless, dark, and unfruitful life."

Again the Shepherd speaks, "Due to their disobedience these sheep have left and wandered away from the fold. They choose to live by their own will, not by obeying their Lord. Remember if you love Me, the Lord, your Shepherd, you will obey and keep My commandments!"

"Only through obedience in Me can this fleshly sheep be restored."

I love *my* Shepherd. *He restored my soul.*

Cynthia Perkins
July 12

NKJV John 14:1 "Let not your heart be troubled …"

I AM REDEEMED

"Let not your heart be troubled!" The Shepherd is smiling as He teaches the blessing of redemption. "You believe in God, believe also in Me. In My Father's house are many mansions; if it were not so, I would have told you. I go now to prepare a place for you. And if I go and prepare a place for you, I will come again and receive you unto Myself; so that where I am, there you may be also." (KJV John 14:1-3)

He lifts His hand and directs us to look at the road up ahead. "I am the Way, the Truth, and the Life. No one comes to the Father except through Me. If you love Me, keep My commandments. The Father has given you another Helper, that He may abide with you forever, the Spirit of Truth, whom you have all met. The world cannot receive Him, because it neither sees Him nor knows Him; but you sheep know Him, for He dwells with you, and is in you."

"The world sees me no more, but you see Me. Because I live, you will live also. At that day you will know that I am in My Father; and you in Me, and I in you. Those who know and love My commandments and keep them, love Me. If anyone loves me, they will keep My word; and My Father will love them, and We will come to them and make our home with them."

The Shepherd waves for the Spirit to step to the front. "The Helper, your Holy Spirit, whom the Father has sent in My Name, will teach you all things. Peace, I leave with you, My peace I give to you; not as the world gives do I give to you. Let not your heart be troubled, neither let it be afraid!" (KJV John 14:1-27)

His words sound like thunder and rings in *our* ears. The joy floods our souls and we clap, shout and yell our love for the Lord, *our* Shepherd, and the Spirit of Truth. The lesson is closed by the singing of the hymn SOMETHING BEAUTIFUL. Perfect for expressing the restoration of our souls from the darkness of evil to the beautiful light.

Something beautiful, something good;
All my confusion He understood;
All I had to offer Him was brokenness and strife
But He made something beautiful of my life.
(By Gloria Gather, Copyright 1971)

July 13

ANT John 15:26 "The Helper, Counselor, Advocate, Intercessor, Strengthener—the Holy Spirit …"

RESTORED

BY THE HOLY SPIRIT

Again, the Holy Spirit is teaching with the Shepherd. *My* Shepherd has already explained that He is the third person of the trinity. He possesses all of God's attributes and is fully God.

The Shepherd introduces the lesson. "Throughout history our Father has acted, revealed His will, empowered individuals, and disclosed His personal presence through the Holy Spirit. I will turn the lesson over to Him to teach about His function in your restored life, as My sheep."

The Spirit is so gentle and dignified. He stands tall and strong before us, His face filled with love, for each sheep believes He is looking directly at them. "All of you know, I'm sure, that I have specific functions. In the Old Covenant, I was given to an individual at a specific time to aid in accomplishing a particular mission. I was not constantly present in the life of every follower of Yahweh."

"However, in the *New Covenant* I was left here to dwell inside of each of you. I indwell all of you believers from the moment your trust is completely put in the Lord, *your* Shepherd. When an individual accepts Jesus as Savior, I come in to dwell in his or her life. Then you are sealed with me."

"I Am your greatest ally. I Am an essential for survival in this sin filled world. I Am your advocate, called to come alongside you as Comforter and Teacher: I will guide you into *all* truth; for I do not speak on My own authority, but whatever I hear I will speak; and I will tell you things to come. I glorify Him." (He smiles pointing to the Shepherd) "For I will take of what is His, and declare it to you. All that the Father has is His. I will take of His, your Shepherds, and declare it to you." (ANT Paraphrased from John 14:15-31)

"I give to you, the Lord's sheep, help and advice for living the Christian life. As moment by moment believers (you) surrender your lives to God you allow yourselves to be used for His service. I, the Holy Spirit, fill you with Myself. Through the filling up of Me, you are controlled by Me, and equipped for service, restored to full spiritual fruition!"

As He finishes, His strength and mighty power is felt in me, and surrounds all of us! His glory comes down so thick and so strong, that we cannot see! We sit still, making no sound. Just soaking in His glory.

Cynthia Perkins

July 14

NKJV John 10:27 "My sheep hear My voice and I know them."

LOOSING "FELLOWSHEEP"

The Shepherd will discuss in today's lesson three kinds of problems we can find ourselves in, on this journey we are about to take *in the paths of righteousness.* He gently speaks, with much compassion and grace.

"You are My sheep. You have given your life up to insure My life in you, but sometimes on the path through *the valley of the shadow of death* you can and will lose your way. You are never out of My reach, but sometimes you venture on a path where you loose sight of Me, forfeiting fellowship with Us.

"Today we will begin discussion concerning three frequent problems that sheep find themselves in where fellowship is lost." He laughs and says, "Some call it '*fellowsheep*'." We all laugh; enjoying His humor.

He becomes very serious as He continues. "The first problem is that many of you are stubborn sheep. You get lost in *your* way. I call this a 'mulish' sheep. Stubborn and confused, this sheep believes his or her way is the only way to go, and end up in sins sudden rockslides, steep ravines, sinking sand, and attacks by wild beasts!"

"The second sheep that has lost fellowship is the sheep that strays away from the fold. This sheep believes that the grass is better a little further out. He or she want to go over that hill, and see what is on the other side. These sheep find themselves in dangerous places. Some fall into pits or become tangled in thorns or vines, or stuck in a trap, breaking their leg, they cannot get out."

"And thirdly, there are sick sheep. If a sheep becomes sick, it is easy for an enemy attack."

The Shepherd brings forward three instruments that He uses: a rod, a staff, and oil. First He holds up the rod. "We have had an entire lesson on this instrument called the *rod*. This is why The Twenty Third Psalm says that the rod comforts. It is used to whirl at the enemy or to restore the sheep to the herd. The rod is used as a weapon to protect you sheep from robbers, or an enemy disguised in sheep's clothing."

"This other part of the instrument is a *staff*. It is a crook called *'the shepherd's crook'* just big enough to grab around the sheep's neck. It is this hook that can retrieve a sheep who has fallen into a pit or off of the side of a cliff. The *'crook'* is used as a guide, and also can lift the sheep out of a predicament where the sheep is tangled, or tied up. The staff guides, guards, lifts and retrieves."

He walks forward, picking up a brand new baby lamb. "Sometimes a ewe will forget her lamb. The crook is used to pull her and her baby back together."

The Shepherd stands, leaning on His rod…"Tomorrow we will continue with the second part of this lesson." He motions for us to rise.

※

We all raise our eyes to the heavens and pray with our Lord, *my* Shepherd.

July 15

NKJV Psalm 23:5 "Thou anoints my head with oil …"

THE OIL

Today the Shepherd continues the lesson concerning how to help hurting and lost sheep. Especially those sheep who are troubled, and have stepped out of fellowship with the Shepherd. This lessons explains restoration and bringing those back home to the fold.

The Shepherd lays down the staff and gets a bottle filled with olive oil. He holds it up and explains. "At night when you sheep are guided back to the sheep fold, I take out My rod and staff, and as you go one by one into the fold, I will:

Count the sheep. For I know exactly how many sheep I have. If even one is missing, I immediately go out to hunt, I find it, and bring it back to the fold.

Call the sheep by name. I have fellowship with My sheep, and know them on an intimate bases.

Touch each sheep. I put My hands on each sheep to look for any wounds. If I find any wounds I pour oil on the wound. The oil soothes medicates, heals, and restores the sheep.

Pour the oil on the head of the sheep to sooth its face and head. I will mix the oil with tar and make it into a paste that I rub on their nose, mouth, and ears to keep off those biting bugs and flies.

In the evening, the Shepherd has us kneel, one at a time, at the gate entrance and anoints us with oil. He makes a paste to rub into our open soars or bits. When He is finished, He looks toward heaven and says in a loud, sobering voice… "My sheep hear My voice, and I know them, and they follow Me. No one is able to snatch them out of My Father's hand. I and My Father are One!" (NKJV John 10:27)

It was so silent that the air became loud like thunder! His Word, *the oil of Joy,* poured over our hearts, souls, and minds. Oh the love of the Lord, *my* Shepherd. Let us sing the chorus OH HOW HE LOVES YOU AND ME:

> *O how He loves you and me.*
> *He gave His life*
> *What more could He give.*
> *Oh how He loves you.*
> *Oh, how He loves me.*
> *Oh, how He loves you and me.*
> *(By Kurt Kaiser, Copyright 1975)*

July 16

NKJV Psalm 23:3 He restores my soul.

RESTORATION

To understand the restoration of our soul, the next few lessons the Shepherd will bring to our minds examples of those sheep who were disciplined and restored; and those who refused discipline and were lost. For the Lord disciplines those who are His sheep. Others who have chosen their own way, rejecting His direction concerning their problems and issues in life, choosing to walk down life's road that leads to destruction and hell. Described as a wide, heavily traveled road.

It is extremely important for all of us to note that there are only two options on the way to eternal life; 1) the broad way that leads to destruction; and 2) the narrow way that leads to eternal salvation. It is that simple. To obey the Shepherd leads to soul restoration: disobeying leads to soul destruction. A soul bound and determined to do their own will.

The two ways shown to us by the Shepherd are both of a religious nature. Both are marked *Heaven;* however, one leads to HELL! The Shepherd said … "Enter by the narrow gate; for wide is the gate, and broad is the way that leads to destruction, and those who enter by it are many. For, the gate is narrow, and the way is hard, which leads to life, and those who find it are few." (RS Matthew 7:13-14)

He issued this warning! "Beware of false prophets, who come to you in sheep's clothing, but inwardly are ravenous wolves. You will know them by their fruits. Do you gather grapes from thorn bushes or figs from thistles? Even so, every good tree bears good fruit, nor can a bad tree bear good fruit. Every tree that does not bear good fruit is cut down and thrown into the fire. Therefore, by their fruits you will *know* them." (RS Matthew 7:15-20)

The Shepherd continues His warnings. "Not everyone who says to Me ... 'Lord, Lord,' shall enter the Kingdom of Heaven." And then He raves, **"BUT THOSE WHO DO THE WILL OF MY FATHER ENTER HEAVEN!"** (RS Matthew 7:21)

See, that's it! The sheep who are righteous obey His will. Only obedience enables us to know and to love His good, acceptable, and perfect will.

July 17

NKJV Luke 22: 48 Jesus asked, "Judas, are you betraying the Son of Man?"

EXAMPLES

JUDAS

Today the Shepherd will present illustrations of those who choose restoration, and those who refused it. Listen, this is important.

"The examples I bring to you are of some who appeared to be sheep, but were not, and some who lost their way and were drawn back into the fold."

"The first is one of My very own disciples, Judas." We could tell our Shepherd's heart was breaking to tell this story. Judas betrayed the Lord, our Shepherd with a kiss. Judas is a prime example of a sheep following his own way.

"For three years Judas followed Me with My other disciples. On the outside he seemed to be a sheep of Mine. However, he is the disciple who was raised in Galilee, which made him an outsider of the group."

"By appearances, one would have believed that Judas shared the hope of My Kingdom. He seemed to believe that I was the Messiah. After all, it appeared, he too had left everything to follow me."

The Shepherd pauses, sits and leans toward us. "Judas saw the miracles. He heard My teaching, and saw those raised from the dead. No one questioned him or his faith. The only one who knew Judas' heart: Me! I knew he was the betrayer."

"Listen! Judas never gave up his life. He was extremely confident in himself! He had an unregenerate heart, and because he chose not to believe Me, but to believe in *his* way, his heart gradually hardened so that he became the man still known today as the Lord's betrayer!" We see the sadness in our Shepherd's eyes. He loves him so.

How sad when one choses to go their own way, even to the point of being a traitor to his best friend. We all sit with our heads bowed low with sorrow, knowing that many are like Judas, *sheep that have gone astray, looking to their own way.*

July 18

NKJV Matthew 26:48 "Now His betrayer had given them a sign, saying, "Whomever I kiss, He is the One; seize Him." Immediately he (Judas) went up to Jesus and said, "Greetings, Rabbi" and kissed Him."

THE KISS OF DEATH

"Judas was a thief and desired wealth and fame. He believed, because of his association with Me that he would become an important person in an earthly kingdom. He believed he would be a powerful ruler of the Kingdom, he thought I would build, on earth. Because of his rebellious, disobedient heart, he could not see the Truth."

"Listen to the song I composed about his sad hypocrisy. PSALM FIFTY FIVE: 12-14 NKJ:

For it is not an enemy who reproaches me,
Then I could bear it;
Nor is it one who hates me
who has exalted himself against Me,
Then I could hide myself from him.

But it is you, a man of equal,
My companion and My familiar friend.
We who had sweet fellowship together,
walked in the house of God in the throng.

The Shepherd begins to cry ... "It would have been better if he had not been born. My Father and I actually allowed Satan to enter Judas, so that all scripture would be fulfilled. Judas helped complete My murder. He took the bribe, and gave Me the *Kiss of Death*, which at that time, was a kiss showing respect. He gave me an embrace, showed warm love, affection and intimacy as though he were an equal. If he would had shown reverence or humility by kissing My hand or the hem of My garment, as a servant before His master, We, the Father and I, could have helped Him. Judas' first love was Judas." (NKJV Matthew 26:24, paraphrased)

"Judas kept up the appearance of a disciple, until the very end. I asked him 'Judas, are you betraying the Son of God with a kiss?' Do what you have come to do!'" He looks at us piercing our very hearts.

"Please remember, a restored soul is a soul that may sin, but when sin is done recognizes Me as their advocate, and the propitiation for their sin. An unrestored soul, like Judas', is in it for what *they* receive. These sheep love the world, and they love darkness rather than the Light of the world, Me, your Shepherd!"

We sit quietly. The Shepherd starts to walk into the mountain to pray. We all find a solitary place, kneel down and pray. The Lord is *my* Shepherd.

July 19

> NKJV Romans 1:1 "Paul a bondservant of Jesus Christ, called to be an apostle, separated to the Gospel of God …"

PAUL

Today is a beautiful day. The Shepherd stands in front of us with an honored guest. It is with much excitement we meet the great apostle Paul. Paul wrote two-thirds of the New Testament, Paul is a shining example of the Shepherd's business of soul restoration.

The class begins. "Today we learn of a soul that became obedient even unto death, Paul!" We all clap and shout in honor of this great apostle. "He will be presenting the lesson today, by explaining how his soul was restored."

As we learn about this apostle, we begin to understand that our Shepherd will go to any length to restore our souls. The Shepherd's dealing with him, was so extreme, his name was changed! His given name was Saul. After the restoration, he became Paul.

Paul means "little," so Paul wanted to be known as the "Little One" of Christ's servants. Because as Saul, he was a powerfully, politically correct man, hunting down and killing Christians. As Paul, his name change showed humility, and obedience.

Listen, as Paul begins speaking. "I was a Pharisee and born a Roman citizen; I was a speaker of five languages. By trade I became a tentmaker and studied with Gamaliel, an extremely respected Jewish teacher of the Law. You could say I was at the 'top of my class.'" We all laugh.

"I am first introduced in the gospel as the one that a mob of Jews … 'laid down their robes at the feet of Saul,' while they stoned to death the first martyred Christian, Stephen." He took a deep breath, to gather his composure, then continued.

"After the death of Stephen, I became a radical persecutor of *The Way*. I invaded homes, and arrested believers, throwing them into prison. Not only the men, but also the women, and the children. I persecuted these sheep, and as they were being slaughtered, I cast my vote against them! I was passionate about *my* work. I was respected by the powers that be. I was known throughout the land as a great Pharisee, who loved God, and proved it by destroying this cult known as *The Way*."

"Then one day as I was breathing threats and murder against the disciples who now were scattered because of persecution, I headed to Damascus to arrest and kill as many of *The Way* as I could find. Then THE SHEPHERD CAME with His staff!" He smiled with tears in his eyes.

"On my way to Damascus to search out and kill more of Christ's followers, I was thrown to the ground when the Lord, our Shepherd basically hit me with His staff!" We all laugh. "I was terrified! He blinded me and He told me to … 'Arise and go to the city'."

"I was blind for three days, and I had nothing to eat nor drink. Then God sent a member of *The Way*, Ananias, to lay hands on me, and to fill me with the Holy Spirit. Immediately scales fell from my eyes, and I could see! I was baptized, for the remission of my sins."

"Immediately I begin to preach the gospel. I was blessed to become an early witness, and missionary to the Gentiles." (NKJV Acts 9:1-19 paraphrased)

The Shepherd gave him a huge hug, saying. "Paul was a chosen vessel of Mine, to bear My name before Gentiles, kings, and the children of Israel. He suffered many things for My sake. As He drew near to his death he said 'I have fought the good fight, I have finished the course, I have kept the faith; in the future there is laid up for me the crown of righteousness, which the Lord the righteous judge will award me on that day.'" They hug and we clap and shout for Paul. He showed us his crown.

What joy this witness brings to us. I pray Paul's final plea, will be my final plea, as I go to *dwell in my* Shepherd's *house forever*.

July 20

NKJV I Peter 1:1 "Peter, an apostle of Jesus Christ …"

PETER

Today, the Shepherd is again teaching about restoration of our soul. He has provided life examples, of those whose souls have been restored. Today He said Peter, the preacher of the first sermon of the Church, is coming to share how he was restored by our Shepherd.

In fact, here they come. The Shepherd smiles as we clap and give praise for Him and the apostle Peter.

"It is with great joy that I bring My brother Peter to bear witness of soul restoration." Peter smiles with love in his eyes for our Lord. "Peter's brother Andrew was introduced to Me by My cousin John the Baptist. When introducing Me He called Me … The Lamb of God. Andrew went immediately to Peter and told him that the Messiah had been found. Then he took Peter to Me, and I looked at Him and said…'You are Simon, the son of John; you shall be called Peter, meaning a stone." (NKJV John 1:36-42) In soul restoration even their name is changed.

"Some time passed and I went to the Sea of Galilee, and there proved to this tough fisherman that I knew how to fish." We all laugh. "My catch was a boatload of fish, so heavy that the boat began to sink!" Peter shakes his head in agreement. Peter immediately accepted My call and left everything to follow Me. That was just the beginning of this man's journey as My witness, and My apostle."

The Shepherd turns to Peter patting him on the back and giving him the floor. "I was the leader of the apostles. I was always up front following *my* Shepherd. I always had something to say. Sometimes the words were well spoken, but mostly not. In the beginning, the problem with my words revealed how they were always about *me*, and how *I* felt." He looked down and paused, chocking up.

"All seemed to go fairly well for three years. Then the Lord headed toward Jerusalem for the Passover celebration. We knew it was a dangerous journey for Him, because the religious sect was after Him, to kill Him. We were afraid for our own safety because we were known as His followers. None of us understood, He was the *Sacrificial Lamb*!"

"We all went with Him to celebrate the Passover. The meal was prepared in an upper room. When we were about to eat, the Shepherd did something that made me very upset. He decided to wash our feet. Well I was not about to allow *my* Lord to wash feet! He was Jesus, our leader, not our servant! My Lord looked at me and said, 'If I do not wash you, you have no part with Me.' I was stunned and hurt, I was being rebuked. Still I pushed."

"As the Lord declared, one of us would betray Him, I told Him, that under no circumstances would I ever betray Him, nor leave Him! This time the Lord replied calling me by my old name, which scared me to death, but I was into *I*, so I ignored it. He said 'Simon, Simon, behold Satan has demanded to sift you like wheat! Soon you will have denied Me three times, and on the third time the cock will crow!'"

CONTINUED TOMORROW!

July 21

RS Luke 22: 57 But he (Peter) denied Him, saying, "Woman, I do not know Him."

DENIED

Yesterday Peter began to tell of His denial of the Shepherd after He had been arrested. He seems sad as He begins. Although, he knows he has been restored, he still regrets how he treated the Lord, *our* Shepherd.

We are all extremely quiet as he begins. "They came and took the Lord, our Shepherd away. Judas was with them. He betrayed Him with a kiss of death." He starts to choke up. "We trusted Judas."

I grabbed a sword and cut off Malchus' ear! The Lord immediately rebuked me and picked up the ear and put it back onto Malchus' head. At that point we ran like a bunch of rats from the light, into the darkness of the garden."

"At a distance, John and I followed the Shepherd. The first stop was Caiaphas' palace court. A slave girl asked me if I was one of this Man's disciples. I said with sarcasm in my voice 'I am not!' Then I headed to the porch, where another servant girl declared, 'This man was with Jesus of Nazareth.' How my temper and frustration flared! I cursed and said I was not an acquaintance of that Man!"

Again he pauses and wipes his face with both hands to dispense of the falling tears.

"About an hour passed and some of those by the fire said, my dialect had the accent of a Galilean, where this Jesus was from. I lost it! I cursed and swore, then declared loudly, **'I do not know the Man!'**"

"Suddenly, I was frozen in time. Everything around me stood still, and as clear as a crystal bell came the voice. It was the voice of a rooster. His crowing was so loud that I had to put my hands over my ears. I closed my eyes, and there before me was the Lord, my Shepherd, holding the rooster in his hand, looking at me with sad eyes, saying: 'Before the rooster crows you will deny me three times.'"

As I opened my eyes to get the picture out of my head, there right before me with the guards, was the beaten, bloody, bruised face of the sacrificial Lamb. His eyes looked straight into mine. I fell down on my face, then jumped up, and ran into the darkest, most remote, place I could find. I tore my clothes and bitterly wept!" (NKJV Luke 22:54-62, paraphrased)

The Shepherd stepped toward Peter and embraced him. They cried.

We all begin to cry. Some sobbing, some crying silently, but there were no dry eyes, as we realized that on a daily bases we deny our Lord, *my* Shepherd. Oh God, may it never be.

July 22

> NKJV John 21: 17 "Simon, son of Jonah, do you love Me?" And he said to Him, "Lord, you know all things; You know that I love you."

RESTORATION

Today, Peter, the great apostle, stands strong and smiling beside the Shepherd. He smiles, because he will be finishing the testimony of his restoration. The Shepherd never leaves us undone, neglected, nor disregarded. He will always bring us home unto Himself.

Now Peter begins the lesson. "After the resurrection, *my* Shepherd, the Lord appeared to me. He called me Simon until the name Peter was restored."

"By the sea of Galilee my Lord came to see us after His resurrection, I had given up and had gone back to my old job of fishing for fish!" We all smile and feel the joy. "When I recognized Him, I jumped out of the boat and into the water, running to shore. He was dead! Now He stands before me preparing a meal."

"After we ate, He said to me, … "Simon, son of Jonah, do you love Me more than these?"

"I said … 'Yes, Lord; You know that I love you.' The Shepherd said 'Feed My Lambs.'"

"He said to me a second time … 'Simon, son of Jonah, do you love Me?' I said 'Yes Lord You know I love you.' The Shepherd said, 'Tend My sheep.'"

"The Lord said to Me the third time … 'Simon, son of Jonah, do you love Me?' I started to cry, and with an intense response said 'Lord You know all things; You know that I love You!'"

"The Shepherd said, 'Feed My Sheep. Most assuredly, I say to you, when you were younger, you girded yourself and walked where you wished; but when you are old, you will stretch out your hands, and another will gird you, and carry you where you do not wish … so FOLLOW ME!' And that is what I did." The Shepherd and Peter look at each other and smile. We all stand and clap at the joy that comes from our Savior's love for each individual sheep. (NKJV John 21: 15-23)

Peter continues … "My Lord asked this question three times, because I denied Him three times. It was confirmation that I had been forgiven of this terrible sin, and was now restored and made whole again." Again we let out a yell of cheers!

"My Lord indicated that day that I should die a martyrs' death by stretching out my hands for my own crucifixion. And eventually, as they were about to hang me on my cross, I asked the soldiers to hang me upside down, because I was not worthy to die as my Lord, *my* Shepherd!"

With much joy, and enthusiasm Peter continues … "The restoration was completed. The Lord allowed me to preach the first sermon of the Church, His Bride! That day over three thousand came to conversion and salvation. As my Shepherd said 'You are Peter, and upon this rock I will build My Church, and the gates of hell shall not prevail against it!' " (NKJV Matthew 16:18)

One of the sheep steps forward and leads us in MY CHAINS ARE GONE:

My chains are gone,
I am set free.
My soul, my Savior has ransomed me.
And like a flood His mercy reigns,
unending love, amazing grace.
(By Chris Tomlin, Copyright 2006)

July 23

NKJV John 21:17 "Lovest thou Me?"

THE UNDEVIATING QUESTION

The Shepherd said. We are to continue our study of restoration. One of His Sheep has written these next three lessons that reach into the soul of restoration.

Peter loved Jesus in the way in which any natural man loves a good man.

That is temperamental love; it may go deep into the individuality, but it does not touch the centre of the person. True love never professes anything. Jesus said, "Whosoever shall confess Me before men," confess his love not merely by his words, but by everything he does.

> *Unless we get hurt right out of every deception about ourselves, the word of God is not having its way with us. The word of God hurts as no sin can ever hurt, because sin blunts feeling. The question of the Lord intensifies feeling, until to be hurt by Jesus is the most exquisite hurt conceivable. It hurts not only in the natural way but in the profound personal way. The word of the Lord pierces even to the dividing asunder of soul and spirit, there is no deception left. There is no possibility of being sentimental with the Lord's question; you cannot say nice things when the Lord speaks directly to you, the hurt is too terrific. It is such a hurt that it stings every other concern out of account. There never can be any mistake about the hurt of the Lord's word when it comes to His child; but the point of the hurt is the great point of revelation. (Oswald Chambers, March 1)*

The Shepherd closes with these remarks "Restoration hurts. And as revealed in the lesson, one must get hurt right out of themselves. It is at the foot of the cross that all deception of one's self must end." We bow as He closes in prayer. "Father these are My sheep. May I abide in them, and they in Me, and all of us in You. Amen"

July 24

NKJV John 21:17 "Jesus said unto him the third time, Lovest thou Me?"

HAVE YOU FELT THE HURT OF THE LORD?

"Today, we study another one of My sheep's writings, which exemplifies Peter's life being restored to a level of love, no other love was ever this strong, except his love for Me. He would soon shepherd many sheep, and this one aspect of his life in Mine must be perfected. Listen as we read the exact description, of what a sheep of mine must learn to love."

Have you felt the hurt of the Lord to the uncovered quick, the place where the real sensitiveness of your life is lodged? The devil never hurts there, neither sin nor human affection hurts there. Nothing goes through to that place but the word of God. "Peter was grieved because Jesus said unto him the third time ... " He was awakening to the fact that in the real true centre of his personal life he was devoted to Jesus, and he began to see what the patient questioning meant. There was not the slightest strand of delusion left in Peter's mind, he never could be deluded again. There was no room for passionate utterance, no room for exhilaration or sentiment. It was a revelation to him to realize how much he did love the Lord, and with amazement he said, "Lord, You know all things." Peter began to see how much he did love Jesus; but he did not say, "Look at this or that to confirm it." Peter was beginning to discover to himself how much he did love the Lord, that there was no one in heaven above or upon earth beneath besides Jesus Christ; but he did not know it until the probing, hurting questions of the Lord came. The Lord's questions always reveal me to myself.

The patient directness and skill of Jesus Christ with Peter! Our Lord never asks questions until the right time. Rarely, but probably once, He will get us into a corner where He will hurt us with His undeviating questions, and we will realize that we do love Him far more deeply than any profession can ever show. (Oswald Chambers, March 2)

The Shepherd ends today's lesson with these words. "Let us rejoice in My Father's Word, because it is the Word of God that searches hearts, minds, and souls, and brings us into the spiritual

July 25

NKJV John 23:36 "Whither I go, thou canst not follow Me now; but thou shalt follow Me afterwards."

INVASION

The Shepherd said, our final lesson from the devotions of His sheep Oswald Chambers, will help us to realize the Spirit has to fill our very being, in every aspect of our lives. Listen to Him.

"Only by leaving yourself behind and picking up your cross and following Me will the restoration be rectified. My sheep put his pen to work and wrote these words that describe the life after restoration."

And when He had spoken this, He saith unto him, "Follow Me." Three years before, Jesus had said, "Follow Me," and Peter had followed easily, the fascination of Jesus was upon him, he did not need the Holy Spirit to help him to do it. Then he came to the place where he denied Jesus, and his heart broke. Then he received the Holy Spirit, and now Jesus says again, "Follow Me." There is no figure in front now saving the Lord Jesus Christ. The first "Follow Me" had nothing mystical in it, it was an external following; now it is a following in internal martyrdom.

Between these times Peter had denied Jesus with oaths and curses, he had come to the end of himself and all his self-sufficiency, There was not one strand of himself he would ever rely upon again, and in his destitution he was in a fit condition to receive an impartation from the risen Lord. "He breathed on them, and saith unto them, 'Receive ye the Holy Ghost.'" No matter what changes God has wrought in you, never rely upon them, build only on a Person, the Lord Jesus Christ, and on the Spirit He gives.

All our vows and resolutions end in denial because we have no power to carry them out. When we have come to the end of ourselves, not in imagination but really, we are able to receive the Holy Spirit. "Receive ye the Holy Ghost", the idea is that of invasion. There is only one lodestar in the life now, the Lord Jesus Christ. (Oswald Chambers, January 5)

Our Shepherd smiled as we finished these lessons. Lessons that prepare us for the journey we are about to undertake down the paths of righteousness, through the valley of the shadow of death.

We bow in prayer. Peter prays. "The Lord is *my* Shepherd …"

July 26

NKJV Luke 15:3 "Jesus told this parable …"

I AM THE GOOD SHEPHERD

The Shepherd sits to teach. "Suppose one of you has a hundred sheep and loses one of them. Don't you leave the ninety and nine in the open country and go after the lost sheep until you find it? And when you find it, joyfully you put it on your shoulders and go home. I tell you that in the same way there will be more rejoicing in heaven over one sinner who repents, than over ninety-nine righteous persons who do not need to repent."

He stands. "Oh you my sheep, I Am the Good Shepherd." He leans into us and there is pure love in His eyes. "The Good Shepherd gives His life for His sheep, but the hireling, he who is not the shepherd, sees the wolf coming and leaves the sheep and flees; and the wolf catches the sheep and scatters them. The hireling flees because he is a hireling and does not care about the sheep."

"I Am the Good Shepherd; and I know My sheep, and am known by My own. As the Father knows Me, even so I know the Father; and I lay down My life for the sheep. The other sheep I have which are not of this fold; them also I must bring, and they will hear My voice; and there will be one flock, *and* one Shepherd."

He stands up and points to the heavens. "My Father loves Me, because I lay down My life that I may take it again. **No one takes it from Me, but I lay it down Myself.** I have power to lay it down, and I have power to take it again. This commandment I have received from My FATHER." (NKJV John 10:11-29)

We all are amazed at His wonderful love. His continuance is glorious, so bright we can barely look at Him.

July 27

NKJV John 10:9 "Jesus said ... 'I Am the Door'."

THE TRUE SHEPHERD

The Shepherd continues explaining who He is. "Most assuredly, I say to you, those who do not enter My sheepfold by the door, but they climb up entering some other way, the same persons are thieves and robbers. But those who enter by the Door are the shepherds of the sheep. To them the Door Keeper opens and the sheep hear their voices; and they call their sheep by name and lead them out."

"And when they bring out their own sheep they go before them, and the sheep follow them, for they know their voice. They will not follow a stranger, but will flee from them, for they do not know the voice of strangers."

The True, and Good Shepherd looks directly at us. "Shepherding is a dangerous tiring job. I as the Example, feed, water, and guard My sheep. And I watch and make sure they do not wander off and get lost. I also protect them from predators, usually wolves in sheep's clothing, wolves carry them off, especially if they are sick, or weak, or young. Caring for My Sheep is a twenty-four hour, seven days a week job."

He stands and waves His hand over the countryside. "I spend all of My time with the flock; I call each sheep, old, or new, by My own descriptive name. They respond *only* to My voice, because they *know* me."

"I go before My sheep to make sure the way is safe. I Am the Door and My sheep enter My sheep fold through Me. If anyone enters by Me, they will be saved, and will go in and out and find pasture. The thief does not come except to steal, and to kill, and to destroy. I have come that they may have life, and that they may have it more abundantly." (NKJV John 10:4-18)

He sits down to finish. "As they enter they are restored. For redemption comes through My blood, the blood of the Lamb. I, who became, and still am, the Sacrificial Lamb, the True Shepherd. I Am the Way of salvation. No one comes to the Father except by ME!" (NKJV Ephesians 1:7/ John 14:6)

We all understand that He is the only Way to the Father. He is our sole advocate who helps us approach the Father with confidence, and unafraid.

July 28

NKJV I Peter 1:16 "Be Holy ..."

PERFECTION—-DIRECTION

The Shepherd has taught us that He has restored our souls. He paid the price. We are to accept and pursue this redemption by obedience and becoming like Him, *holy and acceptable*. Listen closely to Him, because He will shortly lead us *in the paths of righteousness.*

"The Spirit and the Shepherd *never* reject us. ... Like the Holy One who called you, be holy yourselves also in all your behavior; because it is written, 'You shall be holy, for I Am holy ... '" (NLT I Peter 1:15-16)

Because God is holy, those who are working with Him will progress more and more toward holiness. Because God is perfect, those in whom He dwells will move on in the direction of the perfect standard of His will.

According to the Shepherd's Word, the standard of perfection does *not* mean that we can never fail; it simply means that when we do fail, we have an advocate with the Father, who is Jesus Christ the righteous, the Lord, *my* Shepherd. "He is the propitiation, not just for our sins, but for the sins of the whole world!" (The Gospel According To Jesus, John MacArthur)

Those with true faith will fail, in some cases, frequently, but a genuine sheep, will, with a contrite heart, confess their sin, and come to the Father for forgiveness. PERFECTION is the standard: DIRECTION is the test. If a sheep's life does not bloom and grown in grace, righteousness, and holiness, an examination into the reality of their faith is in order, even if it is thought they have done *great things* in the name of Christ.

For it is those who hear and act upon the Words of the Shepherd, *who* are restored. The Shepherd has made it quite clear, "those restored souls, through their obedience, will not fall, because they are wise, and they are founded upon the rock!"

The wise sheep act on the Shepherd's Word. Obeying Him proves a restored soul that is solid, and firmly established. The wise sheep continues steadfast, always moving in faith. This soul is known as His sheep, because he or she keeps His commandments.

The Shepherd calls for a active decision of obedience to His bidding. The test of true faith is whether obedience is produced. That faithful sheep who obeys *will dwell in the house of the Lord, FOREVER*!

Cynthia Perkins

A special song is sung today for we are about to go, *on the paths of righteousness, through the valley of the shadow of death.* COME TO JESUS:

> *Weak and wounded sinner*
> *lost and left to die.*
> *O raise your head,*
> *for Love is passing by.*
>
> *Come to Jesus*
> *and live.*
> (By Christopher M. Rice, Copyright 2003)

July 29

NKJV John 14:27 "My peace I give unto you …"

PRESS ON

The Shepherd has told us to prepare for our walk *in the paths of righteousness*. As we are preparing to go, He is conveying to us final instructions.

"Never look back! Press on toward the mark of excellence. Leave everything behind. Let me remind you of those examples of My sheep who left all and followed Me *in the paths of righteousness through the valley of the shadow of death:*

* Abraham left his home, and his family and went to a place he did not know.
* Peter and Andrew left their fishing nets and their jobs.
* James and John left their boats, nets, and their father.
* The Samaritan woman left her water pots."

"If you are blaming God, that you cannot go because of some perplexing difficulty, in a personal experience, it is not the Father's fault, but yours. There is a problem of your not letting go. You must never try to serve two ends, yourself and God. Our attitude must be one of complete reliance on God. Once you reach this plateau, there is nothing easier then living a holy and acceptable life, pleasing unto God. Difficulty only arises when the Holy Spirit's authority is usurped for *your own will!*"

He stands and continues. "Obeying God brings the Holy Spirit's seal of peace, that *passes all understanding.* I keep you in perfect peace when your mind is *stayed* on Me." (NKJV Isaiah 26:3)

"If any one of you act out of your own will, My peace will not witness: because the Holy Spirit is of *My* will not yours. Every choice and every decision, should come from a broken and contrite heart, covered by the Testimony of the Truth, in-other-words ME!" He smiles.

I choose to leave it all behind, as I *walk in the paths of righteousness for His names sake.* Ah the joy of perfect restoration. *He restores my soul.*

July 30

> NKJV Philippians 3:13-14 "Forgetting those things which are behind and reaching forward to those things which are ahead, I press toward the goal for the prize of the upward call of God in Christ Jesus."

THE UPWARD CALL

The Lord, *my* Shepherd is ready for us to *walk in the path of righteousness.*

He stands with His staff in hand, on the top of the hill, ready to lead us down this road. In preparation for the journey, He delivers the *upward call.*

"Therefore rejoice in Me, the Lord, *your* Shepherd. Be aware of evil wolves. For you must rejoice in Me, Jesus Christ, and have *no* confidence in the flesh!"

"What things were gain for you, now count loss for Me. Count all things loss for the excellence of knowledge of Me, Christ Jesus, your Lord, for whom you have lost all things, and count them as rubbish, that you may gain Me, and be found in Me, not having your own righteousness."

"Your own righteousness is from the law, but that which is through faith in Me, Christ, the righteousness which is from God by faith; through that you may know Me, and the power of My resurrection, and the fellowship of My suffering, being conformed to My death, if, by any means, you may attain to the resurrection from the dead." (NAS Philippians 3: 7-11)

He raises His staff above His head, His face up toward the Father.

"Therefore, press on, that you may lay hold of that for which Christ Jesus, *your* Shepherd, the Lord, has also laid hold of you. Do not count yourself to have apprehended IT; but one thing you do, forgetting those things which are behind, and reaching forward to those things which are ahead, you press toward the goal for the prize of the *upward call* of God, the Father, in Me, Christ Jesus, the Lord, *your* Shepherd." (NAS Philippians 3:12-14)

We begin our walk, as *He leads us in the paths of righteousness, for His name's sake."* We hear the song WERE IT NOT FOR GRACE:

> *Were it not for grace I can tell you where I'd be*
> *Wandering down some pointless road to nowhere*
> *With my salvation up to me*
> *I know how that would go, the battles I would face*
> *Forever running but losing the race*
> *were it not for Grace.*
> *(By David Hamilton and Phill McHugh, Copyright 1997)*

July 31

NKJV Isaiah 40:11 "Like a Shepherd ... He will gather the lambs with His arms and carry them ..."

FOOTPRINTS

Years ago a poem was written by a sheep that describes our walk. It describes the perfect grace and love of the Lord, *my* Shepherd. May these words be a blessing in your life, as you begin to *walk through the valley of the shadow of death:*

> *One night a man had a dream.*
> *He dreamed he was walking along*
> *the beach with the LORD.*
> *Across the sky flashed scenes from his life.*
> *For each scene, he noticed two sets of footprints in the sand,*
> *one belonging to him, and the other to the LORD.*
>
> *When the last scene of his life flashed before him,*
> *he looked back at the footprints in the sand.*
> *He noticed that many times along the path of his life*
> *there was only one set of footprints.*
> *He also noticed that it happened*
> *at the very lowest and saddest times in his life.*
>
> *This really bothered him and he questioned the LORD about it.*
> *"LORD, You said that once I decided to follow You,*
> *You'd walk with me all the way.*
> *But I have noticed that during the most troublesome times in my life,*
> *there is only one set of prints.*
> *I don't understand why when I needed You most You would leave me."*
>
> *The LORD replied, "My precious, precious child.*
> *I love you and I would never leave you.*

During your times of trial and suffering,
when you see only one set of footprints,
it was then that I carried you."
(Author Unknown)

What else can be said? *The Lord, is my Shepherd; I shall not want ... Thou annointst my head with oil, my cup runneth over.* O how I love you *my* Lord, *my* Shepherd.

PART IV

He Leads Me In The Paths Of Righteousness

August

August 1

NKJV Psalm 27:11 "Lead me in a plain path."

THE PATH

Today we are taking our first steps *in the paths of righteousness.* The Shepherd leads. He has given us His Word to guide us each day; the Spirit to provide strength and courage; and Wisdom.

Wisdom calls out to us His will. We are to go where He directs, in the path He chooses for each of us. One of the Shepherd's sheep, George MacDonald wrote a poem to encourage us on our way:

I said: "Let me walk in the field";
God said: "Nay, walk in the town";
I said: "There are no flowers there";
He said: No flowers, but a crown."

I said: "But the sky is black,
There is nothing but noise and din";
But he wept as he sent me back,
"There is more," He said, "there is sin."

I said: "But the air is thick,
And fogs are veiling the sun";
He answered: "Yet souls are sick,
And souls in the dark undone."

I said: "I shall miss the light,
And friends will miss me, they say";
He answered me, "Choose tonight,
If I am to miss you, or they."

I pleaded for time to be given;
He said: "Is it hard to decide?
It will not seem hard in Heaven
To have followed the steps of your Guide."

I cast one look at the field,
Then set my face to the town;
He said: "My child, do you yield?
Will you leave the flowers for the crown?"

Then into His hand went mine,
and into my heart came He:
And I walk in a light Divine,
The path I had feared to see.
(By George McDonald 1824-1905)

We lifted our voices up all at once in a shout. "Praise the Lord, who made heaven and earth. Praise His Holy name!" And we begin our walk.

August 2

NKJV John 10:27 "My sheep listen to My voice. I know them and they follow Me."

WHERE HE LEADS ME

As the Shepherd calls us, we all prepare to worship Him before our journey. All of us are to sing this precious hymn whose lyrics provide the message we are about to perform on the walk.

Please join us in singing WHERE HE LEADS ME:

I can hear my Savior calling,
"Take thy cross and follow, follow Me."

I'll go with Him thru the judgment,
I'll go with Him, with Him, all the way.

He will give me grace and glory,
And go with me, with me all the way.

Where He leads me I will follow
I'll go with Him, with Him all the way.
(E. W. Blandy 19th Century)

As we all sing it sounds like one deep resounding voice, pure, clear, and strong. The Shepherd stands and smiles, and turns to go forward.

August 3

NKJV I John1:7 "Walk in the Light."

WALK WITH LIGHT

The Shepherd is leading. All eyes are fixed on Him. He has told us, "My Father is light and in Him is no darkness…at all! If you say that you have fellowship with Him, and yet you walk in darkness, you lie and do not practice the Truth. But if you walk in the Light, as My Father and I, are in the Light, because of this, we have fellowship with one another, and my blood cleanses all of you who are My sheep, from sin." (NAS I John 1:6-7)

"If anyone of My sheep says they do not have sin, they deceive themselves, and I, the Truth, is not in them. If you confess your sins, I will be faithful and just to forgive them, and to cleanse all of your unrighteousness. If you say that you have not sinned, you make Me a liar, and My word is not in you!" (NKJV I John 1:8-10)

"With me, you have an advocate, I Am the propitiation (appeasement) for your sins, and not just for you My sheep, but for the sins of the whole world. I plead for you before My Father. I Am your intercessor; your advocate (one called alongside), and the Holy Spirit is also in this work. I Am the propitiation (peace maker). Paying the price, I satisfied the judgment of God for all sin, for all time." (NKJV I John 2: 1-2)

"I ask My Father to grant you pardon, because on your behalf, I paid the price for your salvation."

Because of the Light up ahead, I can see, and I know I am walking in these *paths of righteousness*. Because, I am walking with the Light.

August 4

NKJV John 12:35 "Walk while you have the light …"

WALK IN THE LIGHT

As we walk in *the paths of righteousness* our Shepherd is preparing us to walk through *the valley of the shadow of death*. We must learn to walk through this valley, on the right paths.

Listen to His instruction. "Those who love their life here will lose their life, and those who hate their lives in this world will keep it for eternity. If anyone serves Me, let them follow Me; and where I am, there My servants will be also. If anyone serves Me, those My Father will honor."

"Whenever I Am lifted up, I will draw all to Myself. A little while longer the Light is with you. Walk while you have the Light, lest darkness overtakes you; those who walk in darkness do not know where they are going. While you have the Light, believe in the Light, that you may become children of Light."

He cries out to us from the hilltop. "Those who believe in Me, believes not only in Me, but in Him who sent Me. I have come as a Light into the world, so that whoever believes in Me should not abide in darkness. And if anyone hears My words, and does not believe, I do not judge them; for I did not come to judge the world, but to SAVE the world. Those who reject Me, and does not receive My Words, have that which judges them, the Word that I have spoken will judge them in the last day. For I have not spoken on My own *authority;* but the FATHER who sent Me gave Me a command, what I say and what I should speak. And I know that His command is everlasting life. Therefore, whatever I speak, just as the Father has told Me, SO I SPEAK."

He turns and continues on the walk *in the paths of righteousness.* (NIV John 12: 35-55)

"Oh dearest God, I am following the Light of this dark world - you."

August 5

NKJV Ephesians 5:8 "Walk as children (sheep) of Light."

WALK - IN LIGHT

The Shepherd travels ahead as the Light for our journey. For we were once in darkness, but now we are Light in the Lord. We walk as children of Light, each step guided by the Word that expresses what is acceptable to the Lord, our Shepherd. We are to have no fellowship with the unfruitful works of darkness, but we should expose them. For it is shameful even to speak of those things which are done in secret by evil persons dressed in sheep's clothing, but all things that are exposed are made manifest by the light.

Walk in the Light as He, *our* Shepherd is in the Light. Know the Savior, our Shepherd's standards. The Light shines in us when we are lit up by His holy righteousness, produced by the Spirit of Truth. By the power of the indwelling of the Holy Spirit, a sheep can alter the inherent consequences of sin.

The Shepherd says …

"Awake, you who sleep
arise from the dead
and I will give you light."
(NKJV Ephesians 5:14)

Oh may we walk in the Light of the Lord. Radiating so all in the world may see the Shepherd. As we walk we sing PSALM ONE HUNDRED NINETEEN NKJ:

Thy word is a lamp unto my feet
and a light unto my path.
I have sworn and confirmed
that I keep your righteous judgments.
(verse 105)

Revive me according to Your word ...
Your testimonies I have taken as a
heritage forever,
for they are the rejoicing of my heart.
(verse 25 & 111)

I have inclined my heart to perform
Your statutes forever,
to the very end.
... I long for Your salvation, O Lord,
and Your law is my delight.
(verse 112 & 174)

I have gone astray as a lost sheep;
therefore, seek your servant, oh Shepherd;
For I do not forget Your commandments.
(verse 176)

Oh for the joy set before us. The joy of the Lord, who is *my* Shepherd, the giver of Light.

August 6

NKJV Matthew 5:14 "Walk in the Light ... you are the Light of the world."

WALK - LET YOUR LIGHT SHINE

The Shepherd stops, and turns. He waves His hand over all of His sheep, and says: "You are the light of the world. A city that is set on a hill cannot be hidden. Nor does anyone light a lamp and put it under a basket, but on a lamp stand, and it gives light to all who are in the house. Let your light so shine before men, that they may see your good works, and glorify your Father in heaven." (NKJV Matthew 5:14-16)

"Do not think that I came to destroy the law or the prophets. I did not come to destroy but to fulfill. For I say to you, till heaven and earth passes away, one jot or one tittle will by no means pass from the law till all is fulfilled. Whoever breaks one of the least of these commandments and teaches men so, shall be called least in the Kingdom of heaven; but whoever does keep the law and teaches them, he shall be called great in the Kingdom of heaven. For I say to you, that unless your righteousness exceeds the righteousness of the Pharisees (hypocrites), you will by no means enter the Kingdom of heaven!" (NKJV Matthew 5:17-20)

He turns and we continue *the walk in the paths of righteousness.*

We follow. Our life is the light that symbolizes a beacon of purity and revelation, attracting all sinners to come out of the darkness into Life, the Life who is the Light of the Word, the Lord, *my* Shepherd.

Listen as we sing THIS LITTLE LIGHT OF MINE:

This little light of mine
I'm gonna let it shine.
Every day, Every day
I'm gonna let my
Little light shine.
(By Harry Dixon Loes, 1892-1965, Copyright circa, 1920)

August 7

NKJV John 12:35 "Walk while you have the Light, lest darkness overtake you; While you have the light believe in the light.

WALK - WHILE YOU HAVE LIGHT

The Shepherd stops us to rest awhile. He begins to teach us another lesson about the light.

"If I be lifted up from the earth, I will draw all peoples to Myself ... A little longer the Light is with you. Walk while you have the Light, lest darkness overtakes you; Those who walk in darkness do not know where they are going. While all of you, My sheep, have the Light, believe in the Light, that you may become sheep of the Light."

He lifted His head and cried out very loudly to all of us."Lay not up for yourselves treasures upon earth, where moth and rust corrupt, and where thieves break through and steal:but lay up for yourselves treasures in heaven, where neither moth nor rust corrupt, and where thieves do not break through nor steal:For where your treasure is, there will your heart be also.I Am the Light Provider.With Me you will live and be satisfied.Because, you Walk in Me the Light of this world."

He turns around and we all walk in the newness of righteous paths.

As we begin to walk we sing SEND THE LIGHT:

> *Send the light*
> *The blessed gospel light*
> *Let it shine from shore to shore.*
> *Let it shine forevermore.*
> *(By Charles H. Gabriel 1856-1932, Public Domain)*

August 8

NKJV Isaiah 30:21 "This is the Way, walk in it."

WALK - HIS FOOTSTEPS

As we continue to walk in the path of right living we listen as our Shepherd calls out to us, and we follow.

"This is the way. Walk in it, whenever you turn to the right hand, or whenever you turn to the left. As you walk with Me, I will feed you and gently gather the lambs in My arms; and I will carry them in My bosom, *and* gently lead those who are with young." (NKJV Isaiah 40:11)

"Have you not known? Have you not heard? Has it not been told you from the beginning? Have you not understood from the foundations of the earth? It is I who sits above the circle of the earth. To whom then will you liken Me, or to whom shall I be equal?" He suddenly stops and turns around and cries out to us with a voice of joy, waving His hands to the heavens. (NKJV Isaiah 40: 21-22)

"Lift up your eyes on high, and see Who has created these things. Who brings out their host by number; it is I. I call them all by name by the greatness of My might and the strength of My power!" (NKJV Isaiah 40:26)

He again begins the walk. We follow. "Have you not known? Have you not heard? The everlasting God, the Lord, the creator of the ends of the earth, neither faints nor is weary. His understanding is unsearchable. He gives power to the weak, and to those who have no might He increases strength.

Even the youths shall faint and be weary, and the young men shall utterly fall, but those who wait on Me shall renew *their* strength; you shall mount up with wings like eagles; you shall run and not be weary; you shall WALK and not faint." (NKJV Isaiah 40: 28-31)

We feel His strength to walk, we are strong because He provides all of our needs. We are not weary. Today we sing a special song FOOTSTEPS OF JESUS. It is in honor of the Lord, *my* Shepherd.

Sweetly, Lord, have we heard Thee calling,Come, follow Me!
And we see where Thy footprints falling Lead us to Thee.
Footprints of Jesus,That make the pathway glow;
We will follow the steps of Jesus Where'er they go.
(Mary B. C. Slade 1826-1882)

August 9

NKJV Micah 6:8 "Walk humbly with your God?"

WALK - HUMBLY

The paths that lie before us have one way, the way of our Lord, *my* Shepherd. With Him in this path, we are to follow His examples. He walks humbly with God the Father. Therefore, we must do likewise.

He has stated that there are three requirements along *the paths of righteousness.* They are not what we sometimes assume them to be. Big sacrifices of money, or time, or even family; running from here to there, showing how hard we work for Him. Letting the world know that we do these things for God because they are seen by Men! NO!

He said -

#1 "Do Justly:" - allow the Holy Spirit to guide you. In so doing, never take your eyes off the Shepherd, who never takes His eyes off our Father God.
#2 "Love Mercy" - observe as the Shepherd shows mercy to all mankind. Every soul is precious in His sight. He opens up His arms of mercy to all.
#3 "Walk Humbly" - Our Shepherd showed complete humility as He bowed to the Lord and said - "Not My will but Thine be done!" His strength obliterated the horrible consequences of sin once for all. Death and sin was conquered because of the humility of Jesus Christ our Lord, *my* Shepherd.

Look ahead - follow Him - the Lord, *my* Shepherd.

August 10

NKJV Romans 6:4 "We should walk in newness of life."

WALK - IN THE NEW LIFE

As we *walk in these paths of righteousness*, we have begun a new way, with the Shepherd. He told us before the journey these words. "For you are united with Me in the likeness of My death, so now you are certainly in the likeness of My resurrection. You know that Your old selves were crucified with Me, that the body of sin might be done away with, so that you should no longer be slaves of sin. For those of you who have died have been freed from sin. For if you died with the Lamb of God, you believe that you shall also *live* with Me, knowing that I, the Shepherd having been raised from the dead, dies no more. Death no longer has dominion over Me. I died to sin once for all; but the *life* that I live I live to God. Likewise you also yourselves are dead to sin, but alive to God in Me, the Lord, *your* Shepherd." (NKJV Romans 6:5-11)

He said, "Therefore do not let sin reign in your mortal bodies, that you should obey it in its lust, and do not present your members as instruments of unrighteousness to sin, but present yourselves to God as being alive from the dead, and your members as instruments of *righteousness* to God. For sin shall not have dominion over you, for we are not under the law, but under **GRACE**." (NKJV Romans 6:12-14)

"So now, you must present your bodily members as slaves of righteousness, having been set free from sin, and having become slaves of God, you present your lives as holy, and at the end receive everlasting life. For the wages of sin is death, but the gift of God, our Father, is eternal life in Jesus Christ, your Lord, *your* Shepherd." (NKJV Romans 6:20-23)

This is our path, the path of new life, in righteous living. That same life of *our* Shepherd, the Lord. We now will sing the hymn STEPPING IN THE LIGHT:

Trying to walk in the steps of the Savior,
trying to follow our Savior and King;
Shaping our lives by His blessed example,
Happy, how happy, the songs that we bring.
Pressing more closely to Him who is leading,
when we are tempted to turn from the way;
Trusting the arm that is strong to defend us,
happy, how happy, our praises each day.

How beautiful to walk
in the steps of the Savior.
Stepping in the light, stepping in the light.
How beautiful to walk
in the steps of the Savior.
As in paths of light.
(By E. E. Hewitt 1851- 1920)

August 11

NKJV II Corinthians 5:7 "We walk by faith and not by sight."

WALK - BY FAITH

Faith is the evidence of things not seen. The Shepherd is the light showing us the Way in this path of right living. We only see Him. Outside of Him is the cosmos of darkness the world. Complete Spiritual darkness. Therefore, each step is a move, by faith and is not by sight. We are confident, and well pleased to be here at home in the body, but soon, we will be pleased to be absent from this body and present with the Lord.

We who are in this body groan at being burdened, not because we want to be unclothed, but further clothed; that mortality may be swallowed up by Life. As He said … "I Am … Life." Our Shepherd who has prepared this walk, gave us the Spirit, to go along with us, as a guarantee. The Spirit is a counselor and friend, who will walk with us, directing our every step on these paths.

Here are the Shepherd's words of comfort … "For each day our outward nature is passing away, yet the inward nature is being renewed, day by day, step by step. For our light affliction, which is but a moment, is working for us a far more exceeding and eternal weight of glory, while we do not look at the things which are seen, but at the Shepherd whose the Light that shines before us, the *Shakina*. For any of the things seen on the earth are temporary, but the things seen in the Light, our Lord, *our* Shepherd *are* eternal …" (RS II Corinthians, 4:16-18 paraphrased)

We are walking by faith and not by sight. In the Light the *paths of righteousness* are easily seen.

August 12

NKJV Galatians 5:16 "Walk in the Spirit and you shall not fulfill the lust of the flesh."

WALK - IN THE SPIRIT

The Holy Spirit bids us to walk in Him. That simply means, to allow Him to fill us completely, by willing Him complete control of *our* wills. Walking in Him requires a direct confrontation with what our own flesh desires to do. The deeds of the flesh must become unimportant and undesirable as we choose to do the things of the Spirit. Therefore, we follow Love's Way, that of the Shepherd.

Here are His Words. "If you walk in the Spirit, you will not fulfill the lust of the flesh. For the flesh lusts against the Spirit, and the Spirit against the flesh; and these are contrary to each other. (NKJV Galatians 5:16-17) These fleshly works have been listed by the Word. They are evident in the lives of those that choose them."

Here is a list of deeds done in the dark, by those who are of the flesh.

- Adultery
- Fornication
- Uncleanness
- Lewdness
- Idolatry
- Sorcery
- Hatred
- Contentions
- Jealousies
- Outburst of wrath
- Selfish Ambitions
- Derisions
- Heresies
- Envy
- Murders
- Drunkenness
- Revelries

To walk and live in the Spirit, means that the Spirit's fruit is produced, and the flesh with its passions and desires is crucified. The following list are attributes of a sheep's featured characteristics as he or she walks in the paths of righteousness for His name's sake:

- Love
- Joy
- Peace

Long-suffering
Kindness
Goodness
Faithfulness
Gentleness
Self-Control

Wow! This is a no brainer! I'm following Jesus, *my* Lord, *my* Shepherd.

August 13

NKJV Ephesians 5:2 "Walk in love ..."

WALK - IN LOVING KINDNESS

The ultimate path to walk in is the path of love, For we are to be imitators of God as His dear sheep. The Shepherd loves us, and has given Himself for us as an offering and a sacrifice to God.

In His *paths of righteousness*, no uncleanness, fornication nor covetousness, should be among us, as we are saints; also no filthiness, foolish talking coarse jesting, but rather giving of thanks. For the Shepherd has taught us that no unclean sheep nor covetous sheep has any inheritance in His Kingdom. We must *not* be deceived by anyone who comes in sheep's clothing talking with empty words, for the wrath of God our Father comes upon those sheep who disobey. Do not join in their work, because if you do, you are not in His *paths*!

If we have heard Him and have been taught by Him, the Truth and the Way: then we have put off, our former conduct. The old person who grew corrupt according to the deceitful lusts, will be renewed in the spirit of their minds. Therefore they will walk according to the Holy Spirit.

Remember He said "Put away lying. Let each one of you speak truth with their neighbor, for we are members of one another. Be angry, and do not sin, do not let the sun go down on your wrath, nor give place to the devil. Let no corrupt word proceed out of your mouth, but what is good for edification, that it may impart grace to the hearers. Do not grieve the Holy Spirit of God by whom we were sealed for the day of redemption. Let all bitterness, wrath, anger, clamor, and evil speaking be put away from you, with *all* malice (revenge). **Be kind one to another, tenderhearted, forgiving one another, even as God in Christ forgave you.**" (NKJV Ephesians 4:25-32)

We all *walk in the paths of righteousness* with the Shepherd's lead. He lights this walk with pure, unadulterated, absolute loving kindness.

August 14

NKJV Ephesians 5:15 "See that you walk circumspectly; not as fools but as wise …"

WALK - IN WISDOM

The Shepherd has explained, how the path of Wisdom includes all of His Word, from the beginning of time, until His return to take us home. His Words: "Now we must redeem the time, because the days are evil. Those who walk in integrity walk securely."

He also said… "Do not be unwise, but understand what My will is for you. Do not be drunk with wine, in which is dissipation, but be filled with the Spirit, speaking to each other in psalms and hymns and spiritual songs, singing and making melody in your heart to Me, giving thinks always for all things to God the Father in My name, the Lord Jesus Christ, submitting to one another in the fear of God." (NKJV Ephesians 5:17-21)

He further explained that The Church is essential for communication and for edifying one another. The Shepherd encourages all sorts of speech, singing the Psalms; singing hymns, and Spiritual songs (spontaneous, Spirit inspired praise); and just speaking kindly to each other. (NKJV 5:15-21)

"Finally, mutually submit to each other. Submission begins in the family. Fathers, mothers and children submit to God. God's will must be sought in all decisions, for Wisdom is of God, and Me."

As we walk in these *paths of righteousness*, the Shepherd knows what is best. He leads us in paths that are right and good. His will is good and perfect. May we follow in His pathways of right living.

August 15

NKJV Colossians 1:10 "Walk worthy of the Lord …"

WALK - WORTHY

The Shepherd speaks His Word.

"I work in you mightily as you walk worthy of Me, always pleasing Me. We are to be fruitful in every good work, increasing constantly in the knowledge of God; straightened with all might, according to His glorious power, for all patience and long-suffering with joy; giving thanks to the Father who has qualified us to be partakers of the inheritance of the Saints in the light. He has delivered us from the power of darkness, and conveyed us into the Kingdom of the Son, who redeemed us through the blood sacrifice, and gave us forgiveness of sins." (NKJV Colossians 1:10-14)

"For it pleases the Father that in the Lamb, who is His Son, all the fullness should dwell, and by Him to reconcile all things to Himself, by Him, whether things on earth or things in Heaven having made peace through the blood of the Lamb's cross." (NKJV Colossians 1:19-21)

Our Shepherd is the exact replica of God Himself. For by Him all things were created that are in heaven and that are on earth, visible and invisible, weather thrones or dominions or principalities or powers. All things were created through Him, and for Him. The Shepherd is before all things, and in Him all things consist. He is the head of the Body the Church, who is the beginning, the Firstborn from the dead, that in all things He may have preeminence. (NKJV Colossians 1:15-18)

To us, His Saints, His sheep, God willed to make known what are the riches of the glory of this mystery: which is Christ in us, the hope of glory. Him we must preach, warning every person and teaching every person in all wisdom that we may present every sheep perfect in Christ Jesus; our Lord, our Shepherd. To this end we must labor, according to our Shepherd's working which works in His sheep mightily. Walk Worthy … (NKJV 1:27-29 paraphrased)

The above writing is from the Word of *our* Shepherd. He provides the way, because He is the Way!

August 16

NKJV Revelation 3:4 "They shall walk with Me in white, for they are worthy."

WALK - IN ROBES OF WHITE

The Shepherd commands us to walk in the appropriate attire. To be worthy, holy, and pure before God our Father is not a suggestion, it is a requirement. The Shepherd's reputation is built on the activity, well-being, and obedience of His sheep. We should look, act and react exactly as the Shepherd does.

The world gets to know the Shepherd by the actions of His Sheep. The name of our Shepherd is JEHOVAH SAVES. We must never desire to disgrace His name. We must remember whose we are: and who we are; the sheep of His pasture.

The Shepherd has stated over and over that we are the sheep of His pasture. He said "My name is linked to you, I know those who are Mine;" and "Let everyone who names the name of the Lord depart from iniquity." (NKJV II Timothy 2:19)

God our Father, mandates Holiness, in our walk with the Shepherd, through our everyday life. He has set a standard that is different than the standard of the world. His sheep should lead a pure life, in accordance with the Shepherd's call, and commandments. A holy life lived in the white robe is a life set apart, a life of *always* choosing to walk with the Shepherd, the Father, and the Spirit desire.

The Spirit works with the transformed heart of the sheep, so that he or she is no longer conformed to their old desire. This is made possible by the sacrifice of the Lamb, *our* Shepherd.

The Lord is *my* Shepherd. He never commands us to do anything that He does not enable us to do. No sheep can make themselves white; but if we desire to be holy as He is holy, and set our wills down and pick up His will, He will dress us in robes of white.

He ends the lesson with these words. "You shall be holy to Me, for I the Lord am holy, and have separated you from the peoples, that you should be mine."

We all wear our robes of white *walking in the paths of righteousness for HIS NAMES SAKE.*

August 17

NKJV Acts 9:31 "And walking in the fear of the Lord and in the comfort of the Holy Spirit …"

WALK - IN THE FEAR OF THE LORD

We always see *our* Shepherd walking ahead step by step. He is never in a hurry, persevering step after step. We have no fear of the predators, only the respectful fear of Him who sends the Holy Spirit's comfort.

We must absolutely follow the Shepherd. We must never look back or around at the darkness that surrounds us. We observe Him, and we love the Light that is He, the Shepherd, the Light of the world.

The fear of our Lord brings obedience. We seek to obey because nothing can harm us. We are kept safe in His arms, by His rod and staff. As we meditate on His Word, the Spirit and wisdom.

Wisdom teaches us that walking in the fear of the Lord is wise, and not foolish. Listen as she calls out to us, while walking by His side.

The fear of the Lord is the beginning of Wisdom.
And the knowledge of the Holy One is understanding.
Receive My instruction, and not silver,
and knowledge rather than choice gold;
For Wisdom is better than rubies, and all the things
one may desire cannot be compared to Me, Wisdom.

*The fear of the Lord is to hate evil; pride and arrogance, and
the evil way, and the perverse mouth.*

*The Lord possessed Me at the beginning of His way.
Before His works of old.
I have been established from everlasting,
From the beginning, before there was ever an earth.
When there were no depths I was brought forth,
When there were no fountains abounding with water.
Before the mountains were settled, before the hill, I was brought forth;
While as yet He had not made the earth or the fields,
or the primal dust of the world.
When He prepared the heavens, I was there.
When He drew a circle on the face of the deep,
When He established the clouds above,
When he strengthened the fountains of the deep,
When He assigned to the sea its limit,
So that the waters would not transgress His command,
When He marked out the foundations of the earth,
Then I was beside Him as a Master craftsman;
And I was daily His delight, rejoicing always before Him,
Rejoicing in his inhabited world …
(NKJV Proverbs 8:10-9:12)*

To follow Wisdom is an act of faithful and obedient service. The result is comfort, and peace, by the Spirit.

May we all sing TO GOD BE THE GLORY as we continue *to walk in the paths of righteousness*.

*To God be the glory
great things He has done.
So loved He the world
that He gave us His son.
Who yielded His life
and atonement for sin.
And opened the life gate
that all may go in.
(By Fanny J. Crosby 1820-1915)*

August 18

NKJV Psalm 1:1 "Blessed is the person who walks ..."

WALKS

A sheep walks either down the path leading to life, or down the path leading to death.

These ways are clearly defined by the teaching and guidance of our Shepherd.

First: **Avoid destructive relationships.**

> "Blessed is the sheep who walks not in the counsel of the ungodly, nor stands in the *path* of sinners, nor sits in the seat of the scornful ..." (NKJV Psalm 1:1)

Second: **Delight continually in God's Word.**

> "Their delight is in the law of the Lord, and in His law they meditate both day and night." (NKJV Psalm 1:2)

Third: **Achieve stability and productivity.**

> "That sheep shall be like a tree planted by the rivers of water that brings forth its fruit in its season, whose leaf also shall not wither and whatever they do shall prosper. And the Lord, *my* Shepherd knows the way of the righteous." (NKJV Psalm 1:3)

The Shepherd has also warned us of the path leading to death

First: **Experience instability.**

> "They are known as ungodly, sinners, scornful; they are like chaff, rubbish which the wind drives away." (NKJV Psalm 1:4)

Second: **Experience defeat and isolation.**

> "The ungodly shall not sit in the judgment seat, nor stand in the congregation of the righteous." (NKJV Psalm 1:5)

Third: **Experience separation from God and the Shepherd, and shall parish.**

> "The troubled evil doer who rejects God's will, experiences calamity and ultimate ruin." (NKJV Psalm 1:6)

He said "My sheep who knows and does the will of My Father is the essence of Wisdom. Stability and fruitfulness belongs to that sheep who focuses continually on obeying God."

He continues expressing the rejecter's ruin. Because of their path of unrighteousness they deny salvation and refuse to follow our Father God."

I have chosen *the paths of righteousness* where *my* Shepherd leads **His** sheep. I'm walking with Jesus.

We close by singing this hymn. WALKING WITH JESUS:

Walking in the sunrise
Walking in the shadows
Walking with Jesus,
Walking everyday,
All along the way,
I'm walking with Jesus alone.
(Barney E. Warren 1867-1951, Copyright Public Domain)

August 19

NKJV Psalm 23:4 "Yea, thought I walk through the valley of the shadow of death, I will fear no evil."

I WALK - THROUGH

We are now entering the *valley of the shadow of death.* I know the statistics in this valley are that one out of every one person dies. The valley is filled, with sin, and extreme evil as we are all bound for death and the grave.

Satan is the ruler of the valley and he intrigues all travelers with many paths of destruction. Everyone from the beginning of time to the end of time, will walk in this valley.

What is important to my Shepherd, as we walk through the valley of the shadow of death, is that His Wisdom becomes the path we sheep must walk. As described in His Word ... "His wisdom is from above and is first pure, then peaceable, gentle, willing to yield, full of mercy and good fruits, without partiality and without hypocrisy." (NKJV James 3:15-17)

Listen to Him! "The wisdom that is not from above is earthly, sensual and demonic. It produces bitter envy and is self-seeking. Those who choose these paths boast and lie against the Truth, for where envy and self-seeking exist, confusion and every evil thing *are* there." (NKJV James 3:13-16)

The source of the wisdom of this world originates with the devil and his demons. The Wisdom from above originates in the heart and mind of God. Godly Wisdom, communicates concern for others through a gentle, yielding, merciful Spirit; earthly wisdom, is selfish and reveals a bitter jealousy toward detractors; Godly wisdom is productive; earthly wisdom confuses and tears down through evil intent.

The Shepherd has given us complete protection concerning the extreme danger ahead. He has made it quite clear that we should have no fear, because He is with us, every moment of every day until we cross over into *the house of the Lord forever.*

We all sing as we *walk in the paths of righteousness.* Today we will be singing the hymn THIS WORLD IS NOT MY HOME:

> *This world is not my home,*
> *I'm just a passing through,*
> *My treasures are laid up*
> *Somewhere beyond the blue;*
> *The angels beckon me from heaven's open door,*
> *and I can't feel at home in this world any more.*
> *(By J R Baxter, Jr, Copyright 1946)*

August 20

NKJV Psalm 23:4 "Yeah, though I walk through the valley of the shadow of death. I will fear no evil, for Thou art with me."

THE VALLEY

Death is both a stubborn and uncertain fact. No sheep knows the day nor the hour that his or her death will come. The Shepherd holds life and death in His hand. Praise be to the Lord death is but a shadow and that there can be no shadow without a light. A shadow cannot hurt us. It can scare us and make us fearful, but *our* Shepherd has stressed, we're to not fear evil, nor death's shadow.

We will walk by God's saving grace through this *valley of the shadow of death.* Remember His words. "The sheep who walks in darkness sees the great light; all of us dwell in the land of the *shadow of death*, and upon us a light has shined." (NKJV Isaiah 9:2)

*There is therefore now no condemnation to those
who are in Christ Jesus, who do not walk according to the flesh,
but according to the spirit.
For the law of the Spirit of life in Christ Jesus
has made me free from the law of sin and death.
For what the law could not do in that it was weak through the flesh,
God did by sending His own Son in the likeness
of sinful flesh, on account of sin:
He condemned sin in the flesh,
that the righteous requirement of the law
might be fulfilled in us who do not walk according
to the flesh but according to the Spirit.
For those who live according to the flesh
set their minds on the things of the flesh,
but those who live according to the Spirit, the things of the Spirit.
For to be carnally minded is death,
but to be spiritually minded is life and peace.
Because the carnal mind is enmity against God;
for it is not subject to the law of God, nor indeed can be.
So then, those who are in the flesh cannot please God.
But you are not in the flesh but in the Spirit,
if indeed the Spirit of God dwells in you.
Now if anyone does not have the Spirit of Christ,
they are not His. And if Christ is in you,
the body is dead because of sin,
but the Spirit is life because of righteousness.
But if the spirit of Him who raised Jesus from the dead dwells in you,
He who raised Christ from the dead will also give life
to your mortal bodies through His Spirit who dwells in you.
(NKJV Romans 8: 1-11)*

The Shepherd has designed every part of our walk to be one of peace and joy in Him. May we praise and worship Him as we *walk through the valley of the shadow of death.*

August 21

NKJV Romans 8:37 "Yet in all these things we are more than conquerors through Him who loved us."

THE SHADOW OF DEATH

Our Shepherd has given us complete victory over this walk through death's valley. Here are more of His comforting words that explain what is happening as we walk i*n the paths of righteousness, through the valley of the shadow of death.*

What can we ever say to such wonderful things as these?
If God is on our side, who can ever be against us?
Since He did not spare even His own Son for us
but gave Him up for us all,
won't He also surely give us everything else?
Who dares accuse us whom God has chosen for His own?
Will God? No!
He is the one who has forgiven us
and given us right standing with Himself.

Who then will condemn us? Will Christ? NO!
For He is the one who died for us and came back to life again for us
and is sitting at the place of highest honor next to God,
pleading for us there in heaven.

Who then can ever keep Christ's love from us?
When we have trouble or calamity,
when we are hunted down or destroyed,
is it because He doesn't love us anymore?
And if we are hungry, or penniless,
or in danger, or threatened with death, has God deserted us?
No, for the Scriptures tell us that for His sake
we must be ready to face death at every moment
of the day - we are like sheep awaiting slaughter;
But despite all this, overwhelming victory is ours
through Christ who loved us enough to die for us.

For I am convinced that nothing can
ever separate us from His love.
Death can't, and life can't. The angels won't,
and all the powers of hell itself cannot keep God's love away.
Our fears for today, our worries about tomorrow.

*Or where we are - high above the sky, or in the deepest ocean - nothing
will ever be able to separate us from the love of God
demonstrated by our Lord Jesus Christ when He died for us.
(NLT Romans 8:31-39)*

We all sing the hymn THE LOVE OF GOD. The love that is absolutely incomprehensible.

*The love of God is greater far
than tongue or pen can ever tell,
it goes beyond the highest star
and reaches to the lowest hell;
(By Frederick Lehman 1868-1953, Copyright 1917)*

August 22

NKJV Isaiah 9:2 "The people who walked in darkness Have seen a great light; Those who dwelt in the land of *the shadow of death*, upon them a light has shined."

THE VIEW

As we travel *the paths of righteousness*, it becomes evident that in the shadow valley, death is inevitable. The view from this valley of death is fearful!

However, death has no power over those sheep who follow the Shepherd. After all, He has just told us "Those who dwelt in the land of *the shadow of death*, upon them a light has shined ... and those of us who must walk in darkness have seen a great light." He walks His sheep through the dark shadowed valley with the Light. (NAS Isaiah 9:2)

Of course this valley has high mountains on every side, for there can be no valley without mountains, just as there is no evil, without a greater good. Mountains are reflected throughout His Word, to signify glorious Spiritual blessings, embracing God's sovereignty.

The following three lessons will be about mountains that are a part of His teaching. These mountains provide a view of what He has prepared for us now and forever.

Many extraordinary events took place on the Lord's mountains. The Shepherd climbed mountains to change the course of mankind. May we take a closer look at three of these mountains and see our Shepherd's love poured out like a great water fall, into the *valley of the shadow of death*. Bringing grace, mercy, and forgiveness to all who will accept Him *as their* Shepherd.

There He stands at the top of that path leading to the mountain top. We follow, the Lord, *my* Shepherd.

August 23

NKJV Matthew 17: 1 "Jesus … led them up on a high mountain …"

MOUNT OF TRANSFIGURATION

The **Mountain of Transfiguration** took place, approximately one week before His death. He took three witnesses, Peter, James and John, to this miraculous viewing. On this mountain, God reinforced, that His Son, was the One who would pay the price, to transform our souls.

Our Shepherd was changed; His face brightly glowed like the sun; His clothing become so white that it became a flood light!

As the three disciples looked on in awe, they saw the Lord, our Shepherd conversing with Moses and Elijah. Moses represented the Old Testament law, and Elijah represented the prophets.

As they were visiting, a bright cloud completely covered them. God yelled out "This is My Son, My chosen One; Listen to Him!" This confirmed that redemption was from the beginning, and that those who had passed, went directly into the Kingdom of God.

The Apostles, Peter, James and John, represented for that time Israel in the flesh and future Kingdom (NKJV Acts1:6 / Ezekiel 37:21-27); and the crowd at the foot of the mountain represented the nations who are to enter the Kingdom after it is established over Israel; (NKJV Isaiah 11:19-12); and the representation of the second coming, "The Son of Man coming in His glory." (NKJV Matthew 16:28)

The apostles wrote… "We were eyewitnesses of His majesty. For our Lord, *my* Shepherd, received from God the Father, honor and glory, when such a voice came to Him from the excellent Glory: 'This is My beloved Son, in whom I Am well pleased.' "We heard this voice, which came from heaven, when we were with our Shepherd, on the holy mountain."

Peter said this before His death. (NKJV II Peter 1:17-18)

So we all look to the Shepherd and say … "The God of peace who brought up our Lord Jesus from the dead, that great Shepherd of us sheep, through His blood of the everlasting covenant, we are transformed and made complete in every good work to do His perfect will; He works in us what is well pleasing in His sight, through Jesus Christ the Lord *our* Shepherd, to whom be all glory forever, and forever." (NAS Hebrews 13: 20-21)

We shall be eternally transformed, as we *walk in the paths of righteousness*.

August 24

NKJV Psalm 22: 1 "My God, My God why have you forsaken Me?"

MOUNT CALVARY

Our Shepherd built this mountain with His life, as the suffering and sacrificial Lamb who was sacrificed on Mount Calvary. The Lamb of God, *my* Shepherd took away the sins of the world.

He cried out ... "My God, My God, why have you forsaken Me?" (NKJV Psalm 22:1) His voice became soft and weak. "I am poured out like water ... My strength is dried up like a pot shed ... they pierced My hands and feet; they divided My garments among them; and for My clothing they cast lots." (NKJV Psalm 22:14-15)

Here on Mount Calvary He suffered and died. The Lamb of God took away the sins of the world, once for all time. And everyone must bump into Mount Calvary, for it is a mountain of love that is too high, too wide, and too deep for anyone to get through, without first making a choice to either accept that mountain of love, or reject it.

If He is accepted and becomes the Shepherd of your life, then you will no longer fear the walk *through the valley of the shadow of death*. He has paid the price with His precious blood, and washed away the mountain of sin.

We all continue to walk and sing I BELIEVE IN A HILL CALLED MOUNT CALVARY. A perfect song to sing as we walk these *paths of righteousness through the Valley of the shadow of death*. So sing. I BELIEVE IN A HILL CALLED MOUNT CALVARY:

I believe in a hill called Mount Calvary
I believe whatever the cost
And when time has surrendered
And earth is no more
I'll still cling to the old rugged cross
(By Dale Oldham, Gloria Gaither and William J. Gaither, Copyright 1968)

August 25

NKJV Hebrews 12:22 "For you have come right up into mount Zion ..."

MOUNT ZION

On Mount Zion is where the final victory is celebrated. The Lord is sovereign, and He brings all of His sheep to Mount Zion. As we walk *through the valley of the shadow of death* there is only joy and peace, because Mount Zion is our final destination. The Spirit reveals to us, and comforts us, providing assurance that The King of Glory's Kingdom reigns in our heart!

The shepherd, King David, sings of this mountain:

The earth is the Lord's and all its fullness
the world and those who dwell therein.
For He has founded it upon the seas,
and established it upon the waters.

Who may ascend into the hill of the Lord?
He who has clean hands and a pure heart,
who has not lifted up his soul to an idol,
nor sworn deceitfully.
Lift up your heads, o you gates!

Lift up, your everlasting doors!
And the King of glory shall come in.
Who is the King of glory?
The Lord strong and mighty
The Lord mighty in battle.
The Lord of hosts,
He is the King of Glory!
(NKJV Psalm 24:1-10)

But you have come right up into Mount Zion,
to the city of the living God, the heavenly Jerusalem,
and to the gathering of countless happy angels;
and to the church,
composed of all those registered in heaven;
and to God who is Judge of all;
and to the spirits of the redeemed in heaven,
already made perfect;

and to Jesus Himself,
who has brought us His wonderful new agreement;
and to the sprinkled blood
which graciously forgives ...
(NKJV Hebrews 12: 22-25)

We can see Mount Zion the place of our eternal home, ahead. All of us who now follow the Shepherd have our destination in sight. We're on our way through *the valley of the shadow of death.*

August 26

NKJV Isaiah 50:11 " ...walk in the light of your fire, and in the sparks that you have kindled ..."

HIS WAY

God bade me go when I would stay
('Twas cool within the wood).
I did not know the reason why.
I heard a boulder crashing by
across the path where I stood.

He bade me stay when I would go;
"Thy will be done," I said
They found one day at early dawn,
across the way I would have gone,
a serpent with a mangled head.

No more I ask the reason why,
Although I may not see
The path ahead, His way I go;
for though I know not; He doth know,
and He will choose safe paths for me.
(Taken from Streams in the Desert, by Mrs. Charles E. Cowman)

To walk where *He leads me in the paths of righteousness* is a simple walk of faith. No looking to the left nor to the right but straight into the face of the Shepherd. Being still is also necessary. As the writing above explains, not one sheep knows what is happening one second from now.

Time after time, I personally thought I knew what to do or where to go, yet *my* Shepherd would lead otherwise and to my stubborn surprise, just as He promised, His way was good and perfect. All of us sheep follow the Way, *our* Shepherd, who is the Way, the Truth and the Life.

August 27

NKJV Psalm 9:11 "Sing praises to the Lord ..."

PRAISE

As King David writes and sings his Psalm, he is telling us that even though there is evil, Jehovah is with us, individually and collectively. On our journey *in the paths of righteousness* we shall sing the Psalms as we walk. These songs will keep us in perfect peace, and the inner joy of the Lord.

A sheep, Adrian Rogers, expressed it by saying: "He, the Truth is brighter than error; His grace is greater than our sin; *Our* Shepherd is greater than Satan; He, the Everlasting Life is greater than death. Jehovah is with me!"

Here is a list of the *IMAGES OF GOD IN THE PSALMS (NKJ)*:

Images of God	Reference in Psalms
Shield	3:3 / 119:114
King	5:2 / 74:12
Shepherd	23:1 / 80:1
Avenger	26:1
Creator	8:1, 6
Healer	30:2
Protector	5:11
Provider	78:23-29
Redeemer	107:2

Study the promises, *my* Shepherd, and *our* Father, made to *Their* sheep. Then sing out Psalm 100 ... "We are the sheep of His pasture. Enter unto His gates with thanksgiving and into His courts with praise." We all stand and sing I WILL ENTER HIS GATES WITH THANKSGIVING IN MY HEART:

I will enter his gates with thanksgiving in my heart,
I will enter his courts with praise.
I will say this is the day that the Lord has made.
I will rejoice, for He has made me glad.
He has made me glad: He has made me glad.
(By Leona Von Brethorst, Copyright 1976)

August 28

NKJV Psalm 5:8 "Make your way straight before my face."

SING OF - A PRAYER OF GUIDANCE

We are ever singing, as we walk each path, that He leads us on.

PSALM

But as for me,
I will come into Your house in the multitude of Your mercy.
In fear of You, I will worship
toward Your holy temple.
Lead me oh Lord, in Your righteousness, because of my enemies:
Make Your ways straight before my face.

But let all those rejoice who put their trust in You;
let them shout for joy,
because You defend them,
let those who love Your name, be joyful in You.

For You oh Lord, will bless
the righteous with favor
You will surround him
with a shield.
(NKJV Psalm 5:7-12)

As we walk and praise Him in song, we acknowledge God's mercy. His covenant love is often talked about as "loving kindness." He promises forgiveness, compassion, and blessing, and He is ever interceding. We then "fear" the Lord in reverent obedience. Protection, joy, and blessings surround us as we walk in faith, following our Shepherd. We sing at the top of our lungs!

We will continue to praise in Psalm as we are lead *in the paths of righteousness for His names sake.* So sing! I'VE GOT THE JOY:

> *I've got the joy, joy, joy, joy down in my heart,*
> *down in my heart, down in my heart!*
> *I've got the joy, joy, joy, joy down in my heart,*
> *down in my heart to stay!*
> *(By George W. Cooke 1848-1923)*

August 29

NKJV Psalm 18:2 "The Lord is my rock …"

SING OF - THE ROCK

We sing as we walk along the *paths of righteousness*, our songs are about our great appreciation of our Father's protection and His love. David composed this song declaring his love for the Lord and exalting the Lord.

> *Oh come let us sing to the Lord!*
> *Let us shout joyfully to the Rock of our salvation.*
> *Let us come before His presence with thanksgiving;*
> *Let us shout joyfully with Psalms …*
>
> *For the Lord is the great God*
> *and the great King above all gods.*
> *In His hand are the deep places of the earth;*
>
> *The heights of the hills are His also.*
> *The sea is His, for He made it;*
> *and His hands formed the dry land.*
>
> *Oh come, let us worship and bow down;*
> *Let us kneel before the Lord our Maker.*
> *For He is our God,*
> *And we are the people of His pasture,*
> *And the sheep of His hand.*
> *(NKJV PSALM 95:1-7:)*

Singing to our God as we walk on our journey clears our hearts and minds. We acknowledge who He is as we lift up His name in song. All of our singing, goes directly to the nostrils of our Father, and He breaths in the aroma of our sacrifice of praise, and thanksgiving. So sing! Sing unto the Lord, who is *our* Shepherd!

Today I am singing ROCK OF AGES. For He is my Rock of Salvation:

Rock of Ages! cleft for me,
Let me hide myself in Thee.
Let the Water and the Blood,
From Thy riven side that flowed,
Be of sin the double cure;
Saved from wrath and make me pure.
(By Augustus M. Toplady, 1740- 1778)

August 30

NKJV Psalm 3:3 "But you, O Lord, are a shield for Me …"

SING OF - THE SHIELD

Today our song expresses the image of God as our Shield. His shield is the "Shield of Faith." Our faith in Him covers our entire body, spirit, mind and soul. **The Faith Shield** protects us from the fiery arrows of the enemy.

So sing …

PSALM THREE (NKJ)

But you, oh Lord, are a shield
for me, my glory and One who lifts my head.
I cried to the Lord with my voice,
and He heard me from His holy hill.

My voice you shall hear in the morning,
O Lord,
In the morning I will direct it to You,
and I will look up!

Lead me, o Lord, in your righteousness ...
Make Your way straight before my face.
But let all those rejoice who put their trust in you;
Let them ever shout for joy,
because you defend them;
Let those also who love your name
be joyful in You.

For You, oh Lord, will bless the righteous;
With favor you will surround them as with a shield.

Blessed be the Lord
Because He has heard the voice of my supplication!
My heart trusted Him, and I am helped;
Therefore my heart greatly rejoices,
And with my song I will praise Him.

Oh Lord, your music brings joy to my heart and soul. I love to sing of Thy great mercy. You are my strength and my shield. Praise be to the Lord, *my* Shepherd.

August 31

NKJV Psalm 5:2 " ...my King and my God."

SING AND CLAP YOUR HANDS

The King who walks before us is not just *a* king, but the KING OF KINGS. And now, we sing praise to the King!

PSALM FIVE (NKJ)

My King and my God,
for to you I will pray.
My voice You shall hear in the morning, oh Lord;

In the morning I will direct it to you
... I will come into your house
in the multitude of Your mercy;

Cynthia Perkins

> *You are my King, O God;*
> *... In God we boast all day long,*
> *and praise Your name forever.*
>
> *My heart is overflowing with good things;*
> *I recite my composition concerning the King;*
> *My tongue is the pen of a ready writer.*
> *For God is my King ...*
> *working salvation in the midst of the earth.*
>
> *Oh clap your hands, all you peoples!*
> *Shout to God with a voice of triumph.*
> *For the Lord Most High is awesome;*
> *He is a great King over all the earth.*
>
> *... Sing praises to God, sing praises!*
> *Sing praises to our King of all the earth ...*
> *He is greatly exalted.*

Everyone sing CLAP YOUR HANDS:

> *Clap your hands all ye people*
> *shout unto God with a voice of triumph.*
> *Clap your hands all ye people*
> *shout unto God with a voice of praise*
>
> *Hosannah - Hosannah*
> *Shout unto God with a voice of triumph.*
> *Praise Him; Praise Him;*
> *Shout unto God with a voice of praise.*
> *(By James Lloyd Owens, Copyright 1972)*

September

September 1

NKJV Psalm 46:1 "God is my refuge and strength …"

SING OF - THE REFUGE

Every day as we *walk in the paths of righteousness* we need His strength and His covering to protect us. We are refugees fleeing from the flesh. Safety lies in the strength of our Lord, *our* Shepherd. He provides shelter, refuge and protection.

PSALM FORTY SIX (NKJ)

*God is our refuge and strength,
a present help in trouble.
Therefore we will not fear,
Even though the earth is removed
and though the mountains be carried
into the midst of the sea …*

*… The Lord of host is with us,
the God of Jacob is our refuge.*

May we sing the hymn written from the inspiration of this passage, A MIGHTY FORTRESS IS OUR GOD:

*A mighty Fortress is our God,
a bulwark never failing;
Our Helper He amid the flood
of mortal ills prevailing.*

*For still our ancient foe
Doth seek to work us woe
His craft and pow'r are great,
and armed with cruel hate,
on earth is not his equal.*

*Did we in our own strength confide,
our striving would be losing,
we're not the right man on our side,
the Man of God's own choosing.*

Dost ask who that may be?
CHRIST JESUS, IT IS HE.
Lord Sabbath is His name,
from age to age the same,
and He must win the battle.
(By Martin Luther 1483-1546)

We shout! "My refuge is in God." Amen and Amen.

September 2

NKJV Psalm 27: "Though an army come against me I shall not fear …"

SING OF - THE SHEPHERD AVENGER

The Shepherd takes care of all grievances against His sheep. He protects them from the evil one, and from coerced temptation, inflected by the enemy. So sing!

PSALM TWENTY SEVEN (NKJ)

The Lord is my Light and my Salvation;
whom shall I fear?
The Lord is the strength of my life;
of whom shall I be afraid.

When the wicked came against me
to eat up my flesh,
my enemies and foes,
they stumbled and fell.

Though an army may encamp against me,
my heart shall not fear;
though war may rise against me,
in this I will be confident.

One thing I have desired of the Lord,
that will I seek:
that I may dwell in His house
of the Lord all the days of my life,
to behold the beauty of the Lord …

*For in the time of trouble
He shall hide me in His pavilion;
in the secret place ... He shall hide me;
He shall set me high upon a rock.*

*And now my head shall be lifted
up above my enemies all around me;
therefore I will offer sacrifices of joy ...
I will sing praises to the Lord.*

**Teach me Your way oh Lord
and lead me in a smooth path,**
*because of my enemies.
Do not deliver me to the will of my adversaries;
for false witnesses have risen against me,
and such as breath violence.*

I would have lost heart,
*unless I had believed
that I would see the goodness of the Lord
in the land of the living.*

*Wait on the Lord
be of good courage,
and He shall strengthen your heart.*

After we sing, we look up to the One ahead and pray:

*Depart from me, all you workers of iniquity;
for the Lord has heard the voice of my weeping.
The Lord has heard my supplication;
the Lord will receive my prayer.*

*Let all my enemies be ashamed and greatly troubled;
let them turn back and be ashamed suddenly.*

In the name of Him who leads us, the Lord, *my* Shepherd.

September 3

NKJV Job 38:4 "Where were you when I laid the foundations of the earth?"

SING OF – HIS EXCELLENT NAME

As we walk in the *paths of righteousness,* the Shepherd knows what is best. He created us and all that surrounds us on our journey through *the valley of the shadow of death.* So today, we lift up Psalms, and hymns to our God the Creator.

PSALM EIGHT AND ONE HUNDRED FOUR (NKJ)

O Lord, our Lord
how excellent is Your name in all the earth,
You have set Your glory above the heavens!

When I consider Your heavens,
the work of Your fingers,
the moon and the stars, which You have ordained,
What is man that you are mindful of Him ...
for You have made him a little lower than the angels,
and You have crowned him with glory and honor.

O Lord my God, You are very great:
You are clothed with honor and majesty.
Who covers Yourself with light
as with a garment,
Who stretches out the heavens
like a curtain.
He lays the beams of His upper chambers
in the waters,

Who makes the clouds His chariot,
Who walks on the wings of the wind,
Who makes His angles spirits,
His ministers a flame of fire.

He sends the springs into the valleys;
They flow among the hills.
They give drink to every beast of the field; ...
By them the birds of the heavens have their home;

They sing among the branches.
He waters the hills from His upper chambers;
The earth is satisfied with the fruit of Your works.

He causes the grass to grow for the cattle,
and vegetation for the service of man,
that He may bring forth food from the earth ...
The trees of the Lord are full of sap,
where the birds make their nests;
the high hills are for the wild goats;
He appointed the moon for seasons;
the sun knows it's going down.

O Lord, how manifold are Your works!
May the glory of the Lord endure forever;
May the Lord rejoice in His works.
I will sing too the Lord as long as I live;
I will sing praise to My God while I have my being.

Bless the Lord, O my soul!

We sing a hymn Of praise, TO GOD BE THE GLORY:

Praise the Lord, Praise the Lord,
Let the earth hear His voice.
Praise the Lord, Praise the Lord,
Let the people rejoice!

Oh come to the Father, through Jesus the Son,
And give Him the glory—great things He hath done.
(By Fanny Cosby 1820-1915)

September 4

NKJV Psalm 6:4 "O Lord, deliver me!"

SING OF - THE DELIVERER

The Lord, *my* Shepherd is my Deliverer. No matter what problems come, He delivers us from the evil one. His constant protection and His perfect love brings peace and joy to our lives! We are assured of God's presence. He promises us that He will never leave us nor forsake us.

So let us sing this:

PSALM FORTY TWO (NKJ)

As the deer pants for the water brook,
so my soul thirsts for God,
for the living God ...

... Why are you cast down oh my soul?
And why are you disquieted within me?
Hope in God, for I shall yet praise Him
for the help of His countenance.

God is our refuge and our strength,
A very present help in trouble.
therefore, we will not fear,
even though the earth be removed
and though the mountains
be carried into the midst of the sea ...

There is a river whose streams
shall make glad the city of God,
the holy place of the tabernacle
of the Most High.

Be still and know that I AM GOD;
I will be exalted among the nations,
I will be exalted in the earth!

As each day's path is before us, our Shepherd's help is there to guide and deliver us from the temptations and attacks of the evil one. The following, is a list of other Psalms, to sing in difficult times:

1) In time of fear   Psalm 27
2) In time of doubt   Psalm 73
3) In time of illness   Psalm 6
4) In time of trouble   Psalm 46
5) In time of sin   Psalm 51
6) In time of thanksgiving Psalm 32
7) In time of loneliness   Psalm 12

Cynthia Perkins

How good it is to sing unto the Lord. His promises are true; His will perfect! Let us sing! MY DELIVERER:

My Deliverer, you rescued me from
All that held me captive.
My Deliverer, you set me free
Now I'm alive and I can live.
So every moment I will give you Praise
My Deliverer
(By Jason Walker, Tony Wood and Chad R. Cates)

September 5

NKJV Psalm 103: 2-3 "Bless the Lord, O my soul, and forget not all His benefits; … Who heals all your diseases …"

SING OF - THE HEALER

In our walk *through the valley of the shadow of death*, we will become accustomed to diseases and sickness. *In the paths of righteousness* we walk spiritually. Yet we are still constantly dying physically. It is *the valley of death* because sin lives here, and sin loves death.

However, with the leading of *my* Shepherd, we will not fear this sickened world, for He is with us. He heals us and our diseases, and we are not afraid.

So sing …

PSALM ONE HUNDRED THREE (NKJ)

Bless the Lord oh my soul
and all that is with in me, bless His holy name?
Bless the Lord, oh my soul,
and forget not all His benefits:
Who forgives all your iniquities,
Who heals all your diseases.
… So that your youth is renewed like the eagles.

As for His sheep, their days are like grass,
as a flower of the field,
so it flourishes.
For the wind passes over it, and it is gone,
and its place remembers it no more.
But the mercies of the Lord is from
everlasting to everlasting on those who fear Him.

Have mercy on me, oh Lord,
for I am weak,
O Lord heal me,
for my bones are troubled.
My soul also is greatly troubled.
For the Lord has heard the voice of weeping.
The Lord has heard my supplication,
the Lord will receive my prayer.

The chastisement for our peace
was upon Him,
and by His stripes we are healed.
All we like sheep have gone astray;
and the Lord has laid on Him, our Shepherd,
the iniquity of us all.

The Shepherd's Word provides guidelines for enduring any kind of sickness both physical or spiritual:

- Acknowledging the Shepherd is with you, and pray without ceasing. I Peter 5:6-7
- Fellowship with all of like precious faith. In-other-words engage the Church. I Corinthians 10:13
- God knows your limits, and He will protect you. I Corinthians 10:13
- His timing is perfect. Wait upon Him! Psalm 31:14-15/ Psalm 27
- Seek and know the truth. John 8:32
- Keep pure and in the paths of right living. I Peter 2:11-12
- Master anger. James 1: 19-20
- Hope in the Lord your Shepherd. Job 13:15

So sing HE CARETH FOR YOU:

He careth for you,
when the worries and cares of your life
seem to block out the rays of his light,
never forget, never lose sight
for He careth for you.
(By Kurt Kaiser, Copyright 1979)

September 6

NKJV Matthew 6:28 "Consider the lilies of the field, how they grow: they neither toil nor spin ..."

SING OF - THE PROVIDER

OR
CONSIDER THE LILIES

Today as we walk *the path of righteousness* called "provider," we learn to lean on our Lord, the Shepherd, who provides for our *every* need. Listen to His promises as our provider, while we walk on this path:

Here is My consolation, don't worry about things - food,
drink, money, and clothes.
For you already have life and a body - and
they are far more important than what to eat and wear.

Look at the birds! They don't worry about what to eat -
they don't need to sow or reap or store up food -
for your heavenly Father feeds them.
And you are far more valuable to Him than they are.

Will all your worries add a single moment to your life?
And why worry about your clothes?
Look at the field lilies!
They don't worry about theirs.
Yet King Solomon in all his glory
was not clothed as beautiful as they.

And if God cares so wonderfully for flowers that are here today
and gone tomorrow,
won't He more surely care for you,
O sheep of little faith?

So don't worry at all about having enough food
and clothing.
Why be like the heathen?
For they take pride in all these things
and are deeply concerned about them.
But your heavenly Father already knows perfectly
well that you need them.
And He will gladly give them to you
if you give Him first place in your life.
Seek first the kingdom of God,
and HIS RIGHTEOUSNESS;
and all these things shall be added to you.

So don't be anxious about tomorrow,
God will take care of your tomorrow too.
Live one day at a time.

Ask, and you will be given what you ask for.
Seek and you will find.
Knock, and the door will be opened.
For everyone who asks, receives.
Anyone who seeks, finds.
If only you will knock, the door will open.
(NLT Matthew 6:25 – 34 / 7:7 – 8)

Today the Shepherd chose a song that goes with this path - CONSIDER THE LILIES:

Consider the lilies, they don't toil nor spin
And there's not a king with more splendor than them.
Consider the sparrows, they don't plant nor sow,
But they're fed by the Master who watches them grow.
We have a Heavenly Father above
with eyes full of mercy and a heart full of love.
He really cares when your head is bowed low
consider the lilies and then you will know.
(By Joel Hemphill, Copyright 1971)

Cynthia Perkins

September 7

NKJV Psalm 107:2 "Let the redeemed of the Lord say so."

SING OF - THE REDEEMED

The song of our Redeemer proves His magnificent grace. He made us. We got lost on the wrong path. Our Shepherd then redeemed us by becoming **The Sacrificial Lamb** who was slain for the sins of the whole world. He took all our sins and conquered death to provide eternal life for the whole world. Oh what a Savior, *our* Shepherd, *my* Shepherd.

May we now sing this path's

PSALM
ONE HUNDRED THIRTY SIX/ONE HUNDRED SEVEN
(NKJ)

*Oh give thanks to the Lord,
for He is good!
For His mercy endures forever.
Let the redeemed of the Lord say so,
whom He has redeemed from the hand
of His enemy,
and gathered out of the lands,
from the east and from the west,
from the north and from the south.*

*He brought us out of darkness
and* **the valley of the shadow of death**,
*and broke their chains in pieces.
Oh that we would give thanks
to the Lord for His goodness,
He led us forth by the right way,
that we might go to His city
for our dwelling place*

*Let us sacrifice the sacrifices of
thanksgiving,
and declare His works with rejoicing.
Let the redeemed of the Lord say so.*

The song we now will sing is a song expressing just how much the Lord loves us and has set us free. Let us lift up our voices; sing "Redeemed":

I am redeemed, You set me free
So I'll shake off these heavy chains
Wipe away every stain, yeah, I'm not who I used to be
Jesus, I'm not who I used to be
'Cause I am redeemed
Thank God, redeemed.
(By Big Daddy Weave, Copyright 2000-2017)

September 8

NKJV Psalm 23 " ...for His name's sake."

NAMESAKE

Many of my family and friends have names that are passed down from generation to generation. One that has received the same name as another has or had in the family is called a *namesake*.

All of us who are the Shepherds are His namesake. We get our name after Christ, and we are called, Christians. We are the personification of Him. As we walk *in His paths of righteousness* wherever He leads we follow, and we look just like Him who is our namesake.

The way of the cross is the way we go in these paths, for the cross exemplifies our namesake. The way of the cross leads us to our eternal home.

Our namesake, Christ, went to the cross deliberately so that we may abide in it. He made the way through *the valley of the shadow of death*, for every person to walk in righteousness, and commune with God, our Father.

When we get to the cross, we do not go through it;
we abide in this life to which the cross is the gateway.
To be like Him we abide in Him;
we walk with Him;
we talk with Him;
we are His namesake.
When His obedience gave everything, even death,
sinful man merged with God
and at this point
a crash opened the way of righteousness

that every human being may get through
into the likeness of Christ and become a Christian
His namesake.
(Oswald Chambers, April 6)

I love being called a Christian, after my Shepherd, Christ our Lord, the Son of God, *my* Father.

Everyone now will sing the hymn THE WAY OF THE CROSS LEADS HOME:

I must needs go home by the way of the cross,
there's no other way but this;
I shall ne'er get sight
of the gates of light,
If the way of the cross I miss.

The way of the cross leads home,
It is sweet to know as I onward go,
The way of the cross leads home.
(By Jessie Brown Pounds, 1861-1921)

September 9

NKJV Psalm 23:4 " ...the valley of the shadow of death."

ENTER THE SHADOW OF DEATH

Now our walk has become eerie, dark. That is the way of the world; walking in a cover of shadows in, *the valley of the shadow of death.*

We all walk in this valley, partners in death. The statistics on death is that one out of one person dies! Yet most sheep choose to walk the broad and wide path leading to destruction, that *our* Shepherd warned against. Death is a *stubborn* and *uncertain* fact. Death casts a shadow that follows everyone. Death loves to devour everybody!

As we, His sheep, walk in this *valley of the shadow of death*, the only light is *the* Light, *our* Shepherd.

Come now you who say,
'Today or tomorrow we will go to such and such a city,
spend a year there, buy and sell, and make a profit;
*whereas you do not know what **will happen** tomorrow.*
For what is your life? It is even a vapor that
appears for a little time and then vanishes away.

*Instead you **ought** to say, 'If the Lord, who is my Shepherd,*
wills, we shall live and do this or that.'
(NKJV James 3:13-17)

He speaks very gently. "Life is a gift from God our Father. He alone knows the exact time, how you will die, or when or where you will die. After all, this is *the valley of the shadow of death*. But with My help, death is swallowed up in victory!"

The Shepherd continues … "It is appointed for you to die once, and after that the judgment … and just as through one man sin entered the world, then death through sin spread to all mankind, because *all* sinned."

The Shepherd used this analogy to explain our walk.

"There is a valley in Palestine that has a a deep chasm that water flows downward. The chasm is 1,300 feet. The water runs into the Red Sea. Even at high noon there are tremendous shadows. Living in these shadows are bears, leopards, hyenas and robbers. There are steep places, narrow paths and holes that are covered and easy to fall into."

"Every year the shepherds of Palestine lead their sheep through this valley to greener pastures. Confronting the extreme danger, they lead their flock to a place of safety and comfort."

"That is what we are doing as we walk through this valley. I, *your* Shepherd am leading you on *the paths of righteousness* so that you will be safe from harm." We all shout for joy!

Our lives are safe with *our* Shepherd. We have complete victory as *we walk through the valley of the shadow of death*. Our Shepherd never loses a sheep, because He overcomes the shadows of darkness. *His goodness and mercy shall follow us all the days of our lives;* and, at the end, *we will dwell in the house of our Lord forever.*

Cynthia Perkins

September 10

KJV Psalm 23:4 "I will fear no evil …"

DEATH DEFEATED

Although death's valley is a fact, we don't need to be afraid. Look death straight in the eye and shout "Yeah, though I walk! … The Shepherd has said to … fear no evil, for He, Jehovah, … is with us!

We are not ready to live; until we are no longer afraid to die. The evil one desires to keep us in bondage through the fear of death, but, the Shepherd, rendered death to be impotent. Death lost its sting, releasing all of us who are His sheep from its monster grip.

He speaks with much strength and excitement. "For all of you sheep have gone astray, and turned to your own ways. The Lord God has laid on Me, *your* Shepherd all of your iniquity. The following list explains the "no fear" policy of death to all of you sheep that belong to Me."

He points to each variable as He explains:

1) **Death is a delightful friend**. (I Corinthians 3:21-23) For all things are Mine, the Shepherds … the world … life … death. All things present and all things to come.
2) **Death belongs to us**. Death is a servant to help you into the eternal bliss of our heavenly home. I said … "I go to prepare a place for you … and I will receive you unto myself that where I am there you may be also." (NAS John 14:2)
3) **Physically death is gain;** You will be like Me, the Lord, your Shepherd.
4) **Intellectually death is gain;** for you are known as I am known.
5) **Emotionally death is gain;** because I will constantly praise Him.
6) **Socially death is gain;** because I will be with the saints of the ages and my Lord face to face.
7) **Spiritually death is gain;** Temptation and sin will be behind you, and you will be one with God forevermore."

Tomorrow we will continue this lesson expressing His victory over death and the grave. Praise be to the Lord, *my* Shepherd as we sing A BEAUTIFUL LIFE:

Each day I'll do a golden deed,
By helping those who are in need;

My life on earth is but a span,
And so I'll do the best I can.

Life's evening sun is sinking low,
A few more days, and I must go.
(*By William M. Golden 1878-1934 /composed 1918*)

September 11

> NKJV Luke 2: 10-11 "Fear not! For behold, I bring you good tidings of great joy! For unto you is born this day the Savior, which is CHRIST THE LORD."

DEATH IS DEAD

Today we continue this perfect lesson of complete assurance of the victory over death, our dreaded enemy.

Listen as He speaks: "What then shall you say to these things? If God is for you who can be against you? He who did not spare Me, His own Son, but delivered Me up for you all, how shall He not with Me also freely give you all things? Who shall bring a charge against you, God's elect? It is God, our Father who justifies. Who is that person who condemns? It is I, Christ, Your Shepherd who died and furthermore is risen, who is now even at the right hand of God, and I also make intercession for all of you."

"Who shall separate you from My love? Shall tribulation, or distress, or persecution, or famine, or nakedness, or peril, or sword? As it is written …

For Your sake we are killed all day long…
We are accounted as sheep for the slaughter.

Yet, in everything, you are more than conquerors, through Me who loves you."

"For you should be persuaded, that neither death nor life, nor angels, nor principalities, nor powers, nor things present, nor things to come, nor height, nor depth, nor any other created thing, shall be able to separate you, My sheep, from the love of God, our Father, which is in Me, Jesus Christ your Lord, *your* Shepherd!" What an amazing Lord, Jesus Christ, *my* Shepherd. (NKJV Romans 8: 31-39, paraphrased)

Ah, the wonder of it all, that Christ, *our* Shepherd loves us to this extreme. There are no words to express the joy inside as I receive His announcement that my sins are forgiven, I have an eternal home, and that death is not to be an issue in my life, because I have laid down my life, I have been crucified with Christ, and it is not me that lives, but Christ who lives in me. *My* Shepherd made sure that I should have no fear, but perfect peace as I *walk in the paths of righteousness, through the valley of the shadow of death.*

Lift up our voices and sing this hymn, THE WONDER OF IT ALL:

O, the wonder of it all!
The wonder of it all!
Just to think that God loves me.
(By George Beverly Shea, Copyright 1957)

September 12

NKJV Psalm 121: 3 "He will not allow your foot to be moved …"

FOR THOU ART WITH ME

The Shepherd never leaves us nor forsakes us. He leads us and covers us and we need never fear.

His presence is with me. It exudes through every living thing! He is with us individually and collectively. He is *Jehovah Shaman* - The Lord ever present.

His power is with me -

*He strengthens me as we walk.
*His rod protects and disciplines me as we walk.
*His staff draws me to Him and guides the way as we walk *in the paths of righteousness.*
*We sing as we walk.

His purpose is to take us all the way home to His sheep fold on the other side of t*he valley of the shadow of death.* He is leading us to heaven, the place He is preparing:

I go now to prepare a place for you
and when I go I will come back
again and receive you unto
myself that where I am, there
you will be also.
(NKJV John 14:2-3)

We are to listen to the Shepherd, and worship Him. We are to obey His instructions. It is that simple! All we must do is engage in:

*His presence
*His power
*His purpose

Let us sing as we walk, PSALM ONE TWENTY ONE, (NKJ):

I will lift up my eyes to the hills
from whence comes my help?
*My help **comes** from the Lord,*
Who made heaven and earth.

He will not allow your foot
to be moved;
He who keeps you will not slumber.
Behold, He who keeps you
shall neither slumber nor sleep.

*The Lord **is** your keeper;*
*The Lord **is your shade***
at your right hand.
The sun shall not strike you by day,
Nor the moon by night.

*The Lord shall preserve you from **all** evil;*
He shall preserve your soul.
The Lord shall preserve you're going
out and you're coming in.
From this time forth and even
forevermore.

September 13

KJV Psalm 23:4 "Thy rod and Thy staff they comfort me."

COMFORT

Comfort comes from the right relationship with the Father, the Shepherd, and the Spirit. He said … "I will guide them and restore comfort." (Isaiah 57:18)

Paul the Shepherd's apostle explains:

Walk properly, as in the day,
not in revelry and drunkenness,
not in lewdness and lust,
not in strife and envy.

> *But put on our Lord Jesus Christ, the Shepherd,*
> *and make NO provision for the flesh,*
> *to fulfill its lusts.*
>
> *And do this, knowing the time,*
> *that now it is high time to awake out of sleep;*
> *for now our salvation is nearer than when we first believed.*
> *The night is far spent, the day is at hand.*
> *Therefore, let us cast off the works of darkness,*
> *and let us put on the armor of Light.*
> *(NKJV Romans 13:11-14*

His tools, the rod, and the staff bring comfort because they discipline us, guiding us in the right direction. His boundaries guide our lives in the direction of His leading and His light. If a sheep is not chastised or disciplined, that sheep is not the Shepherd's. The discipline of the Shepherd and the Father show true ownership and family. (NKJV Hebrews 12:3-4)

Listen as the Shepherd speaks:

> *My son and daughter, do not despise the chastening of the Lord.*
> *Nor be discouraged when you are rebuked by Him;*
> *for whom the Lord loves He chastens,*
> *and scourges every one whom He receives.*
> *If you endure chastening, God deals with you as with His*
> *children; for what child is there whom a father does not discipline?*
> *But if you are without punishment, of which all have become*
> *partakers, than you are illegitimate and not His child.*
> *Furthermore, we have had human fathers who corrected us,*
> *and we paid them respect. Shall we not much more readily be in*
> *subjection to the Father of spirits and live?*
>
> *For they indeed for a few days chastened us as seemed best to them,*
> *but He for our profit, that we may be partakers of His holiness.*
> *Now no punishment seems to be joyful for the present,*
> *but painful, nevertheless, afterward it yields the peaceable*
> *fruit of RIGHTEOUSNESS to those who have been trained by it.*
>
> *Therefore, strengthen the hands which hang down, and the feeble knees,*
> *and MAKE STRAIGHT PATHS for your feet ...*
> *(NLT Hebrews 12:5-17)*

We are sons and daughters and He restores our fellowship and renews our worship because we are His. When our Father lays His rod on you don't despise it; don't faint; and don't dropout!

We all praise our Shepherd, our Lord, for His constant comfort and guidance. He disciplines us, keeping us *in the paths of righteousness* as we walk.

September 14

NKJV Psalm 130:1 "Out of the depths I have cried to you, O Lord; Lord hear my voice."

THE PIT

Once a sheep fell into an extremely deep pit, and began to scream for help.

A politician came by and heard the screams and yelled "If you had voted for me you would not be in this pit." And he kept walking, never even looking back.

Then a teacher came by and hearing the screams yelled down … "If you had stayed in school, and continued your education, you would not have gotten in this mess of a deep pit." And she kept up her warnings as she walked away.

A preacher came by, and he stopped and listened to the pitiful screams. He knelt down, but instead of helping, he exclaimed, "See this is God's judgment!" You refused to join **my** congregation so you are on your own. You deserve this! He laughed as he shouted, "God will get you for this." and he went on walking down his hypocritical path.

The Shepherd hearing the sheep's cries for help came. He reached down into the pit, grabbing the sheep with His shepherd's crook, and pulled that scared, thirsty, sheep to safety. He pulled the sheep to Himself, up into His arms, then set that sheep's feet on the safety of the ground. No questions; no rhetoric; no harassment; just His undeniable grace.

Immediately the sheep that was once lost begin to sing PSALM THIRTY (NKJ):

I will extol you, O Lord,
for you have lifted me up;
and have not let my foes rejoice over me.
Oh Lord my God, I cried out to you,
and you healed me.

O Lord, You brought my soul up from the grave;
You have kept me alive,

> *that I should not go down to the pit ...*
> *... Weeping may endure for the night,*
> *but joy comes in the morning.*
>
> *You have turned for me my morning into dancing; ...*
> *O Lord my God,*
> *I will give thanks to you forever.*

❦

I am ever so grateful that the Shepherd uses His staff to pull me up out of the pit. The Shepherd's crook is to pull us out of danger, and to keep us from getting away from His flock. With His crook He pulls us into Himself.

I pray ... "Oh God, may you draw me up to you with your mighty right hand. In Jesus' name, amen."

September 15

KJV Psalm 23:5 "Thou prepareth a table ..."

I

SET THE TABLE

The Shepherd has taught us that through death's valley all we are to do is follow Him. He will honor, provide, guide and protect us. See Him there, out front leading us in the paths of right living? We go, not knowing the way He desires us to go, nor the direction, but we follow.

Every day we fellowship with Him at mealtime. Here *our* Shepherd puts on His apron. He sets the table with the best. He makes delicious gourmet food served on exquisite china, crystal and silver, glorious flowers and candles cover the table. A quartet of beautiful instrumental music provides the background for the meals setting; and finally uniformed servants who have been trained in heaven, serve the meal.

He prepares this table out of respect and honor for His sheep, those who He calls friends and the family of God. We are celebrated each and every day with our gathering at the table.

As we look at the Lord *our* Shepherd, we see the fullness that one finds in Him. He satisfies and meets our deepest hungers. Jesus, *our* Shepherd has prepared many feasts for His sheep. The following are a few of His special feedings:

   *The miracle of feeding His Children on their journey to the Promise Land.

   *The feeding of King David as He and his mighty men fled King Saul.

*The miracle of feeding Elijah as he hid from his enemies.

*The miracle of feeding the four and five thousand men, which probably including women and children; was more of a count of 20,000.

*After His resurrection, He prepared a meal for Peter and the disciples.

The purpose of our meal time with our Shepherd is always restoration, both physically and spiritually. May we dine with the Lord who *prepares a table before us.*

Look at this meal! We are hungry for our Shepherd's feeding. So everyone come and dine. We all sing the perfect hymn for this occasion COME AND DINE:

Jesus has a table spread
Where the saints of God are fed,
He invites His chosen people, "Come and dine";
with His manna he doth feed
And supplies our every need:
Oh, 'tis sweet to sup with Jesus all the time!

"Come and dine." The Master calleth
"Come and dine."
You can feast at Jesus table any time.

He who fed the multitude,
turned the water into wine.
To the hungry hear the call
"Come and dine."
(By Charles B. Widmeyer, 1884-1974 Copyright, Public Domain)

September 16

NKJV Psalm 23:5 "Thou prepares a table before me ..."

II

THE LORD'S TABLE

Another table the Shepherd has prepared, is a table representing His life, here in the *valley of the shadow of death*. This table is spread in memory of His Gospel: His death, burial, and resurrection. This table has a special name. It is the table of the *Lord's Supper*.

Cynthia Perkins

The Shepherd actually gave this special dinner significance before He came as the Lamb of God. It was called The Passover; and was established with God's people, the Israelites, just before they left Egypt to journey to the promise land.

The celebration of the meal was called *The Passover* because as His people prepared the meal, they marked their doors with the blood of the lamb, which would be a sign to God, that this house belonged to Him. He said, "When I see the blood, I will pass over you; and the plague shall not destroy your first born…"

Now we move to the Lord, our Shepherd, who became the human Lamb Sacrifice, slain for the sins of the world. He took His apostles to an upper room to celebrate His Passover; and the meal, established our commemoration, of His Sacrifice, forever.

At this meal, He made it clear that He was the new *Sacrificial Lamb*, and they would now eat His body, and drink His blood, as the *New Covenant*.

This is how it was done:

And as they were eating,
Jesus took bread, blessed, and broke it, and gave it
to the disciples and said, "Take, eat, this is My body."

Then He took the cup, and gave thanks,
and gave it to them, saying, "Drink from it, all of you.
For this is My blood of the new covenant,
which is shed for many for the remission of sins."
(NKJV Matthew 26:26-27)

The Lord's supper used two symbols from the *Old Covenant Passover Supper*, the bread and the fruit of the vine. The unleavened bread's new meaning was associated with His body, which would be broken, pointing to His death on the cross. The cup of wine would stand for His blood, which would be shed for the sins of the whole world.

After His resurrection, this supper celebration would look back to the Shepherd's death on the cross; and forward to His return. All of His sheep, the Church, instituted this celebration to be commemorated every first day of the week.

Now we will sing a hymn as they did at the night of the establishment of our *Lord's Supper*. BREAK THOU THE BREAD OF LIFE:

Break Thou the bread of life,
Dear Lord to me,
As Thou didst break the loaves

Beside the sea;
Beyond the sacred page
I seek thee, Lord,
My Spirit pants for Thee,
O living Word.
(By A. Lathbury 1841-1913)

September 17

NKJV Luke 22:14 "And at the proper time all sat down together at the table."

III

THE LORD'S TABLE

My Shepherd expressed the importance of coming to *His* table and the meal *He* has prepared. The call to *His* feast is not an option. To live, one must eat at *His* tables.

The Shepherd taught us these parables to explain about gathering at His table:

THE WEDDING FEAST

"The Kingdom of heaven is like a certain king who arranged a marriage for his son, and sent out his servants to call those who were invited to the wedding; and they were not willing to come. Again, he sent out other servants, saying 'tell those who are invited, See I have prepared my dinner; my oxen and fatted cattle are killed and all things are ready ... '"

"But they made light of it and went their ways, one to his own farm, another to his business. And the rest seized his servants, treated them spitefully, and killed them. But when the king heard about it, he sent out his armies, destroyed those murderers, and burned up their city. Then he said to his servants, 'The wedding is ready, but those who were invited were not worthy. Therefore, go into the highways, and as many as you find, invite to the wedding. So those servants went into the highways and gathered together all whom they found, both bad and good, and the wedding hall was filled with guests!
(NLT Matthew 22: 2-13)

THE GREAT SUPPER

"A certain man gave a great supper and invited many, and sent his servant at supper time to say to those who were invited, 'Come, for all things are now ready.' But they all with one accord began to make excuses. The first said to him, 'I have bought a piece of ground, and I must go and see it. I ask you to have me excused.' And another said, 'I have bought five yoke of oxen, and I am going to test them. I ask you to have me excused.' Still another said, 'I have married a wife, and therefore I cannot come.' So that servant came and reported these things to his master. Then the master of the house, being angry, said to his servant, 'Go out quickly into the streets and lanes of the city, and bring in here the poor, and the maimed and the lame and the blind.' And the servant said 'Master, it is done as you commanded ...'"
(NKJV Luke 14:16-22)

THE BREAD FROM HEAVEN

The Shepherd stands before us exclaiming ... "My Father give you the true Bread from heaven. For the Bread of God is He who comes from heaven and gives life to the world.' I Am the Bread of Life. He who comes to Me shall never hunger, and he who believes in Me shall never thirst."

"...I Am the Bread of Life. Your fathers ate the manna in the wilderness, and are dead. This is the Bread," ... He points to Himself ... "which comes down from heaven, that one may eat of it and not die. I am the living Bread which came down from heaven. If anyone eats of this Bread, they will live forever, and the Bread that I shall give is My flesh, which I shall give for the life of the world."

"Unless you eat the flesh of the Son of Man and drink His blood, you have no life in you. Whoever eats My flesh and drinks My blood has eternal life, and I will raise them up at the last day. For My flesh is food indeed, and My blood is drink indeed. Those who eat My flesh and drink My blood abides in Me, and I in them. As the living Father sent Me, and I live because of the Father, so those who feed on Me will live because of Me. This is the Bread which came down from heaven. Those who eat this Bread will live forever!" (NKJV John 6:32-40)

He is the Bread and the Water of life, none of us have life if we do not dine at His table.

September 18

NKJV Psalm 23:5 " ...before Me,"

AN INVITATION TO ME

The invitation to the prepared table is not only a collective invitation, but an individual invitation. As is noted in the parables, we are invited to come to His table on an individual basis and those who reject the invitation must face the anger of God the Father.

The Shepherd has done all of the preparation - He:

   *Prepared the sacrificial Lamb
   *Prepared the Bread of Life
   *Prepared the Water of Life

The entire meal is manifested in the Shepherd, the Lamb of God. *Our* Father, and *our* Shepherd loves us so very much. It is unthinkable that anyone would reject the personal, loving, invitation to sup with the Lord God, and the Shepherd.

The table is prepared before me. He is feeding me, refreshing and hosting me. At His table we find complete joy, comfort and satisfaction. At His table our every need is met.

The table prepared for me is a table of remembrance, of redemption, and of celebration. As I partake, I remember everything about the Lord, *my* Shepherd. I remember His love, mercy, and grace. His blood spilled out as the sacrifice, and His body broken.

Soon there will come the big feast called, "THE MARRIAGE SUPPER OF THE LAMB," where I and all sheep, the Church, the Bride of *my* Shepherd, will be swept up into His arms, as they step over the threshold of time into their eternal home.

The Lord's supper is so good and beautiful. We are all amazed at the wonder of it all. We sing as we begin the meal. PRAISE GOD FROM WHOM ALL BLESSINGS FLOW:

> *Praise God, from whom all blessings flow;*
> *Praise him, all creatures here below;*
> *Praise him above, ye heav'nly host;*
> *Praise Father, Son, and Holy Ghost.*
> *(By Thomas Ken, 1637-1710)*

September 19

NKJV Psalm 23:5 " …in the presence of *my* enemies, …"

JAHOVAH NISSI

Many enemies come to us *in the valley of the shadow of death*, and they come in many ways. Notice the Shepherd has purposely called these enemies My enemies. All enemies are personal. They come at us from all directions. The greatest and most dreaded enemy is DEATH! No sheep knows the time, where, when or how this enemy will strike!

Our Shepherd does not take us out of this valley, but takes us through it. He has a purpose, and that being for us to be His advocate in *this valley of the shadow of death.* We are the light, and salt, and by following Him, we point the way to life eternal with God our Father. He saves us from our enemies, especially death.

Our Shepherd has taught us to expect the enemies right in the middle of the feast. He has assured us He never leaves us, nor forsakes us, and He provides a banner of protection over us. The name He uses to describe Himself is "Jehovah-Nissi." This banner is huge, and is the covering of the Spirit, the Lamb's blood, and our Creator God.

In all enemy attacks, whether physical, emotional, or spiritual, the Shepherd has provided the following battle strategy:

* The Shepherd, and the Father are my points of reference.
They are our north star. **They** lead us in the right path.

* They are my Rock; my hope!
Psalm 62:5-8
My soul waits silently for God alone.
For my expectation is from Him.
He is my Rock.
He is my defense; I shall not be moved.
The Rock is my strength, and my refuge is in God.

* They are my inspiration.
Psalm 60:4-5
You have given a banner to those who fear You, that it may be displayed because of Truth. That your beloved may be delivered …"

* They are the victory.
I Corinthians 15: 57-58
But thanks be to God, who gives the victory through our Lord Jesus Christ, my Shepherd.

Therefore, beloved sheep, be steadfast, immovable, always abounding in the work of the Lord, knowing that your labor in the Lord, is not in vain.

DEATH IS SWALLOWED UP IN VICTORY!

What peace it is to know we live. There is no death. We will all have new life. Let us all sing the hymn HOW GREAT THOU ART.

Then sings my soul, my Savior God to Thee.
How great Thou Art,
How great Thou Art.
(By Carl Gustav Boberg 1859-1940; Translator: Stuart Hine, 1949; Copyright 1951)

September 20

NKJV Psalm 23:5 " ...in the presence of *my* enemies ..."

ENDURE

There is and always will be excruciating suffering *in the valley of the shadow of death.* Suffering often comes from within; our family, our friends, or our community. Suffering may also come from the outside. The Word teaches us how to endure the suffering.

Our Shepherd has made sure He prepares a peaceful blessed table of fellowship. He never forsakes us. He always provides. He never allows us to be tempted beyond what we can bear. Every promise of His Word is truth. His love never fails. His grace is sufficient. His will is good and perfect. There is never a worry about what we should eat, drink, or wear. He is sovereign.

The following is a chart explaining how He teaches us to deal with suffering. As we follow the Shepherd He says, "I shall instruct you and teach you in the way you should go." This chart will help all of us in time of suffering to endure as we *walk through the valley of the shadow of death.*

HOW TO ENDURE SUFFERING

Wrong Ways	**Right Ways**
Demand to know WHY.	Be content to know WHO is in charge (Romans 8:28-30)
Withdraw from God.	Acknowledge that He is with you (Hebrews 13:5) Pray all the more (I Peter 5:6,7)

Decide your own limits.	Know that God sets His own endurance. and knows your limits (I Corinthians 10:13)
Be impatient with God.	Wait for His perfect timing. (Psalm 31:14,15)
Seek your own remedies.	Trust in the Lord to guide. (Proverbs 3:5-6 (Proverbs 14:12)
Give up to despair.	Wait upon the Lord (Psalm 27)
Delude yourself.	Seek the truth (John 8:32)
Indulge yourself.	Keep pure (1 Peter 2:11,12)
Become angry.	Master the anger (James 1:19,20)
Become depressed.	Hope in the Lord. (Job 13:15)

In times of the enemy's attacks, and there will be many, we should all be able to say with His sheep Job "Though He slay me, yet will I trust Him!" That statement is the essence of endurance!

September 21

NKJV Psalm 138:7 "Though I walk in the midst of trouble, Thou wilt revive me."

EYE OF THE STORM

The storms of our personal lives are the hardest to go through. The wind and rain come pouring in and darkness covers the violent attacks often made on our children, spouses, family, or close friends.

Again it is our focus on *our* Shepherd, and the Word that teaches us that we should … "give thanks to God, who gives us the victory through Jesus Christ, the Lord, *our, my* Shepherd."

Today, we are to reflect on this lovely and meaningful poem, written by a sheep, about our *walk through the valley of the shadow of death.*

THE EYE OF THE STORM

Fear not that the whirlwind shall carry thee hence,
Not wait for its onslaught in breathless suspense,
Nor shrink from the whips of the terrible hail,
But pass through the edge to the heart of the tale,
For there is a shelter, sunlight and warm,
And Faith sees her God through the eye of the storm.

The passionate tempest with rush and wild roar
and threatening of evil may beat on the shore,
The waves may be mountains, the fields battle plains,
and the earth be immersed in a deluge of rains,
Yet, the soul, stayed on God, may sing bravely its psalm,
for the heart of the storm is the center of calm.

Let hope be not quenched in the blackness of night,
Though the cyclone awhile may have blotted the light,
For behind the great darkness the stars ever shine,
And the light of God's heavens, His love shall make thine,
Let no gloom dim thine eyes, but uplift them on high
To the face of thy God and the blue of His sky.

The storm is thy shelter from danger and sin,
And God Himself takes thee for safety within;
The tempest with Him passeth into deep calm,
and the roar of the winds is the sound of a psalm.
Be glad and serene when the tempest clouds form;
God smiles on His child in the eye of the storm.
(Streams in the Desert, April 23, Mrs. Charles E. Cowman, Anonymous.)

Lean on *the* Shepherd. He will cover us all in the eye of the storm and *in the presence of my enemies.*

September 22

NKJV Psalm 138:7 "Though I walk in the midst of trouble, thou wilt revive me."

CONTINUED ... THE EYE OF THE STORM

So sing this song.

PEACE IN THE VALLEY

I am tired and weary but I must travel on,
Till the Lord comes to call me away.
Where the morning is bright, and the Lamb is the light.
And the night is fair as the day.

There'll be peace in the valley for me some day.
There'll be peace in the valley for me, Oh Lord I pray.
There'll be no sadness, no sorrow no trouble I'll see.
There'll be peace in the valley for me.
(By Thomas A Dorsey /pub. by Warner/Chappell Music, Inc., Copyright 1937)

Oh, what complete joy, as we continue on our *paths of righteousness, walking through the valley of the shadow of death.* There is no fear, just His peace. Truly, there will be peace in the valley, for all of us, who are in the hands of the Lord, *my* Shepherd.

September 23

NKJV I Peter 3: 12 "For the eyes of the Lord are on the righteous, and His ears are open to their prayers; but the face of the Lord is against those who do evil."

PATHS TO VICTORY

"It is one thing to choose the disagreeable, and another thing to go into the disagreeable by God's engineering. If God puts you there, He is amply sufficient." (Oswald Chambers)

Suffering comes to us in many forms. In this valley we may suffer for right or for wrong. The Shepherd's eyes are on all of His righteous sheep, and as He leads, His ears are always hearing our cries. His face is against those who do evil toward His sheep and those causing the suffering.

Here in His words we find the answers to deal with all our suffering:

And who is he who will harm you
if you become followers of what is good?
But even if you should suffer for righteousness' sake,
you are blessed.
And do not be afraid of their threats, nor be troubled.
But sanctify the Lord God in your hearts,
and always be ready to give a defense
to everyone who asks you a reason for the hope that is in you,
with meekness and fear; having a good conscience,
that when they defame you as evildoers,
those who revile your good conduct in Christ
may be ashamed. For it is better, if it is the will of God,
to suffer for doing good than for doing evil.

For I also suffered once for sins, the just for the unjust,
that I might bring us to God,
being put to death the flesh but made alive by the Spirit.

Therefore, since I suffered for you in the flesh,
arm yourselves also with the same mind,
for he who has suffered in the flesh has ceased from sin,
that they no longer should live the rest of their time in the flesh
for the lust of men, but for the will of God our Father …

Don't think it strange concerning the fiery trial which is to try you,
as though some strange thing happened to you;
but rejoice to the extent that you pre-take of My sufferings,
that when My glory is revealed
*you may also be glad with exceeding **great joy**.*
If you are reproached for Christ, My Name, blessed are you,
for the Spirit of God, our Father rests upon you.

Let those sheep who suffer according to the will of God, our Father,
*commit their souls to Me in **doing good** …*
(NKJV I Peter 4:12-19)

Suffering is imminent in this *valley of the shadow of death*; yet God's and *our* Shepherd's sovereignty prevails! They, and the Spirit bring meaning into even the worst suffering that human life may bring.

I am filled with joy beyond measure. There is no fear here in our *walk in the paths of righteousness*. Remember what *my* Shepherd has said …

Do not fear the reproach of men
nor be afraid of their insults.
For the moth will eat them up like a garment,
and the worm will eat them like wool.
But My righteousness will be forever,
and My salvation from generation to generation!
(NKJV Isiah 51:7, 8)

Cynthia Perkins

September 24

NKJV Psalm 23:4 "I will fear no evil, for You are with me."

COMFORT FOOD

Today we are to focus on thoughts of comfort and peace that will help us through the tough times ahead. Here are some songs, pomes, and thoughts to reflect upon to keep us focused on the Shepherd during times of suffering.

Sing to the Lord.
When I begin to sing God will set
ambushes against the enemy.
The joy of the Lord is my Strength.

Crises always reveals character.

Confidence in Jesus, believe steadfastly on Him,
and all you come up against will develop faith.
There is continues testing in the life of faith,
and the last great test is death.
May God keep us in fighting trim!
Faith is attainable trust in God,
trust which never dreams that He will not stand by us.

We have the idea that we ought to
shield ourselves from some of the things
God brings round us. NEVER!

In nothing be anxious, worried, or afraid,
but by prayer and supplication,
with thanksgiving, let your request
be made known unto God.

Never choose to set down on your handful of thorns.

OVERHEARD IN AN ORCHARD

Said the Robin to the Sparrow
"I should really like to know
why these anxious human beings
rush about and worry so."

Said the Sparrow to the Robin
"Friend I think that it might be
that they have no Heavenly Father
such as cares for you and me!"
(By Elizabeth Cheney 1422-1473)

※

I WALKED A MILE WITH PLEASURE

I walked a mile with pleasure
she chattered all the way;
but left me none the wiser
for all she had to say.

I walked a mile with sorrow
And ne'er a word said she
But, oh the things I learned from her
when sorrow walked with me.
(By Robert Browning 1812-1889)

※

May these meditations help heal our hearts and minds, while in our valley of death, we walk with the Shepherd. For He is with us, so we will not fear.

September 25

NKJV Psalm 23:5 "You anoint my head with oil."

OIL

The Shepherd is caring for us and He heals the wounds we receive as we *walk the paths of righteousness, through the valley of the shadow of death.*

As we *walk in the path of righteousness, He anoints our heads with oil.* He totally cares for us.

Today in closing we sing: NO ONE EVER CARED FOR ME LIKE JESUS:

I would love to tell you what I think of Jesus
Since I found in Him a Friend so strong and true;
I would tell you how He changed my life completely -
He did something that no other Friend could do.

No one ever cared for me like Jesus,
There's no other Friend so kind as He;
No one else could take the sin and darkness from me -
O how much He cared for me!
(By Charles F. Weigle, Copyright 1932)

When I was a baby, only about one and a half years old, my mother said that she and an aunt of mine would sing this song as a duet. And every time they got to the chorus and sang ... *No one ever cared for me like Jesus* ... I would begin to cry!

I believe, as a very young child, just a little lamb, I recognized the loving care, of the Lord, *my* Shepherd.

Truly now as an adult sheep I can testify that n*o one ever cared for me like Jesus*, the Lord, *my* Shepherd.

September 26

NKJV Psalm 23:5 "You anoint my head with oil;"

THE ANOINTING

The Shepherd taught us while He was on earth, most wealthy homes at the time, had a flask of oil by their entry way. When an honored guest arrived, the host would place a kiss on him, and pour the oil into their hand, then gently rub the oil on their guest's hair and face, to perfume and refresh. The host was demonstrating love for the guest. This was considered a blessing, showing respect and honor.

The Shepherd has taught, how the anointing of oil, was used many times as an expression of ennoblement. For example, kings were anointed as a part of the ceremonial coronation; priests appointed to the office of minister were also anointed.

Fresh oil was used every morning to dress for the day, and was used as an ingredient in daily baking and cooking. Oil was precious and represented goodness and comfort.

The oil that *our* Shepherd provides is that of the Holy Spirit's covering. Holiness describes the character of God, our Father, and is the code for the Shepherd's sheep's conduct.

We, His sheep are set apart unto God. That is the exact meaning of being holy. Holiness is the sheep's individual relationship to God. We are called to behave as the Shepherd leads. We are to be filled by the Spirit, anointed, constantly seeking God's face, never veering to the left nor to the right. We are to keep our eyes on Jesus, who is the Author and Finisher of our faith.

Conforming to a life exemplified by God is made possible by the sacrifice of the Lamb on the cross. When He, the Spirit, comes to dwell in us, He anoints us with His oil. We no longer live; He lives in us. It is called the indwelling of the Spirit.

As the Holy Spirit's oil of joy works over and in us, the Lord, *my* Shepherd responds by leading us in His holy and righteous paths.

Today we sing the special song of the Spirit - BREATHE:

> *This is the air I breathe*
> *This is the air I breathe*
> *Your holy presence living in me*
>
> *This is my daily bread*
> *This is my daily bread*
> *Your very word spoken to me.*
>
> *And I, I'm desperate for you.*
> *And I, I'm lost without you.*
> *(By Llam Howe, Tahlia Barnett, and Timmaz Zolleyn, Copyright 2000-2017)*

Cynthia Perkins

September 27

NKJV Psalm 23:5 " ...my cup ..."

MY CUP

The next part of our Lord's blessing are the lessons concerning the *cup of the Lord*, *my* Shepherd.

First the cup represents the measure of our Lord's grace. There was a law in Biblical times, that if one traveled and came to someone's home, it would be unthinkable of them not to feed the traveler. After the meal the host would take the cup, and if it was filled half full, it meant that the traveler was to leave. If the host filled the cup full to overflowing, it signified "I love you; you are special to me; you are my friend."

The Shepherd has said that He calls us "friends." He loves us. He fills our cup full to overflowing with *the Water of Life*. "No longer do I call you servants, ... but I have called you friends. You did not choose Me, but I chose you, and appointed you that you should go and bear fruit ..." Our Shepherd offers us a personal and intimate relationship with God, our Father and Himself. (NKJV John 15:15)

Our Shepherd fills our cup to overflowing with Himself, the Water of Life. He gives new life, with all of His glorious joy. Our cup overruns with abounding love, grace, mercy, and the Spirit's oil of joy. That is why *my cup runneth over.*

We are all drinking from the cup He provides as we sing FILL MY CUP LORD. It is a perfect hymn describing the blessing of our Lord, *my* Shepherd.

Fill my cup, Lord. I lift it up, Lord!
Come and quench this thirsting of my soul.
Bread of heaven, feed me till I want no more.
Fill my cup, fill it up and make me whole!
(By Richard Blanchard, Copyright 1959)

September 28

NKJV Psalm 23:5 " …my cup runs over."

MY CUP RUNS OVER

Our Shepherd's cup, given to all of us, runs over freely filling our lives. The hand of our Shepherd, and our Father is an open hand giving abundant blessings.

The following, are two examples of His filling others with the cup of blessings, while He *walked through the valley of the shadow of death* …

* At the Cannon wedding feast, He made twelve gallons of wine. He blessed the occasion by answering His mother's request for more wine with a miracle of the very best tasting wine ever served at a Jewish wedding! Our Shepherd never offers us second best. He delights in our being given all the best.

* The miracle of the Prodigal Son, is considered a parable, but is actually a lesson of the Father's overflowing cup of blessings and joy. Here a son that was a rebel, disobedient, and full of himself, turns around and comes home to the Father. The Father greets him with open arms; prepares a homecoming party of the best of everything; best clothes, best food, and best jewelry. It was a celebration of the one lost sheep that returned home! This son's cup was filled to overflowing.

The Shepherd, and the Father, give to their sheep, all they have promised. Every promise is "yeah." And every promise in the Book is mine. They neither one measure Their blessings. The blessings just pour out, *my* cup is miraculously refilled, never running dry, because God is our Father, and Jesus, His Son is *our* Shepherd.

It is to this I testify; *my cup runs over*. The joy of *my Shepherd's* waterfall of blessings cannot be contained, as *we walk through the valley of the shadow of death*.

Cynthia Perkins

September 29

NKJV Psalm 23:5 "my cup runs over."

THE NEW CUP

The Shepherd brought a new cup during His stay on this earth. This cup rejuvenates His sheep, washing away their sins, and breaking the chains of death forever. It is the cup of the *New Covenant*.

The *New Covenant* released us all from sin's bondage and death's evil. Those who drink of His cup have been forgiven and saved from eternal damnation and hell. For this cup is filled with the blood of the Lamb, *our* Shepherd. Who by shedding His blood, put sin into remission, reversing its disease forever!

Our sins were washed away by the blood covering. No longer are we drinking from God's cup of wrath, but we drink of the Water of Life, from the cup of the new pact, contract! Jesus, *my* Shepherd gave the full cup of Himself for all mankind, for all time. The flow is ceaseless.

All of us have gone astray, turning to our own ways, deserving death and hell. But in lieu of this, the Lord, *my* Shepherd stood still while God laid all of these sins, for all time, on Him. He laid on His Son the iniquity of us all bringing into completion the New Covenant Cup.

The Shepherd, Jesus, took a cup, and when He had given thanks, He gave it to them, saying, "Drink from it all of you. This is my blood of the **New Covenant**, which is poured out for many for the forgiveness of sin." (NKJV Matthew 26: 27-28)

That very night He and the Disciples sang a hymn. Today let us all sing this hymn, explaining the cup of the New Covenant. NOTHING BUT THE BLOOD:

What can wash away my sin?
Nothing but the blood of Jesus.
What can make me whole again?
Nothing but the blood of Jesus

Oh precious is the flow
That makes me white as snow;
No other Fount I know.
Nothing but the blood of Jesus.
(By Robert Lowry 1826-1899)

September 30

NKJV Psalm 23: 5 " ...my cup runs over."

THE CUP OF BLESSINGS

Today we celebrate with song. Because of our lessons, the joy of blessings we received from our Lord, the Shepherd, are so overpowering we *must* sing. We can't contain ourselves. We must lift up our voices in Psalms and hymns and spiritual songs.

As the Shepherd leads us *in the paths of right living*, no matter if the path is hard and uncomfortable; or filled with pleasure, joy and victory, we sing praises to His name.

The first hymn is O I WANT TO SEE HIM. A song that describes our constant desire to see Jesus as we *walk through the valley of the shadow of death.*

*As I journey thru the land
singing as I go,
Pointing souls to Calvary
to the crimson flow,
Many arrows pierce my soul
from without, within;
But my Lord leads me on,
thru Him I must win.*

*When in service for my Lord
dark may be the night,
But I'll cling more close to Him,
He will give me light;
Satan's snares may vex the soul,
turn my thoughts aside;
But my Lord goes ahead,
leads what-e'er betide.*

*When in valleys low I look
toward the mountain height,
And behold my Savior there,
leading in the fight,
With a tender hand outstretched*

toward the valley low,
Guiding me, I can see,
as I onward go.

When before me billows rise from the mighty deep,
Then my Lord directs my bark;
He doth safely keep,
And He leads me gently on
thru this world below;
He's a real Friend to me,
O I love Him so.

CHORUS
O I want to see Him
look upon His face,
there to sing forever
of His saving grace;
On the streets of glory
let me lift my voice;
Cares all past, home at last,
ever to rejoice.
(By R H Cornelius, 1916)

Now, just keep singing! Praise Him in song. Just pick one and sing. Go ahead … and if you feel you can't sing then make a joyful noise!

PART V

Eternity Now

October

October 1

NKJV Psalm 23:6 "And I will dwell in the house of the Lord forever."

ETERNITY NOW

We must now start to move into His eternal dwelling that He has prepared for us. So to begin the ending, we will all sing the following song, and dedicate it, to our Lord, our Shepherd. We dedicate ourselves, to walk with Him always. Every day, we will walk where He walks. So sing …

FOOTSTEPS OF JESUS

Sweetly Lord, have we heard Thee calling,
"Come, follow Me!"
And we see where Thy foot-prints falling,
Lead us to Thee

Tho they lead o'er the cold, dark mountains,
Seeking His sheep,
Or along by Siloam's fountains,
Helping the weak.

If they lead thro' the temple holy,
Preaching the Word,
Or in homes of the poor and lowly,
Serving the Lord.

Then at last, when on high He sees us,
Our journey done,
We will rest where the steps of Jesus
End at His throne

Foot-prints of Jesus that make the pathway glow;
We will follow the steps of Jesus where'er they go.
(Mary B. C. Slade 1826-1882)

October 2

NKJV Psalm 23:6 "Surely goodness, and mercy shall follow me all the days of my life."

SECTION I

THE BEST IS YET TO COME

The Shepherd has stopped to teach us that as we go *through the valley of the shadow of death*, we will be protected from the rear. His Spirit will follow as He leads us.

As the Israelites were moving out of Egypt, into the promise land, the cloud and fire led them and covered the front and the rear. While going through the Red Sea, the cloud kept Pharaoh's army from overtaking them and herding them back into bondage. The Spirit is called to surround the Shepherd's sheep to provide safe passage.

The enemy, death, cannot overtake us. Each day with Him, here *in the valley is sweeter than the day before*. The enemy is the counterfeit of *our* Shepherd. He is the wolf in sheep's clothing. He has no happy old people. He is a liar and cannot tell the truth. He starts his charade with the lie of "you are in control," and ends with the fires of hell, burning that sheep for eternity!

Our Shepherd's *goodness and mercy shall follow* us as we grow in the Kingdom of God. Our final destiny is the best, a mansion where we will dwell forever with our Father, the Spirit, the Shepherd and all of their sheep!

He has saved the best for last!

Listen to what He has told us about our dwelling:

*Lay not up for yourselves
treasures upon earth,
where moth and rust corrupt,
and where thieves break through and steal:
but lay up for yourselves treasures in heaven
where neither moth nor rust corrupt,
and where thieves do not break through and steal:
For where your treasure is,
there will your heart be also.
I go now to prepare a place for you,
and if I go I will come again and receive
you unto myself that where I am
there you will be also.
(NKJV Matthew 6:19-21)*

Truly the best is yet to come.

Praise the Lord, *my* Shepherd, I am hemmed in from front to the back. *Goodness and mercy follows me all the days of my life,* as I walk toward my final eternal destination with Him.

October 3

NKJV Psalm 23:6 "Surely goodness and mercy shall follow me …"

SAFE

As we journey on these paths of righteousness, our lives must mirror the Shepherd's. Like Him, our face, set like flint, we go to the cross, to accomplish the Father's bidding.

The earthly shepherd always builds a pin for his sheep, about four feet high out of stone. At night the sheep go inside. The opening was about two feet wide and the shepherd would count the sheep as they went in or out.

The shepherd was the door of that opening. At night he would lie down in the door, to make absolutely sure not one thing would go in or out of that door.

Our Shepherd, the Lord called Himself…"the Door." He provides protection both ways. He guides from the front, and covers from the back. We are surrounded with the goodness and mercy, coming from our Shepherd's grace.

In certain parts of central Africa, if anyone needs help to or from an obscure village or place, people may request the help of that area's most exceptional guide. They will ask if "the way" can take them. As "the way" leads them he takes care to guide them safely on the paths where they are not in danger of being attacked. "The way" knows the safe paths to walk.

This parable is just like *my* Shepherd, who is "The Way, the Truth and the Life." I can fear no evil for He is with me, as I walk through the *valley of the shadow of death.* His *goodness and mercy shall always* follow me.

Cynthia Perkins

October 4

NKJV Psalm 23:6 "Surely goodness and mercy shall follow me …"

AS I JOURNEY THROUGH THE LAND

On my journey through the valley, the Shepherd asked me to lay down my life every day, and to take up my cross and to follow. Reaching down to get the cross causes me to stop and think, before I begin *my* daily walk. I remember His cross, and how He suffered for me.

Commitment demands a choice. The Shepherd has told us "If anyone desires to come after me, let them deny themselves, and take up his or her cross, and follow me. For whosoever desires to save their life will lose it, but whoever loses their life for My sake will find it. For what does it profit anyone if they gain this whole world, and lose their own soul? Or what will a person give in exchange for their soul? For the Son of Man will come in the glory of His Father with His angles, and then He will reward each according to their works." (NKJV Matthew 12:23-26)

While the Shepherd was on the earth, the Roman government, would have the victim of crucifixion, carry his or her own cross beam. This was done for a public declaration of Roman authority. The Shepherd challenges us to put ourselves voluntarily under the Father's authority by doing His will. The commitment to our Shepherd demands action: that would be carrying our cross.

Our commitment to follow the Leader, builds faith, and that faith is a verb. To carry our cross means we are *doing* the will of God our Father. It is an act of faith. Commitment in this way is a lifetime adventure, requiring time, hard work and determination. As our love perseveres, it exemplifies the Shepherd.

All of us realize that we are truly honored to be a part of His Crucifixion. It is no shame to us. He poured out His blood. We pour out our will and pick up our cross and follow. We now will sing the hymn WHEN I SURVEY THE WONDROUS CROSS:

> *When I survey the wondrous cross*
> *on which the Prince of glory died,*
> *my richest gain I count but loss,*
> *and pour contempt on all my pride.*
> *(By Isaac Watts, 1674-1748)*

October 5

NKJV John 10:1 "Most assuredly I say to you …"

THE SHEPHERD, THE DOOR: HIS LIFE LAID DOWN

The Shepherd is teaching us He is in control.

"He who does not enter the sheepfold by the door, but climbs up some other way, the same is a thief and a robber. But he who enters by the door is the shepherd of the sheep. To him the doorkeeper opens, and the sheep hear his voice; and he calls his own sheep by name, and leads them out. And when he brings out his own sheep, he goes before them; and the sheep follow him, for they know his voice. Yet they will by no means follow a stranger but will flee from him, for they do not know the voice of strangers." (NKJV John 10: 1-6)

"Most assuredly, I say to you, *I Am the Door* of the sheep. All who ever came before Me are thieves and robbers. *I Am the Door*. If anyone enters by Me, he will be saved, and will go in and out and find pasture. The thief does not come except to steal, and to kill, and to destroy. I have come that they may have life, and that they may have *it* more abundantly." (NKJV John 10: 7-10)

"*I Am the Good Shepherd*. The *Good Shepherd* gives His life for the sheep. *I Am the Good Shepherd*; and I know *My* sheep; and am known by *My* own. As the Father knows Me, even so I know the Father; and I lay down My life for the sheep. And other sheep I have (the gentiles) that are not of this fold; them also I must bring, and they will hear My voice; and there is one flock *and* one Shepherd." (NKJV John 10: 11-16)

"Therefore, My Father loves Me, because I lay down My life that I may take it again. No one takes it from Me, but I lay it down of Myself. I have power to lay it down, and I have power to take it again. This command I have received from My Father." (NKJV John 10: 17-18)

What beautiful strong words of grace from our Shepherd. So I do likewise; I lay down my life. I take up my cross. I do this daily by an act of faith, as I follow *in the paths of righteousness, for His name's sake; goodness and mercy shall follow me all the days of my life.*

October 6

NKJV John 20:21 "As the Father has sent Me, I am sending you."

SECTION II
LESSONS ON THE ABUNDANT LIFE

SERVICE

In order to have His *goodness and mercy* follow us as long as we are here in time, we must live as He wills. The following lessons are examples of how to have the abundant life offered by *my* Shepherd, and the Father.

This lesson deals with being in the service of *our* Shepherd. The Shepherd has constantly explained that He came as a suffering servant; *not* as a king.

Here in the valley, abundant life comes about by being a servant. We are to serve like the Shepherd. He set the standard of service.

SERVICE UNTO GOD

1. **THE NEED OF SERVICE**: Luke 10:2
   "Therefore said He unto them, the harvest truly is great but, the workers are few: pray ye therefore the Lord of the harvest, that he would send forth laborers unto His harvest."

Are we willing to labor in the service of the Lord encouraging many to come to eternal salvation?

2. **THE SPIRIT OF SERVICE**: Psalms 100:2
   "Serve the Lord with gladness; come before His presence with singing."

Can you serve the Lord without complaints, or the miserable excuses of the idler?

3. **SERVE MOTIVATED BY LOVE**: Galatians 5:13
   "For, brethren, you have been called unto liberty; only use not liberty for an occasion to the flesh, but by love, serve one another."

4. **SERVE IN FAITH**: James 2:18, 19
   "Yes, you may say, I have faith and you have works: show me your faith without your works, and I will show you my faith by my works. You believe that there is one God; You do well; the devils also believe and tremble."

5. **SERVICE HAS IT'S REWARD**: Matthew 25:21
"His Lord said unto him, well done, thou good and faithful servant: You have been faithful over a few things, I will make you ruler over many things: enter into the joy of Me, your Lord."

We are called into service. We are to be glad of the opportunity to be the Shepherd's servants.

To end our lesson for the day let us sing a hymn SO SEND I YOU:

So send I you - to labor unrewarded
to serve unpaid, unloved, unsought, unknown.
To bear rebuke, to suffer
scorn and scoffing
so send I you to toil for Me along.
(By Margaret Clarkson and John Peterson 1982)

October 7

NKJV Matthew 5:6 " …hunger and thirst after righteousness …"

BE HAPPY

The Lord, our Shepherd taught, to follow the paths of righteousness, one must desire to live righteous. We must desire this as we desire food and water, the most needed ingredients for life. Without food one starves to death. Without water one dies quickly. Without righteousness, one lives dead, in sin, and after death lives in eternal damnation. (Adrian Rogers)

The Shepherd has told us, those who hunger and thrust for righteousness; those who seek righteousness; will be happy and full of life.

The most unhappy people in the world are people trying to be happy. Those who seek happiness are never happy, for it is like a bubble or a balloon, popping quickly and NEVER sustained for any length of time.

One can try to find happiness in money, possessions or people. One can try to find happiness in education, strength, beauty, but it is like the wind, passing by quickly and they never see where it goes.

There is something wrong in this valley! It is called sin. The earth is filled with sin's tribulations. Because of sin, the earth is full of pain, destruction and death. Looking for a "happy life" can never happen. No persons worldly possessions can provide complete happiness, because life ends in the most unhappy situation. It ends in DEATH!

True happiness can only be a byproduct of righteousness. When one knows God, one can be happy, not only in this life but in the life to come. We who live for righteousness, because of our Father and the Shepherd, His Son, will dwell in *Their house forever.*

Those sheep who try to be happy in life without God, are treating the symptom; those who seek right living with God, are treating the disease.

This poem describes the happy life lived in the Shepherd. As *goodness and mercy follows us all the days of our lives.*

DRINKING FROM MY SAUCER

I NEVER MADE A FORTUNE
AND IT'S PROBABLY TOO LATE NOW,
BUT I DON'T WORRY ABOUT THAT MUCH
I'M HAPPY ANYHOW.
AND AS I GO ALONG LIFE'S JOURNEY
I'M REAPING BETTER THAN I SOW.
AND I'M DRINKING FROM MY SAUCER
CAUSE MY CUP HAS OVERFLOWED.

AIN'T GOT A LOT OF RICHES,
AND SOMETIMES THE GOING IS TOUGH;
BUT I'VE GOT MY FAMILY AND FRIENDS
THAT LOVE ME,
AND THAT MAKES ME RICH ENOUGH.
I JUST THANK GOD FOR HIS BLESSINGS
AND THE MERCIES HE HAS BESTOWED.
I'M DRINKING FROM MY SAUCER
CAUSE MY CUP HAS OVERFLOWED.

I REMEMBER TIMES WHEN THINGS WENT WRONG
MY FAITH GOT A LITTLE BIT THIN.
BUT ALL AT ONCE THE DARK CLOUDS BROKE,
AND THAT OLD SUN PEEPED THROUGH AGAIN.
SO, LORD HELP ME NOT TO GRIPE
ABOUT THE TOUGH ROWS I'VE HOED.
I'M DRINKING FROM MY SAUCER
CAUSE MY CUP HAS OVERFLOWED

*AND IF GOD GIVES ME THE STRENGTH AND COURAGE
WHEN THE WAY GROWS STEEP AND ROUGH.
I'LL NOT ASK FOR OTHER BLESSINGS,
I AM ALREADY BLESSED ENOUGH.
AND MAY I NEVER BE TOO BUSY
TO HELP ANOTHER TO BEAR HIS LOAD.
AND I KEEP DRINKING FROM MY SAUCER
CAUSE MY CUP HAS OVERFLOWED.
(By John Paul Moore, 18th Century)*

October 8

NKJV Romans 10:13 "Whoever calls …"

JUST CALL

The Shepherd has a line that is never busy. It **always** rings. It is **never** out of order. It **never** puts the call on hold. It **never** goes to voice mail, and He **always** answers!

He says … "Need a helping hand? Call My twenty-four hour helpline:"

1) When you have sinned	call Psalm 51
2) For Happiness	call Colossians 3:12-17
3) When wanting peace and rest	call Matthew 11:25-30
4) When needing courage	call Joshua 1
5) If the pocket book is empty	call Psalm 37
6) When thinking of investments	call Mark 10:17-31
7) When lonely or fearful	call Psalm 23
8) When worried	call Matthew 6:19-34
9) When you're depressed	call Psalm 27
10) When faith needs stirring	call Hebrews 11
11) Feeling down and out	call Romans 8:31-39
12) If the world seems bigger than God	call Romans 8:1-30

13) If prayers grow selfish and narrow   call Psalm 67

14) When God seems far away   call Psalm 139

15) When in danger   call Psalm 91

16) When growing bitter and critical   call I Corinthians 13

17) To become fruitful   call John 14

18) In time of sorrow or death   call John 14

19) When trust is low   call Psalm 119

20) When dying   call G-O-D

Tomorrow we continue this lesson.

October 9

NKJV Romans 10:13 "Call on My name …"

THE ROYAL TELEPHONE

To continue our lesson from yesterday, we will sing an old Gospel hymn, which talks about us calling God our Father. It is a happy song, with great lyrics. So carefully sing ever word.

THE ROYAL TELEPHONE

Central's never "busy,"
Always on the line;
You may hear from heaven
Every single time;
'Tis a Royal service,
free for one and all -
When you get in trouble,
give this Royal line a call.

There will be no charges, telephone is free;
It was built for service,
Just for you and me;
There will be no waiting
On this Royal line -
Telephone to glory,
Always answers just in time.

Fail to get your answer?
Satan's crossed your wire
By some strong delusion
Or some base desire;
Take away obstructions -
God is on the throne -
And you'll get the answer
thru the Royal telephone.

If your line is "grounded,"
And connection true
Has been lost with Jesus,
Tell you what to do;
Pray'r and faith and promise
Mend the broken wire,
Till your soul is burning,
With the Pentecostal fire.

Carnal combinations
Cannot get control
of this line to glory,
anchored in the soul;
Storm and trial cannot
disconnect the line,
Held in constant keeping
By the Father's hand divine.

CHORUS

Telephone to glory,
O what joy divine!
I can feel the current
moving on the line;
built by God the Father
for His loved and own,
We may talk to Jesus
thru this royal telephone.
(By FM Lehman, 1868-1953, Public Domain)

Truly a "Royal service" to connect with God the Father, through Jesus Christ our Lord. At any time, and anywhere. He will **always** answer in His perfect timing.

October 10

NKJV John 14:27 "Peace I leave with you, My peace I give unto you … Let not your heart be troubled."

THE ABUNDANT LIFE OF PRAYER

Do you want an abundant life in this *valley of the shadow of death?* PRAY. Prayer changes things, but mostly it changes us. In prayer, the Spirit enables us to walk in obedience to His every Word. He said "I will give you a new heart, and put a new spirit within you; I will take the heart of stone out of your flesh, and give you a heart of flesh."

With this heart we begin to establish a constant prayer life. Here are helpful suggestions for prayer to become the anchor that holds, providing stability, and confidence in our walk with the Shepherd. So pray.

* When praying, **be thankful for God's promised presence**. "For we do not know how to pray as we ought, but the Spirit Himself intercedes for us. Nothing will be able to separate us from the love of God in Christ Jesus our Lord."

*When praying, **be determined.** Do not be willing to hide behind your timidity or your nervousness.

* When praying, **confess your feelings honestly without embarrassment**. After all you are not praying to people, your praying to Almighty God your Heavenly Father, in the name of the Shepherd.

We will continue tomorrow our lesson, of the life of prayer. Now, let us lift our heads and pray.

Father into thy hands I commend my spirit. (Luke 23:46)
I will seek the Lord while He may be found,
I will call upon Him while He is near.(Isaiah 55:6)
In Jesus' name,
Amen

October 11

NLT Luke 10: 21 "Then He was filled with the joy of the Holy Spirit and said, "I praise You, O Father, Lord of heaven and earth, for hiding these things from the intellectuals and worldly wise and for revealing them to those who are as trusting as little children. Yes thank you, Father, for that is the way You wanted it."

THANK YOU, FATHER

Oh let us be like our Shepherd and be thankful for prayer. Prayer is simply talking to God. Conversation with Him, is such a joy. We listen as He speaks. He listens as we speak. It is the perfect communication; no biases; no retaliation; no "I told you so"; just His good and perfect will, joined with ones heart.

* When praying **be humble**. Your first attempt may be stammering and faltering. Do not apologize for what seems to you to be a feeble attempt. Do your best and leave the rest to God! Believe that next time will be easier and better.

* When praying, **be natural**. Talk to God as you would your best friend. He is just that! Use language familiar to you. Do not try to sound like the minister on Sunday morning.

* When praying, **surrender yourself and your needs**. The more completely you can do this, the more it will not be you doing the praying at all, but the Holy Spirit praying through you. Thoughts come and words flow and you experience the glorious thrill of being a person in God's hands.

* When praying, **have faith**. Your continued prayer can be, "I ask God every day to show me the way, and I know that He will."

* **Keep praying**, when the going gets hard. Jesus commanded His disciples to, "Watch and pray." And at that moment, Jesus Himself kept on praying. We can do no less.

As one sheep put it "You can do more than pray after you have prayed, but you cannot do more than pray until you have prayed." Prayer is infinite power. We have constant access to this power. *My* Shepherd said, "The prayer of a righteous sheep avails much." Prayer is my constant conversation with *the Lord, my* Shepherd.

Cynthia Perkins

October 12

NKJV Luke 18:1 "Always pray and not loose heart."

ALWAYS

Jesus has shown us that there is constant need for communication. Communication keeps the connection of His lifeline to our life. Meditating on His words will answer the questions of where we should or should not go, and what we should or should not do.

The Shepherd, *our* Lord has told us that, "My words are Spirit and Life." From Him we find truth, strength and grace to endure until we enter into eternal life.

The following are three tools needed while following the Shepherd in prayer and supplication:

1) **Be obsessed with the Shepherd.**
Fill every desire and life situation with His saving grace. Know Him and be known by Him, to the point that every first reaction has been chosen before there is a need for it, because the Shepherd's will is yours. Your will is only to know His.

2) **Observe the Shepherd.**
We sheep have bad eye sight. We seem to notice only the things that are important to us. If we lose sight of the Shepherd, then we loose our way. Our heads are always down, greedily getting all we can, before the other sheep grabs it. Look up. Keep your eyes constantly on the very Son of God, *our* Shepherd. We are to imitate Him. We should study Him intently, watching every move He makes and follow. Don't ever take your eyes off the Shepherd, or you will find yourself lost!

3) **Obey the Shepherd.**
To obey, means not only to hear Him, but to listen to Him. Meditate on His every word, then put His Words into action. His words are Spirit and Life. Without obedience to the Shepherd's call and instructions, one becomes anti Spirit fruit. The inside of the sheep becomes a grave filled with death and the stink of evil! Obedience brings pure joy even in the darkness of *the valley of the shadow of death*. It is the incredible miracle of His freedom for us to "Fear no evil, for He is with me."

In conclusion, remember, we must stop *always* trying to get out of trouble; and *always* try to get into righteousness. We should *always* be on the offense, and get off the defense. *Always* be a force for the Shepherd.

Always remember who you are.
Always remember whose you are!

Our Shepherd said … "You are My sheep. The sheep of My pasture. Your name is linked to Mine. Always pray and never loose heart!"

There He is. Look up! We lift up our heads and hands and pray.

October 13

> NKJV I Peter 1:15 "But as He who called you *is* holy, you also be holy in all your conduct. Because it is written, 'Be holy, for I Am holy.'"

HOLY

God the Father has called us to be holy. He has directed the Shepherd to lead His sheep in paths of righteousness, paths that are holy. Holiness defines the character of God, and is the code for every sheep's conduct.

Goodness and mercy follows us, when we, His sheep, follow the Shepherd in obedience. Holiness means we are "set apart" to our Father, God. Therefore, we live in His Way, not the way of the world.

The Shepherd's call is a calling to live according to a different set of principles and standards than the ungodly world. We are to lead a pure life in accordance to His commandments, laws, precepts, mercy and grace.

An obedient sheep, no longer conforms to their personal, earthly desires. His or her pattern of thinking is transformed by the renewing of his or her mind, because he or she is changed by the Holy Spirit. The transformation comes, because the Shepherd was the Lamb, slain for the world. His blood was shed, on His cross, to sanctify and wash us, and make us holy. His death, burial, and resurrection sealed the atoning grace we receive.

The Holy Spirit empowers us to pursue holiness. We are to seek holiness and invite the Spirit to work in us. The Shepherd responds by leading us into His righteousness. He strengthens us to withstand taking our own path that leads to the world's way and our will. These paths are called "Destruction-Hell-Damnation-Death-Sin." Sounds lovely, doesn't it?

The following was written by a sheep describing our desire to be holy.

We cannot make ourselves holy,
but if we desire to become holy
and set our wills toward following the Lord,
He will MAKE us so.

Now we all will sing the old hymn HOLY, HOLY, HOLY:

Holy, holy, holy! Lord God Almighty!
Early in the morning our song shall rise to Thee;
Holy, Holy, Holy! Merciful and mighty!
God in three Persons,
blessed Trinity!
(By Reginald Heber/John Dukes, 1783-1826)

October 14

NKJV Ezekiel 18:31 "Cast away from you all the transgressions which you have committed, and get yourselves a new heart and a new Spirit."

LIVE

As we journey through *the valley of the shadow of death*, goodness and mercy will only follow us if we repent of our selfish way and follow *The Way, our* Shepherd.

God, our Father, is the judge of disobedient sheep. In His Word He called His sheep "A rebellious nation;" and "impudent and stubborn children." Yet His love pours through the darkness as He calls them to turn from their evil ways and to walk again *in the paths of righteousness.*

Joshua, one of our Shepherd's sheep says "Choose this day whom you will serve. If you choose the Lord, you choose Life; if you choose your own way, you choose death." (NKJV Joshua 24:15)

Each and every day we must choose the way to walk. My Shepherd says "I am the Way ... the Truth ... the Life." We have a standing invitation to live the abundant life, now, *through the valley of death's shadow* into the Light of eternal life.

Our Shepherd desires us to "take hold" of our profession of faith and to receive a fresh source of motivation and strength, a new heart and a new Spirit. Today is the day of salvation, so may we keep our eyes on the Author and the Finisher of our faith, The Lord *our* Shepherd, *my* Shepherd.

"Let us pray. We are thanking you today Lord for your words. We turn to You, so we will live! We walk in Your paths, and follow Your Son, the Lord, *our* Shepherd. In Jesus' name, Amen."

October 15

NKJV Isiah 55:2 " ...let your soul delight itself in abundance."

"THE LORD IS MY SHEPHERD, I'VE GOT ALL *I* WANT"

Once a little lamb recited these words ... "The Lord is *my* Shepherd I've got all I want!" The lamb may have had the words mixed up from the Bible passage, but he had the concept right! The Shepherd provides all we need; He covers all our needs, and guides us in a way that is good and perfect.

The following is a daily living path to walk on and fulfills our daily needs:

LIFE SITUATIONS	REFERENCE
In time of fear	Psalm 27
In time of doubt	Psalm 73
In time of Illness	Psalm 56
In time of trouble	Psalm 46
In time of sin	Psalm 51
In time of Thanksgiving	Psalm 32
In time of loneliness	Psalm 13

The abundant life holds ... the secret of satisfaction. The secret? Having the Lord Himself!

Our needs will never be met in the Lord giving us "THINGS." The deepest needs will be met when my heart of hearts desires Him. This *is* the abundant life. In Him ... "I live and move and have my being."

I can truly say with one little lamb ... "The Lord is *my* Shepherd, I've got all *I* want."

October 16

> NKJV Matthew 13: 10 & 11 "Why do you speak in parables? Jesus answered them, 'Because it has been given you to know the mysteries of the Kingdom of heaven.'"

SECTION III

PARABLES

The Lord, our Shepherd, taught many parables, which are designed to reveal Scriptural truths, in a way easy to understand.

Parables are simply short stories in the form of a *type, figure,* or *illustration* with two levels of meaning. They present a comparison or contrast in order to stimulate a thought, a decision, or an action. Parables are the most difficult and the most powerful form of literature to create.

Their power comes from both the simplicity and the brevity of their teaching, as well as in the memory tool they provide. Approximately one-third of the Shepherd's teaching was done in parables revealing the nature of the Kingdom of God.

The Shepherd told us that our eyes are blessed for they see and our ears for they hear. These parables, of our Lord's do just that. They open our eyes and ears teaching us how to live as we *walk in the paths of righteousness* through *the valley of the shadow of death.* And at the end we *dwell in the house of the Lord forever.*

Our Shepherd will be using His parables to teach us to make the right choices as we *walk through the valley of the shadow of death,* He brings us home to our eternal destiny.

As we prepare our hearts let us pray.

> Lord teach us Thy Word. May Your Spirit guide us,
> invading our hearts to be still and know you are our God.
> In Jesus' name, Amen

October 17

NKJV Matthew 7:13 "Enter by the narrow gate ..."

PARABLE

TWO GATES

The Shepherd tells a parable at the end of His famous sermons called "The Sermon on the Mount." After this sermon covering the entire dissertation on how to live a peace filled life, He expresses in the story the way of salvation.

Listen as He speaks.

Enter by the narrow gate;
for wide is the gate and broad is the way
that leads to destruction,
and there are many who go in by it.
Because narrow is the gate
and difficult is the way which leads to life,
and there are few who find it.

The Shepherd is very intense, because which gate to enter is a choice that must be made by every individual sheep. "Salvation is a choice every person must make, but it is not just a momentary decision in the sense we often think of it. It is a once-for-all verdict with ongoing implications and eternal consequences." (John MacArthur, The Gospel According To Jesus)

The Shepherd stands here demanding a deliberate choice of life or death. A sheep must choose to follow the world on easy-street which leads to hell, a road well-traveled; or a sheep can follow Him on the difficult road which is narrow and less traveled. This road was the road He traveled to Calvary.

These roads lead to two gates. The question asked in the parable is ... "Which do you choose?"

The Shepherd said "I Am the Way, the Truth, and the Life; no one comes to the Father but through Me." He is the Gate, and the Way. There is *no* other.

The other choice is the wrong way. It is the broad gate that also invites us to eternal life. It is the way of the religion of self! A way to eternal damnation.

The narrow way and the broad way do not contrast religion with paganism. Both systems claim to be the *way to God*. The wide gate is not marked "This way to hell." It is labeled ... Heaven just as the narrow gate is, but it does not lead there. (John MacArthur, The Gospel According to Jesus)

Cynthia Perkins

The narrow gate is a turnstile. Only one sheep can pass through at a time. No sheep can come into the Shepherd's fold with a group, nor baggage.

To enter the narrow gate is not easy. The Shepherd said, "Strive to enter by the narrow door." He means one must struggle and fight because to enter is to enter the war. It is not easy. He said, "The gate is small and few are those who find it." (NKJV Matthew 7:13-23)

I praise God, *my* Father that I have entered. Let us listen to the song IT'S NOT AN EASY ROAD, a song describing the difficulty of the road and the entering in through the gate. One can only enter this gate by the empowerment of the Spirit, and the grace of our Lord, our Shepherd.

It's not an easy road we are trav'ling to heaven,
for many are the thorns on the way;
It's not an easy road, but the Savior is with us,
His presence gives us joy every day.

Tho' I am often footsore and weary from travel,
Tho' I am often bowed down with care,
Well a better day is coming when home in the glory
We'll rest in perfect peace over there.

No, No It's not an easy Road,
But Jesus walks beside me and brightens the journey,
and lightens every heavy load.
(© 1952 John W. Peterson Music Company. All rights reserved. Used by permission.)

October 18

NKJV Matthew 7:14 "The way is narrow … and few will find it … the way is broad and many find it …"

BROAD vs NARROW

The Shepherd continues the parable of the two ways and two gates. One way is broad and open. The other is small and narrow. One is the way that seems right to all sheep, but is not. The Shepherd said … "There is a way which seems right, but its end is the way of death." (Proverbs 16:25)

The Shepherd's way is a constructed road. It is a narrow path, and it leads to life. The path is narrow because it has no space for **any** deviation.

The Shepherd calls "If anyone comes to Me, and does not hate their own Father and mother, and wife and children, and brothers and sisters, yes, and even their own life, they *cannot* be My disciple. Whoever does not carry their own cross, and come after Me *cannot* be My disciple. Not one of you can be My disciple who does not give up all their possessions." (NKJV Luke 14: 33, 25-27)

The Shepherd leaves no room for a sheep to say "Well, this is too hard. Lord, You never told me it would be hard!" He said "An hour is coming for everyone who kills you to think that he is offering service to God." (NKJV John 16:2)

Following the Shepherd is not a casual walk in the park. Following the Shepherd is a declaration of war on hell! It cost the life of the Sacrificial Lamb, and it costs our very life!

This may sound like a horrible road trip, but it is not. The Lord, our Shepherd said … "My yoke is easy, and My burden is light. I lead the way, and in your weakness, My strength is found."

I follow *my* Shepherd. "For I can do all things through Christ that strengthens me."

Continue singing IT'S NOT AN EASY ROAD:

It's not an easy road there are trials and troubles
And many are the dangers we meet;
But Jesus guards and keeps
so that nothing can harm us,
and smooths the rugged path for our feet.
(© 1952 John W. Peterson Music Company. All rights reserved. Used by permission.)

October 19

NKJV Luke 12:32 "Do not be afraid little flock."

FEW WILL FIND IT

Both roads are marked heaven. The wide road starts out easy but eventually gets extremely hard, and at the end is horrifying. Because it ends in the lake of fire. The narrow gate may seem hard at first, but is the way to the Shepherd's eternal home prepared for His sheep.

The end of the Broad Gate is described as gnashing of teeth, worms, burning fire, and even worse the absence of God.

The narrow gate is described as entering eternal bliss, called heaven. A home filled with streets of gold, angels singing, no pain, perfect love, and the presence of God, the Spirit and Jesus *our* Shepherd. There is nothing more wonderful then what awaits His flock as they walk through that narrow, small Gate.

The Shepherd has asked His sheep to represent Him to the world. Hopefully, by faith, those who are choosing to walk in the Way will see us following the Shepherd, and will make their choice to also follow Him.

Heaven or hell? What will your choice be? These two destinations begin now, while still in *the valley of the shadow of death.* Those who choose to say to the Shepherd, "Thy will be done." are walking on the road that leads to their heavenly destination; those sheep to whom **God** says, "Thy will be done" walk on the way of self-destruction, sin, and hell, having been judged according to *their* wills and *their* ways!

So sing! IT'S NOT AN EASY ROAD:

> *No, no it's not an easy road.*
> *No, no it's not an easy road.*
> *But Jesus walks beside me*
> *and brightens the journey.*
> *And lightens every heavy load.*

October 20

NKJV Matthew 7:24-27 "Whoever hears these sayings of Mine and does them ...
But everyone who hears these sayings of Mine, and does not do them ..."

PARABLE II

THE BUILDERS

Today's Parable speaks to a common problem we sheep have; we are dumb! The Shepherd protects, guides, nurtures, and provides everything for us, and still most of us do not heed, nor listen to His call; that is dumb.

The Shepherd again teaches about the two ways; hearing without obeying; or hearing and obeying. He calls the parable the WISE AND FOOLISH BUILDER.

> *Whoever hears these sayings of Mine, and does them,*
> *I will liken them to a wise person who built their house on the rock;*

and the rain descended, the floods came,
and the winds blew and beat on that house;
and it did not fall, for it was founded on the rock.

But everyone who hears these sayings of Mine,
and does not do them, will be like a foolish person
who built their house on the sand:
and the rain descended, the floods came,
and the winds blew and beat on that house; and it fell.
And great was its fall."
(NKJV Matthew 7: 24-27)

Again the two ways; the *wise* way, or the *fools* way. Both sheep heard the words of the Shepherd, but only the *wise* sheep obeyed. The *wise* sheep responded to the Shepherd's call and acted in humble obedience. Both of these sheep have knowledge; both attended the class; both heard the Teacher's instructions. But, only one obeyed the Shepherd!

Now let's take a deeper look into each sheep's life, the life of the wise sheep; and the life of the foolish sheep. My Shepherd, will teach us a more in-depth lesson, on how to become a *wise* sheep.

October 21

RS Matthew 7:24 "Everyone who hears these words of mine, and acts on them - is a *wise* sheep (person)."

THE WISE SHEEP

Acting upon the Shepherd's word is a matter of eternal consequence. The *wise* sheep built his house right beside the foolish sheep. The difference is the foundation: the *wise* sheep built his house on the Rock. Building on the Rock takes much time, preparation, and thought. The sheep who builds on the Rock digs a deep foundation, He understands the commitment, and desires to build by the instructions given by the Carpenter Shepherd. In other words, the *wise* sheep hears and obeys the Shepherd's call for a decision, an active response of obedience.

Wisdom calls out, "Trust in the Lord with all your heart, and do not lean on your own understanding. The curse of the Lord is on the house of the wicked, but He blesses the house of the just. The just shall live by faith in Him." (NKJV Proverbs 3:5-6; 13-18; 33)

She continues with such persuasion, "Happy is the person who finds Wisdom, and the person who gains understanding. For My proceeds are better than the profits of silver, and my gain than fine gold. I am more precious than rubies, and all the things you may desire cannot compare with

Me. Length of days are in My right hand, in My left hand riches and honor. My ways are ways of pleasantness, and **all My paths are peace**. I am a tree of life to those who take hold of Me, and happy are all who retain Me."

In the *valley of the shadow of death* trouble cannot be avoided. The sheep who stands the test of time in this valley, is the wise sheep who hears and obeys. The winds, floods, and rains of life can rage all they want to, but that sheep's life will not be violated, and that sheep will *dwell in the house of the Lord forever!*

I choose the gift of God, eternal life. Jesus Christ, *my* Shepherd, has given me eternal life now, as *I walk in the paths of righteousness through the valley of the shadow of death.*

October 22

> NKJV Matthew 7:26-27 "Everyone who hears these words of mine and does not act upon them - is a foolish sheep (person)."

THE FOOLISH SHEEP

A foolish sheep is one who hears, the Shepherd's words, but their hearts are empty and hard. The Shepherd is clearly stating that the sheep who do not manifest genuine righteousness will not enter the *house of the Lord* after they leave *the valley of the shadow of death.*

The foolish sheep builds his house right beside the wise sheep. The same problems arises at both homes: floods, winds and rain beat on both houses, but only the fool's house falls.

The foolish sheep builds a life on a sandy foundation that requires no preparation. The foundation is not dug deep so it is stable and secure. The structure is quickly slapped up, bringing quick results. Judgment comes, and that sheep's house falls. It is an eternal damnation that does not end in the house of the Lord; but in the place prepared for the Devil and his followers.

The foolish sheep hears the Shepherd's voice, but refuses to obey. To obey the Shepherd proves that the foundation is built, on the Rock. To disobey proves the foundation is built on sand. These houses may be exactly alike in their appearance, but the fool's foundation is completely unstable, and it falls, here, *in the valley of the shadow of death.*

The question that *our* Shepherd asks is … "Which person are you? The wise sheep, or the foolish sheep?" Listen to Wisdom:

She raises her voice ...
"How long, you simple ones, will you love simplicity?
For scorners delight in their scorning, And fools hate knowledge.
Turn at my rebuke; Surely I will pour out my spirit on you.
I will make my words known to you,
Because I have called and you refused,
I have stretched out my hand and no one regarded,
Because you disdained all my counsel,
And would have none of my rebuke,
I also will laugh at your calamity;
I will mock when your terror comes,
When your terror comes like a storm.
And your destruction comes like a whirlwind,
When distress and anguish come upon you."
(NKJV Proverbs 1: 20-27)

Today, to close, we will sing the chorus about the wise, and the foolish builder. This chorus best explains Wisdom's words. THE WISE MAN:

The wise man built his house upon the rock.
And the rains came tumbling down.
The rains came down as the floods came up.
And the house on the rock stood firm.

The foolish man built his house upon the sand.
And the rains came tumbling down.
The rains came down as the floods came up.
And the house on the sand went splat!

So build your life on the Lord Jesus Christ.
And the blessings will come down.
The blessings will come down
as the prayers go up.
So build your life on the Lord.
(By Ann Omley, 1947)

October 23

NKJV Luke 15:2 "This man receives sinners and eats with them."

PARABLES OF THE LOST AND FOUND

#1 THE LOST SHEEP

Three parables have been presented by the Shepherd dealing with the pursuit of lost sheep. He emulates to all of us His Father's love for sinners, especially the undesirable.

He hates self-righteous unrepentant sin that manifests itself in the hearts and minds of sheep who proclaim to be religious. Those sheep are wolves dressed as sheep who claim compassion for the underdog, but really treat those *sinners* with distain. They believe that they are above the law, and **are merciless**.

The sheep of the Shepherd must uphold these parables that teach how to love the lost. All of the Shepherd's sheep should pursue the lost, just as He does. And when a lost sheep is found, we should rejoice with the angels in heaven.

What person among you, if they have a hundred
sheep and has lost one of them, does not
leave the ninety and nine in the pasture,
and goes after the lost one, until they find it?
And when that lost sheep has been found,
they lay it on their shoulders, rejoicing.
And when they come home, they call together their friends
and their neighbors, saying to them,
'Rejoice with me, for I have found my sheep
which was lost!' I say to all of you
that there will be more joy in heaven over one sinner
who repents than over ninety-nine just persons
who need no repentance.
(NKJV Luke 15: 4-7)

The parable begins with the Shepherd stating that everyone of us, even a common, uneducated, illiterate sheepherder is expected to have compassion for their flock! No shepherd would want to ever lose a sheep. Much time, money, and effort is put into his sheep. A shepherd loves and cares for his own sheep, raising them from babies.

Shepherds live with their sheep in the pasture, protecting them from predators, singing to them, and calling them by name. At night the sheep are counted, and examined as they come into the sheepfold.

If a sheep is lost, the shepherd searches desperately to find it. When he does he has a joyful celebration. He is not just happy for himself, but shares the joy that the lost sheep has been found.

The Shepherd speaks from His heart. "Even the Heavenly angels join God the Father in the celebration of one sheep that is found. In our journey here we are to do the same; we are to be passionate in our seeking and saving those lost sheep, and as we bring them back to the fold we rejoice and shout to all, that the **one lost sheep** has been found!"

You know I was lost, but now I am found. The Lord, *my* Shepherd found me and saved me. We sing AMAZING GRACE:

Amazing grace how sweet the sound.
that saved a wretch like me.
I once was lost, but now am found,
was blind but now I see.
(By John Newton, 1725-1807)

October 24

NKJV Luke 15:8 "She lights a lamp, sweeps the house and searches carefully …"

#2 THE LOST COIN

Today our Shepherd tells the parable of a woman who knows the value of heaven's salvation.

What woman, having ten silver coins,
if she loses one coin, does not light a lamp,
sweep the house and searches carefully until she finds it?
And when she has found it, she calls her friends
and neighbors together, saying 'Rejoice with me,
for I have found the piece which I lost.
Likewise I say to you, there is joy in the presence
of the angels of God over one sinner who repents.'
(NKJV Luke 15:8-10)

He speaks to us of the importance of His, and the Father's loving concern for the lost. In this parable He uses the example of a woman who has lost a valuable coin. A coin that was part of her dowery.

Listen as He teaches. "The woman in the parable loses one of her ten silver coins that are worth a days' wages. These coins represent her savings and probably formed part of her dowry. The issue here is not only the value of the coin, but also the fact that losing part of her dowry is considered shameful."

"She lights a lamp and diligently sweeps every nook, listening for the coins tellable clink and watching for its shine in the lamplight. When at last she finds it, her joy knows no bounds! She yells and announces to everyone … 'Rejoice with me, I have found the piece which I lost!'"

The Lord speaks with much passion. "Again we see the example of what our attitudes should be toward the lost. We *all* are to help seek and save the lost. The Father and the angels share in the joy of just one sinner's return to Him. We, His sheep, know this unconfined joy, as we find the lost sheep, while walking *the paths of righteousness, through the valley of the shadow of death.*"

Every step I take I shout the joy of salvation for all. Praising God I pray that all lost sheep will be found, and that I help.

October 25

NKJV Matthew 13:3 "Behold the sower went out to sow …"

3 EVANGELIZE

The Shepherd has commissioned us to "Go and make disciples of all the nations, baptizing them in the name of the Father, Son, and the Holy Spirit, teaching them to observe all the things that I have commanded you; and lo, I am with you always, even to the end." This command is to pursue the lost as we *walk in the valley of the shadow of death.*

In today's parable He teaches us evangelism. We, as He, should always be seeking and saving the lost, evangelizing the world.

Behold a sower went out to sow;
and as he sowed, some seed fell by the wayside;
and the birds came and devoured them.
Some fell on stony places,
where they did not have much earth.
But when the sun was up they were scorched,
and because they had no root they withered away,
and some fell among thorns,
and the thorns sprang up and chocked them.
But others fell on good ground and yelled a crop

some a hundredfold, some sixty, some thirty.
You who have ears to hear, let them hear!
(NKJV Matthew 13:3-9)

The sowers would broadcast the seed onto the field. Just as we should do as broadcasters of the Shepherd's message. This act is done while we *walk through the valley of the shadow of death*. We continue this lesson tomorrow.

October 26

NKJV Matthew 13:9 "He who has ears let him hear."

THE MESSAGE OF THE SEED AND THE SOWER

The seed in the parable is God, the Father's word. Here it is specifically the Gospel. The Gospel is the death, burial and resurrection of the Lord, *our* Shepherd.

The sowers are us, the sheep of His pasture. We are the ones who plant the seed of the Gospel by broadcasting it on the hearts, of each individual who hears it and is willing to listen.

One sheep said it best … "Seed is an appropriate illustration of the Gospel. It cannot be created; it can only be reproduced. Spreading the gospel is a process of taking that which has been sown and reproduced, and sowing it again. God does not call us to create our own seed or message. His Word is the only good seed. There is no such thing as evangelism apart from God's Word." (John MacArthur, The Gospel According to Jesus)

THE CONDITION Of THE SOIL

The soil is each individual heart. There is nothing necessarily wrong with the sower, nor the seed. The problem lies in the condition of the soil. The soil is pretty much the same in the entire field. The soil is made different by environmental influences. All of the soil prepared for the seed will bear a crop, but unprepared soil will receive the seed, but the seed will not take root or grow, and cannot bear fruit.

It is the same in the hearts of individual sheep. If the heart of a sheep is influenced by conditions of the world and is not responsive to the seed of the sower, that heart will never receive the gospel seed into its soil, and can never become rooted, grow, nor bear fruit, so it withers and dies.

As we walk through the valley of the shadow of death, I see many hearts not accepting the seed of the Gospel. Tomorrow we continue with our Lord, *my* Shepherd explaining the kinds of soil that the seed may fall on and not take root.

October 27

NKJV Matthew 13:3 "Some fell by the wayside, and the birds devoured them."

THE BIRDS

The Shepherd continues our lesson about the heart. "Soil is the issue in the parable of the sower and the soil. First is the wayside soil. It is described as a hardened, unresponsive hearer. A Sheep of this heart is cold and unconcerned. He or she desires his or her own will and own way. This heart is so beaten down with the sin and shame of this world, it cannot ever be forgiven. I call it a heart of stone. Wisdom calls this sheep a fool. She says, 'A fool says in their heart there is no God!'"

"A heart of this caliber cannot be penetrated by My love; My Gospel. The mind is closed; the eyes are blind; the ears are shut. Often these sheep are *religious*. They are in church every Sunday, but they bear no fruit, because they have chosen sin. Sin has hardened their hearts, so that they refuse to respond to our Father God. No matter how much love is poured out on them, they are not restored, nor do they grow. These sheep reject Me, and cling to *the valley of the shadow of death!*" He bows his head.

> *"There is a positive response, but it does not represent saving faith.*
> *No thought is involved, no counting of the cost. It is quick,*
> *emotional, instant excitement without understanding of the*
> *actual significance of discipleship."*
> (John MacArthur, The Gospel According to Jesus)

The Shepherd lifts His head and says, "Many sheep have heart problems. The problem is that the heart is unyielding and rebellious. It is not broken, and filled with Godly sorrow. These sheep start their journey with Me being *their* Shepherd with joy and excitement; however, he or she refuses to come clean and renounce the sin. Their beginning is only rooted in emotion. Emotion is not deep enough to grow. The root of emotion only, is sin! Sin has to be dug up and burned before God's word can take root."

I pray that these lost sheep have heart surgery. One sheep explains in no uncertain terms a lost sheep's predicament.

*If a profession of faith in Christ does not grow
out of a deep sense of lostness; if it is not accompanied
by an inner conviction of sin; if it does not include
a tremendous desire for the Lord to cleanse
and purify and lead; if it does not involve a willingness
to deny self, to sacrifice, and to suffer for His sake,
then it is without a proper root.*
(John MacArthur, The Gospel According to Jesus)

I understand.

October 28

NKJV Matthew 13:22 "The one on whom seed was sown among thorns, this is the sheep who hears the word, and the worry of the world chokes … the Word, and it becomes unfruitful."

A HEART THAT LOVES THE WORLD

Our Shepherd has often spoken this warning … "Be in the world but not of the world." The parable today is about those sheep who desire the world. They are preoccupied with world matters. They are consumed with life *in the valley of the shadow of death.*

The Shepherd looks sad as he speaks of these sheep who love "things." They equate happiness with career; family; money; house; car; clothes; or hobbies. Power or prestige, are their aims. They lust for whatever the neighbors have.

"The germinating seed that looks so good will ultimately be overwhelmed by the thorns of worldliness, and eventually the weedy heart will show no evidence that good seed was ever sown." (John MacArthur, The Gospel According to Jesus)

The seed hits a heart that has no room for growth of the Word, because the world, has first priority. "If anyone loves the world, the love of our Father is not in them." *Our* Shepherd said that we sheep must loose our life to find it. He desires all, *in the valley of the shadow of death,* to be crucified with Him, and to take up their cross and follow Him *in the paths of righteousness.*

If a sheep wants *goodness and mercy to follow them all the days of their life,* that sheep must leave the world behind and press on to *dwell in the house of the Lord forever.*

Cynthia Perkins

October 29

NKJV Matthew 13: " ...the sun v 6; the wicked one v 19; the weeds v 22 ..."

ELEMENTS

The enemies described in His parable are the world, the flesh, and the devil.

*The weeds represent the worry of the world.

*The sun represents the affliction and persecution of the world.

*The birds represents the evil one, Satan.

The Shepherd prays for us as we sow the seeds of the gospel of peace. For He is the one who provides the harvest, and guides us as to where we should walk. May we never become discouraged by the elements of the world, for our Shepherd restores our souls.

The Shepherd's Prayer

*I do not pray for these alone, but also for those who will
believe in Me through their word; that they all may be one as You,
Father, are in Me, and I in You; that they also may be one in Us,
that the world may believe that You sent Me.
And the glory which You gave Me I have given them,
that they may be one just as We are one:
I in them, and You in Me; that they may be made perfect in one,
and that the world may know that You have sent Me,
and have loved them as You have loved Me.*

*Father, I desire that they also whom You gave Me
may be with Me where I am,
that they may behold My glory which You have given Me;
for You loved Me before the foundation of the world.
O righteous Father! The world has not known You,
but I have known you; and these have known that You sent Me.
And I have declared to them Your name, and will declare it,
that the love with which You loved Me may be in them, and I in them."
(NKJV John 17:20-26)*

Still Waters

My question is, how could anyone reject so great a salvation? The Shepherd walks in the Light, because He is the Light, those of us in him do not walk in the darkness, of *the valley of the shadow of death*. We walk in the light, because He is the Light! Let us sing JESUS IS ALL THE WORLD TO ME:

Jesus is all the world to me,
my life, my joy, my all;
I'll trust Him now, I'll trust Him when
life's fleeting days shall end.
Beautiful life with such a Friend.
Beautiful life that has no end.
Eternal life, eternal joy, He's my Friend.
(By Will Thompson, 1839-1900)

October 30

NKJV Matthew 13:23 "The good soil, is the sheep who hears the word and understands it, and bears fruit …"

GOOD SOIL

Our Shepherd exclaims:

Behold I say, lift up your eyes and look at the fields,
for they are already white for harvest!
And those who reap receives wages,
and gathers fruit for eternal life,
that both those who sow
and those who reap may rejoice together.
For in this the saying is true;
'One sows, and another reaps.'
(NKJV John 4:35-37).

The good soil, a heart that receives the gospel seed, is the heart that broadcast this seed onto a huge field cultivated and ready to receive; this field *will* bear fruit.

The Shepherd desires that all of us who labor and plant effectively will produce a great crop. This will be a field as He put it … "Ripe for the harvest!"

Listen as He teaches. "All of us who are of good soil, whose hearts are soft for the gospel to be planted, will bear fruit. For a good plant will bear good fruit; but a rotten or bad plant or weed will not bear fruit. A good plant cannot produce bad fruit, nor can a rotten plant or weed produce good fruit. We all are known by the harvest fruit."

"The proof of your life in Me, your Shepherd, is you were crucified, and transformed. You have been planted into the death, burial, and resurrection, by the watery grave of baptism. Now you are a born again sheep! Your daily walk is *in the paths of righteousness*, journeying through *the valley of the shadow of death.* As you walk in the world, bearing the fruit of righteousness, you will be known by that fruit."

These words from a Shepherd's sheep explains. "I know we all bear different quantities of fruit. Not all of us sheep will bear as much fruit as we could, but we all must be fruitful. The Spiritual fruit of true believers, sets us apart from the hard dirt of the road, or the uselessness of a weed patch. Our fruit is multiplied and abundant, not something you have to look for among thick weeds. We bluntly stand out from the rocky, thorny, and barren earth." (John MacArthur, The Gospel According to Jesus)

Let us pray. "Dearest Father, Please help us as we sow the *Gospel of Salvation* to those who are not yet walking the *paths of righteousness*. In the Shepherd, Jesus' precious name, Amen."

October 31

NKJV Matthew 25: 1-13 "The Kingdom of heaven shall be likened to ten virgins …"

4 THE PARABLE OF PREPARATION

Being prepared for the Shepherd's kingdom is very important. He said that He would come quickly and unexpectedly " …in the twinkling of an eye …" His sheep must maintain our daily walk by a lifestyle of faithful obedience, keeping our eyes on Jesus the author and finisher of our faith. As He leads us, we know that the Spirit will take us *through the valley* until He returns, or until resurrection takes us to live *in the house of the Lord forever.*

In the parable of the "Ten Virgins" *our* Shepherd explains how we must always be prepared for His return, and no one knows the exact time.

The kingdom of heaven shall be likened to ten virgins
who took their lamps and went out to meet the bridegroom.
Now five of them were wise, and five were foolish.
Those who were foolish took their lamps

*and took no oil with them, but the wise took oil
in their vessels with their lamps. But while the bridegroom
was delayed they all slumbered and slept.*

*And at midnight a cry was heard: 'Behold, the Bridegroom
is coming; go out to meet Him! Then all those
virgins arose and trimmed their lamps.
And the foolish said to the wise, 'Give us some of your oil,
for our lamps are going out.' But the wise answered,
saying. 'No lest there should not be enough for us
and you; but go rather to those who sell, and buy for
yourselves.' And while they went to buy, the bridegroom
came, and those who were ready went in with him
to the wedding; and the door was shut.*

*Afterward the other virgins came saying, 'Lord, Lord,
open to us!' But He answered and said,
'Assuredly, I say to you, I do not know you.'
Watch therefore, for you know neither the day
nor the hour in which the Son of Man is coming.
(NKJV Matthew 25: 1-13)*

Tomorrow the Shepherd will explain in detail how we must be faithful in our watch for His return.

November

November 1

NKJV Psalm 23: 6 "All the days of my life;" …

SECTION IV

THE CHURCH

As we travel through the *valley of the shadow of death* we are traveling as the Church, the Bride of Christ, our Shepherd. The Church is made up of sheep who belong to the Shepherd.

His sheep, Paul, wrote these words to the Philippians Church:

> *Whatever things were gained to me,*
> *those things I have counted as lost*
> *for the sake of Christ. More than*
> *that, I count all things to be loss,*
> *in view of the surpassing value of knowing*
> *Christ Jesus my Lord (our Shepherd)*
> *for whom I have suffered the loss of all things,*
> *and count them but rubbish in order that I gain Christ.*
> *(NKJV Philippians 3:7-8)*

The sheep that make up the Church, our Shepherd's Bride, are those who are on the lookout for the enemy called *wolves in sheep's clothing*. Together, the Church, His flock, the sheep of His pasture, are in the world to do His bidding: but the world should not be in the Church. Satan sends his wolves in sheep's clothing everywhere, and therefore, we are told not to share spiritual fellowship with those who are of the world.

Wolves love to eat their victims. They prowl about seeking whom they may devour! Listen to Him " …Do not be unequally yoked together with unbelievers. Those who masquerade as sheep but do not obey the Shepherd. For what fellowship has righteousness with lawlessness? And what communion has light with darkness? … Or what part has a believer with an unbeliever? … Be holy for I Am holy!" (NKJV II Corinthians 6:14)

Today as we walk through the valley of the shadow of death, we are the Church, *our* Shepherd's flock. We are His sheep. We hear His voice and He calls us by name. We all sing THE CHURCH IS ONE FOUNDATION.

The Church's one foundation
Is Jesus Christ her Lord;
She is His new creation
By water and the Word:
From heaven He came and sought her
To be His holy Bride;
with His own blood He bought her,
and for her life He died.
Amen
(By Samuel Stone 1839-1900)

November 2

NKJV Romans 12:2 " ...but be transformed by the renewing of your mind."

OVERCOME EVIL

The Shepherd has made the urgent call to the entire Church to embrace a committed life. God's children should, in gratitude, offer a consecrated lifestyle to Him. All sheep individually and collectively sacrifices their life to God. Then He sets it apart, making them holy, as He is holy.

All sheep experience a transformation, a change, a new way of thinking made possible through the power of the Holy Spirit, who indwells us by the blood of the Lamb, who is *our* Shepherd, and *our* sacrifice. Therein lies the transformation.

He calls out: "Through the grace given Me, to everyone who is among this Church, do not think of yourself more highly then you ought to think, but think soberly, as God has dealt to each one a measure of faith. For as we are many members in one Body, but all the members do not have the same function, so we being many, are one body in Me, Christ, and individually members one to another."

His voice seems to be next to my ear: "Let love be without hypocrisy. Abhor what is evil. Cling to what is good. Be kindly affectionate to one another with brotherly love, in honor giving preference to one another; not lagging in diligence, fervent in spirit, serving the Lord; rejoicing in hope, patient in tribulation, continuing in prayer; distributing to the needs of the Saints, given to hospitality."

He turns and looks toward heaven, continuing in an emphatic tone: "Bless those who persecute you: bless and do not curse. Rejoice with those who rejoice, and weep with those who weep. Be of the same mind toward one another. Do not set your mind on high things, but associate with the humble. Do not be wise in your own opinion."

"Repay no one evil for evil. Have regard for good things in the sight of all people. If it is possible, as much as depends on you, live peaceably with all people ... Do not be overcome with evil, but overcome evil with good." He sits down. (NKJV Romans 12:3-14)

This transformation of our life, our mind, our hearts proves that the good, perfect, and acceptable will of *my* Shepherd, our Father, and the Holy Spirit indwells our very being. We are transformed.

November 3

NKJV I Corinthians 12:27 "Now you are the body of Christ and members individually."

MEMBERS

Here in *the valley of the shadow of death,* His sheep are instructed to be His body, *and* His Bride. His Body is called the Church, the Bride of Christ. He honors us by directing His family of believers through this valley.

He continues to explain.

"We are a building ... living stone, spiritual house ... with parts jointly fitted together, ... a body of Christ, a chosen generation, and a royal priesthood, a holy nation, My own special people that you may proclaim the praises of Me who called you out of darkness into a marvelous light; who once were not a people but are now the people of God, who had not obtained mercy but now have obtained mercy." (NKJV I Peter 2:4-6)

He sits, turns and looks straight into everyone's eyes. "Therefore, be sober and rest your hope fully upon the grace that I have brought to you by My revelation; as obedient sheep ... and as I who call you am holy, you also be holy, in all your conduct knowing, you were redeemed with My precious blood, as a lamb without blemish and without spot." (NKJV I Peter 1: 13-19)

He stands and begins to walk the path back toward us. "Since you have purified your souls in obeying the Truth, through the Spirit, in sincere love of the Church, love one another fervently, with a pure heart, having been born again ... of incorruptible seed, through the Word of God which lives and abides forever, because:

All flesh is as grass, and all the glory of man as the
flower of the grass.
The grass withers, and its flower falls away
But My Word endures forever.

"Now this is My word ..." He points to Himself ... "which by My Gospel is preached to you! (NKJV I Peter 1:22-25)

The Lord, *my* Shepherd brings such joy and kindness to all of us, constantly expressing His and the Father's love for all sheep. We who are His sheep are the Church, His Bride. What joy we have to be in the upcoming wedding celebration when the Shepherd comes for His bride.

November 4

NKJV Romans 13: 14 "But put on the Lord Jesus Christ ..."

POSITIVE ID

We are to be identified with the Shepherd, both as the flock, collectively, called the Church, and as His sheep, individually. New life in Him brings a new identity. Being the Shepherd's sheep, and being called a Christian is not just a matter of getting something; it is a matter of *being someone.* The spiritual process makes for a transformation into His image and likeness. The example in His Word describes the process *like* putting on clothes. Put Him on every day.

Being born again transforms us into someone new. What we receive as His sheep is never the point; the point is who I am! It is not what I do as a Christian sheep, that determines who I am; it is who I am that determines what I do.

New life in the Shepherd results in new titles. We must identify ourselves positively and then live out our I.D. The Shepherd has stated in His teaching who we are.

WHO I AM

* I am the *salt* of the earth:
   The Shepherd ... "You are the salt of the earth." Matthew 5:13

* I am the *light* of the world:
   The Shepherd ... "You are the light of the world ... Let your light so shine before people, that they may see ... your Father in Heaven." Matthew 5:14

* I am a joint *heir* with Christ, the Shepherd:
   "Sharing His inheritance with Him. We are Children of God ... then heirs of God and joint heirs with Christ" Romans 8:17

* I am a *member* of Christ's body:
   "No one ever hated their own flesh, but nourishes and cherishes it, just as the Lord does the Church. for we are members of His body, of His flesh and of His bones." Ephesians 5:30

* I am a *Saint*:
"To the Church of God - to those who are sanctified in Christ Jesus, called to be Saints ..." I Corinthians 1:2

* I am God's *workmanship* - His handiwork:
"For we are His workmanship, created in Christ Jesus, for good works, which God prepared beforehand, so we should walk in them." Ephesians 2:10

The Father loves us so. He has chosen us, and given us our new identity! What a Father! What a God! Let us all sing OUR GOD IS AN AWESOME GOD:

Our God is an awesome God, He reigns from heaven above.
With wisdom, power and love, our God is an awesome God.
(By Richard Mullins, Copyrights; 1988)

November 5

NKJV Hebrews 10:38 "The just shall live by faith."

OUTWARDLY

The Church is us, our Lord's sheep. We are His flock. We are His Bride. We are to exhibit our transformed lives to the world. Our behavior exemplifies what we truly believe, and the faith to act on that belief.

If our belief is self-based and not God based, we will be filled with fear and doubt. This is a result of falling back on what *we* know and not what God our Father has told us. In doing this, we are accepting the doctrine of man, not the Truth of the *all* knowing, and *all* loving God, whose will is *good* and *perfect*!

Living the life that reflects faith in His Word, is like the old adage ... "Actions speak louder than words." Another sheep put it this way; "Preach the gospel; and if necessary use words."

If we follow His Word, living in His will by faith, our identity being with the Shepherd, we will be a force, an unstoppable offense for the Bride, the Church, and the Kingdom of Heaven.

Her are the facts about our identity:

* As the Church individually and collectively we are given the mind of Christ. (I Corinthians 2:16)

* Since we (I) have died, we (I) no longer live for ourselves but for Christ. (II Corinthians 5:14-15)

* We (I) have been crucified with Christ, and it is no longer we (I) who live, but Christ lives in us (me). The life I am now living, is Christ's life. (Galatians 2:20)

Tomorrow we will continue this lesson, concerning our outward appearance, as He teaches us how to live our lives so all will see Him, the Shepherd.

November 6

"If you have faith as a grain of mustard seed…" (Matthew 17:20)

Fearless

Today as we finish the lessons on identity, let us all reflect on whose we are, and how we are to behave as obedient sheep who love the Lord. At the conclusion of our walk, whether at the end of the day or at the end of life, He promises us glorification and complete peace and joy.

Listen to the Shepherd as he continues:

"As the Church collectively and individually, the Word should be our claim. And the Word proclaims that we should pray for each other, and whenever we speak, words will be given to us so that we will fearlessly make known the mystery of the gospel, for which we are both collectively and individually ambassadors."

"Earnestly pray that every single and multiple church sheep will declare My word fearlessly. You must stand firm. Let nothing move you. Always give yourself fully to My work. You know that all of your labor in Me is not in vain" (I Corinthians 15:58)!

He starts walking, turns and continues. "Just step out on that path that I have shown you. My Light will shine for you to see the way. My Light cannot be ignored. For there is nothing that I will not do for My sheep, the sheep of My pasture."

As He finishes, you can hear a pin drop. The silence says it all!

November 7

NKJV Revelation 21:20 "The Lamb is the Light."

THE BRIDE

The Bride of the Lamb has been delegated to be the Temple of God here in the *valley of the shadow of death.* The sheep of His pasture became the Church, the Bride, because the Spirit of God came to dwell in him or her. That is why the *walk through the valley of the shadow of death* is the walkathon of the Church, as well as of the individual sheep.

We are the sheep of His pasture, the Bride of the Lamb, the Church of Christ!

His Word teaches us about three temples. The first temple was a magnificent structure built by Solomon and rebuilt by Herod. The second temple was the temple of Jesus' body. Today a third temple has taken shape, fashioned out of individual human beings who have become His sheep.

The Spirit's work comes through His dumb, dirty, lazy, sheep. He has risked that Gospel message being preached by us, to reach those lost sheep. Our Shepherd's Word calls this plan … "The foolishness of God."

The following is an outline of the Shepherd's plan:

   1) We represent God's holiness on earth. We incarnate God in the world; what happens to us happens to Him.

   2) Human beings do the work of God on earth. He does His Will through us. Without God, we cannot; without us, God will not! (Phillip Yancey, Disappointment with God)

Many great examples of the Shepherd's flock being the witness is found in His word. The following example, is of the sheep the Apostle Paul.

When Jesus appeared to him on the road to Damascus; he was planning to roundup and destroy those cultic Christians. The Shepherd asked: "Saul, Saul why do you persecute me?" Saul replied, "Who are you Lord." "I am Jesus" the Shepherd replied, "whom you are persecuting!"

> *This sentence summarizes as well as anything* the
> change brought about by the Holy Spirit. The Lamb had
> been sacrificed months before. It was the Christians,
> the sheep of His pasture, His flock called "The Way" that Saul
> was after, not Jesus. But Jesus alive again, informed Saul
> that these people, these sheep were in fact His
> own body. What hurt them, hurt Him."
> (Phillip Yancey, Disappointment With God)

A sheep was asked by a friend, "Where is God? Show me. I want to see Him." He answered "If you want to see God, then look at the people who belong to Him. They are His Body."

As we *walk through the valley of the shadow of death*, the only human glimpse of the Shepherd that anyone will see is His sheep.

Oh the joy of being Christ to this world! Let us all sing JOY TO THE WORLD:

> *Joy to the world*
> *The Lord has come.*
> *Let every heart*
> *Prepare Him room.*
> *And Heaven and nature sing!*
> *(By Isaac Watts, 1674-1748)*

November 8

> NKJV Ephesians 6:11 "Put on the whole armor of God" …

TROUBLE

Expect trouble in this world. "In this world will be trouble, but be of good cheer, I have overcome the world."

Satan, the ruler of this world and his demons are the enemy of God. They are actively involved in trying to destroy the Church. Satan's plan is to explain you to yourself, just as he did Eve in the garden of Eden. He told her that she would be *just like* God if she ate the forbidden fruit. He wants all of us to live independently of God, our Father. Trying to legitimatize worldly needs by the flesh, or the Devil, instead of Christ.

Satan and his demons know which buttons to push to activate our selfish will. He knows where the Church family, and individual sheep are vulnerable. The attack will be perfect for the situation.

Listen to what the Shepherd says concerning the trouble, and spiritual warfare we are experiencing in this *walk through the valley of the shadow of death*. But remember, Satan's power over His sheep is no more because of the sacrificial Lamb!

> *I want to remind you that your strength must*
> *come from Me and My mighty power within you.*
> *Put on all of God's armor so that you will be able to stand*
> *safe against all strategies and tricks of Satan.*

For you are not fighting against people made
of flesh and blood, but against persons without bodies
- the evil rulers of the unseen world, those mighty
satanic beings and great evil princes of darkness
who rule this world; and against huge numbers
of wicked spirits in the spirit world.

So use every piece of God's armor to resist
the enemy whenever he attacks, and when it is all over,
you will still be standing up.
(NLT Ephesians 6:10-20)

He looks at us and says … "You are in no trouble." We all smile.

November 9

NKJV Ezekiel 37:1-3 "The hand of the Lord came upon me and brought me out in the Spirit of the Lord, and set me down in the midst of the valley; and it was full of bones. Then He caused me to pass by them all around, and behold, there were very many in the open valley; and indeed they were very dry. And He said to me, 'Son of man, can these bones live?'"

FUNNY BONE

Sometimes we find those Church members who are not completely loyal to the Shepherd. Those who are still swayed by their own ways, and their own wills. One Sheep wrote a funny illustration that demonstrates what the prophet Ezekiel explains in his book chapter thirty-seventh. In the *valley of dry bones* the Lord is showing Ezekiel that due to their disobedience, His people are currently dead and nothing but dried-up bones. Then He shows Ezekiel that because of His grace, they will soon arise and be made whole.

This prophecy is also of the Church. She will struggle here in the *valley of the shadow of death,* but the Lord will soon come back for His Bride, the Church, and She will be restored and given honor as She is taken home with Her husband.

THE CHURCH BONE YARD

The following examples, explain some of these lifeless, and dry bones: plus the bones full of newness of life, that bring joy to the Church.

1. <u>The Wishbone Church</u>.
These members are too lazy to work.
They always wish their church would grow,
but want someone else to do the work.

2. <u>The Funny Bone Church Member</u>.
Always getting their feelings hurt.
The preacher must pamper and beg
these people to come to church
all the time.

3. <u>The Dry Bone Church Member.</u>
Never say amen or show emotion.
These are the same ones who will
shout to the top of their lungs
when their grandson hits the T-ball.

4. <u>The Hip-Bone Church Member</u>.
Touchy about their giving.
Their religion does not even
reach their back pockets.

5. <u>The Jaw-Bone Church Member</u>.
Always think they are God's chosen
one to tell the bad news.
And would never take time out of their
life to tell the good news.

6. <u>The Knee-Bone Church Member</u>.
this is the Wednesday night crowd.
The praying type.
The ones who will pay the price
on their knees for revival.
The ones who are the faithful ones
To Christ and the Church.

7. <u>The Back-bone Church Members.</u>
Christians with real convictions,
like the three Hebrew children,
who will stand true to the end.

Some day our Shepherd will return for His Bride and She will be beautiful, and full of life. She will be dressed in the Spirit wedding gown, adorned for Her Husband, the Lord, *my* Shepherd.

November 10

NKJV Revelation 19:6-8 " …for the marriage of the Lamb has come, and His Wife has made herself ready."

THE BRIDE ADORNED

The Lamb, our Shepherd, is to one day marry the Church, His Bride. He is coming back to take Her from *the valley of the shadow of death* to His house where we will dwell forever. Listen as His Word describes this spectacular wedding event:

And I heard, as it were, the voice of a great multitude,
as the sound of many waters, and as the sound of
mighty thunderings, saying, "Alleluia!
For the Lord God omnipotent reigns!
let us be glad and give Him glory,
for the marriage of the Lamb has come,
and His wife has made herself ready."
And to her it was granted to be arrayed in fine linen,
clean and bright, for the fine linen
is the righteous acts of the saints.
(NKJV Revelation 19:6-8)

The marriage of the Lamb, occurs at His return, when He and His Bride the Church reunite. The voice of a great multitude announces the event. The Shepherd uses His wedding announcement to depict His present, and future relationship to the Church. He continued by saying how the Bridegroom, and His coming Kingdom, will present the wedding feast.

As believers we are married to the Lord, our Shepherd. As He describes in His Word the relationship of Himself to the Church as that of a husband and wife. Believers are the holy, and righteous Saints, the Bride, the Lamb's Wife.

Our Shepherd smiles, and is excited as he talks about His wedding plans. He continues, "At the wedding you will all fall down and say … 'Praise our God, all you His servants, and those who fear Him, both small and great.'"

I am practicing falling before *my* Shepherd now! He is the Lord of my life. Soon, and very soon, He will came and gather us, His Bride, the Church.

Cynthia Perkins

November 11

NKJV Revelation 21 "Then I saw the holy city, New Jerusalem, coming down out of heaven from God, prepared as a bride adorned for her husband."

THE HOLY CITY

The HOLY CITY, is being prepared as a Bride for Christ, the Shepherd. These lyrics describe how one sheep felt after reading the Word of our Shepherd:

THE HOLY CITY

Last night I lay a sleeping there came a dream so fair.
I stood in old Jerusalem, beside the temple there.
I heard the children singing and ever as they sang,
Methought the voice of angels from heav'n in answer rang,
Jerusalem, Jerusalem, lift up your gates and sing.
Hosanna in the highest, Hosanna to your King!

And then methought my dream was changed, the streets
no longer rang.
Hushed were the glad Hosannas the little children sang.
The sun grew dark with mystery, the morn was cold and chill,
As the shadow of a cross arose upon a lonely hill,
Jerusalem, Jerusalem, hark how the angels sing.
Hosanna in the highest, Hosanna to your King!

And once again the scene was changed,
new earth there seemed to be;
I saw the Holy City beside the tideless sea.
The light of God was on its streets, the gates were open wide.
And all who would might enter and no one was denied.
No need of moon or stars by night or sun to shine by day.
it was the new Jerusalem that would not pass away.
Jerusalem, Jerusalem! Sing for the night is o'er!
Hosanna in the highest, hosanna forevermore!
(By Stephen Adams, 1844-1913, Public Domain)

Now let us listen to these lyrics put to music. It is sung in praise and honor to God our Father, who is preparing us a home for eternity. The Shepherd is coming to take His Bride *to dwell in His house forever.*

November 12

NKJV Isaiah 52:7 "How beautiful upon the mountains are those who bring good news …"

BEAUTIFUL

The Church is the Bride of the Shepherd. She stands as a beacon in the darkness of *the valley of the shadow of death.* Our Shepherd has shown Her how to live in the world as His Bride. Stately and poised, She stands, filled with love, grace, and mercy. The Church, is unified with His Body, intimately connected, set apart, and holy unto God. The Church is always pleasing the Son by a lifestyle which expresses sacrificial devotion.

Listen to His call to the Church, His Bride:

I beseech you, by the mercies of God,
that you present your bodies as a living Sacrifice,
holy, acceptable to God which is your reasonable service.
And do not be conformed to this world,
*but be **transformed by the renewing of your mind**,*
that you may prove what is that good,
and acceptable, and perfect will of God.

For I say to everyone who is among you,
not to think more highly then they ought to think, but to
think soberly, as God has dealt to each one a measure of faith.

For as there are many members in one body,
but all the members do not have the same function,
so all being many, are one body in Me,
and individually members of one another.
Having then gifts differing according to
the grace that is given to us, let us use them.

Let love be without hypocrisy. Abhor what is evil.
Cling to what is good. Be kindly affectionate to one another:
not lagging in diligence, fervent in spirit serving me;
rejoicing in hope, patient in tribulation,
continuing steadfastly in prayer; distributing to the needs
of the saints; given to hospitality.

Bless those who persecute you: bless and do not curse.
Rejoice with those who rejoice, and weep with
those who weep. Be of the same mind toward

one another. Do not be wise in your own opinion.
Do not be overcome by evil, but overcome evil with good.
(NKJV Romans 12:1-21)

We the Church, are His beautiful Bride. I am the sheep of His pasture. I am a member of His flock. I am the Church. We are the Church.

November 13

NKJV Hebrews 11:6 "Faith comes by hearing and hearing the word of God - Without faith it is impossible to please God."

FAITH IS THE VICTORY OF THE CHURCH

Regardless of the circumstances of our *walk through the valley of the shadow of death*, we as a sheep, are to love as our Father loved. David, the composer of the Twenty-Third Psalm, said, "Your steadfast love, oh Lord, extends to the heavens." Through His love we are … "steadfast, unmovable, always abounding in the Shepherd's, the Lord's work."

Whether we are in a moment of a dark time of trial, or we are being persecuted, or we are lost and confused about the next step because of intense life fog, if we just scream out to Him, His hook will immediately pull us to Him.

Today's lesson from the Shepherd's Word illustrates the love of God. It is a list of those sheep who remained faithful in the valley, through desperate trials, they chose the paths of faith. They focused on obeying our Shepherd. They lived out their faith by active obedience.

By Faith -
Enoch was taken away so that he did not see death.
By Faith -
Able offered to God a more excellent sacrifice.
By Faith -
Noah prepared an ark for the saving of his household.
By Faith -
Abraham obeyed when he was called to go out
to the place he would receive his inheritance.
By Faith -
Sarah received strength to conceive
when she was past the age.
By Faith -
Moses forsook Egypt.

By Faith -
The walls of Jericho fell.
By Faith -
Rehab did not perish.
By Faith -
Gideon, David, Samuel, the prophets, subdued kingdoms,
worked righteousness, obtained promises,
stopped the mouths of lions, quenched the violence of fire,
escaped the edge of the sword, out of weakness were made strong ...
others were tortured - had trials - were mocked - were scourged –
were chained - were stoned - were sawn in two - were slain –
were destitute - were afflicted - were tormented.

Because all of us are surrounded by so great a cloud of witnesses ...
*let us **run with endurance** the race set before us, looking unto*
Me, Jesus, your Shepherd, the Author and Finisher of your faith,
who for the joy set before Me endured the cross,
and has set down at the right hand of the throne of God.
(NKJV Hebrews 11:5-12:2)

Today we close by singing the old hymn "FAITH IS THE VICTORY!" We must "run with endurance this race set before us, "looking unto the Lord, *my* Shepherd." So sing!!!

Faith is the victory, Faith is the victory.
Oh glorious victory that overcomes the world.
(By John Yates 1837-1900)

November 14

NKJV Matthew 28: 18-20 "All power is given unto Me in heaven and in earth. *Go* and teach all nations."

THE CHURCH MUST GO

Where we are placed in this valley is of no importance when it comes to the will of our Lord. The Lord, our Shepherd does not say that those unsaved will never come to Him if we do not go: He simply says "Go, and teach all nations." Go because I said to. Teach and preach by your life living out Me.

Go means to go with your heart, living as a witness. Where we are placed geographically is of no importance. The Shepherd, directs our path.

Cynthia Perkins

The idea is for us to be still in Him, to face the Shepherd, and put our hands down, and with complete assurance and exact obedience go.

The following poem, expresses how our Shepherd, the Lord, desires for us to follow Him. The poem expresses how our Father God works out His purpose in leading us *on the paths of righteousness*.

I longed to walk along an easy road,
And leave behind the dull routine of home,
Thinking in other fields to serve my God;
But Jesus said, "My time has not yet come."

I longed to sow the seed in other soil,
To be unfettered in the work, and free,
To join with other laborers in their toil;
But Jesus said, "Tis not My choice for thee."

I longed to leave the desert, and be led
To work where souls were sunk in sin and shame,
That I might win them; but the Master said,
"I have not called thee, publish here My name."

I longed to fight the battles of my King,
Lift high His standards in the thickest strife;
but my great Captain bid me wait and sing
Songs of His conquests in my quiet life.

I longed to leave the uncongenial sphere,
Where all alone I seemed to stand and wait,
To feel I had some human helper near,
But Jesus bade me guard one lonely gate.

I longed to leave the round of daily toil,
Where no one seemed to understand or care;
But Jesus said, "I choose for thee this soil,
That thou might's raise for Me some blossoms rare."

And now I have no longing but to do
At home, or else afar, His blessed will,
To work amid the many or the few;
Thus, "choosing not to choose," my heart is still.
(From Streams in the Desert, September 5, Selected)

This concludes the lessons about us the Church. Not a path is easy in this valley. Therefore, I must follow *my* Shepherd. Listen again to this song IT'S NOT AN EASY ROAD. The words perfectly describe our travel as the Church, *in the valley of the shadow of death.*

*It's not an easy road,
we are traveling to heaven
for many are the storms on the way.
It's not an easy road,
but the Savior is with us,
His presence gives us joy every day.*

*No, no, it's not an easy road.
But Jesus walks beside me,
and brightens the journey,
and lightens every heavy load.*
(© 1952 John W. Peterson Music Company. All rights reserved. Used by permission.)

November 15

NKJV John 14: 15-16 "Blessed be the God and Father of our Lord Jesus Christ … who comforts us in all our affliction, so that we may be able to comfort those who are in any affliction, with the comfort with which we ourselves are **comforted by GOD.**"

COMFORT IN THE EYE OF THE STORM

It is a stormy life in this valley. Death is inevitable. Satan, the enemy is prowling around causing havoc, and we His sheep are in constant turmoil with unexpected storms that come and rip and roar through our lives. The Shepherd guides us through everything. He chooses each path in our *walk in the valley of the shadow of death.*

Our provisions on the walk are His promises of Truth that bring us peace, in the eye of the storm. Every promise of His brings goodness, and perfection. They shine through our lives, so all will see our good works and glorify our Father.

His Word is our suitcase as we walk, filled with thoughts and Scriptures that keep our faith, intact. He provides peace and comfort as we dress in Christ Jesus, *our* Shepherd each day. Grace abounds throughout the storm. His grace is sufficient for us, and especially in our weakest moments.

Here are several statements of encouragement from sheep who have *walked **through** the valley of the shadow of death:*

* *There is only one being who can satisfy the last aching abyss of the human heart, and that is the Lord Jesus Christ!*

* *Jesus knows every relationship not based on Himself will end in disaster.*

* *Our Shepherd despaired of no one, He trusted His Father, and that is ALL! That is the bottom line.*

* *If I can stay in the middle of the turmoil, calm, and unperplexed; faith prevails.*

* *All fret and worry is caused by calculating without God! It ends in sin.*

* *Fretting springs from a determination to get our own way. Jesus, the Son of God was "out" to realize God's ideas and follow His way.*

* *Let them that suffer according to the will of God, commit the keeping of their souls to Him in well-doing." (I Peter 4:15)*

* *"The great marvel of Jesus Christ's salvation is that He alters heredity. He does not alter human nature; He alters its mainstream."*

* *"Have confidence in Jesus. Believe steadfastly in Him and all you come up against will develop your faith. There is continual testing in the life of faith, and the last great test is death." May God keep us in fighting trim. Faith is unattainable trust in God, trust which never dreams that He will not stand by us."*

To end the lesson we will hear this beautiful song that echoes how the Shepherd is our shelter in the eye of the storm. Tomorrow the composer Rev. Dr. Charles Albert Tindley will perform his composition for the Lord, *my* Shepherd.

November 16

NKJV John 14: 16 " …we ourselves are comforted by God."

STAND BY ME

What a beautiful day. We are excited to hear our guest sheep sing his song. A perfect Spiritual, with a message of comfort, as *we walk through the valley of the shadow of death.*

When the storms of life are raging,
Stand by me;
When the world is tossing me
Like a ship upon the sea,
Thou Who rules wind and water,
Stand by me.

In the midst of tribulation,
Stand by me;
When the hosts of hell assail,
And my strength begins to fail,
Thou Who never lost a battle,
Stand by me.

In the midst of faults and failures,
Stand by me;
When I do the best I can,
And my friends misunderstand,
Thou who knows all about me,
Stand by me.

In the midst of persecution,
Stand by me;
When my foes in battle array
Undertake to stop my way,
Thou Who saved Paul and Silas,
Stand by me.

When I'm growing old and feeble,
Stand by me;
When my life becomes a burden,
and I'm nearing chilly Jordan,

Cynthia Perkins

*O Thou "Lily of the Valley,"
Stand by me.
(By Charles Albert Tindley 1905)*

These lyrics, illuminate the Light of the Shepherd, as He provides and leads us into the *house of the lord forever.*

November 17

NKJV Job 23:10 "When He has tested me, I shall come forth as gold."

THE STORM SHELTER

* *When I begin to sing God sets ambushes against the enemy.*

* *And the prayer came up to His holy dwelling place, to heaven.*

* *The joy of the Lord is my strength.*

* *In nothing be anxious, but by prayer and supplication, with thanksgiving let your request be made known unto God.*

* *God, our Father has all power to help and to overthrow.*

* *Stand still and see the salvation of the Lord, who is with you. Do not fear or be dismayed; go out against them, for the Lord is with you.*

* *There is continual testing in the life of faith and the last great test, is death. May God keep us in fighting trim.*

* *I, the Shepherd, say to you, that if you would believe, you should see the glory of God.*

I think the following poem provides words of encouragement as we suffer throughout our *walk through the valley of the shadow of death.*

YOU NEVER WALK ALONE

You never walk alone my friend,
though you may think you do,
For in your sorrow and despair
God always walks with you.
There is no hour, no passing day
He is not by your side;
And though unseen He still is there,
To be you Friend and Guide.
So, when you think you walk alone,
Reach out and you will find
The hand of God to show the way,
And bring you peace of mind.
(By Harold Mohn)

November 18

NKJV Matthew 5:1 "He went upon a mountain … He opened His mouth and He taught them …"

JUVENILE

Our Shepherd preached a sermon to express how to live while traveling through the shadow of death's valley. The title of His sermon is THE SERMON ON THE MOUNT. In this sermon He gives specific direction to His flock about how to live in the way of righteousness, and to walk in a new life.

However, sometimes we find ourselves so dumb! We also, mentally are blind and deaf. Self-absorption, causes us to desire our own way, ignoring His Way.

The following excerpt, was written by a sheep, who definitely understands how oblivious we can be, when we lose sight of our Shepherd.

THE LESSON

And seeing the multitudes, He went up into a mountain:
and when He was set, His disciples came unto Him:
and He opened His mouth, and taught them, saying:

Blessed are the poor in spirit:
for theirs is the kingdom of heaven.

Blessed are the meek:

for they shall inherit the earth.

*Blessed are they which do hunger and thirst after righteousness:
for they shall be filled.*

*Blessed are the merciful:
for they shall obtain mercy.*

*Blessed are the pure in heart:
For they shall see God*

*Blessed are the peacemakers:
for they shall be called the children of God.*

*Blessed are they that are persecuted for righteousness sake:
for theirs is the kingdom of heaven.*

*Blessed are they when they revile and persecute you,
and say all kinds of evil against you falsely for My sake.*

*Rejoice, and be exceeding glad:
for great is your reward in heaven.
Remember what I am telling you.*

⇝⇜

*Then Simon Peter said,
"Do we have to write this down?"*

*And Andrew said,
"Are we supposed to know this?"*

*And James said,
"Will we be tested on it?"*

*And Phillip said,
"What if we don't know it?"*

*And Bartholomew said,
"Do we have to turn this in?"*

*And John said,
"The other disciples didn't have to learn this."*

*And Matthew said,
"When do we get out of here?"*

And Judas said,
"What does this have to do with real life?"

Then one of the Pharisees who was present
asked to see Jesus' lesson plan,
inquired of Jesus His terminal objectives
in the cognitive domain,
and asked if His objective
was written on the marker board.

AND JESUS WEPT.

And, so do I! Please let us pray that we all become mature in listening and learning to know the Lord *our* Shepherd.

November 19

NKJV II Peter 1:5 "Add to your Faith …"

A SHEPHERD'S PIE

A sheep's character is very important to the Shepherd. He wants us to grow from the inside out. Growth requires, eating the Bread of Life, and drinking the Water of Life.

All sheep are hungry and thirsty. *Our* Shepherd, and the Spirit, fill up their sheep, those who have become members of the Shepherd's flock. The Church, should see the need and satisfy the sheep. "Where others see rebellion, we see thirst … Where others see apathy, we see yearning … Where others see alienation, we see guest."

The flock provides the living Water of Life that fills up those straying sheep and they *never* thirst again. These sheep are sick and wounded by sin, and when they come to Life's Water, and Life's Bread, they come only because they see in us the character of the Shepherd.

Listen to the Shepherd's Word as He teaches us how to grow in Shepherdly character.

"Add to Your Faith …" (NKJV 2 Peter 1:5-7)

VIRTUE - Quality of life, attitude that's demonstrated in life, that makes someone stand out as excellent, and the God given ability to perform heroic deeds.

KNOWLEDGE - This means understanding correct insight. This virtue involves a diligent study and pursuit of Truth in the WORD OF GOD.

SELF-CONTROL - "Holding ones' self in." All of us know from the age of temper tantrums to the age of our death we want to do what **we** want. Wise choices prove our trust in God.

PERSEVERANCE - That is, patience or endurance in doing what is right. Never giving into temptation or trial. Perseverance is that Spiritual staying power that will die before it gives in.

GODLINESS - To be Godly is to live reverently, loyally, and obediently toward God.

BROTHERLY KINDNESS - Mutual sacrifice for one another. Without the Godliness one cannot and will not add kindness. It will be a superficial on the surface kindness.

LOVE - The Greatest of these. Agape love.

All of the above ingredients poured in by the Spirit, mixed with the Water of Life, make for the Bread of Life, *our* Lord, *my* Shepherd. It is a delicious Shepherd's Pie, and they eat it up!

November 20

NKJV I Peter 5:8 "Your adversary the Devil walks about like a roaring lion."

THE COSTUMED LION VS THE LION OF JUDAH

He warns us over and over again that the Tempter will be relentless as he antagonizes us. The Devil masquerades around roaring and mimicking the Mighty Lion - The Shepherd, as he looks for his prey. He is mimicking the King of Kings, and Lord of Lords, *our* Shepherd.

Here are several ways that he plays out the part of the "roaring lion."

- * His mother tongue is lying. Every word out of his mouth is a lie, so he wants believers to lie. His motto is … "any lie will do, just so you lie." The Church that lies, is his greatest asset. For if the Church does not practice what it proclaims, our Shepherd cannot be seen!

- * He accuses and slanders the flock, the Church, and all the Shepherd's sheep. "Look at all of those hypocrites in His Church, they are no different than you."

* Sexual promiscuity is his favorite temptation. With much flair, he entices the flock to ignore God's direct commands against such sins, and invites all the flock, to ignore the holy mandate that our bodies are one with the body of Christ, *our* Shepherd. The Shepherd has said that these sins are devastating because they affect not only the outside of the body, but also the inside.

* Persecution is his number one tool to kill the Lord's sheep. He, and his demons, study each congregation of sheep, and then plant unspiritual bomb attacks, where they can do the most damage.

* Pseudo sheep are planted among the true flock. They look like sheep, and influence somewhat like the Shepherd's sheep, but truly are wolves in sheep's costumes. They promote confusion and division in the Church, slandering and pilfering, trying to kill the Spirit.

The Shepherd says we should "shepherd the flock of God which is among you, serving as overseers, not by compulsion but willingly … by being examples to the flock; and when I the Chief Shepherd appear, you will receive the crown of glory that does not fade away."

THE LION OF JUDAH is our Lord's name. He is the true King full of strength. So when Satan roars, don't get angry; when he roars, don't lust; when he roars, don't get depressed or become rebellious. Remember whose you are!

November 21

NKJV I Peter 5:8 " …like a roaring lion."

THE COSTUMED LION EXPOSED

Satan prowls around acting like He is the mighty lion. He is impotent. All he has is a loud ugly voice. He is NOT the lion. That would be the Lord, *my* Shepherd - THE LAMB OF GOD - THE LION OF JUDAH.

> Into the den of the costumed lion,
> Satan I march!
> Looking for those in chains of sin.
> Standing with my Sword;
> Dressed with the breast plate that
> covers my heart;
> No fear of death within.

For God has sent me into this hell called earth!
To reflect the bright light
that pierces the dark!
The shining light that screams …
"This way out!"
When they look to the light
the chains drop;
In freedom they depart!

Oh may I never again be afraid;
To stand, to rush, to run for my Lord.
Never knowing what is in front of me.
Through faith and trust
He provides the Spirit sword!

Faith is just this - dark …
one cannot see!
Yes, God knows: who, what, where, how, and when!
In the battle all I must do is fall
on my knees …
and go, quickly
Fighting: Rushing: Running:
Marching: Walking:
In!
(By Cynthia Perkins)

Never fear, Satan is impotent! He cannot touch us, His sheep. The Lord is *our* Shepherd, and The Lord is the Lion!

November 22

NKJV Ephesians 4:30 "Do not grieve the Holy Spirit of God …"

BE FILLED WITH THE SPIRIT

The flock has a helper and companion called the Holy Spirit. We all met Him in the green pasture as we humbly laid down our lives. He came to live in us and with us. Our work here, as we *walk through the valley of the shadow of death,* is to allow the Holy Spirit to daily renew our lives, our minds, and our hearts.

His Person in us will not overpower our own will. We must choose to allow Him to intercede for us with the Shepherd and our Father. As we walk humbly *in the paths of righteousness*, we are not to deviate from His prompting our hearts, as we listen and obey our Shepherd's Word.

If we choose a wrong path, we cause the Spirit to grieve, because He will not be a part of any sin in our lives. The following words of the Shepherd tell us how we must *walk* in the way of the Spirit.

> **WALK IN THE SPIRIT**
> "Let no corrupt word proceed out of your mouth, but what is good for necessary edification, that it may impart grace to the hearers. Let all bitterness, wrath, anger, clamor, and evil speaking be put away from you, with all malice. And be kind to one another, tenderhearted, forgiving one another, even as God in Christ forgives you." (NKJV Ephesians 4:29-30)
>
> **WALK IN LOVE**
> "Be imitators of God our Father as dear sheep. And walk in love, as I the Shepherd has loved you and given Myself for you … but fornication and all uncleanness or covetousness, let it not even be named among you, as is fitting for Saints; neither filthiness, nor foolish talking, nor coarse jesting, which are not fitting but rather giving of thanks." (NKJV Ephesians 5:1-2)
>
> **WALK IN LIGHT**
> "For you were once in darkness, but now you are light in Me. Walk as sheep of light (for the fruit of the Spirit is in all goodness, righteousness, and truth) finding out what is acceptable to our Lord! And have no fellowship with the unfruitful works of darkness, but rather expose them." (NKJV Ephesians 5:8-9)
>
> **WALK IN WISDOM**
> "See then that you walk circumspectly, not as fools but as wise, redeeming the time, because the days are evil. Therefore, do not be unwise, but understand what the will of the Lord is. Be filled with the spirit, speaking to one another in psalms and hymns and spiritual songs, singing and making melody in your heart to the Lord, giving thanks always for all things to God the Father in My name the Lord Jesus Christ, submitting to one another in the fear of God." (NKJV Ephesians 5:15-20)

Though I walk through the valley of the shadow of death, the Spirit overshadows me, and *I will fear no evil.* I choose, the paths of the Spirit and the Lord, *my* Shepherd.

Cynthia Perkins

November 23

NKJV Psalm 100:31 "Make a joyful shout ..."

PURE JOY

As we are walking these paths of righteousness, we are commanded to be filled with the Holy Spirits joy, which has been set before us. The Joy of the Shepherd is our strength in this *valley of the shadow of death*.

All the days of our lives should be showered with this irrepressible joy of satisfaction that comes from the Living Water Fountain, the Water of Life. The Lord, *our* Shepherd and this Water are one and the same.

Today, the Shepherd has asked us to sing these Psalms of praise. We are shouting pure Joy!

PSALM ONE HUNDRED

*Make a joyful shout to the Lord,
all you lands!
Serve the Lord with gladness;
Come before His presence with singing.
Know the Lord, He is God;*

*It is He who has made us, and not we ourselves;
We are His people and the sheep of His pasture*

*Enter into His gates with thanksgiving,
and into His courts with praise.*

*Be thankful to Him, and bless His name.
For the Lord is Good;
His mercy is everlasting,
and His truth endures to all generations.*

Now we sing I'V GOT THE JOY:

*Now I'm so happy, so very happy,
I have the love of Jesus in my heart, yes in my heart.
And I'm so happy, so very happy,
I have the love of Jesus in my heart.
(By George Willis Cook, 1848-1923)*

We are all invited to praise the Lord, because He alone is God the creator; the sustainer of life here, and forever. We are dependent on Him. He is the Good Shepherd who cares for His flock. So SING!!! GOD IS SO GOOD:

God is so good,
God is so good,
God is so good,
He's so good to me.
(By Velna A. Ledin, Public Domain)

November 24

NKJV Matthew 6:8-13 "Lord teach us to pray."

THE LORD'S PRAYER

Our Shepherd says: to rise up early before the morning dawn, and cry for help, and to hope in His Word. He set the example for prayer.

Communication with God was never an issue with the Shepherd. His prayers teach us how to be in constant prayer all the days of our lives.

Today we study a prayer that He taught His disciples when they ask Him to teach them to pray.

LORD TEACH US TO PRAY
Our Father -
who we pray to.

In Heaven -
the place He reigns.

Hallowed be Your Name -
God is all.

Your Kingdom come -
We desire to be with God now and forever.
We desire to have Him now in our heart and now eternally.

Your will be done -
Everywhere God's will is good and perfect.

On earth just like in heaven -
God's will is good and perfect.

Give us today our daily bread -
We are humbly asking for food.
Nothing extravagant. But our need met.
This is also for all "our" bread.

Forgive us our debts -
Our sins. We owe God an apology for our flagrant pride - self-will - and rebellion.

As we forgive our debtors -
For if I forgive men their trespasses,
Your (my) heavenly Father will also forgive you (me).
But, if you (me) do not forgive mankind their trespasses,
Neither will your (my) Father forgive your (my) trespasses.

And do not lead us into temptation -
God does not tempt us!
We are subject to trials that expose us to Satan's assaults.
We must avoid sin altogether.
God knows our needs and He will not "Hang us out to dry."
He will not subject us to more than we can bear.
Also He provides a way of escape,
and our endurance is one of those ways -
"Keep on keeping on!"

Deliver us from the evil one -
He paid the "get out of hell" price.

For Yours is the Kingdom and the power and the glory forever -
God is sovereign -
All, things are possible with God!
Amen
(NKJV Matthew 6:9-13)

In praying we invite our Father's will for us and to show complete reliance on Him, *all the days of our lives, as we walk through the valley of the shadow of death, fearing no evil, till we dwell in His house forever.*

November 25

NKJV Matthew 17: 26 "The Shepherd prays for all believers … 'that the love with which You (the Father) loved Me, may be in them, and I in them.'"

PRAY THAT WE MAY BE ONE

Listen as He prayers:

I pray for those who will believe in Me through the witnesses word; that they all may be one, as you, Father, are in Me, and I in You; that they also may be one in us, that the world may believe that you sent Me. And the glory which You gave me I have given them, that they may be one just as We are One: I in them, and You in Me; that they may be made perfect in one, and that the world may know that you have sent Me, and have loved them as You have loved Me.

Father I desire that they also whom You gave Me may be with Me where I am, that they may behold My glory which You have given Me; for you loved Me before the foundation of the world.

O righteous Father! The world has not known You, but I have known You; and these have known that You sent Me. And I have declared to them Your name, and will declare it, that the love with which you loved Me may be in them, and I in them.
(NKJV John 17:20-26)

I pray "God be in me as you are in the Lord who is *my* Shepherd."

November 26

NKJV I Thessalonians 5:17 "Pray without ceasing."

CONTINUOUSLY PRAY

Dearest Lord,

When I do good and suffer, if I take it patiently, this is commendable before you. For to this I was called, because Christ also suffered for us, leaving us an example that I should follow:

Who committed no sin
nor was deceit found in His mouth!
Who when He was reviled, did
not revile in return;
When he suffered, He did not threaten,
but committed Himself to Him
who judges righteously.

This is my prayer - Oh God.
In Jesus' name,
Amen
(NKJV I Peter 2:22-24)

Dearest Lord,

I shall be holy as You are holy oh Lord. Your aim is to produce Saints. You did not come to save us out of pity: You came to save us because You have created us to be holy. Your atonement has put me back into perfect union with You, because of the death of Your Son, the Lord, my Shepherd, Jesus Christ.

Help me to maintain a controlled, continual watchfulness, so that nothing of which you would be ashamed arises in my life.

Show me your ways, O Lord:
Teach me Your paths.
Lead me in Your truth ...
All the paths of the Lord are mercy and truth ...
My eyes are ever toward the Lord.
(NKJV Psalm 25)

God thank you for your Word. In Jesus' name, Amen.

November 27

NKJV Psalm 27:6 "And now my head shall be lifted up above my enemies all around me …"

AN OVERCOMER'S PRAYER

Dearest God,

Turn yourself to me, and have mercy on me,
for I am desolate and afflicted.
The troubles of my heart have enlarged.

Bring me out of distress!
Look on my affliction and my pain,
and forgive my sins.
Consider my enemies: for they are many;
and they hate me with a cruel hatred.

Keep my soul and deliver me;
Let me not be ashamed, for I put my trust in You.
In Jesus' precious name, Amen
(NKJV Psalm 25:18-20)

Here is the prayer prayed by Stephen, the first martyr, as he was being stoned to death for preaching the gospel.

Dearest God,

As I see Thy glory oh God, I see the heavens open and the son of man standing at Your, my God's right hand! Lord Jesus, receive my spirit. Lord do not charge them with this sin". (NKJV Acts 7:56)

Here is the prayer of the apostles as they went out to preach the Word of God.

"Lord, you are God; who made heaven and earth and the sea,
and all that is in them, who by the mouth of your
servant David has said:"
Why did the nations rage,
and the people plot vain things?
The Kings of the earth took their stand,
and the rulers were gathered together
against the Lord and against His Christ.

For truly against your holy servant Jesus,
whom you anointed all people are gathered together
to do whatever your hand and your purpose
determined before to be done.
Now Lord, look on their threats,
and grant to your servants, your sheep,
that with all boldness we may speak your word,
by stretching out Your hand to heal,
and that signs and wonders may be done
through the name of Your holy Servant Jesus."
In Jesus' name, Amen.
(NKJV Acts 4:24-30)

When they prayed this prayer, the place was shaken; and they were all filled with the Holy Spirit, and they spoke the word of God with boldness!

And so should we.

November 28

NKJV Luke 7:13 "And when the Lord saw her He had compassion on her …"

SHOW COMPASSION

We sheep, the Church, are taught by the Shepherd to have compassion, and to show compassion with our actions. He sends us out, as He did His disciples as they *walked through the valley of the shadow of death* to spread compassion to the then known world. These are His instructions:

Then Jesus, the Shepherd, went about all the cities and villages,
teaching in their synagogues,
and preaching the gospel of the Kingdom …

But when He saw the multitudes,
He was moved with compassion for them,
because they were weary and scattered,
like sheep having NO shepherd.
Then He said …
"The harvest truly is plentiful, but the laborers are few.
Therefore, pray the Lord of the harvest
to send out laborers into His harvest.

He sends us out and commands us:
"Go to the lost sheep - and as you go, preach,
saying
'The kingdom of heaven is at hand.'
Heal the sick, cast out demons.
Freely you have received. Freely give.
Don't take any money with you,
nor even carry a duffel bag with extra
clothes and shoes,
or even a walking stick:
for those you help should feed and care for you."
(NKJV Matthew 10: 5-42)

This lesson concerning the Church exhibiting compassion, will continue tomorrow.

November 29

NKJV Matthew 9:36 "When He saw the multitudes, He was moved with compassion for them, because they were weary and scattered, like sheep having no shepherd."

INTENTIONAL COMPASSION

Today is the continuation of *our* Shepherd's teaching on compassion. To have compassion and a love to spread the Gospel of Salvation to the whole world even under duress or persecution, is to follow Him in His way, as we *walk through the valley of the shadow of death.*

Whenever you enter a city or village,
search for a Godly man
and stay in his home until you leave for the next place.
When you ask permission to stay, be friendly,
And if it turns out to be a godly home,
give it your blessing:
if not, keep the blessing.

Any city, country or home that doesn't welcome you -
shake off the dust of that place from
your feet as you leave.
Truly, the wicked cities of Sodom and Gomorrah will be
better off at Judgment Day than they.
I am sending you out as sheep among wolves.
Be wary and wise as serpents and harmless as doves.

But beware! For you will be arrested
and tried, and whipped in the synagogues.

Yes, and you must stand trial before governors and kings for My sake.
This will give you the opportunity to tell them about Me,
yes, to witness to the world.

When you are arrested, don't worry about what to say at your trial,
for you will be given the right words at the right time.
For it won't be you doing the talking -
it will be the spirit of your heavenly Father speaking through you!
(NKJV Matthew 10:11-20)

We will continue with His lesson on compassionate perseverance tomorrow. We are obligated to show compassion in these desperate times. These lessons make all the *difference* in *the valley of the shadow of death.*

November 30

NKJV Romans 9:36 " ...Like Sheep having no shepherd."

THE SUFFERING SERVANT

The Shepherd starts today with a warning. "This is a hard lesson, because it is the way of the world. Heed My words:"

Brother shall betray brother to death,
and fathers shall betray their own children.
and children shall rise against their parents,
and cause their deaths.
Everyone shall hate you because you belong to Me.
But all of you who endure to the end shall be saved.
When you are persecuted in one city, flee to the next!
I will return before you have reached them all!

A student is not greater than his teacher.
A servant is not above his master.
The student shares his teacher's fate.
The servant shares his master's fate!
And since I, the master of the household,
have been called 'Satan,' how much more will you!

But don't be afraid of those who threaten you.
For the time is coming when the truth will be revealed:
their secret plots will become public information.

What I tell you now in the gloom, shout abroad
when daybreak comes.
What I whisper in your ears,
proclaim from the housetops!

Don't be afraid of those who can kill only your bodies,
but can't touch your souls!
Fear only God who can destroy both soul and body in hell.

Not one sparrow (What do they cost? Two for a penny?)
can fall to the ground without your Father knowing it.
And the very hairs of your head are all numbered.
So don't worry!
You are more valuable to Him than many sparrows.
If anyone publicly acknowledges Me as their friend,
I will openly acknowledge them as My friend
before My Father in heaven.
But if anyone publicly denies me,
I will openly deny them before My Father in heaven.
(NKJV Matthew 10:21-33, Paraphrased)

Our Shepherd, wasted no words telling us that He is Lord and that we must become as He, a suffering servant, as we bring the gospel message of salvation to those who live in the darkness of *the valley of the shadow of death.*

December

December 1

NKJV I Thessalonians 5:17 "Pray continually."

A MARATHON OF PRAYER

Your life, in this valley, is a life of the **Faith Marathon Race**. All the struggle commits us to be constant and faithful in prayer. Our Lord says to keep running in this **Faith Race.** We shall run and not grow weary when following Him. Never shall we give up!

He has told us in His word to "Pray continually," "Keep on praying" and "Devote ourselves to prayer, remaining steadfast, unmovable always abounding in His work." A sheep A. W. Tozer said that our prayer life can grow "from the initial, most casual brush to the fullest, most intimate communion of which the human soul is capable."

In running a marathon, one must *"work out."* Working out and preparation cannot be missed. If a day is missed it takes three days to make up the *workout* that was lost. Also, exercise, and discipline in eating and resting is necessary to develop the body for the race.

The same rules apply in our **Prayer Marathon Race**. Press toward the upward calling. Run the race counting on the Holy Spirit to guide, protect and nurture you as you "work out." The Constant feeding on the "Bread of Life, and "Fruit of the Spirit," and drinking the "Water of Life" builds one up both spiritually, and physically, for the winning of the marathon.

Our Shepherd is also our coach. He will never leave us nor forsake us. He desires close communion with us, so any time we falter, He will pick us up, and we can keep on keeping on!

Deep communion with God, the Father and His Son, the Shepherd, is what we sheep must accomplish in this marathon *walk through the valley of the shadow of death.* For the reward is to *dwell in the house of the Lord* **FOREVER.**

I will run the race. I will finish the course. There is laid up for me a crown of righteousness! Because of Him, I'm a winner.

Cynthia Perkins

December 2

NKJV Proverbs 1:7 "But fools despise wisdom and instruction."

BE MERCIFUL TO ME A FOOL

Here is a poem that describes the power and attitude of a life of prayer and supplication. It is an example of how not to be a fool, and how to pray with a humble and contrite heart and spirit.

The Shepherd recites this poem:

THE FOOL'S PRAYER

*The royal feast was done; the King
Sought some new sport to banish care,
And to his jester cried: "Sir Fool,
Kneel now, and make for us a prayer!"*

*The jester doffed his cap and bells,
And stood the mocking court before;
They could not see the bitter smile
Behind the painted grin he wore.*

*He bowed his head, and bent his knee
Upon the monarch's silken stool;
His pleading voice arose: "O Lord,
Be merciful to me, a fool!*

*"No pity, Lord, could change the heart
From red with wrong to white as wool;
The rod must heal the sin: but, Lord,
Be merciful to me, a fool!*

*" 'Tis not by guilt the onward sweep
Of truth and right, O Lord, we stay;
'Tis by our follies that so long
We hold the earth from heaven away.*

*"These clumsy feet, still in the mire,
Go crushing blossoms without end;
These hard, well-meaning hands we thrust
Among the heart-strings of a friend.*

*"The ill-timed truth we might have kept -
Who knows how sharp it pierced and stung?
The word we had not sense to say -
Who knows how grandly it had rung?*

"Our faults no tenderness should ask,
The chastening stripes must cleanse them all;
But for our blunders - oh in shame
Before the eyes of heaven we fall.

"Earth bears no balsam for mistakes;
Men crown the knave, and scourge the tool
That did his will; but Thou, O Lord,
Be merciful to me, a fool!"

The room was hushed; in silence rose
The King, and sought his gardens cool,
And walked apart, and murmured low,
"Be merciful to me, a fool!"
(By Edward R. Still, 1841-1887)

Prayer changes things, but mostly it changes me! I fall on my face and pray:

"God, be merciful to me a sinner, a fool.
In Jesus' precious and holy name,
Amen."

December 3

NKJV Job 16:21 "O that one might plead for a man with God …"

PRAY – SING - MEDITATE

"The Psalmist had plenty to pray, sing, and meditate about. All of these Psalms were to be in honor and praise to our Lord God. Here are several that will help you on your journey." *Our* Shepherd smiles as He sings, recites and prays.

PRAY
Psalm 90:10-12
The days of our lives are seventy years;
And if by reason of strength they are eighty years,
yet their boast is only labor and sorrow;
For it is soon cut off, and we fly away …
So teach us to number our days
That we may gain a heart of wisdom.

SING
Psalm 39:4-6
Lord, make me know my end.
And what is the measure of my days.
That I may know how frail I am.
Indeed, you have made my days as hand breadths,

And my age is as nothing before you;
Certainly every person at their best state is but a vapor.
Surely every person walks about like a shadow;
Surely they busy themselves in vain;
They heap up riches,
But does not know who will gather them.

MEDITATE
Job 16:21-22
O that one might plead for a man with God,
As a man pleads for his neighbor!
For when a few years are finished,
I shall go the way of no return.

Our Shepherd leads us on our paths with His Word, to keep our hearts in constant contact with Him. He will continue with more tomorrow.

December 4

NKJV Isaiah 46:10 "Be still and know that I Am God …"
II Corinthians 2:15 "We are to God the pleasing aroma of Christ."

PRAY - SING - MEDITATE

"Today I will continue to teach you, so that you may glorify in Me, and come even closer to Me, and never be afraid as you *walk through the valley of the shadow of death.*"

PRAY
NKJV Psalm 9:9-10
The Lord … a refuge in times of trouble.
And I who know your name will put my trust in You;
for you Lord, have not forsaken those who seek you.

SING
NKJV Psalm 56:3-4
*I will trust in You
whenever I am afraid,
In God I will praise His Word,
In God I will put my Trust;
I will not fear.
What can flesh do to me!*

MEDITATE
NKJV Isaiah 46:10
*Be still, and know that I Am God;
I will be exalted among the nations;
I will be exalted in the earth!*

MEDITATE
*Let me say I believe God will supply all my need,
and then let me run dry, with no other outlook,
and see whether I will go through the trial of faith,
or whether I will sink back to something lower.
The final thing is confidence in Jesus.
There is continual testing in God.
Trust which never dreams that He will not stand by us!*
(C.S. Lewis)

As we *walk through the valley of the shadow of death we will fear no evil for our Shepherd is with us.*

December 5

NKJV Psalm 56:3 "I will trust in You."

PRAY - SING - MEDITATE

"See how easy you live with Me as your guide, your friend, your companion. Again today learn to sing and meditate and pray to Me."

PRAY
NKJV Psalm 56: 8-11
"You number my wanderings;
put my tears into Your bottle;
Are they not in Your book?
When I cry out to you,
then my enemies will turn back.
This I know because **God is for me**.*"*

※

SING
NKJV Psalm 55:22-23
Cast your burden on the Lord,
and He shall sustain you,
*He shall **never** permit the righteous to be moved!*

"There is one more important Truth in My word to put on your hearts so that you will know without a doubt that My *goodness and mercy shall follow you all of the days of your life.* So sing this Psalm:"

NKJV Psalm 62
Truly my soul silently waits for God;
*From Him **comes** my salvation.*
*He only **is** my rock and my salvation;*
*He **is** my defense;*
I shall not be greatly moved;
(shaken or demoralized)

※

MEDITATE
NKJV Psalm 56:3-4
I will trust in you
whenever I am afraid,
In God I will praise His Word.
In God I will put my trust;
I will not fear.
What can flesh do to me.

※

We must memorize our Shepherd's words, so that our minds are stayed on Him. To live in joy and peace remember these songs, prayers, and meditations as we *walk through the valley of the shadow of death.*

December 6

NKJV Psalm 23:6 "And I will dwell in the house of the Lord forever."

ODE TO FOREVER

As we walk, I begin to see that soon we will be with Him, the Shepherd, in our eternal home. This poem illustrates our life now and forever. It shows us how death is no more a threat to those of us in the Shepherd's fold.

ODE TO LIFE
Death is dreadful;
Death is mad.
Death is filled
with hearts so sad.

Death is final
Dark and mean.
Death is like
a monster dream.

Oh soul take note!
Death may thus seem
all of the above in
it's deadly scream!

But …

Death is life
in Christ, that is.
Death is dead,
for I will live.

He said to me,
"Death has no sting …
for I've been given
grace that sings -
Of victory over death!"
And thus my battle cry -
"I live!
I shall not die!"
The gift of God
is eternal life,
through Jesus
my Lord, My Shepherd, my Christ."

So …

Death be dreadful? …
Not!
Death be mad?"
No …!
Death is filled
with joy instead
of sadness and tears,
darkness and mean;
for joy, peace and
laughter awaits
heaven's gleam.

The Shepherd, my Lord,
lifts me out
of death's dark walk;
"Freedom I shout!"

Oh, come with me
to heaven's shore,
to dwell in the house
of the Lord forevermore;
forevermore!
(By Cynthia Perkins)

And I will dwell in the house of the Lord forever.

December 7

NKJV Job 16:22 "For when a few years are finished, I shall go the way of no return."

DELIGHT

When all of our days are finished, we begin to realize that the emphasis must not be on any of the things here in this *valley of death*. The emphasis must return to the Holy One who restores that shadowed patch of life called death, to the everlasting light of eternity.

When the Shepherd is leading, life here is complete, abundant. He has said, over and over again, "Do not be afraid. Do not fear, for I am with you." Listen:

*"No weapon formed against you shall prosper, and every
tongue which rises against you in judgment you shall
condemn. This is the heritage of the servants of the Lord,
and their righteousness is from Me.*

*Ho! Everyone who thirsts, Come to the waters;
and you who have no money, come, buy and eat.
Why do you spend money for what is not bread,
And your wages for what does not satisfy?*

*Listen carefully to Me, and eat what is good,
And let your soul delight itself in abundance.
Incline your ear, and come to Me.
Hear, and your soul shall live;
And I will make an everlasting covenant with you -"
(NKJV Isaiah 54:17-55:3)*

"We will continue tomorrow. Study these words of Mine."

I Delight in His Words of comfort as we begin the walk into our eternal dwelling.

December 8

NKJV Psalm 23:6 "And I will dwell in the house of the Lord forever."

GO OUT WITH JOY

The Lord continues with His Joyful words.

*"Seek the Lord while He may be found,
Call upon Him while He is near.
Let the wicked forsake his way,
let him return to the Lord,
And He will have mercy on him;
And to our God,
for He will abundantly pardon."*

*"For My thoughts are not your thoughts,
Nor are your ways My ways,
For as the heavens are higher than the earth,*

*So are My ways higher than your ways,
And My thoughts than your thoughts."*

*"For as the rain comes down, and the snow from heaven,
And do not return there,
But water the earth,
And make it bring forth and bud,
That it may give seed to the sower
And bread to the eater,
So shall My Word be that goes forth from My mouth;
It shall not return to Me void,
But it shall accomplish what I please,
And it shall prosper in the thing for which I sent it."*

**"For you shall go out with joy.
And be led out with peace;
The mountains and the hills
Shall break forth into singing before you,
And all the trees of the field shall clap their hands."**
(NKJV Isaiah 55:6-12)

God's Word never fails to accomplish His purpose. He offers to us all, everything that brings overwhelming satisfaction and we live an abundant life. This is how *goodness and mercy follows us all the days of our lives.* Sing TRUST IN JESUS:

*Trust in Jesus,
My great Deliverer,
My strong Defender.
The Son of God.*

*I trust in Jesus,
blessed Redeemer,
My Lord forever,
The Holy One,
the Holy One.*

(By Mark Lee, David Carr, Mac Buell, Tai Anderson)

December 9

NKJV Isiah 49:2 "He hath - made me a polished shaft.

JUST STONES?

Listen as the Shepherd relates an illustration of how we are molded and changed, constantly being transformed from ashes, to the beauty of God's redeeming grace "takes shape." This is a perfect analogy.

There is a very famous "Pebble Beach" at Pescadero,
on the California coast. The lone line of white
surf comes up with its everlasting roar, and rattles
and thunders among the stones on the shore.
They are caught in the arms of the pitiless waves,
and tossed and rolled, and rubbed together,
and ground against the sharp grained cliffs.
Day and night forever the ceaseless attrition goes on - never any rest.

And the result?

Tourists from all the world flock thither
to gather the round and beautiful stones.
They are laid up in cabinets;
They ornament the parlor mantels.

But go yonder, around the point
of the cliff that breaks off the face of the sea;
and up in that quiet cove,
sheltered from the storms,
and lying ever in the sun,
you shall find abundance of pebbles
that have never been chosen by the traveler.

Why are these left all the years through unsought?
For the simple reason that they have
escaped all the turmoil and attrition of the
waves, and the quiet and peace have left them
as they found them, rough and angular,
and devoid of beauty. **Polish comes through trouble.**

Since God knows what niche we are to fill,
let us trust Him to shape us to it.

*Since He knows what work we are to do,
let us trust Him to drill us to the proper preparation.*

*Nearly all God's jewels are crystallized tears.
(From Streams In the Desert, July 7, Mrs. Charles E. Cowman, Copyright 1928)*

Go! Look up ahead! He, the Shepherd, is leading and guiding us *through the valley of the shadow of death*. Here we are shaped into the glorious handiwork of our Father God. We will not conform to this world, but we are transformed into the Shepherd's Work of Art, and placed into eternal bliss, where peace abounds.

December 10

NKJV I Corinthians 15:42 "The body is sown in corruption. It is raised in incorruption."

DIAMOND STUFF

In our walk with the Shepherd, we are changed, and molded into a beautiful creature. He is our Potter. We are His clay. We are transformed into jewels, and our heart light shines out to the world.

Never more in life, then in the time of our walking through the corridors of time into eternity, do we radiate with the light of the Lord, *our* Shepherd. It is in dying that so many around us see the strength, courage and peace of the Shepherd and His sheep. I personally have witnessed this transformation.

One sheep leaving time who was in the dreaded disease of cancer, gave all of what she considered her precious possessions away. She looked awful, during her final walk in this dark valley. She could not talk. She could not move. Her face dark and dreadful. Her mouth stuck wide open to breath. She laid there taking her small final steps *through the valley of the shadow of death.*

And finally she begin to be released from time, grasping for air. Suddenly the air lifted out of her body, and went upward to the forever *dwelling place in the house of the Lord.*

As she stepped from this valley to her home, her face became soft and glowing, her eyes shut, her mouth closed, like the closing of the door to the room called "time". Complete peace wrapped around her body.

Those around her bed begin to rejoice. We lifted up our hands to heaven and praised *our* Shepherd for His blessed grace. We begin to sing I'LL FLY AWAY:

Some glad morning when this life is o'er,
I'll fly away
To a home on God's celestial shore,
I'll fly away
When I die hallelujah, by and by,
I'll fly away.
(By Albert E. Brumley 1905-1977, Copyright 1932, Public Domain)

Dearest Lord God, I bring you all praise, glory and honor, for the peace you bestow on us who are your sheep. We go forth into the light and life of your salvation. Forever, Yours.

December 11

NKJV Isiah 40:31 "They shall mount up with wings as eagles."

A PARABLE

As we travel in *the valley of the shadow of death*, we can look at the huge mountains on both sides and see circling above, glorious free eagles. They are powerful birds, and they are considered the strongest bird.

The Lord, our Shepherd has used these birds as the example of how He keeps us free and strong.

Listen, as the Shepherd uses a parable to teach this lesson:

A PARABLE

There is a fable about the way the birds
got their wings at the beginning.
They were first made without wings.
Then God made the wings and put them down
before the wingless birds and said to them,
"Come, lift up these burdens and bear them."

The birds had lovely plumage and sweet voices;
they could sing, and their feathers gleamed
in the sunshine, but they could not soar in the air.
They hesitated at first when bidden to take up

the burdens that lay at their feet,
but soon they obeyed, and taking up the wings
in their beaks, laid them on their shoulders to carry them.

For a little while the load seemed heavy and hard to bear,
but presently, as they went on carrying the burdens,
folding them over their hearts,
the wings grew fast to their little bodies,
and soon they discovered how to use them,
and were lifted by them up into the air -

THE WEIGHTS BECAME WINGS

We are the wingless birds, and our duties,
and tasks are the pinions God has made to lift us up
and carry us heavenward.
We look at our burdens and heavy loads,
and shrink from them; but as we lift them
and bind them about our hearts, they become wings,
and on them we rise and soar toward God.

There is no burden which,
if we lift it cheerfully and bear it with love in our hearts,
will not become a blessing to us.
God means our tasks to be our helpers;
to refuse to bend our shoulders to receive a load,
is to decline a new opportunity for growth.
(By J. R. Miller 1840-1912)

One in the flock, F.W Faber said this: "Blessed is any weight, however overwhelming, which God has been so good as to fasten with His own hand upon our shoulders." I concur, as I *walk through the valley of the shadow of death,* that **His** burden is lite and **His** load easy.

December 12

NKJV Matthew 6:5 "Don't prayer like the hypocrites who love to pray standing in the synagogues and on the corners of the streets, that they may be seen by men."

SEEK – KNOCK - FIND

In His teaching today, the Shepherd teaches the Spiritual and physical attitude one should have when coming to God. He provides a list of prayer actions, which are both encouraged, and commanded in His Word:

- *Bowing the knee
- *Looking up
- *Lifting up the soul
- *Lifting up the heart
- *Pouring out the soul
- *Calling upon the name of the Lord
- *Crying to God
- *Drawing near to God
- *With infringed lips
- *With humility
- *In faith
- *With boldness
- *With desire to be answered
- *With earnestness
- *Without ceasing
- *Everywhere
- *In everything
- *With submission to God
- *With truth
- *In a forgiving spirit
- *Beseeching the Lord
- *Seeking His face
- *Making supplication
- *With holiness

He says, "Seek Us, Myself and the Father, for when you seek Us with worship and humility, We will be found."

We all with humble hearts bow before the Lord, *my* Shepherd.

Cynthia Perkins

December 13

NKJV Psal6m 23:6 "I shall dwell in the house of the Lord forever."

VICTORY = HEAVEN

My Shepherd has a house ready for me. He has prepared the place and it is such a joy to know after we leave the valley, He is waiting for us with arms outstretched, to hold us, and to show us our new home.

He told us to never let anything trouble us ... "You believe in God the Father, believe also in Me. In My Father's house are many dwellings; I am preparing a place for you. As soon as the place is prepared for you, I will come again and receive you unto myself. That where I go, you may be also. For I Am the Way, the Truth, and the Life. No one comes to the Father except through Me."

"Heaven is the name of your new home. Heaven is where God's throne sits, on the farthest side of the north, above the clouds. The third heaven (II Corinthians 12:2) is a place further above the clouds, that I named *Paradise*. *Paradise* is the ultimate abode of the just: a place of sheer bliss, a delight, pure joy, and absolute peace. It is a place that is perfect, that your human minds, cannot fathom nor comprehend."

"Stephen who was the first sheep to be a martyred Christian, gazed into heaven while being stoned to death. He saw Me standing at the right hand of God. He asked Me not to hold the murderers accountable for their actions. He asked Me to forgive them. With his face, glowing like an angel, he fell asleep. But his spirit, and soul came immediately to My open arms."

Tomorrow *my* Shepherd will continue to speak of the place that He is preparing for us.

May we sing O THAT WILL BE GLORY:

When all my labors and trials are o'er,
And I am safe on that beautiful shore,
Just to be near the dear Lord I adore
Will through the ages be glory for me!
Oh that will be glory for me!
(by Charles H. Gabriel 1856-1932, copyright Public Domain)

December 14

KJV Psalm 23: 6 " ...the house of the Lord forever."

FOREVER

With pure joy, Rudyard Kipling, a prolific poet, describes in human terms, our eternal Heavenly home:

A CONCLUSION
L'Envoi

When earth's last picture is painted,
and the tubes are twisted and dried,
When the oldest colors have faded,
the youngest critic has died,
We all rest, and, faith, we shall need it-
lie down for an aeon or two,
Till the Master of all good workmen
shall set us to work anew!

And those that were good will be happy:
they shall sit in a golden chair;
They shall splash at a ten-league canvas
with brushes of comets' hair;
They shall find real saints to draw from -
Magdalene, Peter and Paul;
They shall work for an age at a sitting
and never be tired at all!

And only the Master shall praise us,
and only the Master shall blame;
And no one shall work for money,
and no one shall work for fame;
But each for the joy of the working,
and each, in his separate star,
Shall draw the thing as he sees It
for the God of Things as They Are!
(By Rudyard Kipling, 1865-1936)

Just a few more days to labor and we will be there. I thank *the Lord my Shepherd.* We all join in singing JUST A LITTLE WHILE TO STAY HERE:

Just a little while to stay here,
Just a little while to wait.
Just a little while to labor,
In the path that's always straight.

Just a little more of trouble,
In this low and sinful state.
Then we'll enter Heaven's portals,
Sweeping thru the pearly gates.

(By E.M Bartlett, 1885- 1941)

December 15

NKJV Psalm 23:6 "I will dwell in the house of the Lord forever."

THE GRAND FINALE

MORTALITY

We know that death is inevitable. However, by faith, our hope of resurrection is sure. Death is no longer our enemy. The Light and Life of the Eternal Flame has been lit in this valley. The Shepherd broke the chains of death, setting us free! He has captured and defeated the prince of darkness and provided him a home of fire, brimstone, worms, and sores.

As we near the end of *Still Waters* we will let these final days be pure joy, knowing that we are now receiving the glorious victory by entering eternally into the *house of the* Lord, our Shepherd.

Hear Him:

Do not lose heart.
Even though our outward person is perishing,
yet the inward person is being renewed day by day.
For our light affliction, which is but for a moment,
is working for us a far more exceeding
and eternal weight of glory,
while we do not look at the things which are seen,
but the things which are not seen.
For the things which are seen are temporary,
but the things which are not seen are eternal.

For we know that if this earthly house,
this tent, is destroyed,
we have a building from God,
a house not made with hands,
eternal in the heavens.
For in this we groan earnestly desiring to be clothed
with habitation which is from heaven,
if indeed, having been clothed,
we shall not be found naked.
For we who are in this tent groan,
being burdened, not because we want to be unclothed,
but further clothed, that mortality may be swallowed up by life.
He who has prepared us for this very thing is God,
who also has given us the Spirit as a guarantee.

So we are always confident,
knowing that while we are at home in the body
we are absent from the Lord.
For we walk by faith and not by sight.
We are confident, yes,
well pleased rather to be absent from the body
and to be present with the Lord!
(NKJV II Corinthians 4:16-5:8)

After *my* Shepherd spoke these words, a great shout of "Amen" went up! No death! Not me, nor the sheep of His pasture, nor His Church. We live because He lives. Death is a defeated foe. Thank you *my* Shepherd, *my* Lord, and *my* God!

Cynthia Perkins

December 16

NKJV I Corinthians 15:54 "Death is swallowed up in victory."

SMILE AT DEATH

Death is a violent rape of life. Death has been described as chilling. What makes death potent is that it appears so - final. Because of death, life seems fragile. One moment we are enjoying our lives, and then - death! There is no turning around, no heartbeat, no breath, just a cold shell!

Five principles are provided in the Word of *our* Shepherd to help us smile at death:

#1 Accept death as a defeated foe. Look death square in the eye. James 4:13-14

#2 Life here is a vapor that appears for a little time and then vanishes away. James 4:13-14

#3 We have seen a great light, those who dwell in the land of *the shadow of death*, upon us this light has shined. Isaiah 9:2

#4 Death is swallowed up in victory. We will be changed in the twinkling of an eye—in a moment. I Corinthians 15:54

#5 The dead in Christ will rise—incorruptible; we will be changed. I Corinthians 15: 50-52

Jesus exclaims with a big smile: "Death is dead. My Word has finished him off. So My beloved, be steadfast, immovable, always abounding in My work. Knowing that your labor is not in vain in Me, the Lord, *your* Shepherd."

We are filled with joy as we lift our voices singing. BLESSED ASSURANCE:

Blessed assurance Jesus is mine
Oh what a foretaste of glory divine.
Heir of salvation, purchase of God,
Born of His Spirit, washed in His blood.

This is my story
This is my song
Praising my Savior
All the day long
(By Fanny Crosby 1820-1915)

December 17

NKJV I Corinthians 15: 55 "O Death, where is your sting?"

SMILE

Many sheep have written songs and poems about death. In today's lesson two poems are spoken by the Shepherd. We are nearing our dwelling; we are preparing to go through the entry door called "DEATH." These poems have meaning that provide reflection of this inevitable experience as we go through *the valley of the shadow of death* into the *House of the Lord*, forever!

He is speaking. "For the death that I died, I died to sin once for all: but the life that I live, I live to God. Likewise, you also reckon yourselves to be dead indeed to sin, but alive to God in Me, Christ Jesus your Lord. So listen. These pomes reflect the attitude of the fallen world, and how the fear of death is removed by taking the road called the **WAY OF SALVATION**."

THANATOPSIS

So live that when thy summons comes to join
The innumerable caravan that moves
To that mysterious realm, where each shall take
His chamber in the silent halls of death,

Thou go not, like the quarry-slave at night,
Scourged to his dungeon, but, sustained and soothed
By an unfaltering trust, approach thy grave
Like one who wraps the drapering of his couch
About him, and lies down to pleasant dreams.
(By William Cullen Bryant 1794-1878)

I know that "Death" has a scary and eerie ring. However, *our* Shepherd, who became the spotless, Sacrificial Lamb, gave His life in death to explode into Resurrection! We follow Him! We are SAVED from death.

Cynthia Perkins

December 18

NKJV I Corinthians 15:55 "The gift of God is eternal life, through Jesus Christ our Lord."

WITH A SMILE

Today we continue to smile at death.

This poem expresses perfectly, how we as His sheep should face death.

HOW DID YOU DIE?

Did you tackle that trouble that came your way
With a resolute heart and cheerful?
Or hide your face from the light of day
With a craven soul and fearful?
Oh a trouble's a ton, or a trouble's an ounce,
Or a trouble is what you make it.
And it isn't the fact that you're hurt that counts,
But only how did you take it?

You are beaten to earth? Well, well, what's that?
Come up with a smiling face.
It's nothing against you to fall down flat,
but to lie there - that's disgrace.
The harder you're thrown, why the higher you bounce;
Be proud of your blackened eye!
It isn't the fact that you're licked that counts;
It's how did you fight and why?

And though you be done to death, what then?
If you battled the best you could;
If you played your part in the world of men,
Why, the Critic will call it good.
Death comes with a crawl, or comes with a pounce,
And whether he's slow or spry,
It isn't the fact that you're dead that counts,
But only, how did you die?
(Edmund Vance Cooke 1866-1932, Copyrighted 1903)

The Shepherd says, "So come on. Don't be afraid. I bring life more abundantly."

We will sing that old hymn that perfectly describes how I feel about death. DEATH WILL NEVER KNOCK ON HEAVENS DOOR:

There is hope beyond this vale of tears,
Yes, beyond the silent grave;
For the ones who die in Christ the Lord,
Had His blood applied to save,
In a little while we'll see the face
of our Savior on that shore;
There to rest assured that the hand of death
Never knocks on Heaven's door.
(Hartford Music, J. A. McClung 1891-1942)

December 19

NKJV Deuteronomy 11:11-12 "The land whither you go to possess it is a land of hills and valleys and drinking water of the rain of heaven: A land which the Lord thy God cares for …"

THE COMPANY IN THE HOUSE OF THE LORD

On earth *our* Shepherd spoke of the earthly King David who is now in heaven's company. King David said this about his baby boy who died soon after birth. "While he was alive I wept (because he was sick and dying). But now he is dead - I shall go to him!" The household of God is filled with this kind of grace.

Listen as *our* Shepherd describes the event of resurrection. "On the other side of *the valley of the shadow of death* you will meet your loved ones and those who you have learned about in My Word. Your sisters and brothers who are the sheep of the flock. You will meet many for the first time and instantly know them. All who have gone before you through death's valley following My Way will be dwelling in My house."

He turns and looks us in the eye. "In My Word I told you about the *transfiguration,* which was My appearance with Moses and Elijah. Peter, James, and John who were watching, even though they had never seen Moses and Elijah, instantly they knew them. In your new home, you will instantly know who people are, and how they worshiped and followed Me, the Shepherd."

"Just think of all those in the Church." He waves His hand over us "Those whom you have had fellowship with in your lifetime, all of those sisters and brothers who you have come in contact with, on your walk through *the valley of the shadow of death*, will join you there. You will see them face to face."

※

Just like the joy here when one arrives home to family from a long trip, we finally have come to the place of love, comfort, and completeness. Our arrival in heaven will be so rewarding that words cannot express what our overwhelming joy of praise will be, as we behold the Lord. The King, the Lamb of God, *our* Shepherd in all of His glory will welcome us home.

December 20

NKJV John 11:26 "And whoever lives and believes in me shall never die."

THE PARADE

Today our Shepherd is describing our homecoming:

"I am the resurrection and the life. Those who believe in me, though they die, they shall live. And whoever lives and believes in Me shall never die. If anyone keeps My word they shall not see death." (John 11:25-26 / John 8:51)

The joy that shouts out as we complete the walk is described in the following poem:

MARCHING IN

I'm here today by the power of God
As I marched through the heavenly clouds.
And in His home on streets of gold I trod
As joy surrounds my soul like a shroud.

To you oh God I have come home
And stand by your heavenly throne.
I run right into your open arms
As you welcome me to my home.

Marching in - Marching in
Marching in to my heavenly home.
Here I live; Here I live!
Here I stay; Here I stay!
In this house of the Lord's
Marching home.

My home right here is filled with the Light,
of God the Father, and God the Son.
And there is the Dove who takes His flight,
God the Spirit, Three in One.

No tears, no death only love, and grace;
To live and never die.
I March to the front of His Heavenly space,
And shout while the angels fly!

Marching in - Marching in,
Marching in to my heavenly home.
Here I live; Here I live!
Here I stay; Here I stay!
In this house of the Lord's
Marching home.
(Anonymous)

Everyday I'm marching on to Zion. Personally I can't wait to *dwell in the house of the Lord forever*. So sing WE'RE MARCHING TO ZION:

Come we that love the Lord, and let our joy be known.
We're marching to Zion, beautiful, beautiful Zion.
We're marching upward to Zion, the beautiful city of God.
(Isaac Watts/Robert Lowry 1674-1748)

December 21

NKJV Revelation 1:12 "One like the Son of Man …"

THE LAMB

Today our Shepherd came dressed in the attire of deity. This garment is like the garment of the High-Priest. A flowing robe down to His feet, with a golden sash across His chest that completes the apparel. His hair and head are white like wool, as white as snow. His eyes are like a flame of fire. His feet are like fine brass, as if refined in a furnace, and His countenance is like the sun shining in its strength!

His voice has totally changed! It is loud, like the sound of many waters. He explains "I am coming in the clouds, and every eye will see Me … I Am the Alpha and the Omega, the Beginning and the

End, who is, and who was to come, the Almighty…I Am He who lives, and was dead, and behold, I Am alive forevermore. Amen." (NKJV Revelation 1:7-8)

A NEW SONG

John the Apostle saw and wrote all about this moment. "He had in His right hand seven stars, out of His mouth went a sharp two-edged sword. I looked and behold in the midst of the throne … and in the midst of the elders, stood a Lamb as though it had been slain, having seven horns and seven eyes, which were the seven Spirits of God sent out into *all* the earth." (NKJV Revelation 1:16/5:6)

John continues …

We all fell down before the Lamb,
each having a harp, and golden bowls of incense
which are the prayers of the Saints,
and we sang a new song saying:

"You were slain,
and have redeemed us to God by your blood,
Out of every tribe and tongue, people and nation,
Worthy is the Lamb who was slain
to receive power and riches and
wisdom and strength and honor and glory
and blessing!"

John said …
"Every Creature which is in heaven and on the earth
and under the earth and such as are in the sea,
and all that are in them, I heard saying:

"Blessing and honor and glory and power
Be to Him who sits on the throne
and to the Lamb, forever and ever!"
(NKJV Revelation 5:8-13)

Our Shepherd is the Lamb without spot or blemish, who redeemed us by His precious blood so that our faith and hope are in God our Father. We are here at last, dwelling with Him in the house of the Lord forever.

December 22

NKJV Revelation 19:7 "The marriage of the Lamb has come …"

THE BRIDE AND GROOM

Today we will be attending the wedding of the Lamb and His Bride, the Church. Listen as John the Revelator describes this event:

And I heard the voice of a great multitude,
as the sound of many waters,
and as the sound of mighty thunderings saying,
'Alleluia! For the Lord God Omnipotent reigns!
Let us be glad, rejoice and give glory,
for the marriage of the Lamb has come,
and His Wife has made Herself ready!
And to Her it was granted to be arrayed in fine linen,
clean, and bright, for the fine linen is
the righteous acts of the Saints.

Blessed are those who are called to the
marriage supper of the Lamb!
He is the King of Kings and Lord of Lords.

Then one of the angels said 'Come I will show you the Bride,
the Lamb's Wife.'
He showed me the great city, the holy Jerusalem,
descending out of heaven from God,
having the glory of God.
Her light was like a most precious stone,
like nine jasper stones, clear as crystal.
Also she had a great and high wall with twelve gates,
and twelve angels at the gates,
and names written on them,
which are the names of the twelve tribes of the children of Israel.

The Bride, the city, is laid out in a square.
The walls Jasper. The city pure gold.
The foundations made of precious stones:

Jasper
Sapphire
Chalcedony
Emerald

Sardonyx
Sardius
Chrysolite
Beryl
Topaz
Chrysoprase
Jacinth
Amethyst

The twelve gates were twelve pearls and the streets pure gold.
The City, has no temple, because the
LORD GOD ALMIGHTY AND THE LAMB ARE ITS TEMPLE.
The City had no need of the sun or the moon,
for the glory of God illuminated it.
The Lamb is its light.
There shall enter in those who are written in the
LAMB'S BOOK OF LIFE.
(Selections taken from the NKJV Revelation 19:6-10/ 21:1-27)

I cannot grasp it. I can't wait to see for myself, as I enter the gates with the glorious wedding party, of the Bride and the Lamb.

December 23

NKJV Revelation 21:1 "I saw a new heaven and a new earth."

HEAVEN

The Shepherd continues to explain about our heavenly home. "Your eyes cannot see, nor ears hear what I, *your* Shepherd and God, *your* Father have in store for you as we come to dwell in His house. The splendor of it all, this City, is unsurpassed."

She stands in glorious radiance, a Bride adorned for Her Husband, marrying the Lamb, our Lord, the Shepherd. We all stand still and sing "HOW BEAUTIFUL HEAVEN MUST BE." Read, listen, and sing these words:

HOW BEAUTIFUL HEAVEN MUST BE

We read of a place that's called heaven,
Prepared for the pure and the free;
These truths in God's word He has given,
How beautiful heaven must be.

In heaven, no drooping nor pining,
No wishing for elsewhere to be;
God's light is forever there shining,
How beautiful heaven must be.

The angels so sweetly are singing,
Up there by the beautiful sea;
Sweet chords from their gold harps are ringing,
How beautiful heaven must be.

CHORUS
How beautiful heaven must, must be,
Sweet home of the happy and free;
Fair haven of rest for the weary,
How beautiful heaven must be.
(By A. P. Bland, Copyright 1903)

This hymn describes Heaven's beauty, where we will *dwell in the house of the Lord forever.*

Cynthia Perkins

December 24

NKJV Revelation 2: 4 "And God shall wipe away every tear from their eyes, there shall be no more death, nor sorrow, nor crying. There shall be no pain ..."

THE NO MORES

As we step out of *the valley of the shadow of death* into eternal bliss, we step into the *no mores*. There will be no more sorrow; for sorrow, in all of its forms will end.

"He has sent Me to heal the broken hearted, ... to comfort all who morn; to console those who morn; to give beauty for ashes; the oil of joy for morning; and the garment of praise for the spirit of heaviness."

Today the Shepherd teaches about these *no mores*.

NO MORE SORROW: Just think how sorrow bleeds into this dark life in *the shadow of death*: we experience death, tears, oppression, sickness, grief, and depression. As we step into the Lord's dwelling place, we **never** remember these experiences again. All is gladness, comfort and joy!

NO MORE CURSE: The earth will become another Garden of Eden. The curse will have ended. Creation will be perfect again! Sin will not enter the garden. The river, the water of life, is pure, crystal clear, and running *from* the throne of God, and the Lamb. In the middle of the streets of gold, and on either side of the river, the tree of life stands. It bears twelve fruit, each tree yielding its fruit every month. The leaves of the fruit are for the healing of the nations. All shall see His face and His name shall be on our foreheads.

NO MORE DARKNESS: No darkness shall surround us. No lamp, no light from the sun is needed. No one has to yell ... "Turn on the light!" For the Lord God will be the giver of light. All will see the Father, the Son and the Spirit. There will be no more walking in shadowy darkness. The veil will have been lifted from all darkness of sin!

Tomorrow our Lord is teaching the choir a song called NO MORE NIGHT.

We will all sing of the joy of our new home, and the "no mores."

December 25 CHRISTMAS

NKJV Luke 2:14 "Glory to God in the highest. Peace and good will to everyone."

NO MORE

After our lesson yesterday, we will all turn to a song that spotlights the *no mores* that awaits us in *the house of the Lord. Our* Shepherd is singing with us.

NO MORE NIGHT

The timeless theme, Earth and Heaven will pass away.
It's not a dream, God will make all things new that day.
Gone is the curse from which I stumbled and fell.
Evil is banished to eternal hell.

No more night, no more pain,
No more tears, never crying again.
And praises to the great, "I AM."
We will live in the light of the risen Lamb.

See all around, now the nations bow down to sing.
The only sound is the praises to Christ, our King.
Slowly the names from the book are read.
I know the King, so theres no need to dread.

See over there, there's a mansion
Oh, thats prepared just for me
Where I will live with my Savior eternally.
(By Walt Harrah, 1984, Word Music, LLC Admin. by WB Music Corp)
(All Rights Reserved. Used By Permission)

Sing at the top of your lungs! For there is NO MORE_____. You fill in the blank.

Cynthia Perkins

December 26

NKJV Revelation 22:17 "And the Spirit and the Bride say come."

COME

All of those sheep who thirst, and desire to quench that thirst, should come now! The Shepherd's words of invitation are faithful and true. He said … "I am coming quickly! blessed are they who keep the words of the prophecy of this book!" He holds up His Word, the BIBLE.

"I am coming quickly, and My reward is with Me to give to everyone according **to their work.** Blessed are those who do My commandments, who wash their robes, that they may have the right to the tree of life, and may enter through the gates into the city. But outside are dogs, and sorcerers, and the sexually immoral, and murderers, and idolaters, and whoever loves and practices a lie."

"I," He puts His hand on His chest, " …Jesus, have sent My angel to testify to you these things in the Churches. I am the … Bright and Morning Star. The Spirit and the Bride say, 'Come!' And let him who thirst come. Whoever desires, let them take of the water of life freely."

He stands very tall and looks at all of us. His voice sounds like thunder. We all fall to the ground as He speaks. "Do not add nor take away from this Book. If anyone does add or take away the words of this book, of this prophecy, God shall take away their part from the book of life, from the Tree of Life, from the Holy City, and from all things written in this Book!"

The plea from the Lamb is urgent. He is coming quickly. Creation and all of His sheep groan for this great day, when they will be released from sin, death and shame. Whether it is our time to go from here to eternity, or He comes back for us, His Bride, the Church. He says … "I am quickly coming." (NKJV Revelation 22:12-21)

A RED SEA PLACE

Have you come to the Red Sea place in your life,
Where, in spite of all you can do,
there is no way out, there is no way back,
there is no other way but through?
Then wait on the Lord with a trust serene
Till the night of your fear is gone;
He will send the wind, He will heap the floods,
When he says to your soul, "Go on."

And His hand will lead you
Through - clear through -
Ere the watery walls roll down,

No foe can reach you, no wave can touch,
no mightiest sea can drown;
The towing billows may rear their crests,
Their foam at your feet may break,
But over their bed you shall walk dry shod
In the path that your Lord will make.

In the morning watch, 'neath the lifted cloud,
You shall see but the Lord alone,
when He leads you on from the place of the sea
to a land that you have not known;
And your fears shall pass as your foes have passed,
You shall be no more afraid;
you shall sing His praise in a better place,
A place that His hand has made.
(By Annie Johnson Flint, 1866-1932)

December 27

NKJV Psalm 23:6 "And I will dwell in the house of the Lord forever."

HOME

ETERNAL LIFE

There He stands, tall on the mountain, looking toward His sheep who are standing in *the valley of the shadow of death.*

"Dear sheep, remember that I am your SONG IN THE NIGHT. You are like a bird that has had its cage covered. In darkness you sang the entire song of life. Through the darkness of this shadowed land, you learned by the study of Me, the Word, to follow Me, the Light of the world."

It is the stroke of midnight and He says ... "Come, behold the bridegroom cometh; come out to meet ME. It is true that all of you came to know the love of the Father through the Son, and the guidance of the Spirit, while walking in this valley where the sky is dark, and clouds are low. Light comes out of darkness, morning out of the womb of night." (NKJV Matthew 25:6)

He smiles and reaches to take our hands and guide us as we start to walk into our new homes. He says "There is a place there in the valley where roses are gathered in the darkest hours, because if they are gathered in the light of day they lose most of their fragrance."

"As I gather you out of the shadowed darkness of death valley, My sheep's fragrance is a sweet smelling aroma that goes upward to our Father. So when you step from the dark into the light, you will be in full bloom. The fog will be gone forever. You will be beautiful, perfectly anointed with the aroma of heaven, and with an eternal body."

"For I, the LAMB, in the midst of the throne, will shepherd you and lead you to living fountains of waters, and God will wipe away every tear from your eyes."

He turns, and walks; we follow, to *dwell in the house of the Lord forever*!

Let us sing! I CAN ONLY IMAGINE:

I can only imagine what it will be like,
When I walk by your side.
I can only imagine what my eyes will see,
When Your face is before me.

Surrounded by Your glory, what will my heart feel.
Will I dance for You Jesus, or in awe of You be still.
Will I stand in Your presence, or to my knees will I fall.
Will I sing hallelujah, will I be able to speak at all.

I can only imagine when that day comes
and I find myself standing in the sun.
I can only imagine when all I would do,
Is forever, forever worship You!

I can only imagine!
(By Bart Millard)
(Copyrighted 2001 Simpleville Music ASCAP)

December 28

NKJV Revelations 4: 10 " ...fall down before Him ... saying 'Holy, holy, holy, Lord God Almighty, who was, and is, and is to come!"

I BOW ON MY KNEES

As we enter the eternal homeland, our joy is overwhelming. These words explain exactly what we see as we take hold of our Shepherd's hand, and enter our new home. All of us are now wearing our new robes. They are white like snow because they have been washed in the blood of the Lamb.

I BOWED MY KNEES AND CRIED HOLY

I dreamed of a city called Glory,
So bright and so fair.
When I entered that gate I cried, "Holy"
The angels all met me there:
They carried me from mansion to mansion,
And oh what sights I saw,
but I said, "I want to see Jesus,
He's the One who died for all."

Then I bowed on my knees and cried,
"Holy, Holy, Holy."
Then I clapped my hands and sang,
"Glory, Glory to the Son of God."
Then I bowed on my knees and cried,
"Holy, Holy, Holy."
then I clapped my hands and sang,
"Glory, Glory to the son of God."

I thought as I entered that city,
My friends all knew me well.
They showed me the streets of Heaven;
such scenes too numerous to tell;
I saw Abraham, Isaac, and Jacob,
Mark, Luke and Timothy.
But I said, "I want to see Jesus,
He's the One who died for me."

Then I bowed on my knees and cried,
"Holy, Holy, Holy."
Then I clapped my hands and sang,
"Glory, Glory to the Son of God."
(Nettie Dudley Washington, Public Domain)

There He is! Standing before the Throne of Grace with God our Father, and the Holy Spirit, The Lamb of God, *our* Savior, the Lord who is *my* Shepherd.

December 29

NKJV Revelation 21: 1 "I saw a new heaven and a new earth …"

NEW

Then there I was in the new heaven and new earth, for the first heaven and the first earth had passed away, and there was no longer any sea. I saw the Holy City, the new Jerusalem, coming down out of heaven from God prepared as a bride beautifully adorned for her husband.
(NKJV Revelation 21:1-2)

"Look!" I shout! "God's dwelling place is now among the people, and He will dwell with them. They are all His people, and God will be with them and they with God. For the old order of things has passed away."

He said to me: "It is done. I am the Alpha and the Omega, the Beginning and the End. To the thirsty I will give water without cost from the spring of the water of life … I will be their God and they will be my children."

The Shepherd began with the crownings.

* **The crown of rejoicing**, given as a reward for winning others to Christ;

* **The crown of life** awarded to those who have suffered persecution or martyrdom for they faith;

* **The crown of mastery** awarded to those who have disciplined the body and been victorious over it;

* **The crown of glory** awarded to those church leaders who have faithfully cared for the sheep.

As I look around I know everyone! But mostly I love everyone! Truth lives, there is no shame, for Truth is standing right in front of me. *And I will dwell in the house of the Lord forever*! This is my perfect destiny.

December 30

FOREVERMORE

The description of the Holy City can only be captured in a song. Just like the song of the Twenty-Third Psalm, which describes our *walk through the valley of the shadow of death*, and crossing over to our *dwelling in the house of the Lord*. So sing, THE HOLY CITY:

And once again the scene was changed,
new earth there seemed to be;
I saw the Holy City beside the tideless sea.
the light of God was on its streets,
the gates were open wide.
And all who would might enter and no one was denied.
No need of moon or stars by night or sun to shine by day.
It was the new Jerusalem that would not pass away.
(By Weatherly & Adams, Copyright 1959)

Sing JUST OVER IN THE GLORY LAND:

With the blood-washed throng I will shout and sing,
Just over in the glory land;
Glad hosannas to Christ, the Lord and King,
Just over in the glory land;

Just over in the glory land,
I'll join the happy angel band,
Just over in the glory land;

There with the mighty host I'll stand,
Just over in the glory land.
(By James W. Acuff, Copyright 1906)

Look there is the Shepherd, the Church, Wisdom, the Word, the Holy Spirit, and THE LORD GOD, *our* Father. Words are out of the question. The only thing coming out of my mouth is our songs of praise to the KING OF KINGS, AND THE LORD OF LORDS!

The STILL WATERS of the sea of glass is before His throne. We all are baptized in the glorious grace of our precious Lamb of God, the Lord, who is *my* Shepherd.

December 31

POSTLUDE

Psalm 23 is eternal. The Shepherd stands ahead, His arms open wide, dressed in glistening pure bright white. We begin with *our* Shepherd, in time; and we end with *our* Shepherd, in eternity.

He lifts His staff and says. "As you enter, may we all sing My favorite Psalm, the Twenty-Third." The Shepherd directs and King David played on his harp:

> *The Lord is my Shepherd*
> *I shall not want.*
> *He makes me to lie down in green pastures.*
> *He leads me beside the still waters.*
> *He restores my soul.*
> *He leads me in the path of righteousness for His name's sake.*
> *Yeah, though I walk through the valley of the shadow of death.*
> *I will fear no evil,*
> *For You are with me.*
> *Your rod and Your staff they comfort me.*
> *You prepare a table before me in the presence of mine enemies.*
> *Thou anoint my head with oil.*
> *My cup runs over.*
> *Surely goodness and mercy shall follow me all the days of my life.*
> *And I will dwell in the house of the Lord forever.*
> *Amen*

SOURCES

GOD'S TREASURY OF VIRTUES. 1995. Tulsa, Oklahoma; Honor Books Inc..

Chambers, Oswald. MY UTMOST FOR HIS HIGHEST. 1935. Renewed 1963. Uhrichsville, Ohio. Barbour Books. Discovery House Publishers. Grand Rapids, Michigan.

Cook, Roy J. Compiled by. ONE HUNDRED AND ONE FAMOUS POEMS. 1958. Chicago, Illinois. The Reilly and Lee Company Publishing.

Cowman, Mrs. Charles E. STREAMS IN THE DESERT. 1928, 1965 by Cowman Publications Barbour Publishing. Inc. Uhrichsville, Ohio. Edition issued by Zondervan Publishing House, Grand Rapids, Michigan.

Duke, Michael Van. THE STORY OF DIETRICH BONHOEFFER. 2001. Uhrichville, Ohio. Barbour Publishing, Inc..

THE LAYMAN'S PARALLEL NEW TESTAMENT. The New King James; The Amplified New Testament; The Living New Testament; The Revised Standard Version. 1972. Grand Rapids, Michigan. Zondervan Publishing House.

Lewis, C. S. MERE CHRISTIANITY. 1943. New York, New York. Collier Books, Macmillan Publishing.

MacArthur, Jr., John F.. THE GOSPEL ACCORDING TO JESUS. 1988. Grand Rapids, Michigan. Academic Books, Zondervan Publishing House.

MacArthur, John. THE MACARTHUR STUDY BIBLE. 1997. NKJV. Nashville, Tennessee

MacArthur, John. PARABLES, The Mysteries of God's Kingdom Revealed Through the Stories Jesus Told. 2015Nashville, Tennessee. Thomas Nelson, Inc.

Marshall, Catherine. BEYOND OUR SELVES. 1961. Old Tappan, New Jersey. Fleming H. Revell company. A Chosen Book.

Marshall, Catherine. SOMETHING MORE. 1974. Carmel, New York. McGraw - Hill Book Company, Inc.. Guidepost Associates, Inc.

Morgan, Robert J. 2003. THEN SINGS MY SOUL. Nashville, Tennessee. Thomas Nelson, Inc.

Patterson, Dorothy Kelly, General Editor. Kelley, Rhonda Harrington, Managing Editor. THE WOMAN'S STUDY BIBLE. The New King James Version. 1995. Nashville, Tennessee. Thomas Nelson. Inc.

Rogers, Adrian. THE SECRET OF SATISFACTION. 1988. Memphis, Tennessee. Love Worth Finding Ministries.

Yancey, Phillip. DISAPPOINTMENT WITH GOD. 1988. Grand Rapids, Michigan. Zondervan.

Yancey, Phillip. THE JESUS I NEVER KNEW. 1995. Grand Rapids, Michigan. Zondervan.

Yancey, Phillip. VANISHING GRACE; What Ever Happened To The Good News?. 2014. Grand Rapids, Michigan. Zondervan.

Yancey, Phillip. WHAT GOOD IS GOD?. 2010. Nashville, Tennessee. Faith Works, a Division of Hachette Book Group, Inc.

Oswald Chambers' devotionals are "Taken from *My Utmost for His Highest* by Oswald Chambers, edited by James Reimann, 1992 by Oswald Chambers Publications Assn., Ltd., and used by permission of Discovery House Publishings, Grand Rapids Mi 49501. All rights reserved.

Cynthia Ann Perkins PhD grew up in the Southeastern corner of Oklahoma, in the Kiamichi Mountains. There, her family were missionaries in a small community called Zafra. Her beginning education was in the Zafra one room school house.

At the age of eighteen she left for college where she met her husband Kent Perkins. They both embraced the ministry. After marriage she received her PhD in Music Education from The University of Oklahoma.

They have been missionaries in both Nicaragua and the Kiamichis. She has taught music to all ages, in public schools, colleges, and Churches. Also, she has been the Christian Education Minister in the churches that her husband has been called to minister. Dr. Perkins has been published by Standard Publishing Company, and numerous community newspapers and magazines.

Dr. Perkins has two children Ann Marie Brown married to Sig; and Keri Lynn Lawson, married to Jake. She has four wonderful grandchildren; Brodie and Audrey Anna Brown; and Dewey Wayne and Lucille Lynn Lawson.

She lives with her husband Kent between Nashoba and Honobia, Oklahoma. They currently minister at the Zafra Church, in Zafra, Oklahoma, the Church of her childhood.